day trips® from atlanta

help us keep this guide up to date

We would love to hear from you concerning your experiences with this guide and how you feel it could be improved and kept up to date. Please send your comments and suggestions to:

editorial@GlobePequot.com

Thanks for your input, and happy travels!

day trips® series

day trips® from atlanta

first edition

getaway ideas for the local traveler

janice mcdonald

travel

Guilford, Connecticut

All the information in this guidebook is subject to change. We recommend that you call ahead to obtain current information before traveling.

Editor: Amy Lyons
Project Editor: Heather Santiago
Layout: Joanna Beyer
Text Design: Linda R. Loiewski
Maps: Mapping Specialists, Ltd. © Morris Book Publishing, LLC
Spot photography throughout licensed by Shutterstock.com

ISBN 978-0-7627-7305-3

Printed in the United States of America
10 9 8 7 6 5 4 3 2 1

contents

northeast

day trip 01

day trip 02

day trip 03

day trip 04

east

day trip 01

day trip 02

day trip 03

day trip 04

south

day trip 01

day trip 02

day trip 03

day trip 04

day trip 05

southwest

day trip 01

about the author

Janice McDonald has called Atlanta her home for more three decades and has spent countless hours exploring the city along with the towns and countryside around it. A seasoned traveler and accomplished writer and video producer, Janice has written about journeys on all seven continents but continues to be enchanted with the places she finds so close to her own backyard.

Janice is author of Globe Pequot's *Insiders' Guide to Atlanta* as well as the *Insiders' Guide to Myrtle Beach*, the town in which she grew up. She has authored three historical photograph books for Arcadia Publishing, including *The Varsity* about the world's largest drive-in located in Atlanta, *The Myrtle Beach Pavilion* (coauthored with Lesta Sue Hardee), and *Aiken* (coauthored with Paul Miles).

acknowledgments

I could not have written this book without the help of all of those nameless friendly folks who provided their insider tips along the way as I zigzagged around the state and the smiling staff at the numerous visitor centers who were more than happy to share the wonders of their towns. Kim Hatcher of the Georgia Department of Natural Resources and Stephanie Paupeck of the Georgia Department of Economic Development were amazingly helpful and timely when I needed a little extra clarification.

My apologies to friends who endured me as I went underground for deadlines. Thanks to my mother, Dorothy McDonald, and sisters, Anna Boyce and Paula Miles, who offered advice along the way; Steve Green, Barbara Lynn Howell, John Vlahakis, Karen Rosen, Sheila Hula, Susan Hancock, and Karen Lennon, who shared their own love and suggestions for some of these spots; and to Anna Rice, who stepped in at the last minute to help me verify some of the facts.

I'm coming up for air again and ready to get back on the road thanks to you all.

introduction

These day trips cover an amazing amount of territory from Central Georgia to North Georgia and an incredible array of sites and activities. We've limited ourselves to making sure the places we have included didn't exceed more than a 2- to 2.5-hour radius from Atlanta.

Even for those of us who have lived here for so long, it's hard to choose just which direction to go when we have a day or days to spend away from the city. All of these trips can be driven in a day, but the time you spend along the way will determine just how long that day is. That's why we have given you options on where to stay in the towns we have included. Almost every town or city outlined in a given trip would be worthy of a whole day's visit.

A few themes you will notice cropping up consistently in almost every town are their Native American past, the arrival of a railroad, and how the Civil War shaped them. These factors should not be ignored because they really do define what the towns and areas have become today.

North Georgia in particular has a rich Native American heritage. Back in the 1700s, this *was* the Wild West. Things ended rather tragically for the Creeks and Cherokees, who were not just driven from the lands but literally marched away on the "Trail of Tears." Still, many locations owe their names to these early habitants.

While many claim the South still fights the Civil War on a daily basis, as you travel around Georgia you might almost understand why it remains in the forefront: Northern and Central Georgia were reshaped entirely by "Sherman's March to the Sea." Entire towns were destroyed, in addition to the countless lives lost. Almost every town bears the evidence of before and after the war. Some thriving communities poised to become big cities then are now just sleepy little crossroads.

You may know that Atlanta was a hub for the railroads when it was established. In fact, its original name was Terminus. All railroad lines lead here, so as you spiral out on day trips, you'll find that roads followed the rails and a lot of the places you'll visit owe their very existence to the arrival of that all-important train and its train depot.

These day trips range from the flatlands of the south to the lush mountains in the north. As such, there is a huge contrast in the topography you will experience, and since it would literally take you months to see all the places we recommend, we suggest you mix it up and find a favorite in each direction to get a true change of scenery.

Which direction you go will sometimes determine the difficulty you might experience while driving, especially in the northern part of the state. The real beauty of these trips is that

day trips from atlanta

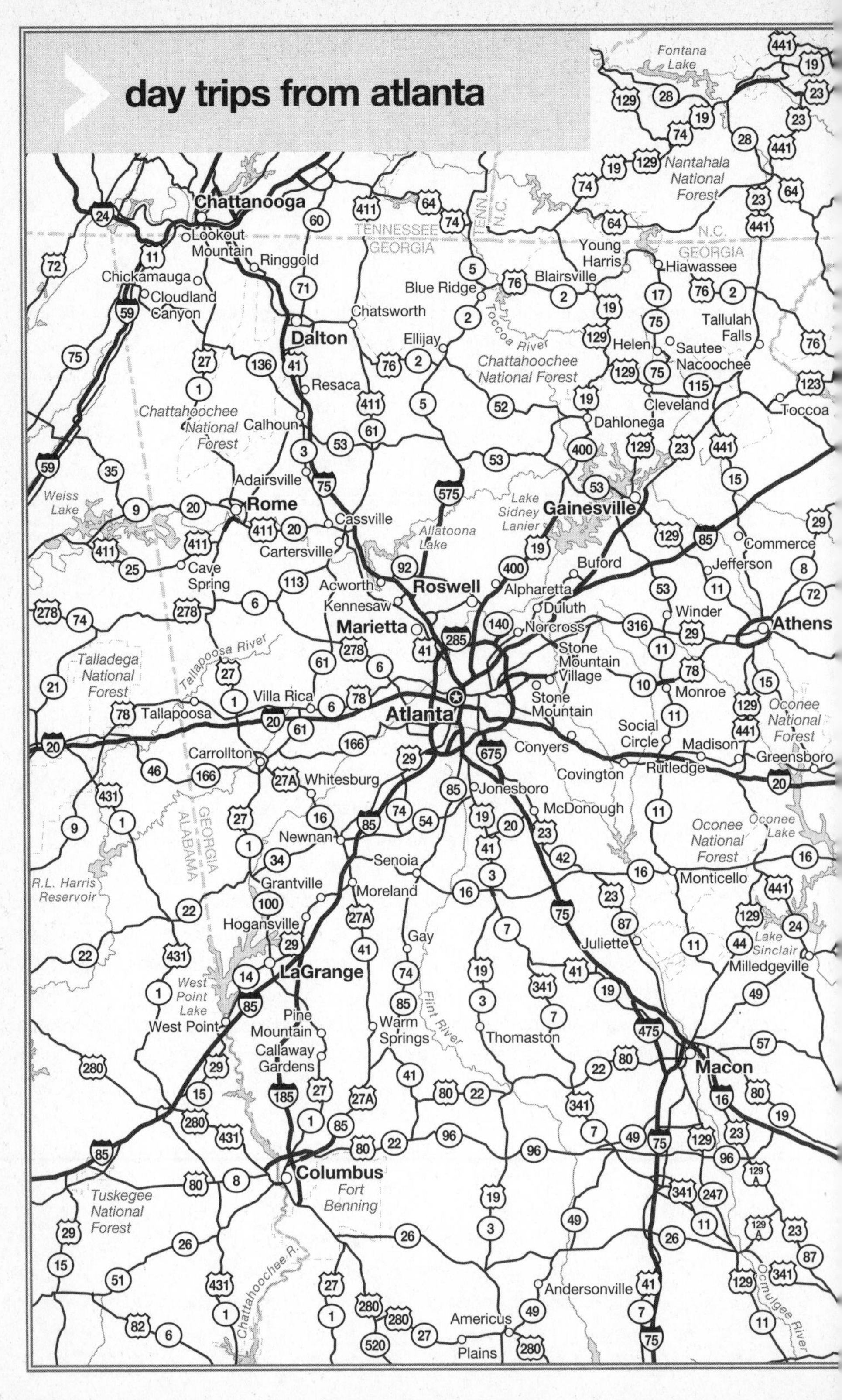

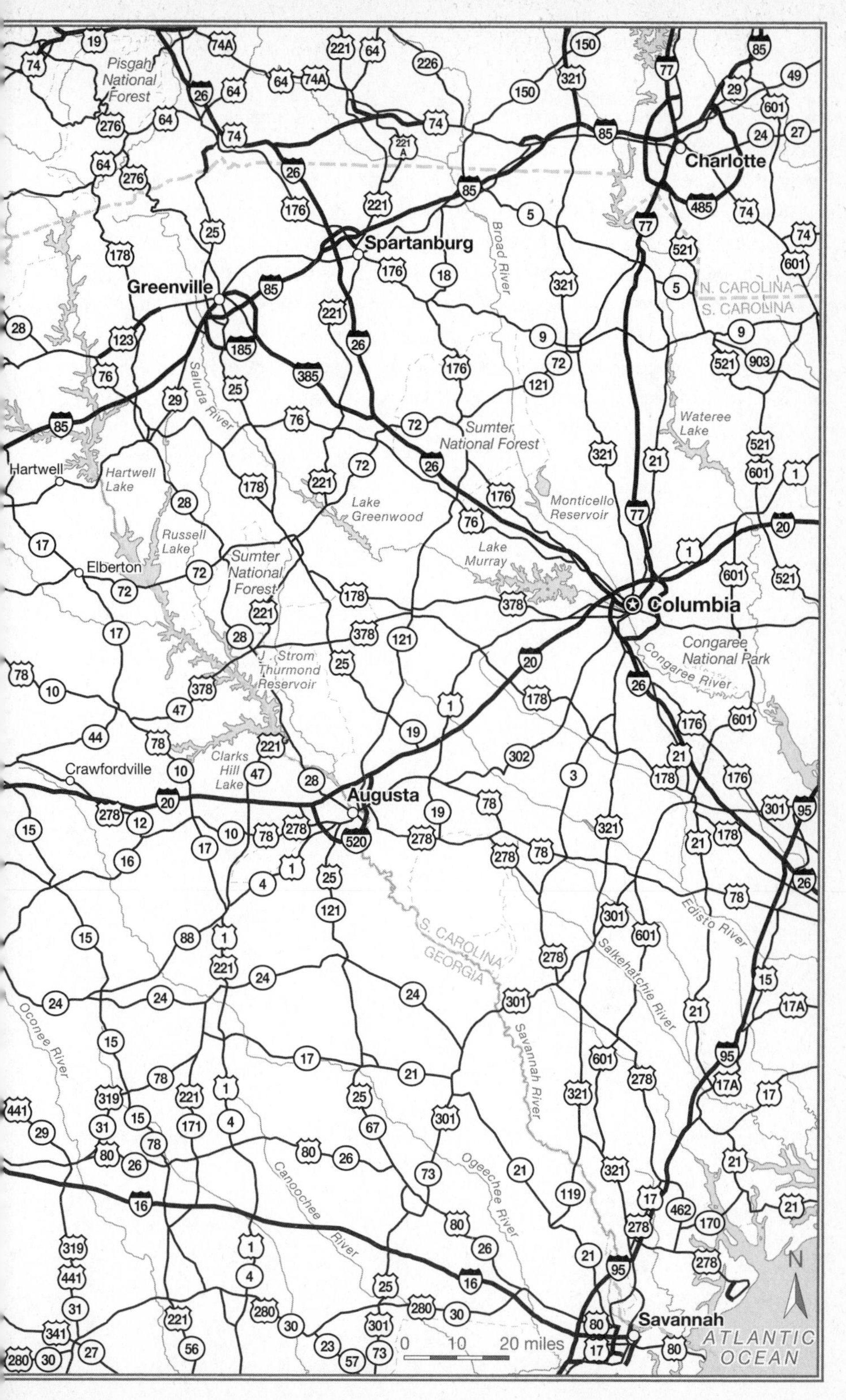
Pisgah National Forest
Charlotte
Spartanburg
Broad River
Greenville
N. CAROLINA
S. CAROLINA
Saluda River
Wateree Lake
Sumter National Forest
Hartwell
Hartwell Lake
Lake Greenwood
Monticello Reservoir
Russell Lake
Sumter National Forest
Lake Murray
Elberton
Columbia
J. Strom Thurmond Reservoir
Congaree National Park
Congaree River
Clarks Hill Lake
Crawfordville
Augusta
Edisto River
S. CAROLINA
GEORGIA
Salkehatchie River
Oconee River
Savannah River
Ogeechee River
Canoochee River
Savannah
ATLANTIC OCEAN
N
0 10 20 miles

they are connected via those famous Georgia back roads. While interstates may save you some time from point to point, we say, "Why would you want to?"

Finally, there is a reason why people want to move and settle here: Georgia is a beautiful state. There are countless little parks, big parks, and viewing points along the way, and we have tried to include most of the key ones worthy of stopping. The Georgia State Park system has done a fabulous job of preserving the state's natural wonders and history. Make sure you pack your hiking shoes in case you get weary of meandering through towns and want to just get out and experience the wilds of Georgia.

Try as we might, we could not include every town in this book worthy of your time. But we have tried our darndest to pack in as many adventures as possible.

using this guide

Atlanta's original name was Terminus because it was where all the railroads came together. On the basis of that early model, roads and highways now shoot out in all directions from Atlanta like spokes on a wheel. So we've grouped the day trips according to what makes sense for a targeted spot on the map. Instead of just a general North-South-East-West designation, we've also indicated some areas in between and the best ways to get there. There is a lot to see around Atlanta!

When choosing one day trip, you may find yourself passing a town or place listed with another trip. Feel free to deviate from the itineraries and explore!

hours of operation, prices, credit cards

To help you in your planning, we have provided hours of operation and general pricing with each listing for attractions, restaurants, and hotels. All accept credit cards unless otherwise noted. We've also listed phone numbers and Web addresses where possible, so feel free to call ahead or scout out details online. All of this information was valid as of the time of publication.

pricing key

We've tried to keep this simple. Just keep in mind the value of a $ sign for food differs greatly from one for accommodations!

accommodations

Based on the average cost per night for a standard room for two adults. Unless otherwise noted pricing does not include local occupancy and/or tourist taxes. Don't forget to ask for special discounts (military, senior, corporate, or AAA) in some locations.

$	Less than $100
$$	$100 to $175
$$$	More than $175

restaurants

The restaurant pricing guide is designed to give you a sense of the cost of a single entree at that particular location. Amounts do not include appetizers, cocktails, or gratuity.

$	Less than $10
$$	$10 to $25
$$$	More than $25

attractions

This code designates the average price for one adult entry and does not include taxes. Group and family pricing may also be available as well as travel discounts.

$	Less than $5
$$	$5 to $10
$$$	More than $10

driving tips

Perhaps because Georgia is a big state, most drivers seem to want to get where they are going as fast as they can. But take heed: Even though you may have people passing you as though you were backing up, there is a law designed to target lead-footed drivers and put a world of hurt on their wallets. It's called the "Super Speeder Law" and has been in effect since January 1, 2010. Any driver convicted of speeding at 75 mph or higher on any two-lane road OR convicted of speeding at 85 mph and higher anywhere in Georgia, faces *an additional $200 fine* on top of what they would already be charged for speeding. Failure to pay the fine ups the fee another $50.

Generally, if you are doing 5 miles over the speed limit, officers deem you are hardly worth the trouble of stopping, but be careful about having that speedometer creep higher. You'll find most Georgia highways have posted speed limits of 65–70 mph.

road hazards

Throughout Georgia, you can call 511 for real-time traffic and construction information, or visit **www.511ga.org.**

In case of an accident or car problems, dial 911. Major highways around Metro Atlanta are serviced by rapid responders called Highway Emergency Response Operators or HERO units.

highway designations

The area around Atlanta and North Georgia in general is dissected by three major interstates: I-75 (North/South), I-85 (North/South), and I-20 (East/West). Knowing what parts of the state these cut through can help you utilize them to bypass some smaller roads and get around the state faster. I-75 and I-85 both have offshoots as they make their way out of Atlanta: I-575 north of Marietta and I-985 heading toward Gainesville. Atlanta itself is completely encircled by I-285.

Which brings us to key phrases to know: "The Perimeter" and "The Connector." The Perimeter is I-285 as it circles the edges of Atlanta. You may also hear someone refer to "The Connector." This is I-75/85 where they run together through the heart of town. "Spaghetti Junction" is the mind-boggling twist of on- and off-ramps at the convergence of I-285 and I-85 on the north end of Atlanta as I-85 heads north to South Carolina.

Most smaller highways have route numbers with a US Highway designation (US) and/or a Georgia State Highway designation (GA); for example, US 78 or GA 10. State highways generally show the route number within an outline of the state map. And if that isn't enough, you may also encounter County Roads, such as CO 122.

Also, don't get confused if the name of a street suddenly changes after you cross a major thoroughfare in some towns. For example, you may be driving down Boulevard and suddenly find yourself on Monroe Avenue instead, or you are on Briarcliff Road at first and then it becomes Moreland. These things happen often in Georgia. It's an issue dating back to segregation when white homeowners didn't want to share a street address with blacks.

travel tips

area codes

If you choose to call ahead to any of the businesses mentioned in this book, you'll find locations within Atlanta itself have a 404, 678, or 770 area code. When you venture outside I-285, you will encounter a wide variety of area codes:

- **706:** Most of North Georgia (Athens, Augusta, Columbus, Dalton, LaGrange, Rome)
- **229:** Albany, Valdosta
- **476:** Macon, Warner Robins
- **912:** South Georgia (Savannah, Statesboro, Hinesville)

sales tax

Georgia has a statewide sales tax of 4 percent (3 percent on grocery items), but allows counties to tack on a little extra. And they all do. County taxes range from 1 to 3 percent, so the cost of the same item could vary by a few cents just from crossing over a county line.

where to get more information

Explore Georgia
Georgia Department of Economic Development
75 5th St. Northwest, Ste. 1200
Atlanta, GA 30308
(404) 962-4000
travel@exploregeorgia.org
www.exploregeorgia.org/VisitorInformationCenter

Georgia Department of Natural Resources
State Parks & Historic Sites
2 MLK Jr. Dr. Southeast, Ste. 1252
Atlanta, GA 30334
(800) 864-7275
(404) 656-2770
www.gadnr.org

Georgia Historical Society
260 14th St. Northwest, Ste. A-148
Atlanta, GA 30318
(404) 382-5410
www.georgiahistory.com

Georgia Innkeepers Association
www.inngeorgia.com

National Register of Historic Places
www.nationalregisterofhistoricplaces.com/ga/state.html

Winegrowers Association of Georgia
PO Box 808
Helen, GA 30545
(706) 878-9463
www.georgiawine.com

northwest

day trip 01

northwest

getting on the dixie highway:

marietta, kennesaw

The Dixie Highway actually runs from Atlanta to Chattanooga with these stops marking the beginning of a journey that could take you a week if you were so inclined. The name has roots going back to 1912 when plans were laid to connect Michigan with Florida, a route that would ultimately become I-75. On the southern end, a Dixie Highway Association was formed to help plan a path tourists would enjoy, much of it along the line of Civil War campaigns. The old Georgia towns of Marietta and Kennesaw are only the tip of the Dixie Highway outside of Atlanta, but yet could be a world away.

marietta

Marietta got its start as a frontier town in Indian territory in the early 1800s, and the square it grew up around remains the center of activities today. While the city is the bustling seat of Cobb County, the historical downtown area could easily be seen as a sleepy, old Southern town.

Downtown Marietta has five districts (and 50 homes) listed on the National Historic Register. Self-guided tours have been laid out by the visitor center to help you navigate them all. Old Marietta developed as a resort, followed by a railroad town, and subsequently became the place where General William Tecumseh Sherman launched his destructive March to the Sea during the Civil War.

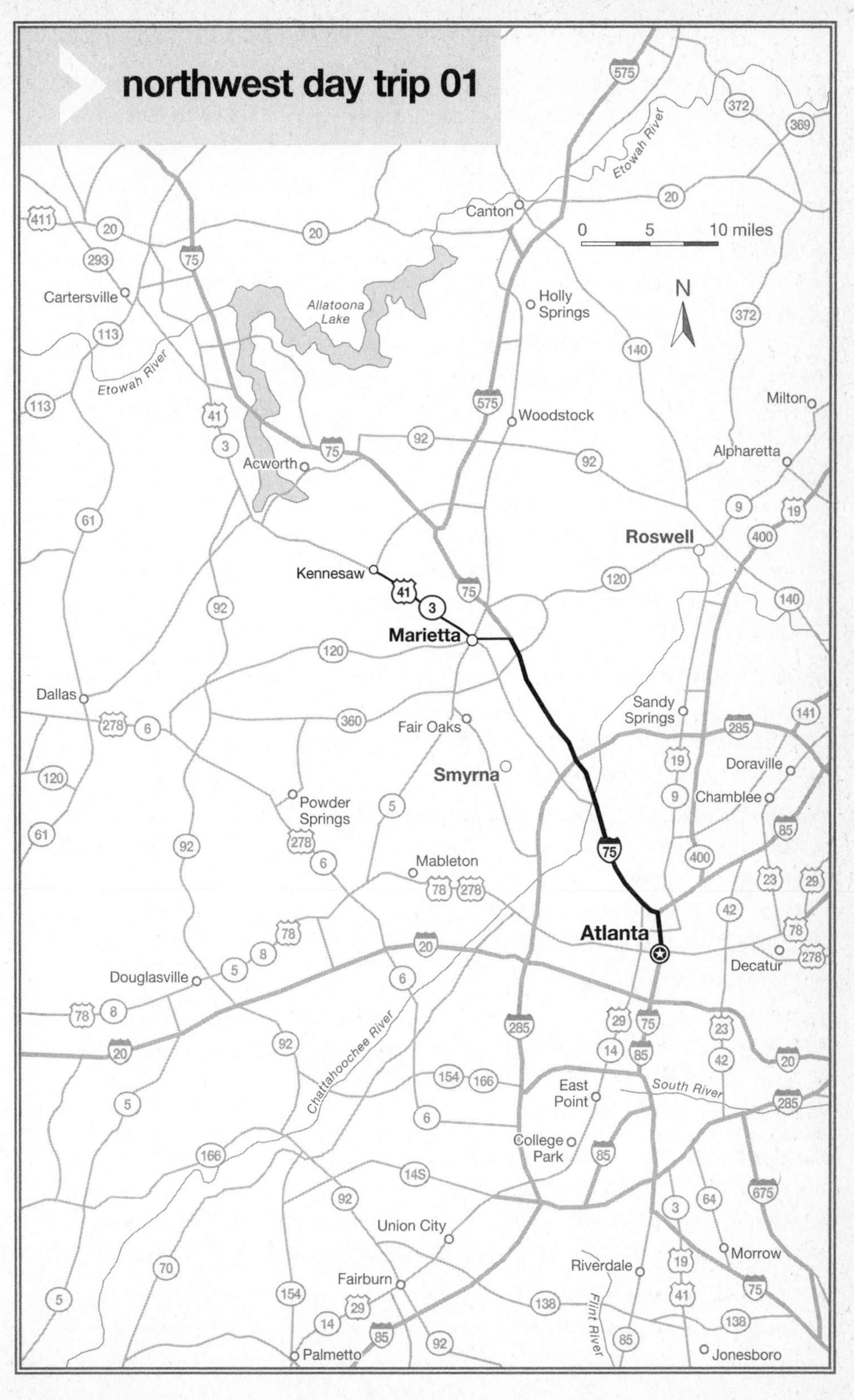
northwest day trip 01
0 5 10 miles
N
Canton
Holly Springs
Cartersville
Allatoona Lake
Etowah River
Woodstock
Milton
Alpharetta
Acworth
Roswell
Kennesaw
Marietta
Dallas
Sandy Springs
Fair Oaks
Smyrna
Doraville
Chamblee
Powder Springs
Mableton
Atlanta
Decatur
Douglasville
Chattahoochee River
East Point
South River
College Park
Union City
Riverdale
Morrow
Fairburn
Flint River
Palmetto
Jonesboro

The town rose from the ashes of that era to become an industrial center. Bell Aircraft Corporation built a plant here to produce B-52s during World War II, and now Lockheed Martin remains a large employer for the area.

getting there

Only about a 20-minute drive from downtown Atlanta, take I-75 north toward Chattanooga. About 4 miles after you pass over I-285 you will see exit 263 called GA 120 Loop. Take the second exit (263) under the bridge and clover-leaf up toward Marietta/Southern Polytechnic. Take this for 3.6 miles. Turn right on Cherokee Street and you will find yourself on the square.

where to go

The Marietta Welcome Center and Visitor's Bureau. 4 Depot St.; (770) 429-1115 or (800) 835-0445; http://mariettasquare.com. Located in the town's 1898 train depot, the visitor center is well equipped to advise you on where to spend your time either walking or driving. They also have a Heritage Passport available which provides discounted entry to local museums, including the Marietta History Museum right next door.

Marietta/Cobb Museum of Art. 30 Atlanta St.; (770) 528-1444; http://mariettacobbart museum.org. If you are a fan of American art, this is a must. Housed in Marietta's first post office, it contains pieces described as Warhol to Wyeth. Tues through Fri 11 a.m. to 5 p.m.; Sat 11 a.m. to 4 p.m.; Sun 1 to 4 p.m. $$.

Marietta Gone with the Wind Museum. 18 Whitlock Ave.; (770) 794-5576; www.gwtw marietta.com. You can't be in Georgia without getting your *Gone with the Wind* fix. Called Scarlett on the Square, this collection contains everything from movie props to posters and even Scarlett's honeymoon gown worn by Vivien Leigh. Remember, the book author, Margaret Mitchell, was from Atlanta, after all. Mon through Sat 10 a.m. to 5 p.m. Closed major holidays. $$.

The Marietta Square. 104 Lawrence St.; http://mariettasquare.com/events.html. The heart of downtown Marietta, the square is surrounding by historical sites, shops, and restaurants. There is a constant array of activities on the square itself, so check the calendar on the website.

Old Zion Baptist Church Heritage Museum. 165 Lemon St.; (770) 427-8749, ext. 114. This building dates to 1866 when the church was founded by freed slaves. The museum is dedicated to the preservation of black history, art, and culture and often hosts special events. Thurs 10 a.m. to 2 p.m. or by appointment. Free (donations accepted).

The Root House Museum. 145 Denmead St.; (770) 426-4982; www.cobblandmarks .com/root-house.php. You can take a step back in time here and get a sense of life in a middle-class home of the 1850s. The house was built in 1845 by Hannah and William Root and now functions as a living history museum. Visitors can explore the house or walk among the gardens and see the everyday lifestyle of that period. Wed through Sat 11 a.m. to 4 p.m. $$.

Theatre in the Square. 11 Whitlock Ave.; (770) 422-8369; www.theatreinthesquare.com. If you plan on being in Marietta in the evening, it is worth checking out the performance schedule here. The theater is housed in an old cotton warehouse, and for a small troupe, they put on high-caliber productions. Matinee performances available. $$–$$$.

the cemeteries

Marietta City Cemetery & Marietta Confederate Cemetery. 395 Powder Springs St.; www.mariettaga.gov. A unique way to get insight into Marietta's history is to wander through the graves in this cemetery dating back to the 1830s. Of note is the Old Slave Lot, created at a time when no other major cemetery in Georgia allowed people of African descent to be buried in the same graveyard as whites. Adjacent to the city cemetery is the Confederate Cemetery. With more than 3,000 graves, it is the largest Confederate cemetery south of Richmond. Free.

Marietta National Cemetery. 500 Washington Ave.; (770) 428-5631 or (866) 236-8159; www.cem.va.gov/CEM/cems/nchp/marietta.asp. This National Cemetery was established in 1866 to handle the Union casualties from the Civil War. Federal officials didn't like the idea of burying Confederate and Union soldiers side by side, so only the Union soldiers were laid to rest here—more than 10,000 of them. This cemetery contains more than 17,000 graves in all. Mon through Fri 8 a.m. to 4:30 p.m. Free.

where to shop

Marietta is noted for its antiques shops, and here are a few of the tried and true.

Castaway Antiques. 87 Church St.; (678) 355-0703. Located in a historic building near the square, offering collectibles, antiques, and gifts. Tues through Sat 10:30 a.m. to 6 p.m.; Sun noon to 6 p.m.

Cobb Antique Mall. 119C N. Cobb Pkwy.; (770) 590-8989; http://cobbantiques.com. With 80 vendors and more than 36,000 square feet of space, you could spend a day under this one roof looking at antiques. Items include everything from European pieces to Americana. Mon through Sat 10 a.m. to 6 p.m.; Sun noon to 6 p.m.

Dupre's Antique Market. 17 Whitlock Ave.; (770) 428-2667; www.dupresantiquemarket.com. This 14,000-square-foot antiques mall has booth after booth of every item imaginable from antique jewelry to collectible porcelains and, of course, furniture. Mon through Sat 10 a.m. to 6 p.m.; Sun 11 a.m. to 6 p.m.

High Cottage. 101 Church St.; (770) 426-9910. Don't let the small storefront fool you. There are great treasures to be found here. Mon through Sat 11 a.m. to 5:30 p.m.; Sun 1 to 5 p.m.

Willow, Too. 113 Church St.; (770) 426-3099. This small store carries antiques and gifts ranging from country to formal. Tues through Sat 11 a.m. to 5 p.m.; Sun 1 to 5 p.m. Closed Mon.

where to eat

Australian Bakery. 48 South Park Sq.; (678) 797-6222; http://australianbakery.com. The Aussies have ruled the Marietta Square for decades with unique offerings from Down Under. Open for breakfast and lunch with a great bakery selection. Try the Australian meat pie! Mon through Fri 7 a.m. to 5:30 p.m.; Sat to Sun 8 a.m. to 4 p.m. $–$$.

The Big Chicken. 12 Cobb Pkwy.; (770) 422-4716; www.mariettasquare.net/bigchicken.html. Technically speaking, this is a Kentucky Fried Chicken, but the massive chicken head, complete with moving beak, was constructed in 1963 to draw people to the restaurant that previously stood here. The 7-story-tall chicken has been through a few incarnations, but it is such a landmark it is said that airline pilots use the chicken to line up their approach to Hartsfield-Jackson Airport.

Johnnie MacCracken's Celtic Firehouse Irish Pub. 15 Atlanta St.; (678) 290-6641; www.johnniemaccrackens.com. Make this your neighborhood pub while in Marietta. It has the best pub grub this side of Dublin with an extensive beer list. Live music on weekends. Mon through Thurs 3 p.m. to 3 a.m.; Fri 1 p.m. to 3 a.m.; Sat 11 a.m. to 3 a.m. Closed Sun. No children allowed. $$.

La Famiglia. 45 W. Park Sq.; (770) 425-9300; www.mylafamiglia.com. Bring your appetite for old-style Italian cuisine. Lunch Tues through Sat 11:30 a.m. to 3 p.m.; dinner Tues through Thurs 5 to 9 p.m., Fri through Sat 4 to 10 p.m., Sun noon to 8 p.m. Closed Mon. $$–$$$.

Nik's Place. Back Porch Cafe; 645 Whitlock Ave.; (770) 792-6666; http://niksplace.com. This is one of those hole-in-the-wall places you love to love. It serves authentic Greek cuisine and hosts live music in the evenings in a historic home on the road to the Kennesaw Battlefield. Mon through Sat 11 a.m. to 3 a.m., Sun noon to midnight. $–$$.

Simpatico. 23 N. Park Sq.; (770) 792-9995; www.willieraes.net/simpatico.htm. A great dinner location, but reservations are recommended for the Mediterranean-meets-Pacific-Rim-style food selection. Tues through Thurs 5:30 to 10 p.m., Fri through Sat 5:30 to 11 p.m. Closed Sun. $$–$$$.

Sugar Cakes Patisserie. 101 N. Park Sq.; (770) 218-9994; www.sugarcakespatisserie.com. If you are starting early, this is a great brunch location; otherwise, you can't miss here for soups and sandwiches. Tues through Thurs 7 a.m. to 6 p.m., Fri 7 a.m. to 9 p.m., Sat 8 a.m. to 9 p.m., Sun 8 a.m. to 4 p.m. Closed Mon. $–$$.

The Vineyard Gift Shop & Cafe. 21 W. Park Sq.; (678) 581-3777; www.thevineyardcafe.com. Homemade soups and dangerous desserts. Oh, and all in addition to great gift shopping. Open for lunch and tea. Cafe hours 11 a.m. to 3 p.m. Mon through Sat; closed Sun. Gift shop open Mon through Thurs 10 a.m. to 5 p.m., Fri through Sat 10 a.m. to 7 p.m., Sun noon to 5 p.m. $–$$.

where to stay

The Stanley House B&B. 236 Church St.; (770) 426-1881; www.thestanleyhouse.com. Located in the heart of Marietta, the Stanley House is a gorgeous Victorian bed-and-breakfast. A favorite for events and weddings, it offers 5 individual rooms as well as an efficiency apartment. $–$$.

Whitlock Inn B&B. 57 Whitlock Ave.; (770) 428-1495; www.whitlockinn.com. This charming inn right near the square has 5 distinctive rooms. It's a popular site for weddings and events. Breakfast is included with the room. Credit cards accepted, but no online transactions. $$.

kennesaw

For such a peaceful town, it's hard to imagine that Kennesaw is best known for its battles and guns. A focal point during the Atlanta Campaign, more than 4,000 soldiers from both sides lost their lives in the Battle of Kennesaw Mountain. The town was originally called Big Shanty, but changed its name following the war to *Kennesaw*, a name derived from the Cherokee "Gah-nee-sah," which means "burial ground."

You may also recognize the name because of a controversial law unanimously passed by the city requiring that every household needed to have a gun and ammunition. Though not strictly enforced, it is still in place. Kennesaw has the lowest crime rate in Cobb County.

Despite this history, the Kennesaw of today is a quaint Southern town which is regularly listed as one of the Best Towns in America for Families. The downtown area has numerous events to bring the whole gang together.

getting there

Only 10 minutes from Marietta. Leaving Marietta Square, turn left (or north) on Cherokee Street until it merges with Cobb Parkway (US 41/GA 3). Stay left or north. After 3 miles, bear right on Old 41 which becomes Main Street, Kennesaw.

where to go

Kennesaw Mountain National Battlefield Park. 900 Kennesaw Mountain Dr.; (770) 427-4686; www.nps.gov/kemo. Kennesaw is noted for the vicious 2-week battle that took place here in 1864 when Confederate soldiers were able to temporarily halt Gen. Sherman's

March to the Sea. There is a steep mile-long interpretive path up the mountain. Confederate-dug trenches are still visible on top as well as some Union rifle pits. While Civil War buffs flock to this 2,888-acre national park, there is a great deal of natural beauty to enjoy here as well. The visitor center is open Mon through Fri 8:30 a.m. to 5 p.m., Sat through Sun 8:30 a.m. to 6 p.m.; the lot and battlefield ground: 7:30 a.m. to 8 p.m. daily. Free.

Smith-Gilbert Gardens. 2382 Pine Mountain Rd.; (770) 919-0248; www.smithgilbert gardens.com. A 13-acre collector's garden, Smith-Gilbert features more than 3,000 species of plants. The grounds surround a home on the National Register of Historic Places built in 1880. Mon through Sat 9 a.m. to 4 p.m., Sun 11 a.m. to 4 p.m., except holidays. $$.

The Southern Museum of Civil War and Locomotive History. 2829 Cherokee St.; (770) 427-2117; www.southernmuseum.org. A member of the Smithsonian Affiliated Programs, this is a must for train buffs and could easily convert nonbelievers. It houses "The General," which was at the center of what became known as "The Great Locomotive Chase." Mon through Sat 9:30 a.m. to 5 p.m., Sun 1 to 5:30 p.m. $$.

where to eat

Big Pie in the Sky Pizzeria. 2090 Baker Rd. Northwest, #103; (770) 420-8883; www .bigpieinthesky.com. New York–style brick oven pizzas and calzones. Fast and filling. A local favorite. Mon through Sat 11 a.m. to 10 p.m., Sun noon to 9 p.m. $–$$.

Big Shanty Smokehouse. 3393 Cherokee St.; (770) 499-7444; www.bigshantybbq.com. Mouthwatering barbeque ranging from chopped pork to ribs and chicken. Tues through Thurs 11 a.m. to 8:30 p.m., Fri through Sat 11 a.m. to 9 p.m., Sun noon to 5 p.m. Closed Mon. $–$$.

Trackside Grill. 2840 S. Main St. Northwest; (770) 499-0874; www.tracksidegrill.com. Southern dining with a flair, offering generous portions in a historic atmosphere. Mon through Thurs 11 a.m. to 3 p.m., 5 to 9 p.m.; Fri through Sat 11 a.m. to 3 p.m., 5 to 10 p.m.; Sun 10 a.m. to 3 p.m. $–$$.

Whistle Stop Cafe. 1200 Ernest W. Barrett Pkwy. Northwest; (770) 794-0101. Good home cooking, Southern-style, at good prices. Plan for lines at peak hours, but it's worth the wait. Open for breakfast and lunch only 7 a.m. to 3 p.m. daily. $.

where to stay

Hill Manor Bed & Breakfast. 2676 Summers St.; (770) 428-5997; www.hillmanor.com. With its wraparound porch and quiet setting, this 1898 Victorian B&B offers a great retreat. It's also a popular wedding venue. $$.

day trip 02

northwest

the other big "a"s:
acworth, lake allatoona

About 35 miles north of Atlanta on I-75 you'll find yourself driving over a gorgeous lake that meanders for miles through rolling foothills. Welcome to Lake Allatoona. This day trip to the northwest of Atlanta explores what is one of the most visited Army Corps of Engineers lakes in the nation and the little town that claims it as its own—Acworth.

Allatoona is a man-made lake with 270 miles of shoreline and countless recreational opportunities. But long before the lake was created between 1941 and 1950, the area was rich in natural beauty and a history that included Native Americans, gold discoveries, Civil War battles, and so much more.

Even if you never put your toe (or boat) in the water, this trip is worth the time to take in the lake as well as the town of Acworth. Less than a mile from Atlanta, this little slice of Georgia will astound you.

acworth

Acworth has been dubbed an "All-American City" by the National Civic League, and as you stroll the streets of this town on the shores of two lakes, you'll understand why. It is as welcoming and, dare we agree, as "All-American" as they come. Great time and effort has gone into developing businesses and preserving the history in the downtown area.

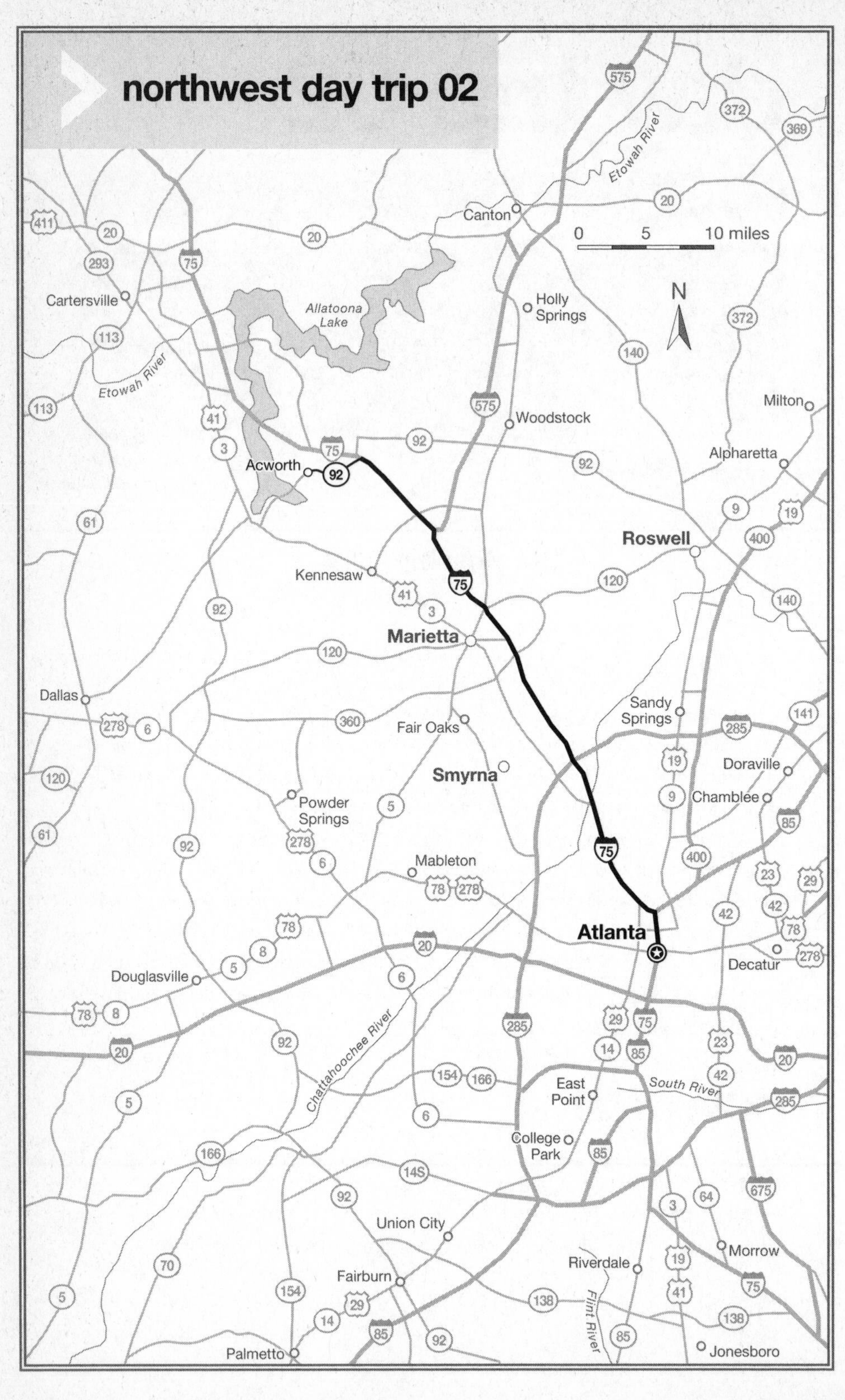

northwest day trip 02
Canton
Holly Springs
Allatoona Lake
Cartersville
Etowah River
Woodstock
Milton
Alpharetta
Acworth
Roswell
Kennesaw
Marietta
Dallas
Sandy Springs
Fair Oaks
Smyrna
Doraville
Chamblee
Powder Springs
Mableton
Atlanta
Decatur
Douglasville
Chattahoochee River
East Point
South River
College Park
Union City
Fairburn
Riverdale
Morrow
Flint River
Palmetto
Jonesboro
0 5 10 miles
N

Main Street was part of the original "Dixie Highway" prior to the development of I-75. As such, Acworth is now part of the Main Street America initiative that seeks to make sure the area is not just preserved, but celebrated.

This little town in Georgia is a far cry from New Hampshire, but that is where the name originated. Atlantic Railroad engineer Joseph Gregg renamed what had been called Northcutt Station after his hometown of Acworth, New Hampshire, while he was working the line in 1860. Prior to the 1840 arrival of the railroad, this had been the Cherokee Nation Territory, part of what was vacated during the tragic Trail of Tears.

The railroad changed the course for Acworth, making it a prosperous business hub. Its path changed again when Gen. Sherman targeted the town during the Civil War, and its previous growth was pretty much stopped dead in its tracks.

The coming of Lake Allatoona and the smaller Lake Acworth in the 1940s were game changers, and the historic town is now known for its numerous recreational activities both on and off the lake: swimming, fishing, boating, golf . . . or even visiting some of the eclectic shops downtown.

getting there

Acworth is only 32 miles from downtown Atlanta via I-75 North. Take exit 277 and make a left at the top of the ramp onto Cowan Road to head right into downtown Acworth.

where to go

Acworth Area Convention and Visitors Bureau. 4415 Senator Russell Ave.; (770) 974-3112; www.acworth.org. Learn about Acworth as well as the lake. Those all-important maps and insider tips can be picked up here. Mon through Fri 8 a.m. to 5 p.m.

Acworth Mill. 4271 Southside Dr. Originally a steam-driven gristmill, this brick and heavy timber structure was built by John Cowan in 1873. Cowan had earned fame as a gold prospector who had helped found Helen, Georgia, with three friends and had struck gold at Last Chance Gulch. Over its more than a century of history, this mill was used for making hosiery and tapestries and later as a warehouse before it was converted to a restaurant. (See Mill Pub in the restaurant section.)

Cedar Plantation. 4610 Northside Dr.; (770) 917-0067. This elegant 1870s antebellum plantation is a favorite site for weddings these days but is open for tours most days. Mon through Sat 10 a.m. to 4 p.m. $$.

Lake Acworth. 2293 Beach St.; (770) 917-1234; www.acworth.org/aprd. You could call Lake Acworth Lake Allatoona's kid brother. The shore of this 90-acre lake is right in downtown Acworth, and Acworth Beach in Cauble Park on its north shore affords a relaxing place to escape. The white-sand beach has an area roped off for swimming and boating; fishing and picnicking are both encouraged. Lake Acworth is separated from Allatoona by a 1,500-foot-long dam which also doubles as a bridge on Lake Acworth Drive (GA 92). The park is open year-round; the beach, from Memorial Day through Labor Day 7 a.m. to 11 p.m.

Liberty Hill Cemetery. Cemetery Street; (770) 974-3112. The earliest grave in this historic cemetery dates to 1799. Founded as the church cemetery for the Liberty Hill Baptist Church, Liberty Cemetery has been managed by the city since the church was destroyed during the Civil War. Burials still take place here. Open daily dawn until dusk.

where to eat

Acworth Fish Camp. 5989 Groovers Landing Rd.; (770) 917-8806; www.acworthfishcamp.com. Located at Holiday Harbor Marina, this place is good fun. They serve everything from oysters on the half shell to Philly cheesesteaks. Thurs through Fri 11 a.m. to 10 p.m., Sat 11 a.m. to 11 p.m., Sun 11 a.m. to 9 p.m. $–$$.

Bar-B-Cutie. 3466 Cobb Pkwy. Northwest, Ste. 100; (770) 917-8436; www.bar-b-cutie.com. They claim to have the World's Best barbeque since 1950, and some would say that is an accurate assessment. Mon through Sat 11 a.m. to 9 p.m. $.

Daddy's Country Kitchen. 4525 S. Main St.; (770) 974-2281. Great Southern food. The corn bread dressing is the best around. Mon through Sat 6 a.m. to 8 p.m. $.

The Fish Head Grille. 4220 S. Main St.; (770) 975-7708. Good times and good food can be had at this local seafood restaurant. The bar area is a happening spot. Mon through Thurs 11 a.m. to 10 p.m.; Fri through Sat 11 a.m. to 11 p.m.; Sun noon to 10 p.m. $$.

Fusco's Via Roma. 4815A S. Main St. Northwest; (770) 974-1110; www.fuscosviaroma.com. Awesome Italian. Lunch includes sandwiches and paninis. Tues through Thurs 11 a.m. to 10 p.m., Fri through Sat 11 a.m. to 11 p.m., Sun 4 to 9 p.m.

Henry's Louisiana Grill. 4835 N. Main St.; (770) 966-1515; www.chefhenrys.com. Cajun country in North Georgia. Great Louisiana-style food for breakfast, lunch, and dinner. Henry's is hopping with live music on the weekends. Mon through Thurs 11 a.m. to 10 p.m., Fri and Sat 11 a.m. to 11 p.m., and Sat brunch 9 to 11:30 a.m.

The Mill Pub. 4271 Southside Dr.; (678) 388-1630; www.acwortholdmill.com. One of Acworth's oldest buildings, the pub capitalizes on the atmosphere while offering spectacular pub grub. Open daily for lunch and dinner. $–$$.

Oak Barrel. (770) 974-7720; www.theoakbarrel.net. It is all about the wine here. There is great food to go along, but the Oak Barrel features wines for every budget. Wine tastings Tues through Thurs 11 a.m. to 6 p.m., Fri 11 a.m. to 9 p.m., Sat 11 a.m. to 8 p.m. $–$$.

where to stay

Best Western Acworth Inn. 5155 Cowan Rd.; (770) 974-0116 or (800) WESTERN; http://bestwestern.com/acworthinn. Near the interstate and downtown Acworth. The Best Western also has an outdoor pool. $.

EconoLodge. 4980 Cowan Rd.; (770) 974-1922 or (800) 4CHOICE; www.econolodge.com. Good for business travelers and families. Continental breakfast and pool. $.

worth more time

Woodstock. Woodstock Downtown Development Authority; 8632 Main St., Ste. 160, Johnston Bldg., Woodstock 30188; (770) 924-0406; http://oldetownewoodstock.com. A little off any beaten path, Woodstock is a small town on Lake Allatoona 10 miles due east of Acworth on GA 92. Known for its quaint streets and antiques store, this is a good detour if you want to take in another small Southern town on this day trip. The visitor center is in a 1906 store. Mon through Fri 8 a.m. to 5 p.m.

Woodstock is also home to the Dixie Speedway, a ⅜-mile banked clay oval that hosts weekly stock car racing along with special events. Races Sat nights May through Oct. 150 Dixie Dr., GA 92; (770) 926-5315; http://dixiespeedway.com.

lake allatoona

Lake Allatoona covers more than 12,000 acres, stretching for more than 35 miles along the Etowah River in North Georgia. Its official name is Allatoona Lake, but no one really calls it that except the Army Corps of Engineers, who created it by building a dam on the river as part of the Flood Control Acts of 1941 and 1946. The dam began blocking the river in 1949 and went online to generate power in 1950.

Since then, Lake Allatoona has become a premier recreational area. More than 7 million visitors a year come to swim, boat, and fish in these waters. That makes it the most used of all of the Corps' 450 lakes in the US.

Spend time driving around it, and you can see its appeal. Bring your bathing suit and take a dip, or just enjoy the scenery.

getting there

The best way to get to Lake Allatoona from Atlanta is to go via exit 277 as outlined above and head south into Acworth to wander the numerous streets that are on its shores. Or go one exit further to number 278 and Glade Road, turn right and head north. There are several access points along this road and it leads directly into Red Top Mountain State Park, which is a peninsula on the lake.

where to go

Lake Allatoona Visitor Center. 1138 GA 20 Spur; (678) 721-6700; http://allatoona.sam.usace.army.mil. The Lake Allatoona—or as the Corps of Engineers called it, Allatoona Lake—Visitor Center gives you historic perspective about the formation of this lake and will explain how power is generated by the dam. You can also learn the best areas for picnicking, hiking, boating, and camping along its shore. Open daily 8 a.m. to 4 p.m.

Allatoona Pass Battlefield. Old Allatoona Road; (770) 975-0055; www.evhsonline.org/allatoona/index.shtml. There is a 3.4-mile interpretive path through this man-made gorge dug by slaves in the 1830s and then the site of a bloody Civil War battle that was the beginning of the Nashville Campaign. Two earthen forts, miles of earthworks, and the graves of 21 Confederate soldiers are found along the trail, which lore says is haunted. The parking lot and the dyke that creates Lake Allatoona are located where warehouses were built to hold the food for Union troops in Marietta and Atlanta. Open daily. Free.

Lake Allatoona Recreation. There are 8 marinas around the lake and 11 Army Corps of Engineers parks. Any park with a beach requires a $4 a day usage fee.

Acworth Beach, Cauble Park. Beach Street, Acworth, northern shore. Managed by Acworth Parks and Recreation, this beach features a roped-off swimming area and includes a bathroom, changing station, and showers all located adjacent to the beach. There are also 2 playgrounds, picnic facilities with grills, and a gazebo. Paddleboat rentals are available during the summer. The beach is open Memorial Day weekend through Labor Day, from 8:30 a.m. to 6 p.m. $10 parking on weekends.

Dallas Landing. 5120 Allatoona Dr., Acworth; (770) 917-1234. Managed by the City of Acworth, this park has a very large swimming area, picnic tables with grills, a volleyball court, a horseshoe pit, and a group pavilion. $5 parking fee during summer months.

Proctor Landing. Proctor Landing Drive, Acworth; (770) 917-1234. Proctor Landing is another busy park because of its location. It features a swimming beach, individual picnic tables, 2 group picnic areas, a fishing jetty, and volleyball and horseshoe courts. No alcohol is allowed in the park, and you are not permitted to use any amplified music systems.

South Shore. Ragsdale Road, off GA 92. It is just opposite Cauble Park/Acworth Beach. One strip of the park is best known for shoreline fishing.

Galt's Ferry. Rocky Lane, Acworth; (678) 721-6700. Galt's Ferry is popular during the summer because of its large beach. It also has individual picnic tables, a 3-lane boat ramp, a fishing jetty, and group picnic facility found in the park. Galt's Ferry is open daily from 8 a.m. to 9 p.m. There are a few bathrooms in the park.

Bartow Carver Park. Bartow Carver Road, 2 miles east of Red Top Mountain; (770) 974-6053. This large park includes a beach, picnic area, hiking trails, 2 playgrounds, a boat ramp, and 2 rental facilities that are available for parties.

Bartow Gatewood Park. Bartow Beach Road in Cartersville (north of the dam); (770) 387-5163. This park is more isolated and not as busy as the others. In addition to the boat ramp, picnic area, and playgrounds, there are some camping facilities including RV hookups.

Cooper Branch #1. GA 20 Spur, just before the Etowah Dam and the US Corps of Engineers Allatoona Lake Visitors Center; (678) 721-6700. The picnic area of this park has some of the best views around of the lake. There is also a boat ramp at this location.

Cooper Branch #2. GA 20 Spur, north of Cooper Branch #1 and Allatoona Lake Visitors Center; (678) 721-6700. This park actually connects to the visitor center via trails. It is one of the smaller parks, but does have individual picnic areas and a pavilion available for rental.

Fields Landing. Fields Landing Drive, Canton; (770) 924-7768. Managed by Cherokee County, this small park offers numerous amenities. There is a small single-lane boat ramp, a floating fishing dock, individual picnic tables and grills, a children's playscape, and a horseshoe court.

Kellogg Creek. Old Highway 41, #1. This is one of the less popular parks because it doesn't have much of a view. There is a swimming beach, picnic tables, and a boat launch.

Sweetwater. Sweetwater Creek Drive, Canton; (678) 721-6700. The main attraction at Sweetwater Park is its swimming beach. There is also a nice group picnic pavilion with a volleyball court and 2 horseshoe courts adjacent to its seating area. There are bathrooms.

Tanyard Creek. Tanyard Creek Road. Acworth Tanyard includes a protected swimming area (no lifeguards), a 3-lane boat ramp, and a playground.

Victoria Park. This day-use facility offers a swimming beach, a fishing jetty, and 2 boat launches. There are bathrooms located in a building just off of the main parking lot. There is a $4 per vehicle fee for entry into the park. This can be paid at the park entry booth or, on days when it is not staffed, at self-serve collection boxes.

Red Top Mountain State Park. East of I-75, exit 285; (770) 975-4226 or (800) 864-7275; www.redtopmountainstatepark.org. Red Top Mountain State Park on Lake Allatoona is easily accessible from I-75, making it a popular spot for those wanting to get to Lake Allatoona quickly. In addition to boat ramps, there are 12 miles of hiking trails and a reconstructed 1860s homestead. Red Top originated as a mining site for iron ore, and the red soil in the area reflects its rich iron content. Those who want to stay longer than the day can rent cabins at Red Top (see "Where to Stay"). Open daily 7 a.m. to 10 p.m. $.

where to eat

Little River Sports Bar. 6979 Bells Ferry Rd., Canton, GA 30114-9701; (770) 345-4444; http://littleriverbigfun.com. Located at the Little River Marina, this restaurant is right on the water where boats pull up to dine. They have a great deck that is perfect for watching a sunset over the lake. Good food from the wings to the salads and the steaks. There are nightly specials. Sun through Thurs 11 a.m. to 11 p.m., Fri and Sat 11 a.m. until close. $–$$.

Sunset Grille. Victoria Harbor, 1000 Victoria Landing, Woodstock, GA 30189; (770) 926-7718; www.victoriaharbourmarina.com. A favorite for even those not boating. Good food with a great view of the lake. Sunsets here over the northern part of the lake are a must. Sun through Thurs 11 a.m. to 9 p.m., Fri and Sat 11 a.m. to 11 p.m. $–$$.

where to stay

Lake Allatoona Inn. 632 Old Allatoona Rd.; (770) 943-0171. This 1800s Victorian inn sits on a 16-acre farm right on Lake Allatoona. The rooms are large, and there is also a lakefront cabin available. $$.

Red Top Mountain Cabins. East of I-75, exit 285; (770) 975-4226 or (800) 864-7275; www.redtopmountainstatepark.org. There are 18 fully furnished, self-catering cottages in Red Top Mountain State Park, 2 of which are dog friendly. $–$$.

day trip 03

not italy:
rome, cave spring

Today you'll venture to a part of Northwest Georgia that is known for its natural beauty as well as its cosmopolitan lifestyle, all close to Atlanta, but far enough away to maintain a distinctly different culture and lifestyle.

For many, the city of Rome can be as remote as its Italian counterpart, although it is still only a 90-minute drive from Atlanta, while the tiny community of Cave Spring is like stepping back in time. Both towns are nestled in the foothills of the Appalachians and are known for their surroundings as well as the waters which define them: Rome, for its three rivers, and Cave Spring, for the never-ceasing pure mineral springs.

This is a day trip that will leave a real smile on your face and will have you recommending other people venture along this same path.

rome

If you go to the courthouse in Rome, Georgia, you will see the same Romulus, Remus, and their wolf nursemaid statue that you'll find everywhere in Rome, Italy, but that is about where the similarity between the two cities end. The town's name was literally drawn out of a hat in 1832 when it was decided that Indian lands in North Georgia needed to be confiscated to make way for more settlers.

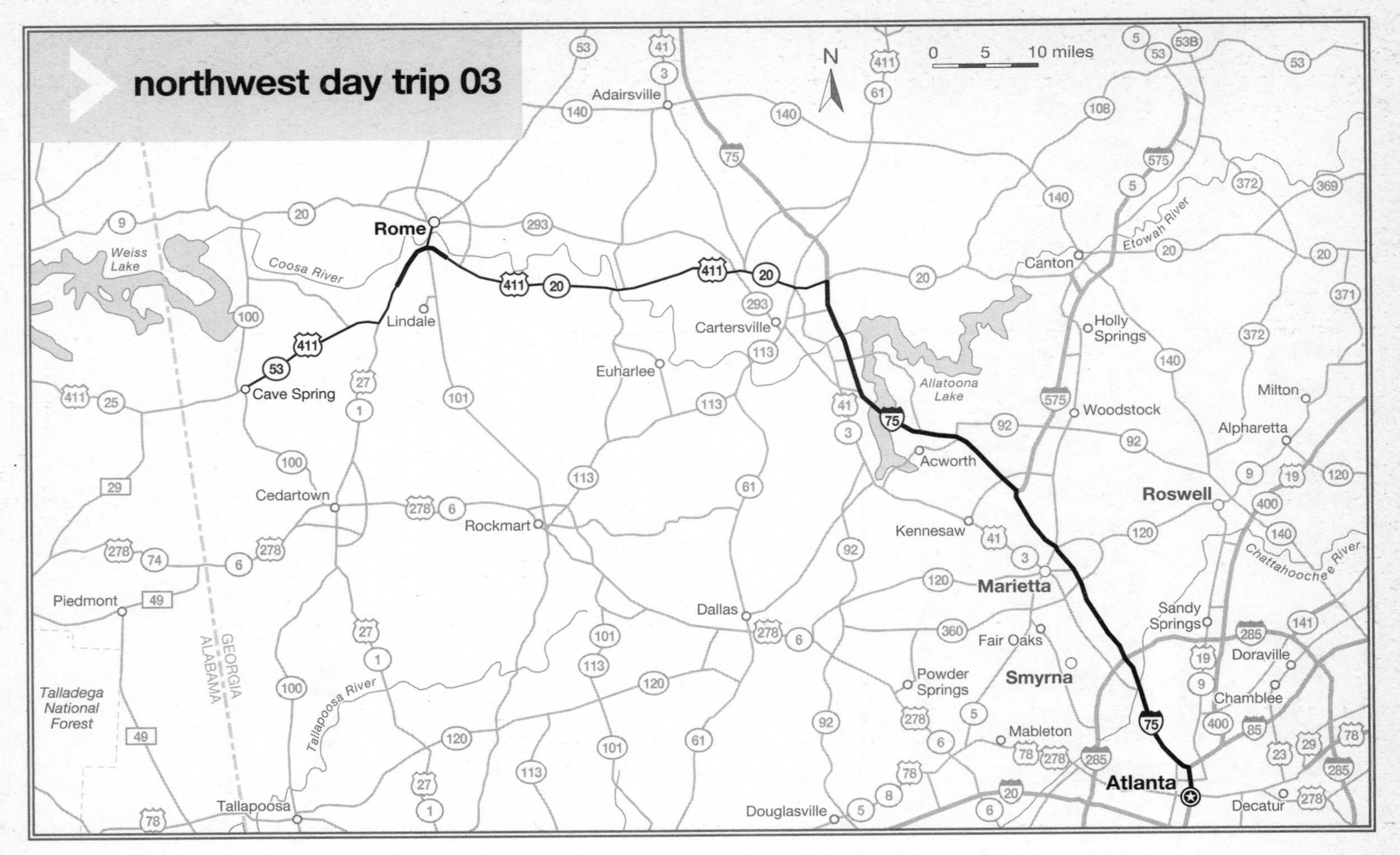
northwest day trip 03
N
0 5 10 miles
Rome
Adairsville
Cartersville
Euharlee
Lindale
Cave Spring
Cedartown
Rockmart
Piedmont
Tallapoosa
Dallas
Douglasville
Powder Springs
Kennesaw
Acworth
Marietta
Smyrna
Fair Oaks
Mableton
Atlanta
Decatur
Chamblee
Doraville
Sandy Springs
Roswell
Alpharetta
Milton
Woodstock
Holly Springs
Canton
Weiss Lake
Coosa River
Allatoona Lake
Etowah River
Chattahoochee River
Tallapoosa River
Talladega National Forest
GEORGIA
ALABAMA

In a valley in the foothills of the Appalachians, the Etowah, Oostanaula, and Coosa Rivers come together in a place the Cherokees called "The Enchanted Land." It's easy to see why the area was so coveted.

Rome has played an important role throughout Georgia's development, from the Revolutionary War to the Civil War and forward. These days the historic town is known as the Capital of North Georgia, with residents coming to capitalize on its medical, educational, recreational, and cultural services. A visit here blends small-town charm with some big-city sophistication, allowing you to enjoy mountains, rivers, and Southern hospitality with a unique cultural flair.

getting there

Rome is only 80 minutes from the heart of Atlanta. Take I-75 North for 40 miles to exit 290/GA 20 and go left toward Rome–Canton. Rome is 25 miles from I-75.

where to go

Greater Rome Convention and Visitors Bureau. 402 Civic Center Dr.; (706) 295-5576 or (800) 444-1834; www.romegeorgia.org. In a nod to the importance of the railroads to Rome's development in the 1800s, the visitor center is housed in a 1901 train station and caboose. Mon through Fri 9:30 a.m. to 5 p.m., Sat 10 a.m. to 3 p.m.

Chieftains Museum/Major Ridge Home. 501 Riverside Pkwy. It was Cherokee chief Major Ridge who wrote the law that called for death for any Cherokee selling land. He also signed the New Echota Treaty which led to the ouster of the Cherokees from this area in the "Trail of Tears," and he was assassinated by his people for it. This National Historic Register home was where Ridge lived, and it contains artifacts and exhibits on the Ridge and the Cherokee story. Wed through Sat 10 a.m. to 5 p.m. Call for fees.

DeSoto Theatre. 530 Broad St.; (706) 295-7171; www.romelittletheatre.com. Built in 1928, the historic DeSoto Theatre was designed after New York's Roxy Theatre. Planned as a "talkie" theater for movies, it is now home to live theater and the Little Rome Theatre group. Mon through Fri 10 a.m. to 4 p.m.; check schedule for performances.

Eubanks Museum and Gallery. 315 Shorter Ave.; (706) 291-2121; www.shorter.edu. This natural history museum features the collection of J. Robert Eubanks, a benefactor of Shorter University. It includes personal artifacts from around the world such as trophy animals from Africa and India as well as early American hardware and Native American pottery, tools, and hunting items.

Historic Clock Tower. Noble Hill; (706) 295-5576; www.romegeorgia.org. Rising more than 100 feet, this brick clock tower is a symbol of the city. It was built by James Noble Jr. not just for the clock, but to serve as a water cistern for the city and did so for 30 years. The clock continues to tell time for the city from its place atop the hill at the end of 5th Avenue.

The clock tower is not open regularly for visitors but if you want to explore it, the Visitor's Center will provide you with a key.

Marshall Forest. Horseleg Creek Road; (404) 873-6946 or (404) 253-7216; www.nature.org/georgia. Go hiking in one of the few remaining old-growth forests in the Ridge and Valley Province, a corridor that runs from Pennsylvania to Alabama.

Myrtle Hill Cemetery. Myrtle and Broad Streets; (706) 295-5576; www.romegeorgia.org. Some call this the most beautiful cemetery in the country. Sitting high on a hill overlooking the Etowah and Oostanaula Rivers, this location combines gorgeous views and impressive funerary art. The 32-acre cemetery dates from 1857. Self-guided tours include grave notes for many of the older areas. Myrtle Hill is the final resting place for almost 400 Civil War soldiers.

Noble Brothers Foundry. 1st and Broad Streets. There isn't much left of what was a huge ironworks foundry next to the depot begun in 1855 by James Noble Sr. and his six sons—William, James Jr., Stephen, George, Samuel, and John. Charged with making cannons during the Civil War, the foundry was destroyed by Gen. Sherman's men in 1863.

Oak Hill and the Martha Berry Museum. 24 Veterans Memorial Hwy.; (706) 368-6789; http://berry.edu/oakhill. Oak Hill is the 170-acre estate of Martha Berry, the founder of nearby Berry College. Oak Hill's beautiful Greek Revival home and its grounds have been perfectly preserved as they were at the time of her death in 1942. The grounds feature a carriage house with vintage vehicles, Aunt Martha's Cottage (where her beloved cook and house servant, Martha Freeman, lived), formal gardens, and nature trails. The museum on the grounds houses an impressive collection of art, including memorabilia from Martha Berry's founding of the Berry Schools. Mon through Sat 10 a.m. to 5 p.m. $.

Rome Area History Museum. 305 Broad St.; (706).235-8051; www.romehistorymuseum.org. This museum in the heart of downtown is arranged chronologically and will guide you through Rome's history from the time of the Native Americans to DeSoto's visits to the present day. The amount of information here is impressive, and a visit is almost a must. Thurs through Fri 10 a.m. to 5 p.m., Sat 10 a.m. to 2 p.m. $.

Rome Speedway. 1900 Chulio Rd.; (706) 235-2541; http://raceromespeedway.com. The half-mile speedway is listed as the world's fastest dirt track. Special Sunday night events. Call or visit the website for a schedule, event information, and fees.

State Mutual Stadium. Braves Boulevard Northeast; (706) 368-9388; web.minorleaguebaseball.com/index. Home to the minor league baseball team the Rome Braves, the stadium hosts the Braves during baseball season and also is used for concerts and other events. Call or visit the website for a schedule, event information, and fees.

where to eat

Country Gentleman Restaurant East. 26 Chateau Dr. Southeast; (706) 295-0205. Famous in Rome for Italian and seafood, Country Gentleman also offers steaks and sandwiches. Tues through Sat 11 a.m. to 2 p.m. and 5 to 10 p.m., Sun 11 a.m. to 2:30 p.m. $–$$.

The Gravy Boat. 1413 Dean Ave. Southeast; (706) 235-4242. This little country restaurant will satisfy your hunger. Try the biscuits and gravy! Breakfast and lunch; closed Sun. $.

Harvest Moon Cafe. 234 Broad St.; (706) 291-4224; www.myharvestmooncafe.com. Wonderfully creative food bought from local suppliers. Try the pimento cheese spread or the fish tacos; for dinner, it's all about the grilled fish or steaks. Sun through Mon 11 a.m. to 2 p.m., Tues and Wed 11 a.m. to 9 p.m., Thurs through Sat 11 a.m. to 10 p.m. $–$$.

The Homestead. 1401 Kingston Rd. Northeast; (706) 291-4290; http://thehomesteadrestaurant.webs.com. Locally owned and operated, The Homestead serves up steak and seafood. Tues through Thurs 5 to 9 p.m., Fri and Sat 5 to 10 p.m., Sun 11:30 a.m. to 2:30 p.m. $$.

Jefferson's Restaurant. 340 Broad St.; (706) 378-0222; www.jeffersonsrestaurant.com. Their motto is "Peace, Love and Hot Wings," but also expect burgers, fresh oysters, and more. Lunch and dinner daily. $–$$.

Schroeder's New Deli. 406 Broad St.; (706) 234-4613; www.schroedersnewdeli.com. Serving pizzas, calzones, sandwiches, soups, and salads, this popular place stays busy for good reason. Mon through Thurs 11 a.m. to 10 p.m., Fri and Sat 11 a.m. to 11 p.m. $.

where to stay

The Claremont House Bed & Breakfast. 906 E. 2nd Ave.; (706) 291-0900 or (800) 254-4797; www.theclaremonthouse.net. You'll feel right at home in this historic property in the heart of Rome. Four guest rooms and a cottage are available at this beautiful home. $–$$.

Country Inn & Suites Rome East. 15 Hobson Way; (706) 232-3380; www.countryinns.com. Right in the downtown Rome area, the inn is convenient to most locations. $.

Hampton Inn. 21 Chateau Dr.; (706) 232-9551 or (800) HAMPTON; www.hamptoninn.com. Right downtown, clean and comfortable. Pool and fitness facilities on-site. $.

Jameson Inn Rome. 40 Grace Dr. Southeast; (706) 291-7797. Located downtown. Jameson has a fitness center, and breakfast is included with room. $.

cave spring

Native Americans were drawn to this place rich in fresh mineral water, and everyone else simply followed. There are still old Cherokee roads in the woods of the surrounding areas. But what this place is best known for is the cave around which this tiny, historic community sprang up.

People still come to fill jugs from this bubbling spring which produces 2 million gallons of pure water daily. But in addition to drinking it yourself and exploring the cave, roam around this quaint little mountain town and also sample some of its history. You'll feel like you've stepped back in time. There are parks along Cedar Creek and beautiful historic buildings to discover.

getting there

Cave Spring is 14 miles southwest of Rome. Take US 441/GA 53 West. From Atlanta, the drive is about 1 hour and 45 minutes. Follow the directions to Rome from I-75, taking exit 290 and GA 20 west. Travel 22 miles and take a left on US 441/GA 53. At Six Mile, bear Right and Cave Spring is 20 miles from Six Mile. If you are continuing to Cave Spring from Rome, then take US 441/GA 53 south.

where to go

Museum/Welcome Center. 4 Rome Rd.; (706) 777-8608; www.cavespringgeorgia.com. Stop here to get a sense of what all is available to see and experience in Cave Spring. The museum does a good job of telling about the cave's discovery and how it became an attraction. Open daily 11 a.m. to 4 p.m.

Cave Spring Depot. Alabama Street (US 411 South/GA 53) at Lee Street and Perry Farm Road. This wooden depot was constructed in 1880 to serve the East Tennessee, Virginia, and Georgia Railroad. It later served ETV&G's successor the Southern Railway, which operated from 1894 until it was bought by Central of Georgia Railway in 1964.

Cave Spring's Cave. Rolater Park; (706) 777-9944; www.cavespringgeorgia.com. Step into this cool cave and taste its waters, but also explore and see its stalagmites and legendary "Devil's Stool" formation. The cave's stream flows into a reflecting pond and then a shallow stream which ultimately lets out into the swimming lake. Daily May through Sept and by appointment at other times.

The Hearn Academy. 13 Cedartown Rd.; (706) 777-8865. In 1838, the Baptist Church established what was then called the Manual Labor School for boys to teach the skills of farming and other ways to make a living. The school, whose grounds included the cave and spring, was later renamed Hearn Academy when Lott Hearn bequeathed money to the school, and it ultimately became a college prep school around 1902. The school closed in 1925, but its historic buildings remain in use as shops as well as an inn.

Old Cave Spring Baptist Church. Rolater Park. Not to be confused with Cave Spring Baptist on Cedartown Road, this old church dates to 1850. The boxy building is made of red bricks handmade by slaves. Services are held in the other church, which was built in the 1930s, but this structure is used for events like weddings. It has stained-glass windows, a balcony, and wide, pine-planked floors.

Rolater Park. (706) 777-9944; www.cavespringgeorgia.com. This 29-acre park is at the center of everything and is where the cave of Cave Spring is located. It is named for Dr. J. B. Rolater, who owned the land and deeded it to the city in 1929. Cedar Creek runs adjacent to the park, which includes picnic areas, a duck pond, a fish pond, and a 1.5-acre swimming lake, the second largest in the state. The pool complex includes a snack bar, volleyball area, bathhouse, and picnic tables.

where to eat

Cave Spring Cafe. 20 Broad St.; (706) 777-9917. Homey atmosphere for serving country breakfast, lunch, and dinner with daily specials. They do not accept credit cards but will take checks. $.

Creekside Restaurant. 23 Cedartown St.; (706) 777-0041. With home-style meals, Creekside is open all day. $–$$.

La Cabana. 118 Gadsden Rd. Southwest; (706) 777-8876. Serving authentic Mexican dishes. Open daily 11 a.m. to 10 p.m. $.

Tumlin House Restaurant. 38 Alabama St.; (706) 777-0066 or (800) 939-3880; http://tumlinhouse.com. Fine dining in historic Cave Spring at the historic Tumlin House Inn is a regular activity for many residents, so make sure you have reservations for the 6-course event. Sat evening, 7 p.m. reservations only. $$.

where to stay

The Guest House. 30 Fannin St.; (706) 777-3871. The Guest House is an entire home available for rent in downtown Cave Spring. Self-catering, it has 4 bedrooms and 2 baths and is fully furnished for your stay. $$.

The Historic Hearn Inn. (706) 777-8865; www.cavespringgeorgia.com. The Hearn Inn was built by the Baptists as a dormitory for the Manual Labor School and is located in Rolater Park. When the school closed, the building was converted into apartments and remained as such until the 1960s. The inn has served as a bed-and-breakfast since its restoration in the 1980s. $.

Tumlin House Bed & Breakfast. 38 Alabama St.; (706) 777-0066 or (800) 939-3880; http://tumlinhouse.com. Parts of this inn date back to 1842, and it was added onto over the next century. The historic Victorian structure with its wraparound porch has 4 guest rooms named after relatives of the 1886 owners of the home. There is a pool on-site as well as a restaurant for breakfast daily and dinner on Saturday. $.

day trip 04

the indian trail:

cartersville, cassville, calhoun

The North Georgia mountains are filled with Indian lore and evidence of these first inhabitants. This day trip is designed to take you to some key locales which are very significant in Native American history.

Dating back more than 1,000 years, North Georgia's first settlers were Native Americans known as Mound Builders. Evidence of their settlements is found in several locations across the region. The Mound Builders gave way to the Creek Nation, who were later replaced by the Cherokee, who dominated until they were displaced by the white man by the Trail of Tears. Each of these groups can be traced to unique sites which might otherwise be overlooked while exploring northwest of Atlanta.

cartersville

The rolling foothills on the banks of the Etowah River no doubt played a role in drawing Native Americans to this area of Georgia for centuries. And while there are remnants of ancient settlements dating back millennia, Cartersville's official establishment traces back to 1850 when wealthy businessman Farish Carter suggested the developing new town be named in his honor. As a key stop on the Western and Atlanta Railroad run between Chattanooga and Atlanta, the little town grew quickly.

Cartersville was also among those towns hit hard by Gen. Sherman's March to the Sea, but it quickly recovered due to its railroading endeavors. Even today, it is a busy hub

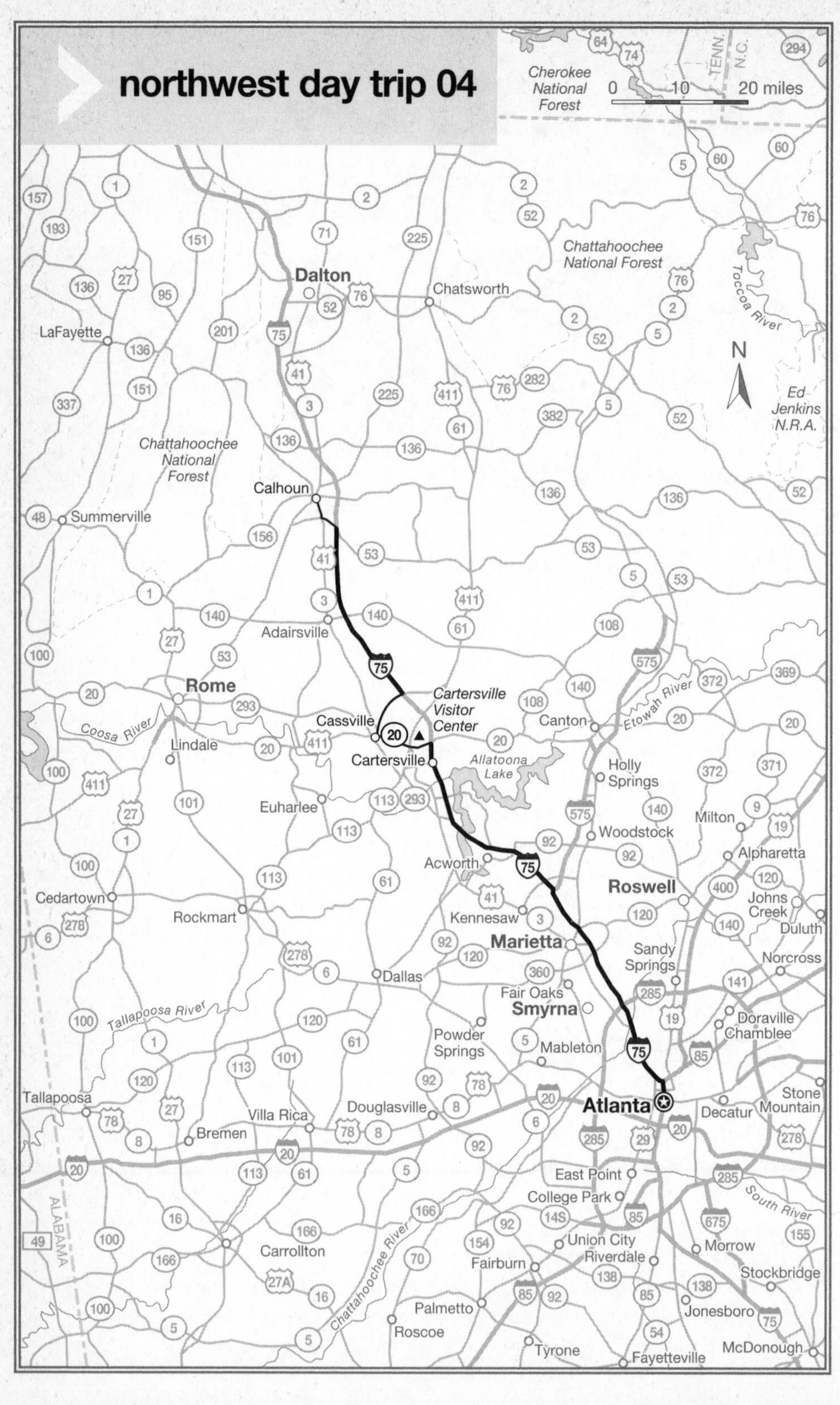
northwest day trip 04
Cherokee National Forest
0
10
20 miles
TENN.
N.C.
Chattahoochee National Forest
Toccoa River
N
Ed Jenkins N.R.A.
Dalton
Chatsworth
LaFayette
Chattahoochee National Forest
Calhoun
Summerville
Adairsville
Rome
Coosa River
Lindale
Cassville
Cartersville Visitor Center
Cartersville
Allatoona Lake
Canton
Etowah River
Holly Springs
Woodstock
Milton
Alpharetta
Roswell
Johns Creek
Duluth
Euharlee
Acworth
Kennesaw
Marietta
Cedartown
Rockmart
Dallas
Sandy Springs
Norcross
Fair Oaks
Smyrna
Doraville
Chamblee
Tallapoosa River
Powder Springs
Mableton
Tallapoosa
Villa Rica
Douglasville
Bremen
Atlanta
Decatur
Stone Mountain
East Point
College Park
South River
ALABAMA
Carrollton
Chattahoochee River
Union City
Riverdale
Morrow
Fairburn
Stockbridge
Palmetto
Jonesboro
Roscoe
Tyrone
Fayetteville
McDonough

of rail traffic and more than 50 trains cut through the town each day. The bustling burg makes the most of its location both with industry and recreation. You'll find a host of parks in the area.

getting there

Cartersville is a 50-minute drive from downtown Atlanta, heading straight up I-75 North. There are several Cartersville exits, but if you take exit 290 onto GA 20, you can stop by the visitor center.

where to go

Georgia Visitor Information Center inside the Clarence Brown Conference Center. 5450 GA 20; (770) 387-1357; www.brownconferencecenter.com. On exit 290 off I-75, this is a good place to stop to get oriented on all things Cartersville as well as the region. It is an official Georgia Local Welcome Center and includes free Wi-Fi, picnic areas, and its own nature trails. Mon through Fri 8:30 a.m. to 5 p.m., Sat 11 a.m. to 4 p.m. Free.

Carterville Visitor Center. 1 Friendship Plaza; (770) 387-1357; http://notatlanta.org. Next to the 1850s train depot, the visitor center can guide you to places to see in and around Cartersville. It's on Friendship Plaza, which was created by Mark Cooper, who is credited with bringing trains to Cartersville, and honors the 38 friends who helped him during financial difficulties. Mon through Fri 9 a.m. to 5 p.m., Sat 11 a.m. to 4 p.m.

Bartow History Museum. 4 E. Church St.; (770) 382-3818; www.bartowhistorymuseum.org. In the 1867 Old Cartersville Courthouse, the museum contains artifacts, archives, and oral histories dating to prehistoric times. The museum store is a great place to shop. Mon through Sat 10 a.m. to 5 p.m. Closed Sun. $$.

Booth Western Art Museum. 501 Museum Dr.; (770) 387-1300; www.boothmuseum.org. The Booth is the second largest art museum in Georgia and houses the largest permanent exhibition space for Western art in the US. An affiliate of the Smithsonian Institution, it also boasts a presidential gallery with a photograph and original signed letter from all 43 US presidents. Tues, Wed, Fri, and Sat 10 a.m. to 5 p.m.; Thurs 10 a.m. to 8 p.m.; Sun 1 to 5 p.m. Closed Mon. $$.

Etowah Indian Mounds. 813 Indian Mound Rd. Southeast; (770) 387-3747; www.gastateparks.org/EtowahMounds. The 6 earthen mounds in this park are believed to date back to AD 1000 and can be traced back to what is called the Native American Mississippian culture. This 54-acre site contains the mounds, a plaza, village area, borrow pits, and a defensive ditch, and is the most intact site of its kind in the US. The highest mound reaches 63 feet. Wed through Sat 9 a.m. to 5 p.m. $.

Rose Lawn. 224 W. Cherokee Ave.; (770) 387-5162; www.roselawnmuseum.com. This beautiful Victorian mansion was the home of noted evangelist Sam Jones, who lived here in the late 1800s. Nashville's Union Gospel Tabernacle (Ryman Auditorium) was built for Jones. The Ryman would later become the Grand Ole Opry. Jones coined the phrase, "The path to hell is paved with good intentions." You may also want to wander across the street to the First Baptist Church where there is a monument to Baptist missionary Lottie Moon. Tues through Fri 10 a.m. to noon and 1 to 5 p.m. $.

Tellus Science Museum. 100 Tellus Dr.; (770) 606-5700; www.tellusmuseum.org. Occupying more than 125,000 square feet, the Tellus is devoted to minerals, fossils, transportation technology, and hands-on science experiences. This Smithsonian Institute affiliate also features the first digital planetarium in North Georgia. Daily 10 a.m. to 5 p.m. $$.

Young Brothers Pharmacy. 2 W. Main St.; (770) 382-4010. Most of Young Brothers' visitors aren't there to shop; they are there to take pictures. On the side of the building is the world's first Coca-Cola outdoor wall advertisement. Painted in 1894 by a Coca-Cola syrup salesman named James Couden, it has been carefully restored in recent years. Pictures turn out best in the morning light. The pharmacy is open Mon through Fri 8 a.m. to 6:30 p.m., Sat 9 a.m. to 2 p.m., Sun 1:30 to 3 p.m.

where to shop

B & B Antiques and Collectables. 16 S. Wall St.; (770) 386-3232. A friendly shop offering American and French country antiques, vintage jewelry, and more. Mon through Sat 10 a.m. to 6 p.m.

Bradford Place Antiques. 121 Postelle St.; (770) 607-6692. There is something for everyone in this antiques shop. Think decorative furniture, pottery, and antique books. Mon through Sat 10:30 a.m. to 6 p.m.

Cartersville Antique Gallery. 9 E. Main St.; (770) 607-8040; www.cartersvilleantiquegallery.com. Considered one of the top destinations for antiques in the area, it carries a wide selection of quality pieces ranging from period antique furniture to early crock pottery and renowned Gordy pottery, elegant glassware, and much more. Mon to Sat 11 a.m. to 5 p.m. or by appointment.

Under the Bridge. 10–20 E. Church St. Under the Bridge is an eclectic group of shops located literally under the Church Street Bridge in downtown. They include the **Lulu Boutique** (770-386-5898), **Meg Pie** (770-386-1231), and **Periwinkle** (770-607-7171). Mon through Thurs 10 a.m. to 6 p.m., Fri and Sat 10 a.m. to 8 p.m. Closed Sun.

where to eat

Antonino's Italian Grotto. 28 S. Wall St.; (770) 387-9664. Homemade Italian cuisine including fresh pasta, soups, and salads as well as desserts. Tues through Thurs 11 a.m. to 2 p.m. and 5 to 9:30 p.m., Fri 11 a.m. to 2 p.m. and 4:30 to 10 p.m., and Sat 11:30 a.m. to 10 p.m. Closed Sun and Mon. $$.

Appalachian Grill. 14 E. Church St., "Under the Bridge"; (770) 607-5357. In a quaint storefront Under the Bridge, call this food Southern and soul. Fish, chicken, and steak all have a touch of Southern extras. Mon through Thurs 11 a.m. to 9 p.m., Fri 11 a.m. to 10 p.m., Sat noon to 10 p.m. Closed Sun. $–$$.

Bartow Diner. 957 Joe Frank Harris Pkwy., across from Cartersville Medical Center; (770) 607-7775. There is something for everyone on this diner menu from burgers to potpie. The milkshakes alone are worth the visit. Sun through Thurs 7 a.m. to 10 p.m., Fri and Sat 7 a.m. to 11 p.m. $–$$.

Cody J's. 675 Erwin St.; (770) 387-0208. This is a classic meat-and-three Southern diner. In other words, you can get a dinner order than includes a choice of meat and 3 vegetables. Homemade desserts are also a must. Drive-through window available. No alcohol. Mon through Wed and Fri 6 a.m. to 2 p.m., Thurs 6 a.m. to 9 p.m. Closed Sat and Sun. $–$$.

Doug Jr's. 300 S. Tennessee St.; (678) 721-4200. Southern home-cooking at its best. (Doug's is in nearby Emerson.) Open only for breakfast and lunch. You can't beat the fried chicken. Mon through Fri 7 a.m. to 2 p.m. $.

Four Way Lunch. Main Street and Gilmer Street; no phone. Open since 1931, this former fruit stand is a must in Cartersville. The menu is basic, mostly hot dogs (great chili dogs!), burgers, french fries, and fried pies. There are only 8 stools in the place, but the turnover is fast. Cash only. Mon through Sat 6 a.m. to 3 p.m. $.

Jefferson's. 28 W. Main St.; (770) 334-2069. For juicy burgers and spicy chicken wings, this sports bar and grill is the place to be. But don't overlook the fresh seafood or cool desserts. Sun through Wed 11 a.m. to 10 p.m., Thurs through Sat 11 a.m. to 11 p.m. $–$$.

Ross's Diner. 17 Wall St.; (770) 382-9159. Another local favorite, Ross's has been in business since 1945. A great place for meat-and-three or just burgers and hot dogs. Visa and MasterCard only. Mon through Sat 6:30 a.m. to 2:30 p.m. Open until 8 p.m. on Fri. $.

Scott's Walk-Up Bar-B-Q. 206 N. Tennessee St.; (770) 382-1600. A hometown barbeque favorite. The smoked pork is to die for, and ribs are fall-off-the-bone tender. Tues and Wed 10:30 a.m. to 2:30 p.m., Thurs and Fri 10:30 a.m. to 8 p.m., Sat 10:30 a.m. to 2:30 p.m. $–$$.

Wall Street Cafe. 25 N. Wall St.; (770) 386-3100; www.wallstreetcafecartersville.com. Daily sandwich specials with ample portions. Homemade soups and salads as well as scrumptious desserts. Tues through Sat 10:30 a.m. to 3 p.m. $.

where to stay

Days Inn. 5618 GA 20 Southeast; (770) 382-1824; www.daysinn.com. Complimentary breakfast included. Kids stay free. Pool on-site. $.

Hilton Garden Inn. 24 Liberty Dr.; (770) 382-9787; www.hilton.com. Just 1 mile from the heart of downtown. Clean and comfortable. $–$$.

Lake Allatoona Inn. 632 Old Allatoona Rd.; (770) 943-0171. This 1800s Victorian inn sits on a 16-acre farm right on Lake Allatoona. Rooms are large, and a lakefront cabin is also available. $$.

worth more time

Euharlee Covered Bridge. Covered Bridge Road, west of Cartersville. In the tiny town of Euharlee is a landmark of Georgia's Covered Bridge Trail. Listed on the National Register of Historic Places, the Euharlee Covered Bridge was built in 1886 by Washington W. King, a black contractor. The Euharlee History Museum offers free tours Tues through Sat 10 a.m. to 5 p.m. and Sun 1 to 5 p.m. Closed Mon. To get there from Cartersville, head south on GA 113 approximately 4.5 miles, then right on Euharlee Road. Go 5.5 miles on Euharlee Road, then turn left on Covered Bridge Road.

cassville

To look around tiny Cassville today it is almost hard to believe that this town used to be the cultural capital of North Georgia. Founded in 1832 by the state legislature, it was the county seat for Cass County (now Bartow), which was carved from the former Cherokee territory. It its heyday, the town consisted of two colleges (male and female), four churches, a newspaper, and four hotels.

Then came the Civil War.

On October 30, 1864, orders were issued to destroy Cassville. Residents were given only 20 minutes' notice that their town was to be burned. When Gen. Sherman was through with Cassville, all that remained was three homes, two churches, and a Confederate cemetery. Rather than rebuilding, residents shifted to neighboring Cartersville, which had access to the railroad, and many simply never came back.

The Cassville of today is a sleepy community paying tribute to its past.

getting there

Cassville is 5 minutes from Cartersville; take US 41 North 5 miles to Cassville Road. From Atlanta it's just under an hour drive. Take I-75 North to exit 290 for GA 20 toward Rome. Go 2 miles and take US 41 North for 5 miles to Cassville Road.

where to go

Cassville Baptist Church. 1663 Cassville Rd. Northwest; (770) 382-6739. The redbrick Baptist church stands on the site where the original church was built in 1832. Although the building survived the burning of Cassville by Sherman, it had to be razed in 1910 and rebuilt in its present form.

Cassville United Methodist Church. 52 Church St. Cassville United Methodist Church was established in 1833 and operated the Female Methodist College in town until that was burned down during the Civil War. The church survived, and its white wooden structure remains almost unaltered since that day.

Confederate Cemetery at Cassville. Cassville and White Roads. There are more than 300 graves of unknown Confederate soldiers as well as CSA Brig. Gen. William T. Wofford here in this country cemetery. Many of the dead fought in the Battle of Chickamauga and were moved to local hospitals where they died. Most were buried without a headstone, but in May 1899 the Cassville Chapter of the United Daughters of the Confederacy began making sure every grave was marked. Daily dawn to dusk.

Noble Hill-Wheeler Memorial Center. 2361 Joe Frank Harris Pkwy.; (770) 382-3392; www.noblehillwheeler.com. Built in 1923, this was the first school in northwest Georgia constructed with what were called "Rosenwald" funds—financing dedicated specifically to the education of black children. The school was at that time called the Noble Hill Rosenwald School. The history museum and cultural center is dedicated to black educational history and is on the National Historic Register. Tues through Sat 9 a.m. to 4 p.m. Closed Sun and Mon. Wheelchair accessible. No admission charged, although donations are accepted.

Old Cassville Post Office Museum. 1813 Cassville Rd.; (678) 322-6967. The Old Post Office was occupied by the US Postal Service until the mid-1990s. Now operated by the Cassville Historical Society as a museum, exhibitions here not only trace the history of the post office, but Cassville itself. Among the items inside are an original wanted poster for Martin Luther King Jr.'s assassin, James Earl Ray. Sat 10 a.m. to 2 p.m. (except holidays).

Old Presbyterian Church. 1718 Cassville Rd. The Old Cassville Presbyterian Church was built in 1833 and was one of the three Cassville churches that Gen. Sherman did not burn. This church is now known as St. James AME Church.

where to eat

There are no restaurants or hotels in Cassville. We recommend you look at those sections in Cartersville.

worth more time

Kingston. Rich in antebellum history, Kingston is just 20 minutes west of Cartersville out Cherokee Avenue (GA 293). Visit Kingston Woman's History Museum and Annex or the Martha Mulinex Annex for free exhibitions on the town's history before and after the Civil War (13 E. Main St.; 770-336-0380; http://notatlanta.org; Sat and Sun 1 to 4 p.m.).

calhoun

Calhoun dates back to the heyday of the Cherokee Nation when it was known as Oothcalooga. It was near here that the Cherokees had their capital of Echota. But even after they were driven out of the area, Calhoun grew in prominence thanks to the railroad. These days, its central location halfway between Atlanta and Chattanooga makes it a great place to escape.

The courthouse stands in the center of downtown, and traffic must go around on either side. It makes for a great area to stroll and check out the shops, restaurants, and historical sites. As with much of this part of Georgia, Calhoun had its own role in the Civil War, and there are many monuments to commemorate this era in its history.

getting there

Calhoun is only 30 miles from Cassville. Take Cass White Road north and get back on I-75 North. Get off at exit 312 for GA 53 and turn left toward Calhoun. Go 3 miles and turn right on US 42 into Calhoun. Or you may choose to meander up US 41, which runs parallel to I-75. It will take you 15 to 20 minutes longer than taking I-75. If you are coming directly from Atlanta, the dirive will take you about 1 hour and 15 minutes. Take exit 312 and follow the above directions.

where to go

Gordon County Convention and Visitors Bureau. 300 S. Wall St.; (800) 887-3811; www.exploregordoncounty.com. In the heart of town, stop here for extra insight into activities taking place while you are visiting. They will also provide maps of the area. Mon through Thurs 8:30 a.m. to 5 p.m.

Calhoun Memorial Arch. GA 225 and US 41. This arch was built in 1927 and features a Confederate soldier, a World War I doughboy, and Sequoyah, the Cherokee who invented the Native American alphabet. The arch was built by W. I. Hillhouse for the Calhoun Women's Club.

Gordon County Historical Society. 335 S. Wall St.; (706) 629-1515. The historical society is in a beautiful old antebellum home called Oakleigh, which was used by Gen. Sherman as his headquarters during the Civil War. In addition to historical records, the building is home to a collection of 1,500 dolls. Mon through Fri 10 a.m. to 5 p.m.

Harris Arts Center. 212 S. Wall St.; (706) 629.2599; www.cgarts.org. In the restored Rooker Hotel, the Harris Arts Center features a gallery as well as artists' studios and a 250-seat theater.

New Echota Historic Site. 1211 Chatsworth Hwy. Northeast; (706) 624-1321; www.gastateparks.org/NewEchota. From 1825 until the time they were removed in the Trail of Tears, New Echota served as the capital of the Cherokee Nation. It was home to the first Indian-language newspaper office. Visitors can learn about the Cherokees' removal and the Trail of Tears while visiting 12 original and reconstructed buildings. Thurs through Sat 9 a.m. to 5 p.m. $.

Pure Oil Gas Station. Wall Street and US 41. This old gas station is a classic example of those that used to line the Dixie Highway. Designed by self-taught architect Carl Peterson in 1927, it is one of literally hundreds of similar English-cottage-motif stations built across the South and Midwest. It is now home to the Moon Rogers Motor Company.

Roland Hayes Museum. 212 S. Wall St.; (706) 629-2599; www.cgarts.org. A museum honoring classical singer Roland Hayes (1887–1977). An African American from Gordon County, Hayes opened doors for blacks in the performing arts arena. At the height of his half-century career, he was one of the world's highest paid singers, performing throughout the US and Europe. Mon 10 a.m. to 6 p.m., Tues through Thus 10 a.m. to 4 p.m., Fri 10 a.m. to 2 p.m., Sat by appointment only.

where to shop

For antiques lovers, there is a host of shops around Calhoun through which to browse, but most shoppers come to the area for:

Calhoun Premium Outlets. 455 Belwood Rd., exit 127 off I-75; (706) 602-1305; www.premiumoutlets.com. More than 50 stores offering up to 65 percent discount off of the retail price. This place is a mecca for those shopping for designer brands. Mon through Sat 10 a.m. to 9 p.m., Sun 11 a.m. to 7 p.m.

where to eat

Dub's High on the Hog. 349 S. Wall St.; (706) 602-5150. Finger-licking good barbeque and some of the best around. It gets crowded, but is worth the wait. Mon through Sat 11 a.m. to 9 p.m. $–$$.

Echota Smoke House. 1214 US 41 North; (706) 629-5660. Specializing in barbeque, it has numerous other home-style foods from which to choose. Mon through Sat 7 a.m. to 9 p.m. $.

Gondolier Pizza Italian. 427 GA 53 East; (706) 625-2322; www.gondolierpizza.com. Originally started in the 1980s in Cleveland, Tennessee, Gondolier has established itself as a favorite in Calhoun. A combination of traditional Italian and Greek foods are filling and tasty. Sun through Thurs 11 a.m. to 10 p.m., Fri and Sat 11 a.m. to 11 p.m. $–$$.

Mama's Home Cooking. Gordon Hills Shopping Center, 100 Peters St., #8; (706) 625-1588. Home-style cooking and fast service. Dig into the meat loaf, salmon patties, Salisbury steak, barbeque chicken, and homemade corn bread. There are 4 types of homemade soups daily. Daily 11 a.m. to 8 p.m. $.

Thurston's. 114 Court St.; (706) 602-4401. Thurston's makes up for its tiny space with great taste. This deli and coffee shop in the heart of town offers fresh baked goods and wonderful sandwiches. Try the sweet potato fries! Mon through Sat 11 a.m. to 3 p.m. $–$$.

Yellow Jacket Drive-in. 801 Oothcalooga St.; (706) 629-4347. The Yellow Jacket is an old-fashioned diner and a favorite among the locals. It serves up family-style foods with a meat-and-three as well as typical diner fare. Cash only. Daily 6 a.m. to 8 p.m. $.

where to stay

Days Inn. 915 GA 53 East Southeast; (706) 629-9501; www.daysinn.com. The Days Inn Calhoun is off of I-75 exit 312 on GA 53. Walking distance to the outlets, the Days Inn offers breakfast, an outdoor pool, and free Internet with your stay. $.

Hampton Inn. 115 Jamison St. Southeast; (706) 629-0999; http://hamptoninn.hilton.com. This hotel features 65 clean and comfortable rooms. Includes a pool, fitness center, and free Wi-Fi. Restaurant on-site. $.

Ramada Calhoun. 1204 Red Bud Rd. Northeast; (706) 629-9207; www.ramadainn.com. Located at exit 315 on I-75, this 45-room hotel has free Wi-Fi and an outdoor pool. Laundry service is available on-site. $.

day trip 05

marked in history:
adairsville, resaca

For history lovers, this is the perfect little day trip. The towns on this journey—Adairsville and Resaca—may not be known by many but between them, they have numerous historical markers you'll find along the way. We admit that much of them have to do with the Civil War, but not everything. In fact, not even close. Remember, this area was the wild frontier back in the 1700s and 1800s.

Each of these towns has its own distinct history, and you'll be charmed by both the towns and the people who live there. You'll have a hard time deciding which is your favorite between them and may have trouble pulling away from one to go on to the next. Don't worry, you don't have to. Feel free to linger.

adairsville

Adairsville was the first town in Georgia to be listed in its entirety on the National Register of Historic Places, and it is easy to see why. A quaint town, it is steeped in history. Built on the site of a Cherokee town called Oothcalooga Village, it is named for Chief Walter Adair, a Scottish settler who was married to a Cherokee woman. Its position along the Western and Atlantic Railroad allowed it to thrive and become the "Granary of the State." But, during the Civil War, much of the area was destroyed when Gen. Sherman discovered the townspeople had been supplying arms to the Confederates.

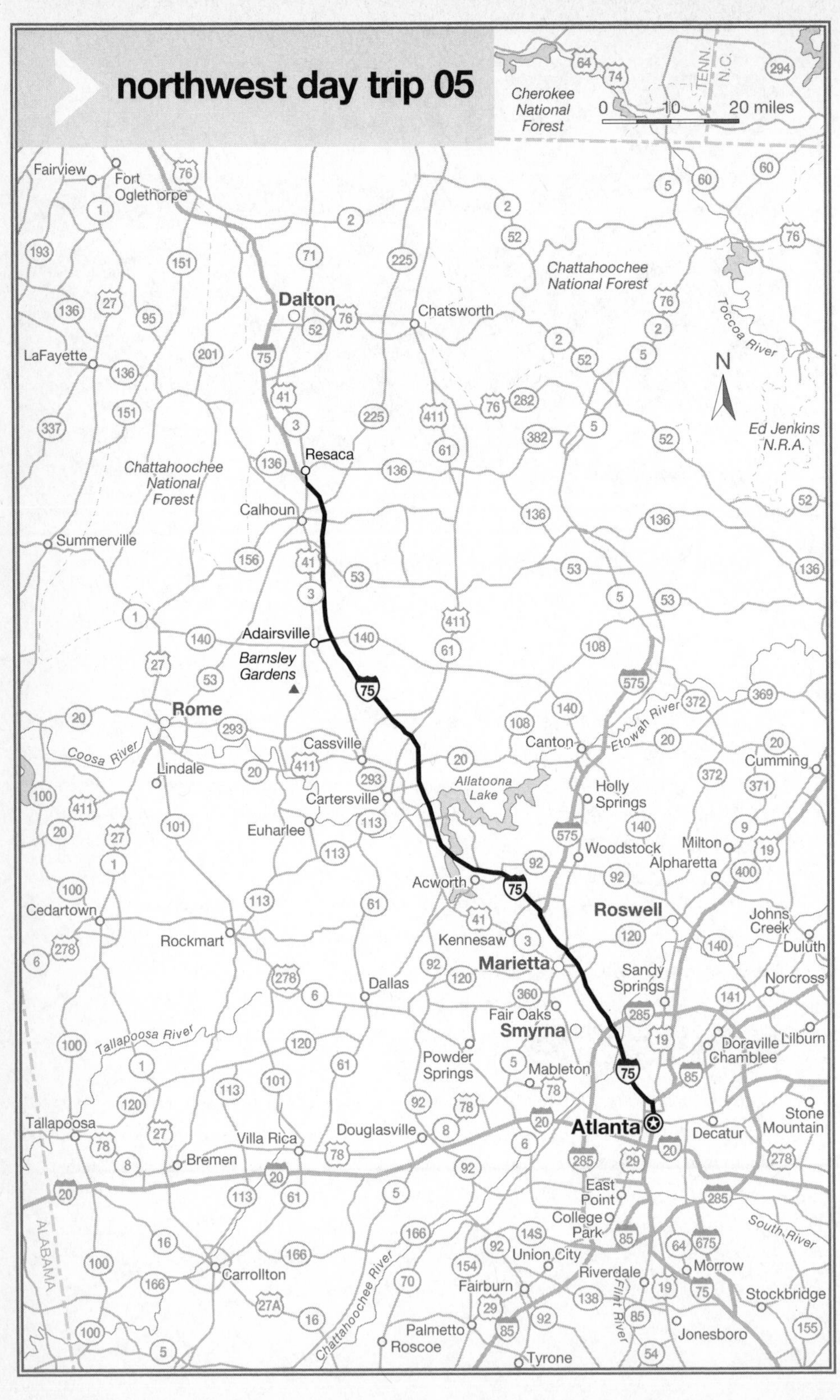
northwest day trip 05
Cherokee National Forest
0 10 20 miles
TENN.
N.C.
Fairview
Fort Oglethorpe
Dalton
Chatsworth
Chattahoochee National Forest
Toccoa River
LaFayette
N
Ed Jenkins N.R.A.
Resaca
Chattahoochee National Forest
Calhoun
Summerville
Adairsville
Barnsley Gardens
Rome
Coosa River
Cassville
Lindale
Canton
Etowah River
Cumming
Allatoona Lake
Cartersville
Holly Springs
Euharlee
Woodstock
Milton
Alpharetta
Acworth
Cedartown
Roswell
Johns Creek
Rockmart
Kennesaw
Duluth
Marietta
Sandy Springs
Norcross
Dallas
Fair Oaks
Smyrna
Lilburn
Tallapoosa River
Powder Springs
Doraville
Chamblee
Mableton
Stone Mountain
Tallapoosa
Atlanta
Decatur
Villa Rica
Douglasville
Bremen
East Point
College Park
South River
ALABAMA
Union City
Carrollton
Riverdale
Morrow
Chattahoochee River
Fairburn
Flint River
Stockbridge
Palmetto
Jonesboro
Roscoe
Tyrone

Rebuilding came quickly with the help of that ever-present railroad, and Adairsville thrived on textiles (in particular—chenille) and farming. At one point, it was known as "The Peach Center of the World," bragging that its peaches were served at tables in Europe.

These days, as in the past, the town's activities center around its historic square.

getting there

Adairsville is just more than an hour from Atlanta. Take I-75 North to exit 306, and go left on GA 140 towards Adairsville/Summerville for just more than a mile. Cross over US 41 and make a left on Main Street, which is the next street. Within a half a mile you'll be in the heart of Adairsville.

where to go

Adairsville Depot Visitor's Center and Age of Steam Museum. 101 Public Sq.; (770) 773-1775; http://adairsvilledepot.garlandlink.com. Built in 1847, the W&A Railroad Depot has been a centerpiece of Adairsville since it was conceived. The welcome center can fill you in on activities around town, but make sure you visit the museum, which traces the town's history and highlights Adairsville's role in the Civil War railroad espionage caper known as *The Great Locomotive Chase.* Tues through Fri 10 a.m. to 5 p.m. Free

Barnsley Gardens. 597 Barnsley Gardens Rd.; (770) 773-7480; www.barnsleyresort.com. Barnsley Gardens is named for Geoffrey Barnsley, a Savannah businessman who built this estate as a tribute to his wife Julia, who died before work could begin. Barnsley said he still felt her presence and erected the mansion and gardens according to her wishes. There are occasional ghostly sightings in the mansion ruins. After its heyday, the property fell into disrepair until 1988 when it was bought by Prince Hubertus Fugger-Babenhausen of Germany. Now owned by a Dalton group, the Barnsley has been developed into a world-class resort with a spa, golf course, accommodations, and on-site restaurants.

1902 Stock Exchange. 124 Public Sq.; (770) 773-1902. As a restored mercantile on the town square, the 1902 Stock Exchange is listed on the National Historic Register. It currently houses a gallery of shops, which include a bookstore, an antiques store, a tearoom, and even a seasonal dinner theater upstairs in the Opera House. Folks are friendly here, and if you want to know anything about Adairsville, just ask. Tues through Sat 10 a.m. to 5 p.m.; Sun 1 to 5 p.m.

Pumpkin Patch Farm. 230 Old Dixie Hwy. Northwest; (770) 773-2617; www.pumpkinpatchfarm.net. Pumpkin Patch Farm helps celebrate fall, and you'll wish it could be October year-round. The Pumpkin Patch's entry fee includes hayrides, an animal barnyard, a hay maze, and a pumpkin ring toss, gourds, Indian corn, cornstalks, hay, and much more. Weekends in Oct 10 a.m. to 5 p.m. $$.

where to eat

Adairsville Inn Restaurant. 100 S. Main St.; (770) 878-9695; www.adairsvilleinnrestaurant.com. Enjoy Southern cooking on the veranda of this home built in 1855. The grounds are almost as pretty as the cooking is good! Tues through Sat 11 a.m. to 2 p.m. and 5 to 9 p.m., Sunday buffet noon to 2:30 p.m. $–$$.

Maggie Mae Tea Room and Cafe. 124 Public Sq., inside 1902 Stock Exchange; (770) 773-1902. Tucked in the back of the 1902 Stock Exchange are homemade salads and sandwiches that will draw you in, even if you are not shopping. Mon through Sat 11 a.m. to 3 p.m. $–$$.

Rice House Restaurant. Barnsley Gardens Resort, 597 Barnsley Gardens Rd.; (770) 773-7480; www.barnsleyresort.com. Fine dining in a resort atmosphere, the Rice House features a menu that ranges from wild game to steaks and seafood. 5:30 p.m. to 10 p.m. $$–$$$.

Sage Cottage Restaurant. 212 N. Main St.; (770) 877-5995; www.sagecottagerestaurant.com. You'll delight in the fine dining that includes steak and seafood as well as crepes and homemade desserts. Owners Jim and Sharon Sutherland will make you feel right at home. Tues through Fri and Sun 11 a.m. to 2 p.m., Tues through Sat 5 to 9:30 p.m. $$–$$$.

Woodlands Grill. Barnsley Gardens Resort, 597 Barnsley Gardens Rd.; (770) 773-7480; www.barnsleyresort.com. The Woodlands Grill has the air of an English hunting lodge and serves meals ranging from burgers and salads to steaks. Attached to the grill is Dugan's Tavern where you can enjoy a game of billiards. Daily 7 a.m. to 11 p.m. $–$$$.

where to stay

Barnsley Gardens. 597 Barnsley Gardens Rd.; (770) 773-7480; www.barnsleyresort.com. Barnsley is a destination unto itself with its spa, golf course, and restaurants. There are 87 rooms and suites from which to choose with most decorated in period furniture. $$–$$$.

resaca

Resaca gets its name from a group of inductees from the Mexican-American War and a battle they fought in 1846. In fact, sadly, wars have brought Resaca its greatest recognition.

Most people recognize the name because the first battle of the Atlanta Campaign of the Civil War was fought just outside of downtown. These days, the town of fewer than 1,000 is a sleepy little community that is generally visited by Civil War buffs and antiques hunters.

getting there

Resaca is 20 minutes north of Adairsville and just over an hour from the heart of Atlanta. Head straight up I-75 North and get off at exit 320. The town is to the east of the interstate on GA 136, while the battlefield is to the west.

where to go

Confederate Cemetery, Battle of Resaca. Confederate Cemetery Road Northeast; (706) 625-3200; www.resacabattlefield.org. Each May, reenactors bring the battlefield back to life as they re-create the Battle of Resaca and educate visitors with living history displays. Even if you are not visiting during that time, you can't help but be moved by the cemetery which stands as its memorial. The more than 2.5-acre grounds are surrounded by a stone wall while the entrance is an imposing stone arch bearing the Southern Cross of Honor constructed of Stone Mountain granite. Many of those resting in the cemetery were buried personally by Mary and Pyatt Green and their African-American cook and maid. The girls and their family returned home after the 1864 battle to find many bodies still uninterred. Mary helped raise funds through the Georgia legislature to start this cemetery, which also houses soldiers who died at Chickamauga.

Little River Farms. 669 Nickelsville Rd.; (706) 629-9688; www.littleriverfarms.com. Little River Farms allows visitors to immerse themselves in rural living. There is a wide variety of activities, many of which depend on the season, but there is always horseback riding and the petting zoo as well as picnicking on the river. If you want to stay longer, there is an inn on-site (see below). $.

Monastery of the Glorious Ascension. 5052 S. Dixie Hwy.; (706) 277-9442; www.monastery.org. Situated on more than 100 wooded acres in North Georgia, this working monastery is home to a small group of Russian Orthodox brothers. Guests are welcome to be a part of the religious services each day, which include vespers, liturgy, and Trapeza, but it's best to check with the monastery because schedules do change. There is a small store on-site which sells books and beeswax candles.

where to eat

Bowman's. 868 County Line Rd. Northeast; (706) 624-3255; www.bowmansrestaurantandcatering.com. Great home cooking with daily specials. Chicken-fried steak to die for. All the vegetables and many of the meats come from their farm. All the desserts are homemade, so leave room. Thurs through Sat 11 a.m. to 9 p.m., Sun 11 a.m. to 3 p.m. $–$$.

where to stay

Country Inn at Little River Farms. 669 Nickelsville Rd., GA 136; (706) 280-7393; www.littleriverfarms.com. There is no end of activities at Little River Farms, but the inn offers large furnished bedroom suites, a full kitchen, and a porch where you can relax and enjoy views. $–$$.

day trip 06

peacocks & pine trees:
dalton, chatsworth, ringgold

As we get closer to the Tennessee border with this day trip, you'll notice the hills rolling more and the towns getting more and more spread out. Those tall Georgia pines you've heard so much about are everywhere. It's easy to see why this area of Georgia was once considered the frontier. It was the Enchanted Lands of the Cherokee at one time, and this day trip will take you to some of their favorite areas to see just how much they have changed, and in some cases, stayed the same.

We will start at a small, unassuming town that the world relies on for its carpets. Yes. Carpets. Dalton, Georgia, stumbled into this industry quite by accident and is now the world leader in carpet making. The industry spreads into the neighboring town of Chatsworth, which is better known for its Native American legacy.

The final stop is a town few have heard of: Ringgold. This little burg has big history to explore, so come along and head northwest one more time.

dalton

These days Dalton is known as the Carpet Capital of the World, and with 150 mills in the area, 90 percent of the functioning carpet in the world comes from this little town. That milling history can be traced back to a wedding gift in 1895: Teenager Catherine Evans Whitener wanted to give her brother Henry something special for his wedding, and she created a tufted bedspread by using a quilt pattern clipping cotton yarns that she'd sewn onto it.

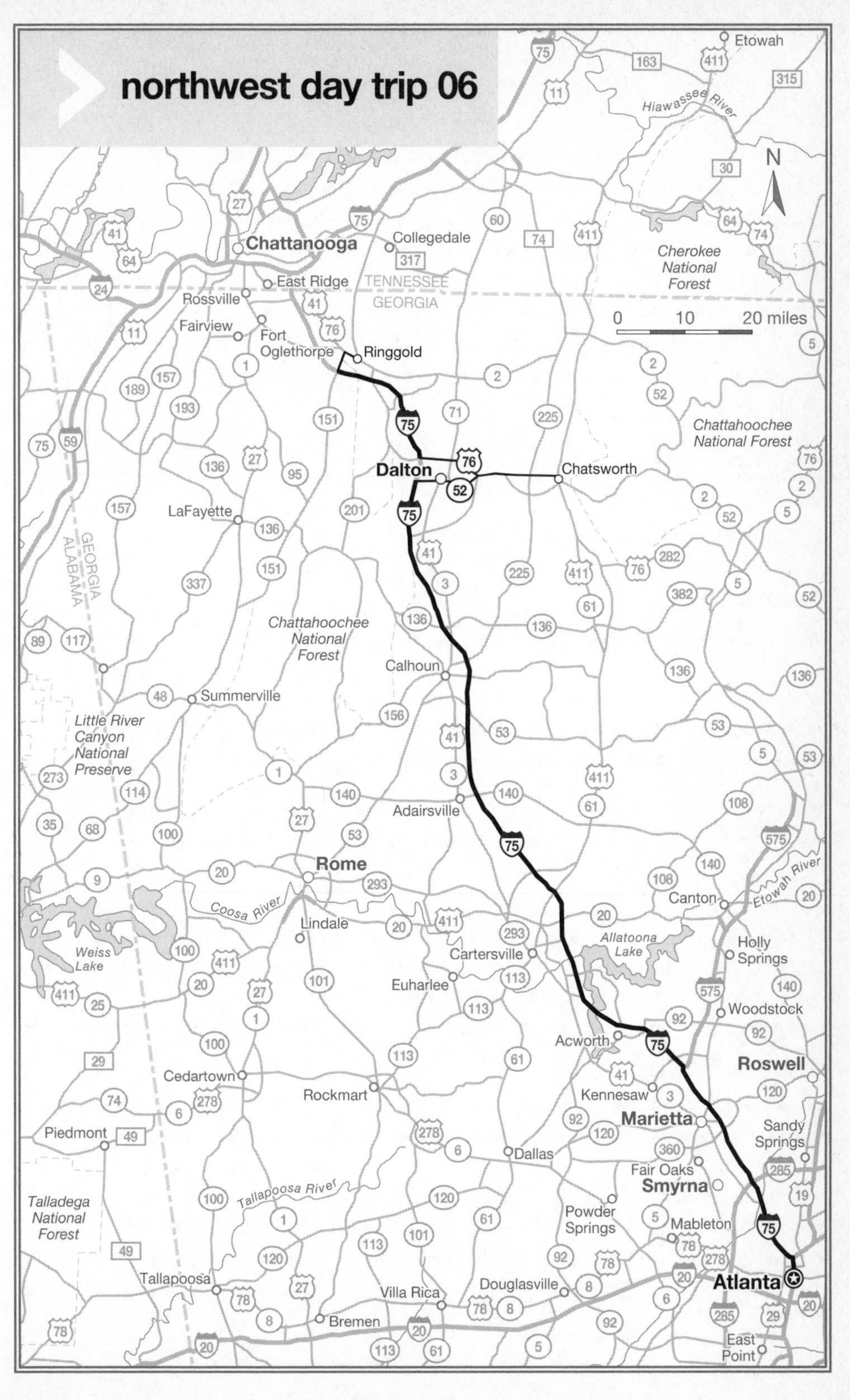
northwest day trip 06
Chattanooga
Collegedale
East Ridge
TENNESSEE
GEORGIA
Rossville
Fairview
Fort Oglethorpe
Ringgold
Dalton
Chatsworth
LaFayette
Calhoun
Summerville
Adairsville
Rome
Lindale
Cartersville
Euharlee
Canton
Holly Springs
Woodstock
Acworth
Kennesaw
Marietta
Roswell
Sandy Springs
Fair Oaks
Smyrna
Mableton
Atlanta
East Point
Dallas
Powder Springs
Douglasville
Villa Rica
Bremen
Tallapoosa
Cedartown
Rockmart
Piedmont
Etowah
Hiawassee River
Cherokee National Forest
Chattahoochee National Forest
Little River Canyon National Preserve
Talladega National Forest
Weiss Lake
Coosa River
Tallapoosa River
Etowah River
Allatoona Lake
GEORGIA
ALABAMA
N
0 10 20 miles

Her bedspread proved so popular that a cottage industry of nearly 10,000 area "tufters"—men, women, and children—began producing chenille bedspreads. When automobiles started making their way through Dalton, the bedspreads were sold off clotheslines to tourists. A popular pattern was that of a peacock, and the area around Dalton became known as "Peacock Alley" or even "Bedspread Boulevard."

Tufting for bedspreads gave way to tufting for carpets in the 1950s, and a new industry was born, one that has transformed Dalton to a world-renown giant.

As staggering as the carpet figures are, Dalton has another claim to fame: its history dating back to the time of the Cherokee. A visit to Dalton doesn't revolve just around carpets.

getting there

A straight shot from downtown Atlanta, the journey will take you 90 minutes. Take I-75 North for 86 miles to exit 333/GA 52 toward Dalton.

where to go

Visitors Bureau/Visitor Center. 305 S. Depot St.; (706) 270-9960 or (800) 331-3258; http://visitdaltonga.com. Stop here not just for maps and advice, but for a nice little gift shop as well. Among the most popular items is a self-guided driving tour of the area's significant Civil War sites, mainly focusing on the Atlanta Campaign. Mon through Fri 8:30 a.m. to 5 p.m. (gift shop Mon through Sat 9 a.m. to 5 p.m.).

Blunt House. 506 S. Thornton Ave.; (706) 278-0217. The first 2-story house in Dalton was built in 1848 by the town's first mayor Ainsworth Emery Blunt, who also served as postmaster. Blunt was known teaching carpentry, blacksmithing, coopering, and religion to the Cherokees. The home was used by the Union Army as a hospital during the Civil War, and the Blunt family returned and repaired it after the war was through. On the National Register of Historic Places, the house has been a museum since 1978. Visitors can get a sense of life over the decades in this house through viewing vintage clothing and accessories, antique toys and tools, family linens, antique kitchenware, and much more. Fri 10 a.m. to 4 p.m. and by appointment.

Crown Gardens and Archives. 715 Chattanooga Rd.; (706) 278-0217. Even if you aren't interested in exploring the archives, this place is worth a stop. The 1890s mill was part of the booming chenille fabric industry in Dalton, which predated its carpet industry. The mill contains a museum tracing local history as far back as the Cherokees. Next door is the mill office, which is home to the Crown Gardens and Archives. This is also the location of the Whitfield-Murray Historical Society, which operates the archives as a depository for historical records and research material relating to the history of Whitfield and Murray counties.

There is a gift shop on-site where you can purchase publications about the county. Tues through Fri 10 a.m. to 5 p.m., Sat 9 a.m. to 2 p.m. Free.

Dalton (West Hill) Cemetery. Emory Street; (800) 331-3258; http://visitdaltonga.com. The West Hill pays honor to the battles fought in Dalton, Rocky Face, Chickamauga, and Resaca. Because Dalton was a major medical center during the Civil War, many of the wounded were brought here from battles in the surrounding areas in Tennessee and at Chickamauga. As such, 421 unknown Confederate soldiers, 4 known Confederate soldiers, and 4 unknown Union men were buried here between 1862 and 1864. Confederate general Bryan M. Thomas was interred here upon his death in 1905. There is a self-guided walking tour of West Hill Cemetery, featuring 25 of its most interesting characters. There is also a Memorial Wall near the entrance. Dawn to dusk. Free.

Dug Gap Battle Park. Dug Gap Battle Road; (706) 278-0217 or (800) 331-3258; http://visitdaltonga.com. This park still has more than 1,200 feet of the original stone wall that Confederates soldiers built between November of 1863 and May of 1864 to try and protect themselves from the Union. There is a scenic overlook from atop Dug Gap and hiking trails. Daily. Free.

Hamilton House Museum. 701 Chattanooga Ave.; (706) 278-0217. This antebellum home is next to Crown Gardens. With parts of the home dating to 1840, it is considered Dalton's oldest. A tour of the Hamilton House museum treats visitors to antiques, chenille bedspreads and tufting artifacts, and historical memorabilia including Civil War artifacts. The entire upstairs is dedicated to the chenille-making process from tufting to folk-rafting methods. Tues through Fri 10 a.m. to 5 p.m., Sat 9 a.m. to 2 p.m. Free.

Historic Dalton Depot. 110 Depot St.; (706) 226-3160. This historic 1847 Atlantic and Western depot was ground central for more than 100 years for shipping of Dalton's chenille and later carpet products. It was one of the few Victorian train depots to survive Sherman's March to the Sea. The depot is now home to the Dalton Depot Restaurant. Mon through Thurs 11 a.m. to 10 p.m., Fri and Sat noon to 11 p.m.

Prater's Mill. 500 Old Praters Mill Rd. Northeast; (706) 694-6455; www.pratersmill.org. Now a heritage center which focuses on maintaining the crafts and culture from the 1800s, this historic gristmill was built in 1855 by slave labor. Visitors can fish in Cohulla Creek or go hiking along a scenic nature trail. From May to October each year, Prater's Mill also hosts the Prater's Mill Country Fair, featuring local arts, crafts, and musical performances.

Tunnel Hill Heritage Center. 215 Clisby Austin Rd.; (706) 876-1571; www.tunnelhillheritagecenter.com. The small center has a surprising amount of history. The main draw is the 1,477-foot railroad tunnel which was dug in 1848 through the base of a mountain, ultimately connecting Atlanta to the Midwest. There is also a historic antebellum home on the grounds. Mon through Sat 9 a.m. to 5 p.m.; closed Sun. $.

where to shop

Market Street Shops of Dalton. 1001 Market St.; (706) 277-2688 or (800) 409-7029. Just off exit 333, this outlet area has 3 dozen designer stores and specialty shops. Daily 10 a.m. to 9 p.m.

where to eat

Dalton Depot Restaurant. 110 Depot St.; (706) 226-3160. This restaurant is housed in the nationally registered historic depot and serves everything from hamburgers and pasta to steak and seafood. A great place to dine in a historical setting. Mon through Thurs 11 a.m. to 10 p.m., Fri and Sat noon to 11 p.m. $–$$.

Cremo Drive-In. 125 E. Morris St.; (706) 278-6316. Cremo's is an institution. Their foot-long chili dogs alone are worth the drive. Open daily for breakfast, lunch, and dinner. $.

Cubby Hole Cafe. 229 N. Hamilton St.; (706) 226-8886. Comfortable and good, serving homemade soups, salads, and sandwiches. Mon through Fri 11 a.m. to 2:30 p.m. $–$$.

Miller Brothers Rib Shack. 606 E. Morris St.; (706) 278-7365. Barbeque cooked low and slow. Miller Brothers is family run and still a shack after 3 decades of serving some of the finest barbeque around. But that's part of the charm. Lunch and dinner. Closed Sun. $–$$.

Oakwood Cafe. 203 W. Cuyler St.; (706) 529-9663; www.oakwoodcafe.net. This family-owned and -operated cafe serves up good Southern fare from pot roast and fried chicken to barbeque and ribs. Very popular among locals. Mon through Fri 6 a.m. to 8 p.m., Sat 7 a.m. to 8 p.m. $–$$.

Peacock Alley Cafe. 311 S. Hamilton St.; (706) 279-1022; www.peacockalleycafe.com. In an old hardware store, Peacock serves hot and cold sandwiches, quiches, and homemade soups and desserts. Mon through Fri 10 a.m. to 4 p.m. $$.

Powell's Country Kitchen. 116 W. King St.; (706) 278-1545. "Great people, great food, great prices," they say at this local favorite. Southern food served home-style. Mon through Fri 6 a.m. to 2 p.m. $.

where to stay

Days Inn. 1518 W. Walnut Ave.; (706) 278-0850 or (800) DAYSINN; www.daysinn.com. Convenient to the outlet mall and I-75, the Days Inn has a continental breakfast and an outdoor pool. $–$$.

Hampton Inn. 1000 Market St.; (706) 226-4333 or (800) HAMPTON; www.hamptoninn.com. Near downtown, the Hampton Inn has 124 guest rooms/suites, free continental breakfast, an outdoor pool, and a fitness center. $.

Holiday Inn & Suites. 879 College Dr.; (706) 529-6000; www.holidayinn.com. This hotel includes a 24-hour business center, indoor heated pool, fitness center, restaurant, and lounge among its amenities. $–$$.

La Quinta Inn & Suites. 715 College Dr.; (706) 272-9099 or (800) SLEEPLQ; www.lq.com. In the heart of downtown, La Quinta offers breakfast and has an outdoor pool and fitness center. $–$$.

chatsworth

While Chatsworth itself was founded in 1906, its history goes back much further because of the surrounding Cherokee lands, and some of the best-known landmarks in the area are of Native American origin. Local lore states Chatsworth got its name from a sign that fell off a passing train. (Others claim it was the name of a railroad official.) Whatever the real story, Chatsworth has made its own name in the textile industry. There are eight textile mills in and around the town, which employ a large percentage of the population.

The historic downtown area is centered around the Murray County Courthouse, an imposing redbrick structure with white columns, built in 1917.

getting there

Chatsworth is just 10 minutes from Dalton. From downtown Dalton, take E. Morris Street to GA 52/US 76 and make a left towards Chatsworth. If you are coming directly from Atlanta, the drive will take you about an hour and 45 minutes. Take I-75 North to exit 333/GA 52 towards Dalton and follow GA 53/US 76 for 15 miles into Chatsworth.

where to go

Chief Vann House. 82 GA 225 North; (706) 695-2598; www.gastateparks.org/ChiefVannHouse. Considered a showplace of the Cherokee Nation, the 2-story Federal brick home was built in 1804 by Chief James Vann. Vann was a trader and one of the wealthiest men in the still-young US. This was the largest, most prosperous plantation within the Cherokee Nation. Vann was instrumental in helping educate Cherokee youths. Open Thurs through Sat 9 a.m. to 5 p.m. $.

Fort Mountain State Park. 181 Fort Mount Park Rd.; (706) 422-1932; www.gastateparks.org/FortMountain. Fort Mountain is named for a mysterious 855-foot-long wall constructed along the western slope of the peak. While its origins are unclear, most authorities believe the wall was constructed by Woodlands-era Indians between 500 BC and AD 500. The park includes wonderful hiking and horseback riding trails as well as cabins and camping areas. Another feature is a stone fire tower built by the Civilian Conservation Corps. Daily 7 a.m. to 10 p.m. $.

where to eat

Four Way Drive-In. GA 225 South; (706) 695-4935. An old-time drive-in selling burgers and hot dogs. You can't beat their corn dogs. Daily 11 a.m. to 9 p.m. $.

Little Rome. 1201 N. 3rd Ave.; (706) 695-7309. Little Rome is a favorite for Italian. The lasagna is meaty, and the pizza is about the best you'll find. Tues through Sun 11:30 a.m. to 9 p.m. $–$$.

Lou's Burger Hut. 13 Spring Place Smyrna Rd.; (706) 517-1536. A classic hamburger stand that has survived for decades as a stop along the Dixie Highway. Daily 10 a.m. to 8 p.m. $.

Village Cafeteria. 121 N. 2nd Ave.; (706) 695-6356. If you are looking for country cooking, look no further. The cafeteria features 9 meats and 16 veggies daily. And don't forget desserts! Mon through Fri 11 a.m. to 8 p.m., Sun 11 a.m. to 6 p.m. $–$$.

where to stay

Fort Mountain State Park. 181 Fort Mountain Park Rd.; (800) 864-7275; www.gastateparks.org/FortMountain. This 3,700-acre state park has 3 two-bedroom cottages available for rent in addition to campsites. $.

The Hearthstone Lodge. 2755 GA 282; (706) 695-0920; www.thehearthstonelodge.com. This pine-log mountain lodge offers 3 beautiful rooms in a wonderful setting. Sit by a fire or out on the deck. The grounds are gorgeous and include a waterfall. $$.

The Overlook Inn. 864 Wilderness View; (706) 517-8810; www.theoverlookinn.com. This bed-and-breakfast nestled in the foothills is incredibly inviting and offers wonderful views of the mountains. Each comfy room has its own porch and a gas fireplace. $$–$$$.

worth more time

Fort Mountain State Park. 181 Fort Mountain Park Rd.; (800) 864-7275; www.gastateparks.org/FortMountain. Just 8 miles southeast of Chatsworth, Fort Mountain State Park contains one of those ancient mysteries that leave even historians stumped. Stretching 855 feet and zigzagging along the highest point on Fort Mountain is a wall made of rocks. Many believe it was built by Indians for ceremonial purposes during the Woodland period at least 1,000 years ago. In addition to the mountain, the park encompasses camping, streams, and a lake within the Chattahoochee National Forest.

ringgold

This tiny town was hit hard by tornadoes in the spring of 2011, and while much of the business area off of I-75 was destroyed, the historical center was left almost untouched. The town itself was originally called "Crossroads," so named because the Cherokees allowed the US to build a federal highway through their lands in 1805, intersecting other highways in this area.

In the mid-1800s, the bustling community was larger than Chattanooga. Ringgold's position near the Tennessee border also earned it the dubious honor of being the first town in Georgia to burn during Gen. Sherman's March to the Sea.

These days, Ringgold is known as not just a place for history buffs, but for those seeking to get married quickly. The town's short waiting period for marriage licenses has made it "The Wedding Capital of the South."

getting there

Ringgold is about 15 minutes from Dalton straight up I-75, so it's best to go back to Dalton from Chatsworth by retracing your steps on GA 52. Once you're back on I-75, get off at exit 348, GA 151. If you are coming from Atlanta, the drive will take you just over an hour and a half.

where to go

The Battle of Ringgold Gap Confederate Park. US 41, 3 miles north of Ringgold. This 150-acre park on US 41 commemorates the Battle of Ringgold Gap, fought November 23, 1863. There are several historical markers and statues on the site, and it is also the location of the Battle of Ringgold Civil War Festival held each October. Free.

Creek Walk. Paralleling Lafayette Street, Creek Walk is a nice way to get from between Ringgold's Highway Commercial District to the Historic Downtown District. The paved path follows Chickamauga Creek and crosses over the Old Federal Bridge to explore historic downtown Ringgold. Creek Walk is part of a larger project called the Richard Taylor Nature Trail that will eventually connect the Ringgold ball fields with the Ringgold Gap Battlefield. The walk is open year-round.

Georgia Winery Tasting Center. 6469 Battlefield Pkwy.; (706) 937-WINE. Georgia has a well-developed wine industry, and here you can sample a variety of offerings from it. They also have custom-made gift baskets and wine-making supplies. They specialize in Southern-style wines like muscadine and scuppernong. Mon through Sat 10 a.m. to 6 p.m.

The Old Stone Church. 41 Old Cohutta Rd.; (706) 935-5232. The church dates back to 1837 when it was known as the Chickamauga Presbyterian Church. During the Civil War, it was used as headquarters by both sides, later becoming a hospital and then a Methodist church. It is now a museum housing artifacts from the Civil War. Tues through Sat 10 a.m. to 6 p.m. $.

Ringgold Depot. 155 Depot St.; (706) 935-3061. Constructed in 1849 by the Western and Atlantic Railroad, the depot also houses the Ringgold Visitor's Center. The Ringgold Depot is one of the few antebellum-style railroad depots in Georgia. The stone depot was damaged by a cannonball bombardment during the Civil War, but it was restored and is now home to the visitor center. Daily 8:30 a.m. to 5:30 p.m. Closed holidays. Free.

The Wedding Chapel. 7683 Nashville St.; (706) 935-8199; www.ringgoldweddingchapel.net. Most infamously Tammy Wynette and George Strait exchanged vows in this chapel. More than 3,000 couples a year come to Ringgold to get hitched, and this is the prime location to do so. Weekdays 8:30 a.m. to 5 p.m.; Sat 10 a.m. to 4 p.m. $$–$$$.

The Whitman-Anderson House. 309 Tennessee St. A private residence, this 1858 antebellum house is notable because it is the only place Union general Ulysses S. Grant ever stayed in Georgia during the Civil War. He overnighted here during the Battle of Ringgold. General William T. Sherman later used the house as his own headquarters. Not open to the public.

where to eat

Aunt Effie's. 5287 Alabama Hwy.; (706) 935-6525. If you want true Southern cooking, come here. Small and simple, the food alone is worth the drive. Mon through Sat breakfast and lunch. $.

Choo Choo Bar-B-Que. 1670 Old Mill Rd.; (706) 937-5777. Authentic 'que at great prices. You can even buy it by the pound and take it with you. Mon through Fri 10:45 a.m. to 8 p.m., Sat 11 a.m. to 9 p.m. $.

Cook's Bbq. 2929 US 41; (706) 965-5099. Smoky goodness, Cook's has great chopped pork and rib plates. Mon through Fri 11:30 a.m. to 8 p.m., Sat 11 a.m. to 9 p.m. $.

Hilly Billy Cafe. 6977 Nashville St.; (706) 965-4673. Friendly and fast. Southern cooking served up for breakfast, lunch, and dinner. $.

Richard's Restaurant. 906 Lafayette St.; (706) 937-7434. A great restaurant frequented by locals. A wide selection of vegetables from which to choose. Mon through Fri 6:30 a.m. to 2 p.m., Sat 7 a.m. to 2 p.m. $.

where to stay

Home Town Inn. 22 Gateway Business Park Dr.; (706) 937-7070; www.hometowninnringgold.com. Newly renovated, this hotel is friendly and clean. It offers a continental breakfast and an outdoor pool for guests. $.

day trip 07

sky views:
lookout mountain, chickamauga, cloudland canyon

We head into North Georgia's mountains today for some of the most spectacular scenery you will find. If you name a place Lookout Mountain, then you know there must be plenty to see. In fact, the view in all directions seems almost endless and encompasses parts of three states: Georgia, Tennessee, and Alabama.

Lookout's beauty is only surpassed by its history. Here you will see a place commemorating the bloodiest battle of the Civil War, but yet you'll also discover Georgia's own version of the Grand Canyon; only this one is covered in pine trees. They call it Cloudland Canyon for good reason. The views above and below in Cloudland Canyon are like none you will ever see. You'll be right on the Tennessee line here, and this trip will possibly have you crisscrossing the border.

lookout mountain

It can get a bit confusing because there is a Lookout Mountain, Georgia, and Lookout Mountain, Tennessee. They are both the same mountain, just on opposite sides of the state line. The mountain was originally called "Chatanuga" by the Native Americans, meaning "mountains looking at each other." It referred to the rugged rock faces on the side of the mountain.

So treacherous were the roads around it, that early settlers would be warned to "look out" for bandits and warring Indians while crossing the region. The name stuck.

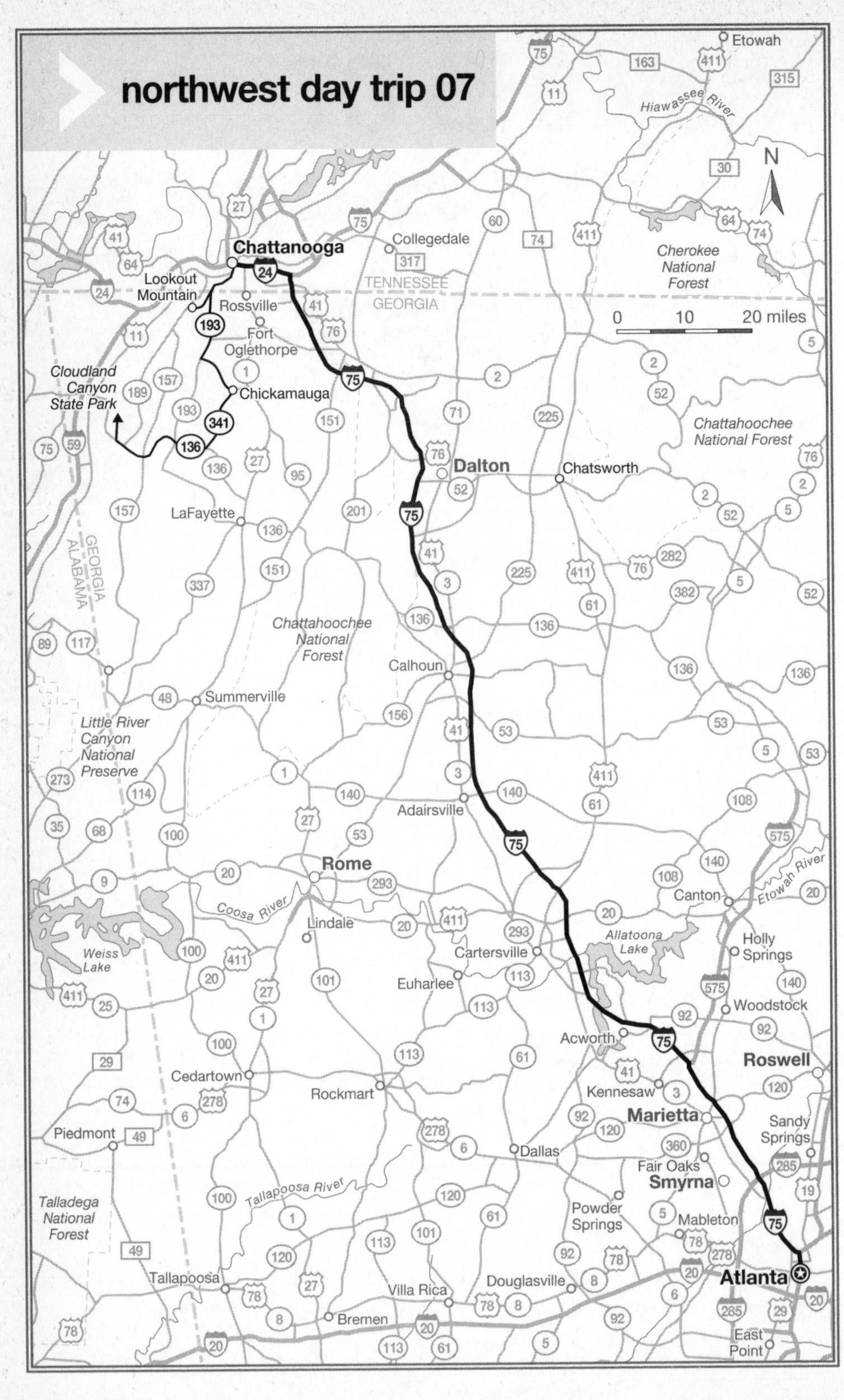
northwest day trip 07
Chattanooga
Collegedale
Lookout Mountain
Rossville
Fort Oglethorpe
TENNESSEE
GEORGIA
Cherokee National Forest
Hiawassee River
Etowah
Cloudland Canyon State Park
Chickamauga
Dalton
Chatsworth
Chattahoochee National Forest
LaFayette
Calhoun
Summerville
Little River Canyon National Preserve
Adairsville
Rome
Coosa River
Lindale
Weiss Lake
Cartersville
Euharlee
Allatoona Lake
Canton
Etowah River
Holly Springs
Woodstock
Acworth
Roswell
Kennesaw
Marietta
Cedartown
Rockmart
Piedmont
Dallas
Sandy Springs
Fair Oaks
Smyrna
Talladega National Forest
Tallapoosa River
Powder Springs
Mableton
Tallapoosa
Villa Rica
Douglasville
Atlanta
Bremen
East Point
0 10 20 miles
N

Lookout Mountain came to national attention during the Civil War due to a bloody 3-day confrontation that took place there. The fight was waged from the foothills to just below the crest of the mountain in a conflict that would later be known as the "Battle Above the Clouds." In the years following, tourists began coming to the area, and the National Battlefield Park was established. Eventually a luxury hotel was built on the mountaintop and a rail system put in place to help guests reach it.

In the 1920s, Florida businessmen O. B. Andrews and Garnet Carter conceived the idea of developing a residential area here to allow people to live on the mountain and enjoy the natural beauty year-round. They bought the land that now makes up the almost 3 square miles of the town of Lookout Mountain. The town itself maintains a laid-back lifestyle, and the residents are used to the fact that tourists still come to see the battlefield and then decide to stay to enjoy the incredible natural wonders around it.

getting there

Just about 2 hours from Atlanta, the quickest route is to take I-75 north for 110 miles into Tennessee. Take I-24 West after you cross the Tennessee border. Within 6 miles, you will see exit 178, US 27 toward downtown and Lookout Mountain. US 27 will merge into TN 57. Once you cross back into Georgia, TN 57 becomes GA 157 and will take you into Lookout Mountain.

where to go

Lookout Mountain Incline Railway. 827 E. Brow Rd., Lookout Mountain, TN 37350; (423) 821-4224; www.ridetheincline.com. They call it America's Amazing Mile. The Lookout Mountain Incline Railway Company was built in 1895 to bring people to the top of the mountain and a luxury hotel resort which had been built here. A technical marvel at the time, it has changed little in more than 100 years of operation. The railroad reaches an incline of 72.7 percent at some points, making it the steepest passenger railway in the world. The incline operates between St. Elmo Station in Chattanooga and the Lookout Station on top of the mountain. Memorial Day through Labor Day 8:30 a.m. to 9:30 p.m.; Apr, May, Sept, and Oct 9 a.m. to 6 p.m.; Nov through Mar 10 a.m. to 6 p.m. $$.

Rock City. 1400 Patten Rd., Chattanooga, TN 30750; (706) 820-2531; http://seerockcity.com. Right on the side of Lookout Mountain, Rock City is something you have to see to truly understand. A combination of incredible rock formations, woodland paths, caves, and breathtaking views, Rock City also is home to gardens with more than 400 native plant species. Oh, and the view! On a clear day, you can see 7 states. Be forwarned that you'll see plenty of "See Rock City" signs on houses, barns, and birdhouses long before you actually see Rock City. Daily 8:30 a.m. to 8 p.m. $$$.

Ruby Falls. 1720 S. Scenic Hwy., Lookout Mountain, TN 37350; (423) 821-2544; http://rubyfalls.com. Ruby Falls are actually located within Lookout Mountain. The 145-foot-high falls are part of an underground limestone cave system. The caves were discovered in 1928 when speleologist Leo Lambert was attempting to locate a larger passage to the neighboring Lookout Caverns. Visitors can combine trips to Ruby Falls and Rock City. Daily 8 a.m. to 8 p.m. $$.

where to eat

Cafe On the Corner. 826 Scenic Hwy., Lookout Mountain, TN 37350; (423) 825-5005; www.cafeonthecornerlookoutmountain.com. Southern dishes "cooked with style and grace and a bit of flair." Mon through Thurs 11 a.m. to 9 p.m., Fri and Sat 11 a.m. to 10 p.m., Sun 11 a.m. to 3 p.m. $$.

Dilly Deli. 9090 Scenic Hwy.; (706) 398-2330. Dilly Deli is a perfect place to grab a quick sandwich or even buy a picnic to take to the top of Lookout Mountain. Daily for lunch. $.

Yellow Jacket Cafe. 212 Fairy Ln.; (423) 702-5517. Southern cooking in a friendly atmosphere featuring daily specials. Breakfast and lunch daily. $.

where to stay

Chanticleer Inn. 1300 Mockingbird Ln.; (706) 820-2015. This charming inn offers 18 large rooms, most with private baths. The beautiful grounds include a swimming pool. $$–$$$.

Garden Walk Bed & Breakfast. 1206 Lula Lake Rd.; (706) 820-4127; www.gardenwalkinn.com. This gorgeous little inn with cottages offers a variety of accommodations from which to choose, each more comfortable and welcoming than the next. The inn itself has 12 rooms, and the small cottages on the grounds offer more privacy. $–$$$.

Hidden Hollow Resort. 463 Hidden Hollow Ln.; (706) 539-2372; http://hiddenhollowresort.com. The resort includes several cabins, a music hall, a chapel, and a 5-acre lake. $$.

The Preserve at Rising Fawn. Lookout Mountain Resort, LLC, 66 Lakeview Dr.; (706) 462-2051; www.lookoutmountainresort.com. The preserve is located amid a 28,000-acre resort on the eastern side of Lookout Mountain. Cabins are available for guests. $$$.

worth more time

Chattanooga. Chattanooga Area Convention and Visitors Bureau, 215 Broad St., Chattanooga, TN 37402; (423) 756-8687; www.chattanoogafun.com. Well, you are right there, and it is so tempting! On the Tennessee River, Chattanooga is a trip unto itself. Visit the amazing aquarium, ride the Chattanooga Choo-Choo, or visit one of its many museums.

chickamauga

The little town of Chickamauga is the site of an old plantation which grew up in the heart of what had been Cherokee lands. But the quaint and scenic historic mill town is not what draws people to the area. This is where the bloodiest 2-day battle of the Civil War was fought in 1863.

As if people could possibly forget, Chickamauga is also home to the oldest, largest, and most visited national military park in the US, the Chickamauga/Chattanooga National Battlefield Park. The town and the park are contrasts of sorts: the town being a quaint reminder of days gone by and the park, a solemn reminder of some of the darkest times in US history.

getting there

From Lookout Mountain the trip is about a half an hour. You'll need to retrace your footsteps back into Tennessee on GA 157 which will become TN 58 at the border and just 2 miles later you'll make a right on Elmo St./TN 17. Follow TN 17 (becoming GA 193) to GA 341 into Chickamauga. From Atlanta, take I-75 North, taking exit 350 toward Ft. Oglethorpe on GA 2/Battlefield Parkway. Follow GA 2 for 6 miles to US 27 toward Chickamauga. The town will be in another 6 miles.

where to go

Chickamauga/Chattanooga National Military Park. (706) 866-9241. This national military park is the first and the largest military park in the US, straddling the Georgia-Tennessee border. It commemorates the Civil War battles for Chattanooga that took place in 1863, including a 2-day battle on September19–20 at Chickamauga, which was the last major Confederate victory and the bloodiest battle of the war. The park itself was dedicated just

preserving history

Chickamauga became the United States' first National Military Park in 1890, but three others soon received the same designation: Shiloh in1894 (Virginia), Gettysburg in 1895 (Pennsylvania), and Vicksburg in 1899 (Mississippi). There are now 24 battle sites in the US which are preserved by the government because of their national and historic importance. Another located in Georgia is Kennesaw National Battlefield. Covering more than 5,200 acres, Chickamauga remains the largest of the preserved battle sites.

32 years later and features 1,400 monuments and historical markers on the battlefields. A 7-mile auto trail will take you to key sites in the park. Multimedia programs are available to enhance your visit including a "dial and discover" cell phone line. The park has numerous self-guided tours, trails, and roads for hiking, biking, running, and horseback riding. The visitor center is open daily from 8 a.m. to 4:45 p.m.; the park daily from dawn to dusk. Free.

Coke Ovens. GA 341. Just north of downtown you will see a 2-acre park with 36 large brick beehive-looking structures. These are what remain of the Durham Iron and Coal Company. The ovens were designed to turn coal into coke for use in the iron and steel foundries in nearby Chattanooga and operated between 1897 and 1929. Twice a day, trains would bring coal from the Durham coal mines on nearby Lookout Mountain. By 1904, the mines were producing 700 to 1,000 tons of coal per day and one-fifth of that was manufactured into coke. The ovens were restored in the 1990s, and the area around them is now a public park.

Gordon-Lee Mansion. 217 Cover Rd.; (706) 375-4728; http://gordonleemansion.com. The Gordon Lee Mansion is one of the South's older and more historic antebellum plantation houses. Set on 7 manicured acres, this is where the town of Chickamauga began. The mansion itself was built in 1847 by James Gordon, who in 1836 purchased 2,500 acres from settlers who had won it in the Cherokee land lottery. At the time, the house was engineered to have running water coming in from nearby Crawfish Spring. It was on the plantation's grounds that the fierce Battle of Chickamauga took place. The mansion served as a Confederate Army hospital during the battle, and amazingly, the mansion itself was not destroyed. The house has been totally restored with museum-quality furniture. The grounds include a formal English and Southern vegetable garden. Every Sat 11 a.m. to 3 p.m. $.

Lee and Gordon's Mills. 71 Red Belt Rd.; (423) 304-1722; www.leeandgordonsmills.com. About 2 miles east of the center of town on the west bank of the Chickamauga Creek, this is one of the oldest mills in the state of Georgia. The mill was built by James Gordon, who came from Gwinnett County, Georgia, in 1836. It served as the first general store in the area and as a stagecoach stop. During the Battle of Chickamauga, the mill served as the headquarters of the Confederate Army of Tennessee, and later Union forces occupied the mill. It now houses a store and gift shop with a Veterans of All Wars Museum on the upper floor. Tues through Fri 10 a.m. to 4 p.m., Sat 10 a.m. to 3 p.m., Sun 2 to 3 p.m. $.

Walker County Regional Heritage & Model Train Museum. 100 Gordon St.; (706) 375-4488. Housed inside the 1890s train depot, this museum features a wide variety of exhibits including Native American artifacts and Cherokee arrowheads, Civil War and WWI memorabilia, antique guns and furniture, and a complete working display of Lionel Old Gauge model trains that date back to 1947. Model train engines, cars, and parts are also sold in the depot. During the summer months, a steam engine carries passengers on excursions and day trips from Chattanooga. Tues through Sat 10 a.m. to 4 p.m. $.

where to eat

Choo Choo Bbq & Grill. 13070 N. US 27; (706) 375-7675. Delicious food and plenty of it. Great barbeque and crispy potato logs. Lunch and dinner. $$.

Crystal Springs Smokehouse. 505 W. 9th St.; (706) 375-9269. Barbeque, burgers, etc. Open lunch and dinner. $.

Deb's Kitchen. 510 W. 9th St.; (706) 375-7777. Family owned and operated. Southern food for breakfast, lunch, and dinner. $.

Emma's. 110 Cove Rd.; (706) 375-1800. Sandwiches and more. Daily specials for lunch and dinner. $.

Pie Slingers Pizzeria. 110 Cove Rd.; (706) 375-9182; www.pieslingers.com. Fabulous pizzas with some great combinations. These folks take serious pride in their dough. Mon through Sat 10 a.m. to 10 p.m., Sun noon to 10 p.m. $$.

where to stay

Best Western Battlefield Inn. 2120 Lafayette Rd., Fort Oglethorpe; (706) 866-0222; www.bestwestern.com. Just 4 blocks from the battlefield, this inn is in Ft. Oglethorpe. Complimentary breakfast and an outdoor pool. $.

EconoLodge. 118 General Bushrod Johnson Ave.; (706) 375-7007. Easy access to all the area attractions. Clean and comfortable. $.

cloudland canyon

Cloudland Canyon is aptly named because when you stand on the edge of this spectacular canyon, you can find yourself above the clouds. Looking down into the gorge below, you will see rugged geology, cascading waterfalls, and unbelievable hiking opportunities. Yet, some of the best views require little effort to get to.

The 3,485-acre park is at the western edge of Lookout Mountain where Daniel Creek and Bear Creek cut gorges through the rock of Lookout Mountain Plateau and converge to form Sitton Gulch Creek below. Cloudland straddles the creek, and elevation varies from 800 to more than 1,800 feet. There are numerous trails and picnicking options.

Cloudland Canyon first became a park in 1939 when Georgia purchased the land from the three families who owned it. It has expanded periodically since then, as caretakers seek to preserve more and more area of this gorgeous part of North Georgia. Because it is relatively remote, Cloudland is not very crowded, so make the effort and enjoy the views. There are two main roads in Cloudland, both of which leave from the visitor center. One road travels on the east rim, and the other, on the west. There are overlooks, picnic tables, and trails off of both.

getting there

The trip to Cloudland from Chickamauga takes about 40 minutes. Head south on GA 341 for 6 miles and make a right on GA 136 which will take you to the town of Rising Fawn. The official address is 122 Cloudland Canyon Park Rd, Rising Fawn, GA, 30738. From Atlanta, the drive is just more than two hours. Take I-75 North to exit 320/GA 136. Make a left and follow GA 136 to the town of Rising Fawn (706-657-4050; www.gastateparks.org/CloudlandCanyon). Open daily 7 a.m. to 10 p.m.

where to go

Interpretive Center. Adjacent to the main parking lot, this center gives the history on how Cloudland was formed and the story of the park itself. It also provides information about picnicking, camping, and hiking in the park. The park picnic areas include a group pavilion, tennis courts, a children's playground, and a disc golf course. Annual events hosted in the park include a Wildflower Program in April, Adventure Weekend (also in April), and a Kids' Catfish Rodeo in May.

Hiking trails within Cloudland include:

Sitton's Gulch Loop Trail. This trail is 5 miles long and considered strenuous due to several steep grades, including 1,200 steps. It starts as part of the second waterfall trail and follows Daniel Creek down through limestone crevices. You pass several small waterfalls, and the wildflowers can be amazing.

Two-Mile Backcountry Loop Trail. Rated moderate, this is actually more like 2.5 miles. It includes secluded camping and pristine hemlock groves. The trail passes through open woods, progressing down a moderate grade into a hollow filled with spring and summer flowers. The trail then loops back among oaks and hickories, and eventually back to the parking area.

Waterfalls Trail. Rated strenuous, this 2-mile hike begins at the main overlook and goes down 1,200 gravel and stone steps to the canyon floor below. The payoff is seeing Hemlock and Cherokee falls from below.

West Rim Loop Trail. This 5-mile loop is moderate to strenuous but is considered one of the most scenic hiking trails in the nation. It starts out at the Daniel Creek Bridge and climbs onto the plateau, providing magnificent views of Trenton, Georgia, neighboring Sand Mountain, and Cloudland Canyon itself. Cottages, the west rim, and walk-in camping areas are accessible via the West Rim Loop.

where to eat

Canyon Grill. 28 Scenic Hwy.; (706) 398-9510; http://canyongrill.com. In an old grocery store, the Canyon Grill has been listed as one of the Top Ten restaurants in all of Georgia. Fresh fish and steaks with a creative menu. Since no alcohol is allowed in the county, Canyon Grill is BYOB. Wed through Sat 5 p.m. to 9 p.m. $$.

Depot Diner. 4356 GA 11; (706) 462-2301. Family owned and operated, they will treat you like family as well at this Southern-style diner. Serving breakfast, lunch, and dinner; closed Sun. $.

Geneva's Restaurant. 12136 GA 136; (706) 398-1749. Down-home Southern food. Open for breakfast and Lunch. $.

Lazy Bones BBQ. 317 CO 120; (706) 462-2096. Barbeque and Southern food for breakfast and lunch. $.

Lobo's BBQ. 10998 GA 157; (706) 398-0895. Hickory-smoked and family-run, Lobo's barbeque serves up ribs and chopped pork. $.

where to stay

Canyon Ridge Club & Resort. 14653 GA 157, Rising Fawn; (706) 398-0882; www.canyonridgeclub.com. This resort and private golf club is located in Rising Fawn, not far from Cloudland's main entrance. $$.

Cloudland Canyon. Reservations, (800) 864-7275; park, (706) 657-4050. There are numerous options for staying within the park itself, ranging from a group lodge to 16 cottages as well as 73 tent, trailer, and RV sites, 30 walk-in campsites, and 11 backcountry campsites for backpackers. There are bathing facilities near the campsites. $.

General Woods Inn. 1346 Deer Head Cove Rd.; (706) 462-2686; www.generalwoodsinn.com. This beautiful inn was built in the style of an antebellum mansion in the foothills of the Appalachian Mountains and includes a balconied porch with gorgeous views. It offers 4 rooms for guests, 3 of which have private baths. $–$$.

north

day trip 01

north

milling around:
roswell, alpharetta

There is no easier day trip than heading straight north up GA 400 from Buckhead, making your way to the towns of Roswell and Alpharetta. The good news, too, is that if you are heading out in the morning, you will be going against all of that traffic coming into the city via GA 400.

These two little cities are filled with people who commute to Atlanta to work, but love living in here because of what all the area has to offer.

roswell

The beautiful streams and lush surroundings of Roswell are what drew wealthy planters to the area in the late 1700s. Eventually textile magnet Roswell King felt those streams had potential to power industry and established a New England–style mill town in the area. Much of the labor was done by women, making Roswell a unique area.

The mills also made Roswell a target for the Union during the Civil War, and after Gen. Sherman discovered Confederate insignias on cloth made in local establishments, he had 400 women and children workers arrested, charged with treason, and shipped to prisons in the North.

These days the cosmopolitan city has a 640-acre historic district that highlights both the good and the bad of its past. There are 122 acres listed on the National Register

north day trip 01

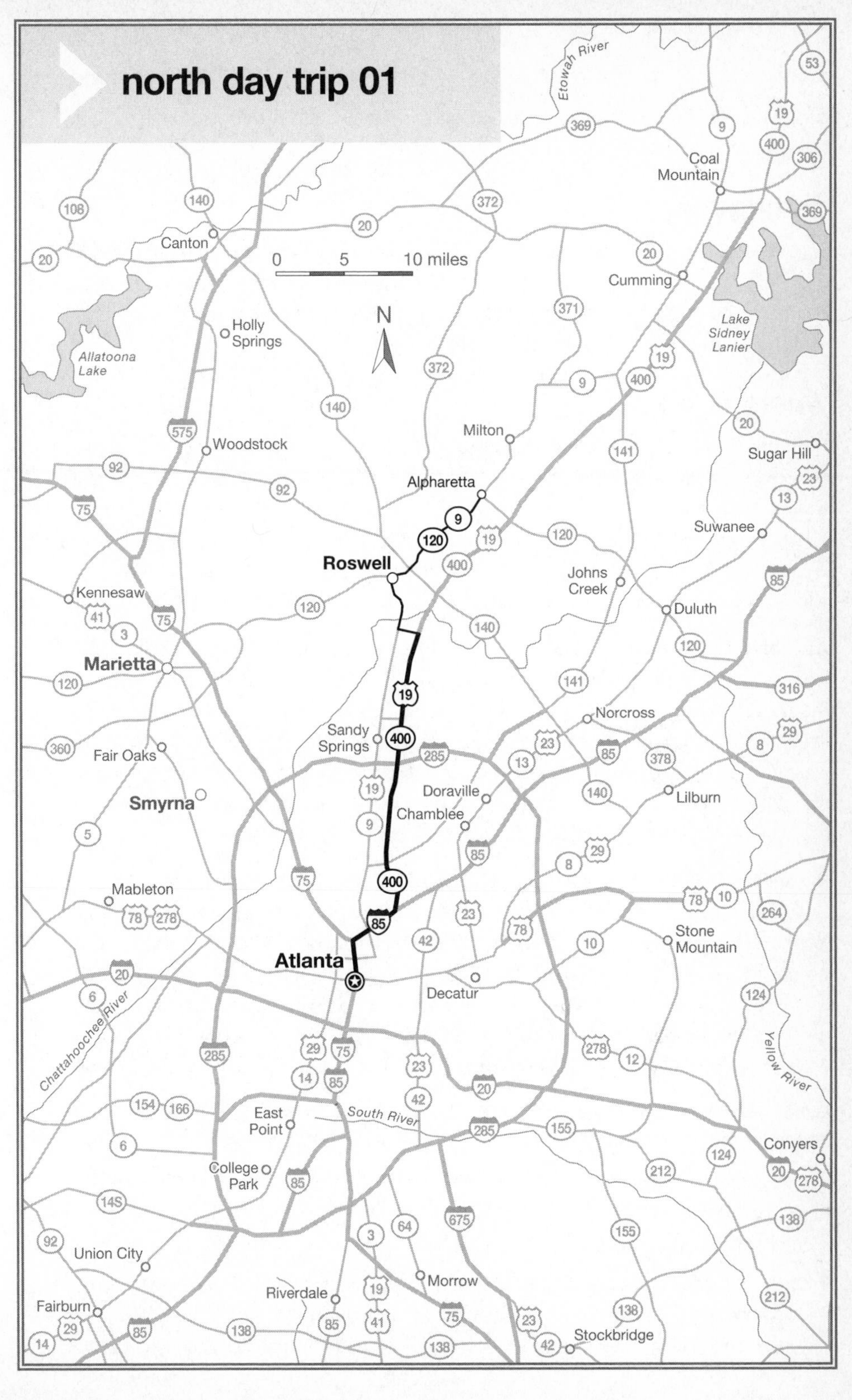

of Historic Places, which include vintage homes, historic sites, museums, monuments, churches, and cemeteries.

getting there

Roswell is 35 miles from the heart of Atlanta. Take I-85 north from downtown and then the GA 400 tollway. You'll travel 10 minutes outside the perimeter and then take the Northridge Road exit (exit 6). Go right on Northridge Road and follow it to Roswell Road/GA 9. Make a right, and 3 miles later you will be in the heart of Roswell.

where to go

Heritage Center at Roswell Visitors Bureau. 617 Atlanta St.; (770) 640-3253 or (800) 776-7935; www.visitroswellga.com. The Heritage Center at Roswell Visitors Bureau really should be your first stop because it can provide you with self-guided tour maps and discounted visitor passes. The center itself contains exhibits showcasing the history of the Roswell Mills and Mill Life. Mon through Fri 9 a.m. to 5 p.m., Sat 10 a.m. to 4 p.m., Sun noon to 3 p.m. Free.

Archibald Smith Plantation. 935 Alpharetta St.; (678) 639-7500; www.southerntrilogy.org. Owner Archibald Smith was a founding father of Roswell and divided his time between this plantation and one in coastal St. Mary's. Three generations of Smiths lived here before the home and its grounds were turned into a monument to the lifestyles of the 1800s. The wooded grounds and gardens include the perfectly preserved 2-story farmhouse, complete with outbuildings such as slave quarters, a well, springhouse, cookhouse, barn, and carriage house. Mon through Sat 10 a.m. to 3 p.m.; Sun 1 to 3 p.m. $$.

Barrington Hall. 535 Barrington Dr.; (678) 639-7500; http://barringtonhall-roswell.com or www.southerntrilogy.org. Barrington King was son of Roswell founder Roswell King and a textile giant in his own right. This Greek Revival home was built in the 1830s on the highest point overlooking the new town. Its gardens maintain the same regal air they did when they were first developed. The Roswell Manufacturing Company was a leading supplier of goods to the Confederacy. Six of Barrington King's sons served in the Confederate forces; 2 were killed and 2 were injured. Mon through Sat 10 a.m. to 3 p.m., Sun 1 to 3 p.m. $$.

Bulloch Hall. 180 Bulloch Ave.; (800) 776-7935; www.visitroswellga.com or www.southerntrilogy.org. This beautiful antebellum home was the childhood residence of Theodore Roosevelt's mother, Mittie Bulloch Roosevelt. Built in 1840, it also served as headquarters for Federal soldiers during the Atlanta Campaign. Mon through Sat 10 a.m. to 3 p.m.; Sun 1 to 3 p.m. $$.

Founder's Cemetery. Sloan Street. Just across the street from the Roswell Mills ruins is the entrance to the Founder's Cemetery. Started in 1840, it was Roswell's first public cemetery, and among the graves are those for Roswell King and Major James Stephens Bulloch.

Old Roswell Cemetery (1848). Woodstock and Alpharetta Streets. Once known as the Methodist Cemetery, this burial site holds more than 2,000 graves. Still an active cemetery, it's a favorite spot for ghost hunters.

Pleasant Hill Cemetery. Old Roswell Place. Pleasant Hill was established in 1855 when African-American members of the Lebanon Baptist Church organized their own church. The old cemetery is adjacent to the Town Center Shopping Center.

Roswell Fire and Rescue Museum. 1002 Alpharetta St.; (770) 641-3730; www.roswellgov.com. Probably not the most frequented museum around, it is a very interesting place if you love fire department history. This small local museum focuses on the history of the Roswell Volunteer Fire Department. Daily. Free.

Roswell Mills & Sloan Street Park. Sloan Street. Just down the street from the visitor center along the banks of Vickery's Creek is a city park where you can see the ruins of the Roswell Mills. Collectively known as the Roswell Manufacturing Company, they were built starting in 1839. The mills were destroyed during the Civil War, and only the 1853 cotton mill was rebuilt. It is now offices and an events facility. A staircase walkway will lead you down to the site. Free.

Teaching Museum North. 793 Mimosa Blvd.; (770) 552-6339; www.teachingmuseumnorth.org. This museum's mission is "to teach the mind and touch the heart." There is a vast array of exhibits here to do both on political, social, and historical interests documenting the history of the US, Georgia, and Roswell. Focal points include US presidents, Georgia authors, an Anne Frank exhibit, and more. Mon through Fri 8 a.m. to 4 p.m. $.

where to eat

Dreamland Bar-B-Que. 10730 Alpharetta Hwy.; (678) 352-7999; www.dreamlandbbq.com. This place started in Tuscaloosa, Alabama, but its goodness could not be contained. Awesome barbeque in a rustic atmosphere. Mon through Sat 10 a.m. to 10 p.m.; Sun 11 a.m. to 9 p.m. $$.

Fickle Pickle. 1085 Canton St.; (770) 650-9838; www.ficklepicklecafe.com. In an 1800s-era Victorian house in historic Roswell, you'll feel right at home as you chow down on their wonderful sandwiches and salads. Mon 11 a.m. to 3 p.m.; Tues to Sat 11 a.m. to 9 p.m. $–$$.

Inc. Street Food. 948 Canton St.; (770) 998-3114; www.incstreetfood.com. The name hails from the menu which replicates street foods from Latin American locales like Peru, Chile, and Argentina. The great variety ranges from Cuban sandwiches to shrimp tacos to calamari rellenos. Mon through Thurs 11 a.m. to 10 p.m., Fri and Sat 11 a.m. to 11 p.m., Sun noon to 10 p.m. $–$$.

Oak Street Cafe. 45 Oak St.; (770) 594-1300; www.oakstcafe.com. If you are hungry for a juicy burger while in Roswell, look no further, and their homemade fries are to die for. Mon 9 a.m. to 3 p.m.; Tues and Wed 9 a.m. to 3 p.m., 5:30 to 9:30 p.m.; Thurs and Fri 9 a.m. to 3 p.m., 5:30 to 10 p.m.; Sat 11 a.m. to 3 p.m., 5:30 to 10 p.m.; Sun 10 a.m. to 2 p.m. $.

Pastis. 928 Canton St.; (770) 640-3870; www.pastisroswell.com. Consistently good, this French-style bistro stays busy with regulars. Fine French cuisine without the Parisian prices. Tues through Thurs 11:30 a.m. to 2:30 p.m., 5:30 to 9:30 p.m.; Fri and Sat 11:30 a.m. to 2:30 p.m., 5:30 to 10:30 p.m.; Sun 11:30 a.m. to 2:30 p.m., 5:30 to 9 p.m. $$.

Salt Factory Pub. 952 Canton St.; (770) 998-4850; http://saltfactorypub.com. Extremely friendly with a warm atmosphere, Salt is in the heart of historic Roswell. The pub offers everything from pasta to potpies, a great beer selection, and fun happy hour. Mon through Thurs 11 a.m. to 11 p.m.; Fri and Sat 11 a.m. to midnight; Sun noon to 10 p.m. $–$$.

Swallow at the Hollow. 1072 Green St.; (678) 352-1975; www.theswallowatthehollow.com. In a rustic cabin underneath old oak trees, you'll swear you are down in a hollow somewhere. Great home-style barbeque and the trappings with live musical performances. Wed through Thu, Sun 11 a.m. to 9 p.m.; Fri and Sat 11 a.m. to 10 p.m. $$.

where to stay

Best Western, Roswell Suites. 907 Holcomb Bridge Rd., near GA 400; (770) 552-5599 or (800) SUITE21; www.bestwestern.com. All the comforts of home, including hot waffles in the morning. $.

Comfort Suites. 3000 Mansell Rd.; (770) 654-6060 or (800) 228-5150; www.choicehotels.com. Great for families because of the suite-style rooms. $.

Doubletree by Hilton. 1075 Holcomb Bridge Rd.; (770) 992-9600 or (800) 222-TREE; www.doubletree.com. Clean and comfortable with hot cookies at the front desk. $$.

alpharetta

What's not to love about the rolling hills and beautiful countryside surrounding Alpharetta? Now one of Atlanta's most affluent suburbs, a good deal of the residents live here because of just how much land they can claim as their own.

Land and its availability are what shaped Alpharetta from the beginning. This area was settled through the land lotteries of the 1830s when the Cherokee Nation was displaced from North Georgia. Back then, the pioneers called the town "Milton," changing the name in the 1850s.

The origin of the current moniker is the subject of conflict. But both of the two popular versions are the result of inaccuracies. One attributes the name to a popular song at the time called “The Blue Juniata,” which featured a character named “Alfarata.” The city’s official site claims the name is a combination of the Greek words for “first” and “town.” That said, “town” in Greek is “Poli” or “Polis” and “Retta” is not even a Greek word.

No matter where the name comes from, Alpharetta these days does its best to live up to its self-proclaimed title of “Awesome Alpharetta,” as it offers a vibrant arts community, fantastic restaurants, and entertainment and plenty of history to accent the present.

getting there

To get to Alpharetta from Roswell, head north on Alpharetta Street for about 14 miles. From Atlanta, the drive is about 30 miles. Go north on I-85 to GA 400 to exit 9/Haynes Bridge Road and turn left on Old Milton Parkway. Make your first right onto Main Street.

where to go

Alpharetta Convention and Visitor’s Bureau. Park Plaza, 178 S. Main St., Ste. 200; (678) 297-2811; www.awesomealpharetta.com. Though this is an Alpharetta information center, they are prepared to help you find anything you want within a 60-mile radius. Maps, discounts, and advice all available. Mon through Fri 9 a.m. to 5 p.m., Sat 10 a.m. to 4 p.m.

American Girl Boutique and Bistro. Northpoint Mall, 1202 North Point Circle; (877) 247-5223; www.americangirl.com. This is the only place like it in the Southeast, and if you have a doll lover with you or know a doll lover, this could be a must. You can dine in the bistro and shop till you drop. Have you doll’s hair styled or pick up the latest accessories. Check with the store to see the American Girl hotels they feature, and you may be able to get a package deal with the hotel to enhance your experience.

Historic Mansell House and Gardens. 1835 Old Milton Pkwy.; (770) 475-4663. This lovely old farmhouse was built in 1910 by Mr. and Mrs. Robert Henry Mansell from timbers on the Mansell farm. The farm is gone, but this Queen Anne–style home will help you get a sense of that era. Stroll the award-winning gardens which always seem to have something in bloom. A highlight of the property is a massive 125-year-old oak tree. Walking tours of this historic home and gardens are available Mon through Fri 10 a.m. to 2 p.m. Free.

Milton Log Cabin. 86 School Dr.; (770) 475-4663. Dating back to 1934, this log structure was built by the Future Farmers of America as a hands-on project that involved the entire community. The rock foundation was hand-laid, and the students hand-cut and hauled the pine trees for the actual building. The cabin is the only remaining FFA-constructed log cabin still in use today in the US. Call the historical society for a visit.

Publix Apron’s Cooking School. Alpharetta Commons, 4305 State Bridge Rd.; (770) 751-8560; www.publix.com/aprons/schools. This is a unique little experience. The Publix grocery store in Alpharetta Commons is home to an Apron’s Cooking School. Classes are designed for all levels of cooks to help you improve your skills and enjoy your time in the kitchen. Instruction covers every sort of cuisine and technique taught by accomplished professionals. Check the schedule for what is available. Reservations are required. $$.

Verizon Wireless Amphitheatre. 2200 Encore Pkwy.; (404) 733-5010; www.vzwamp.com. The 12,000-seat Verizon Wireless Amphitheatre is one of Atlanta's premier concert venues. Set on 45 acres of beautifully landscaped wooded land, the venue features performances by top acts in pop, rock, country, and Christian music as well as the Grammy-winning Atlanta Symphony Orchestra. Check the calendar for show and event prices.

Walk of Memories. American Legion Post 201, 201 Wills Rd.; (770) 475-9023. Honoring Georgia's military, this little park was created by members of American Legion Post 201, near where it stands. It displays 7,220 bricks, each with the name of a Georgia serviceman or servicewoman engraved on it, including those soldiers from Georgia who have died in the war in Iraq. The Walk of Memories also features a display of military equipment, the highlights of which are a 96-ton Korean War Abrams tank, a 40mm 16,000-ton antiaircraft gun, and a Huey helicopter.

Wills Park. 454 Wills Rd.; (678) 297-6120. With 100 acres, Wills has a never-ending list of activities to enjoy. There is an Olympic-size public swimming pool, an equestrian center, baseball, tennis, and Frisbee golf to go along with the playgrounds and hiking trails.

Wills Park Equestrian Center. 11915 Wills Rd.; (678) 297-6120. Alpharetta is known to be horse country, and the Wills Park Equestrian Center affords guests the opportunity ride and to take riding lessons. The 50-acre center has a total of 298 stalls, 3 show rings (one covered), and 2 separate schooling rings. Call for rates.

where to eat

Alpha Soda. 11760 Haynes Bridge Rd.; (770) 442-3102; www.alphasoda.com. In business since 1922, this traditionally Southern restaurant is a staple in Alpharetta. Breakfast is served anytime you want it. There are blue plate specials every day. Daily, breakfast, lunch, and dinner. $–$$.

Buca di Beppo. 2335 Mansell Rd.; (770) 643-9463; www.bucadibeppo.com. Family-style Italian. Great pasta and a good family restaurant. Mon through Thurs 4 to 10 p.m.; Fri 4 to 11 p.m.; Sat 11 a.m. to 11 p.m.; Sun 11 a.m. to 9 p.m. $$.

Smokejack. 29 S. Main St.; (770) 410-7611; www.smokejackbbq.com. Award-winning barbeque, awesome ribs, and great sandwiches. Mon through Thu, Sun 11 a.m. to 9 p.m.; Fri and Sat 11 a.m. to 10:30 p.m. $.

Village Tavern. 11555 Rainwater Dr.; (770) 777-6490; www.villagetavern.com. A great place to go for comfort food in a relaxing atmosphere. Mon through Thurs 11 a.m. to 10 p.m.; Fri and Sat 11 a.m. to 11 p.m.; Sun 10 a.m. to 10 p.m. $$.

where to stay

Hilton Garden Inn. 4025 Windward Plaza; (770) 360-7766 or (800) HILTONS; www.hilton gardeninn.com. Comfortable and close to GA 400, this inn features a 24-hour business center, indoor pool, fitness center, coin laundry, and a restaurant that is open 24 hours as well. Children under 18 stay free with parents. $$.

Wingate Inn. 1005 Kingswood Place; (770) 649-0955 or (880) 228-1000; www.wingate inns.com. The Wingate has a business center and fitness center with spa. A complimentary wine and beer reception is held Mon through Wed. $$.

worth more time

Polo Club of Atlanta. 5890 Polo Dr., Cumming, GA 30040; (770) 344 0274; www.polo clubofatlanta.com. The club is just north of Alpharetta in the town of Cumming. The entire area is horse country, which makes a great location for these fields. Internationally recognized polo players come here to train and play, and there are numerous matches during the season so check the schedule. The grounds are also available for private events such as corporate picnics, fund-raisers, and even children's birthday parties. There are 25 horses in the stables as well as a petting zoo.

day trip 02

north

wine, wine, wine & gold:
dahlonega

North day trip 02 takes you farther up into the North Georgia mountains to a town that has made quite a name for itself by its past and its present. Dahlonega was the site of the Great Georgia Gold Rush in the 1800s and grew up as a gold-mining town. Since then it has struck gold with what is above ground, not below: grapes. This part of Georgia is prime territory for cultivating grapes and producing wine, and in the last 20 years, Dahlonega has become a wine-tasting destination.

The drive is a quick one, just over an hour. By the time you reach the end of GA 400, you'll be in the mountains. The scenery here is spectacular with lush, green hills and stunning rivers and creeks.

This is an area of Georgia you may want to spend more time in and explore. Note the offerings in the **Worth More Time** section. In the summer, a trip here is a nice way to beat the heat and crowds of Atlanta for a day. In the winter, it's a mountain retreat within easy reach.

dahlonega

Dahlonega is the gateway to the Appalachians, and after spending some time in this little town, you'll be tempted to go no farther. It really does have it all.

The historic downtown will let you learn all about the gold-mining industry that created Dahlonega in the early 1800s, but you'll also find a town that is still alive in the present day.

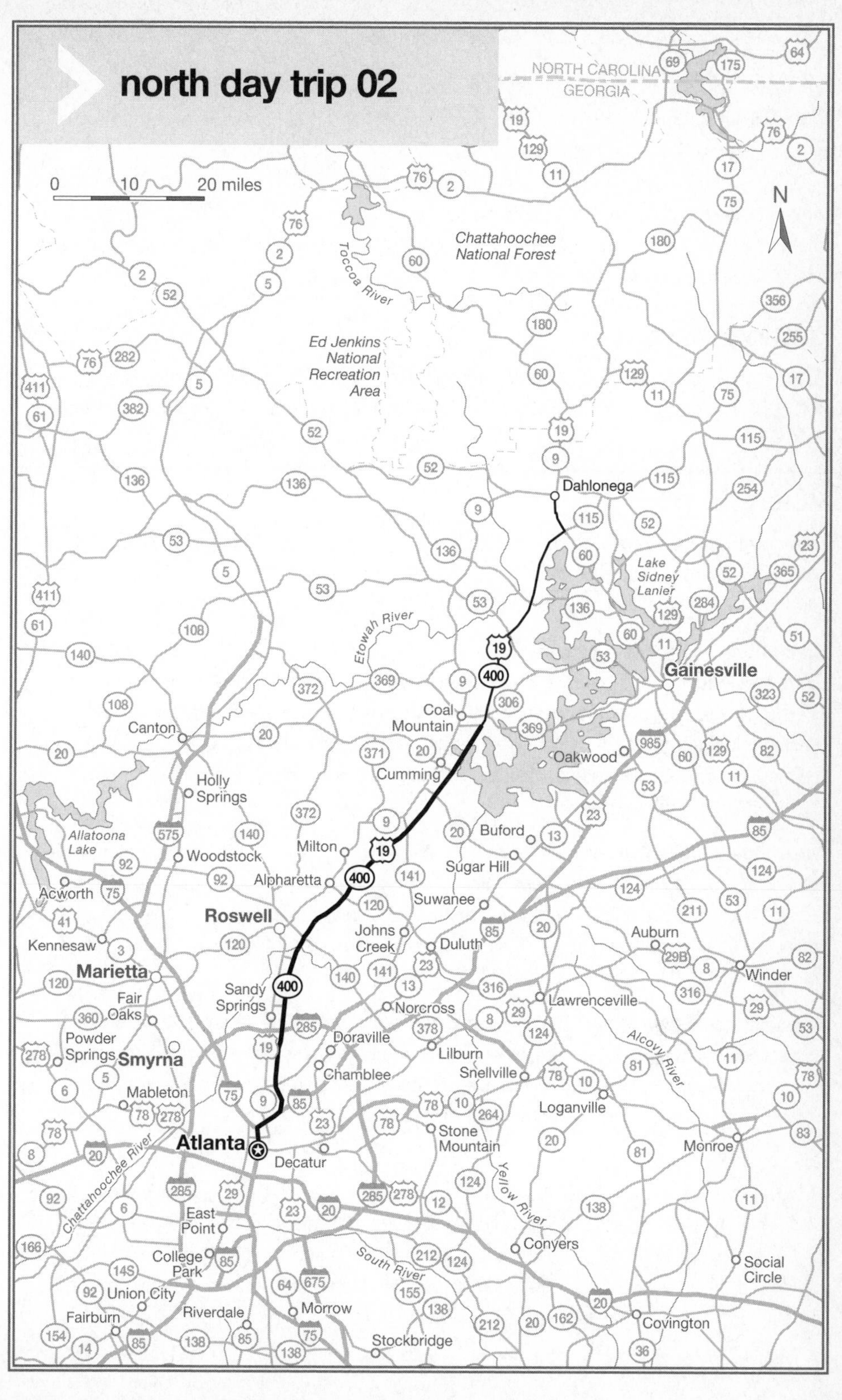
north day trip 02
NORTH CAROLINA
GEORGIA
0 10 20 miles
N
Chattahoochee National Forest
Toccoa River
Ed Jenkins National Recreation Area
Dahlonega
Lake Sidney Lanier
Etowah River
Gainesville
Coal Mountain
Canton
Cumming
Oakwood
Holly Springs
Allatoona Lake
Milton
Buford
Woodstock
Sugar Hill
Alpharetta
Acworth
Suwanee
Roswell
Johns Creek
Kennesaw
Duluth
Auburn
Marietta
Winder
Sandy Springs
Fair Oaks
Norcross
Lawrenceville
Powder Springs
Smyrna
Doraville
Chamblee
Lilburn
Alcovy River
Snellville
Mableton
Loganville
Stone Mountain
Atlanta
Decatur
Monroe
Chattahoochee River
Yellow River
East Point
Conyers
College Park
South River
Social Circle
Union City
Fairburn
Riverdale
Morrow
Covington
Stockbridge

It is bustling with activity from art galleries, shopping, and great restaurants to numerous outdoor events. There are also several spas in the area to help you unwind.

Oh, and let's not forget the wine! Dahlonega's wineries have begun to define the region. Downtown has several tasting rooms if you can't make it out to the vineyards. But you'd be remiss if you did not. Even if you don't drink, you should visit the vineyards for the beautiful scenery each affords. And all of them have places to dine.

getting there

Dahlonega is just over an hour from downtown Atlanta. Take I-85 to GA 400, then follow GA 400 north for almost 50 miles. Turn left on US 19/GA 60, and follow it toward Dahlonega for 5 miles.

where to go

Dahlonega-Lumpkin Welcome Center. 13 S. Park St.; (706) 864-3711 or (800) 231-5543; www.dahlonega.org. With so much to see and do (and taste), come here to get a sense of how to best spend your day. Daily 9 a.m. to 5:30 p.m.

BlackStock Vineyards and Winery. 5400 Town Creek Rd.; (706) 219-2789; www.bsvw.com. BlackStock was the first of the present-day vineyards in Dahlonega to make a success out of raising quality grapes for consumption. Their example has led others to follow. BlackStock has a tasting room and restaurant and a 2,000-square-foot deck overlooking the mountains. They feature many blends and varieties. Mon through Sat 10 a.m. to 6 p.m., Sun 12:30 to 6 p.m.

Chestatee Wildlife Preserve. 469 Old Dahlonega Hwy.; (678) 537-6765; www.chestateewildlife.com. Dedicated to the preservation of exotic and domestic wildlife, this preserve seeks to educate the public about such animals by allowing them to see many up close. Animals who have homes here include black bears, white tigers, and camels. Daily 10 a.m. to 4 p.m. $$.

Consolidated Gold Mines. 185 Consolidated Gold Mine Rd.; (706) 864-8473; www.consolidatedgoldmine.com. This property hosted gold-mining operations in the late 1800s and was reopened in the 1980s to help share the history of mining in Dahlonega. Visitors can tour underground tunnels, learn about miners, and pan for gold. Tennis shoes are recommended. Daily, summer 10 a.m. to 5 p.m., winter 10 a.m. to 4 p.m. $.

Crisson Gold Mine. 2736 Morrison Moore Pkwy. East; (706) 864-6363; www.crissongoldmine.com.The Crisson Gold Mine is an open-pit mine that was started in 1847 and continued operating until the 1980s. Today's setup allows visitors to see Georgia's only working stamp mill, a 125-year-old machine used to crush rock and remove gold. Pan for gold and gemstones. Daily 10 a.m. to 6 p.m. $$.

Dahlonega Gold Museum State Historic Site. 1 Public Sq.; (706) 864-2257; www.georgiastateparks.org. Inside the Old Lumpkin County Courthouse, this museum tells the tale of America's first gold rush—20 years before the famed California stampede of 1848. The building is also the oldest courthouse in Georgia, and visitors can get a look inside the old judge's chambers. Mon through Sat 9 a.m. to 5 p.m., Sun 10 a.m. to 5 p.m. $.

Frogtown Cellars. 700 Ridge Point Dr.; (706) 865-0687; www.frogtownwine.com. This 57-acre estate features 40 acres of vineyards with 17 varieties of grapes. The scenic spread has a tasting room and restaurant and hosts events and weddings. Mon through Fri noon to 5 p.m., Sat noon to 6 p.m., Sun 12:30 to 5 p.m.

Funky Chicken Art Project. 1538 Wesley Chapel Rd.; (706) 864-3938; www.funkychickenartproject.com. This is one of your more unusual art experiences. Funky Chicken is a working studio and gallery located in an old chicken house. Around the side there is a beautiful sculpture garden and a chicken house than holds poultry of several kinds from Bantam roosters to peacocks. Workshops are available. Call for hours and fees.

Historic Holly Theater. 69 W. Main St.; (706) 864-3759; www.hollytheater.com. The Holly Theater has been the cultural epicenter of the community since the 1930s. When movies became popular, a local businessman converted the bottom floor of the Pierce Building to a theater. It's been there ever since, hosting plays, musicals, first-run movies, and concerts. Box office open weekdays 10 a.m. to 5 p.m.; otherwise check the schedule.

Montaluce Winery & Estates. 501 Hightower Church Rd.; (706) 867-4060; www.montaluce.com. Montaluce is not just a winery, but also a development where you can live with the vineyards in your backyard. The gravity-flow winery produces some of the best wines you will find in not just Dahlonega, but the world. And their Le Vigne Restaurant offers world-class dining with spectacular views. Montaluce is also a wedding destination. Mon through Thurs 11 a.m. to 5 p.m., Fri through Sun 11 a.m. to 9:30 p.m.

Three Sisters Vineyards. 439 Vineyard Way; (706) 865-WINE; http://threesistersvineyards.com. Three Sisters is one of the more modest of the wineries in Dahlonega and brags about its back road location on an old family farm. Family-operated, their motto is "fine wines and fun times." The 184-acre vineyard estate offers tastings and tours. Package deals are available. Thurs through Sat 11 a.m. to 5 p.m., Sun 1 to 5 p.m., Mon through Wed by appointment.

Wolf Mountain Vineyards & Winery. 180 Wolf Mountain Trail; (706) 867-9862; www.wolfmountainvineyards.com.Wolf Mountain wines have won more than 100 medals in wine-tasting events. Enjoy wine tours and tastings and take time to eat at the Vineyard Cafe. This vineyard hosts special events, Sunday brunches, and vineyard weddings. Tastings Thurs through Sun noon to 5 p.m.; tours Sun at 2 p.m.

where to shop

Gateway Antiques. 75 E. Main St.; (706) 867-8816. Right on the square in downtown, Gateway has more than 50 dealers under one roof. You'll find everything from fine furniture to collectibles and jewelry. Mon 10 a.m. to 7 p.m.; Tues through Thurs 10 a.m. to 6 p.m.; Fri and Sat 10 a.m. to 8 p.m.; Sun noon to 7 p.m.

where to eat

Crimson Moon Cafe. 24 N. Park St.; (706) 864-3982; www.thecrimsonmoon.com. Crimson Moon bills itself as a "cafe, concert hall, coffeehouse, and turn-of-the-century saloon," and that's an accurate description. Open all day, the cafe also has regular acoustical performances. The food has a distinctive Southern flair. Mon through Thurs 8 a.m. to 11 p.m., Sun 11:30 a.m. to 8:30 p.m. $.

Historic Smith House Inn. 84 S. Chestatee St.; (706) 867-7000. People drive to Dahlonega just to eat at the Smith House with its family dining offering Southern recipes used since 1898. The house opened as an inn in 1922. The structure was built on top of a rich vein of gold, and the original mine shaft is now open for display. Tues through Thurs 11 a.m. to 3 p.m.; Fri 4 to 8 p.m., 11 a.m. to 3 p.m.; Sat 11 a.m. to 8 p.m.; Sun 11 a.m. to 7:30 p.m. $$.

Johnny B's Beef-n-Brew. 438 W. Main St.; (706) 864-2400; www.johnny-bs.com. Johnny's B's is a favorite bar in Dahlonega, serving an extensive list of wing selections as well as burgers, salads, and pizza. Mon through Fri 11 a.m. to 1 a.m.; Sat 11 a.m. to midnight; Sun 12:30 p.m. to midnight. $–$$.

Piazza. 24 E. Main St.; (706) 867-9881; www.piazza-restaurant.com. Authentic Italian made from scratch daily right on the square. Daily 11 a.m. to 9 p.m. $$.

Porter House Restaurant. 24 E. Main St.; (706) 867-0448; www.phsteakhouse.com. Great steaks and burgers in a fabulous location on the square. Live music on weekends. Daily 11 a.m. to 9 p.m. $$.

Yahoola Creek Grill. 1810 S. Chestatee St.; (706) 482-2200; www.yahoolacreekgrill.com. Yahoola serves up casual fine dining creek side. The menu is seasonal but includes such yummy Southern fare as chicken and waffles, made with Southern-fried Springer Mountain Farms chicken breast, savory waffles, andouille sausage, spinach, and sausage gravy. Mon through Thurs 11 a.m. to 2 p.m., 5 to 9 p.m.; Fri and Sat 11 a.m. to 10 p.m.; Sun 10 a.m. to 3 p.m. $$.

where to stay

Bend of the River Cabins & Chalets. 319 Horseshoe Ln.; (706) 219-2040; www.bendoftheriver.net. Bend of the River features 8 distinctive cabins which range in size from 1 to 3 bedrooms. Sited on wooded lots, you can swim, fish, tube, hike, or even pan for gold right at your door. $$–$$$.

Carson's Run Mountain Rental. 206 Cedar Mountain Rd.; (401) 290-8337; www.escape2carsonsrun.com. Carson's Run is right on the side of Cedar Mountain overlooking the valley. There are 3 suites available by the night or the week. $$–$$$.

Dahlonega Spa Resort. 400 Blueberry Hill; (706) 865-7678 or (866) 345-4900; www.rrresorts.com. This wellness retreat center and bed-and-breakfast spans 72 acres. The main house is a reproduction 1920s-style farmhouse with a wraparound porch, and 8 cottages are available. The spa features traditional yoga classes and numerous spa treatments. $$$.

Historic Worley B&B Inn. 168 Main St. West; (706) 864-7002; www.bbonline.com/ga/worley. This inn was built in 1845 as the home of Captain Jasper Worley, CSA. Meticulously restored, it features cozy, romantic rooms, some with fireplaces, each with a private bath. A full country breakfast is offered. All-inclusive packages are available. $$.

Lily Creek Lodge B&B. 2608 Auraria Rd.; (706) 864-6848; www.lilycreeklodge.com. Just 4 miles from the square, Lily Creek Lodge is a European-style bed-and-breakfast. The acreage on which it sits has a swimming pool with waterfall, a tree house, and a wildlife sanctuary with hummingbirds, hawks, rabbits, squirrels, and deer. There are 13 guest rooms or suites. Some suites have kitchenettes. $$.

Top of the Square Bed-and-Breakfast. 90 N. Public Sq.; (706) 867-5009; www.topofthesquare.com. This is the square's only bed-and-breakfast. In the historic 1881 Hall House building, the B&B offers 2 rooms which are within walking distance for anything in downtown. $$.

worth more time

Appalachian Outfitters. 2084 S. Chestatee/GA 60; (706) 864-7117; www.canoegeorgia.com. Take a day and explore the Chestatee River by canoe or kayak. The journey from the outpost is 6 miles and takes between 2 and 3 hours. Schedules based on time of year.

Appalachian Trail Trailhead. Amicalola Falls State Park and Lodge, 418 Amicalola Falls Lodge Rd.; (706) 265-8888 or (800) 864-7275; www.georgiastateparks.org or www.nps.gov/appa/index.htm. The 2,000-mile-long Appalachian Trail gets its start in this gorgeous park just west of Dahlonega. The park itself is simply stunning with the falls themselves as the highlight. This 729-foot waterfall is the highest in the Southeast. Amicalola hosts a mountaintop lodge with a restaurant, cabins, and a hiking lodge only accessible by foot. Daily 7 a.m. to 10 p.m. $5 parking.

The Frog Hollow Company. 900 Frog Hollow Rd.; (706) 244-4372; www.froghollowflyfishing.com. The Chestatee River hosts some great fly-fishing opportunities, and if you want to give it a try, sign up for a guided half-day, full-day, or twilight fly-fishing adventure. Lodging available. Catch and release only. $$$.

Kangaroo Conservation Center. 222 Bailey Waters Rd., Dawsonville, GA 30534; (706) 265-6100; www.kangaroocenter.com. Yes, those are kangaroos you see hopping around the North Georgia hillsides. More than 600 of them to be exact. This is the largest kangaroo population outside of Australia. The conservation center breeds 'roos and other exotics and helps educate the public about their plight. By appointment only Thurs through Sat 9 a.m. to 5 p.m. $$.

North Georgia Canopy Tours. 5290 Harris Rd., Lula, GA 30554; (770) 869-7272; http://northgeorgiacanopytours.com. Zip through the treetops in this exciting way to get some spectacular views of the North Georgia mountains. Reservations required. Daily 9 a.m. to 5 p.m.

day trip 03

an edge of blue:

ellijay, blue ridge, blairsville, young harris, hiawassee

This day trip packs a lot in, but has you wandering through some of North Georgia's most scenic little towns and exploring the fabulous Blue Ridge Mountains. The Blue Ridge is the leading edge of the Appalachians and gets the name because of the peaks' distinctive blue appearance on the horizon. If you want to know what causes that, it is the trees. Their sheer numbers release an organic compound into the atmosphere, changing the color of the range.

These places we're visiting today are nestled in the middle of the Chattahoochee National Forest, so you will travel through lush peaks and valleys to see lakes, waterfalls, and rivers as well as some of the most amazing vistas in the region. Take note that the 2,000-mile-long Appalachian Trail starts along this day trip.

The picturesque mountain town of Ellijay is the teaser of what is to come on your journey and only minutes from the town of Blue Ridge, considered the gateway to these mountains. A visit to Blue Ridge will simply whet your appetite to travel a little deeper into the mountains to Blairsville, Young Harris, and Hiawassee.

This day follows a meandering path designed to let you get a flavor of these quaint little towns, so stay as long or as little as you want in each. Once you are here, you will see signs to many of the other day trip destinations listed later in this chapter, so you may want to extend your visit and play. Go sightseeing. Go antiquing. Go apple picking. Simply go and enjoy yourself.

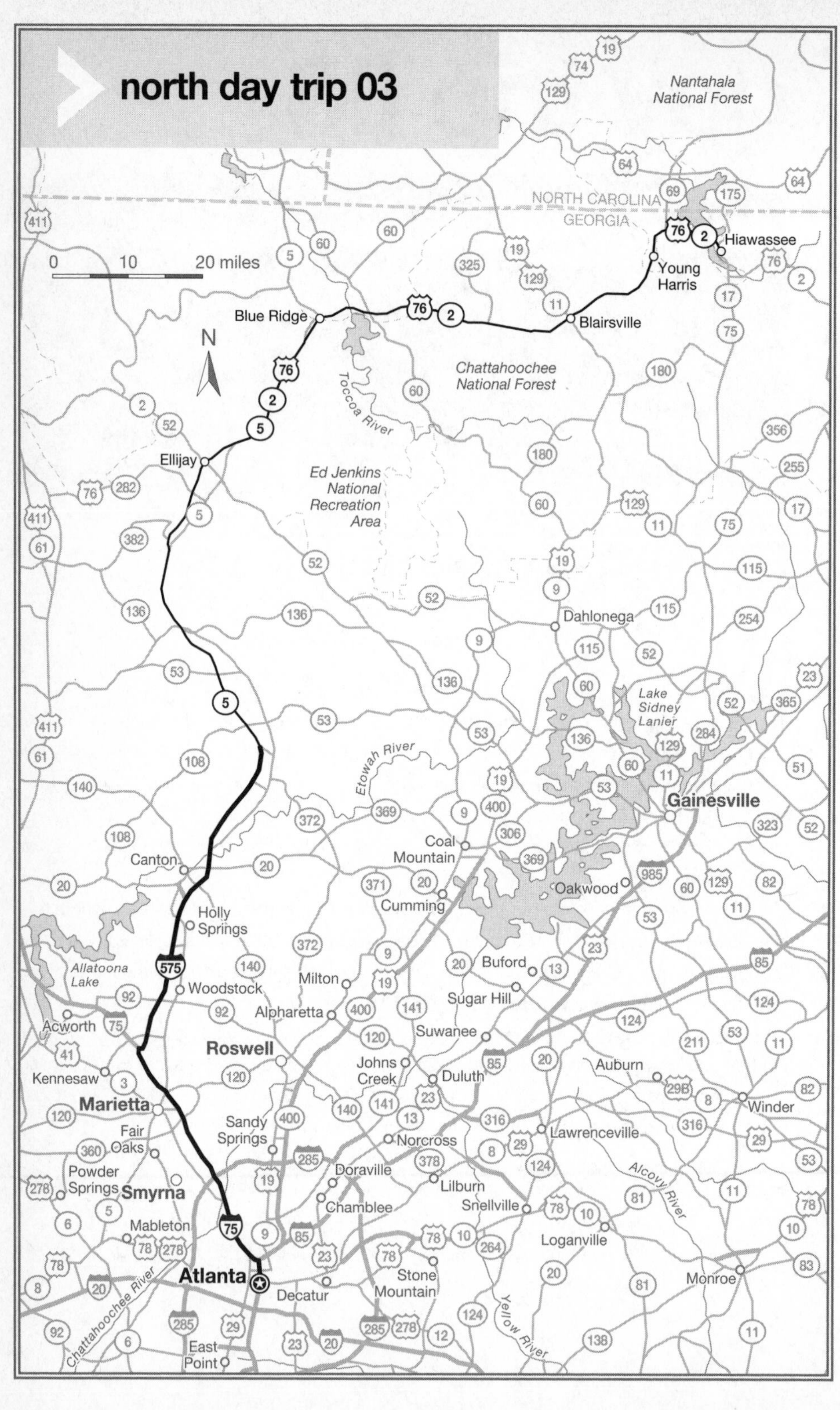

north day trip 03
Nantahala
National Forest
NORTH CAROLINA
GEORGIA
Hiawassee
Young
Harris
Blairsville
Blue Ridge
0
10
20 miles
N
Chattahoochee
National Forest
Toccoa River
Ellijay
Ed Jenkins
National
Recreation
Area
Dahlonega
Lake
Sidney
Lanier
Etowah River
Gainesville
Coal
Mountain
Canton
Cumming
Oakwood
Holly
Springs
Allatoona
Lake
Woodstock
Milton
Buford
Sugar Hill
Alpharetta
Acworth
Suwanee
Roswell
Johns
Creek
Duluth
Auburn
Kennesaw
Marietta
Winder
Fair
Oaks
Sandy
Springs
Norcross
Lawrenceville
Powder
Springs
Smyrna
Doraville
Lilburn
Alcovy River
Chamblee
Snellville
Mableton
Loganville
Atlanta
Stone
Mountain
Monroe
Decatur
Chattahoochee River
Yellow River
East
Point

ellijay

Ellijay sits in the middle of what is called the "Apple Capital of the World," Gilmer County. Each year, more than 600,000 bushels of apples come from this area of the Blue Ridge, and you will see plenty of orchards as you drive through this beautiful country. The little mountain town of Ellijay (and its smaller neighbor East Ellijay) is known as a retreat for many Atlantans who have cabins up here and take advantage of the small-town atmosphere as an escape from the city.

In addition to being a mountain town, Ellijay is a river town. The Ellijay and the Cartecay come together here to form the Coosawattee River. With the rivers, mountains, and the Chattahoochee National Forest right here, there are countless opportunities to get out and hike, camp, fish, and explore. In town, it's all about the square and its friendly, small-town atmosphere.

getting there

Ellijay is about 90 minutes north of Atlanta. Take I-75 north to I-575. When I-575 ends, it becomes GA 5/515. GA 5/515 will take you to East Ellijay. Take a left on GA 52 into Ellijay.

where to go

Gilmer Arts and Heritage Association. Heritage Museum of Gilmer County, 207 Dalton St.; (706) 635-5605; http://gilmerarts.org. This is a small building, but worth a stop. The Gilmer Arts and Heritage Association houses a permanent art gallery and a small theater for plays and musical events, as well as the Heritage Museum of Gilmer County. The museum contains artifacts tracing the region's history back 12,000 years. Mon, Tues, Thurs, Fri 9 a.m. to 4:30 p.m. Free.

Hillcrest Orchards. 9696 GA 52 East; (706) 273-3838; www.hillcrestorchards.net. Hillcrest is considered the most popular apple orchard in North Georgia and not just because of its apples, but because of all of the activities that it offers. In business since 1946, Hillcrest Orchards has grown from its original 15 acres to 80 acres today and produces more than 20 varieties. It hosts several festivals throughout the year, so check schedules.

Olde Downtown Square. Ellijay has been the county seat of Gilmer County since it was founded in 1832 and grew up around the town square. Most of the buildings were destroyed by a fire that ravaged the city in 1912. The buildings lining the square today date back to that period and are home to antiques stores, specialty shops, and restaurants. Take time to just wander the square and the surrounding streets.

where to eat

Colonel Poole Barbeque. 164 Craig St., East Ellijay; (706) 635-4100; www.poolesbarbq.com. This place is easy to spot with its Pig Hill Hall of Fame, and you'll smell the hickory smoke before you see the pigs. Poole's is a "must stop" for its barbeque. Thurs 11 a.m. to 6 p.m., Fri and Sat 11 a.m. to 8 p.m., Sun 11 a.m. to 7 p.m. $$.

Corner Stone Cafe. 76 N. Main St.; (706) 636-2230. Home cooking and the best breakfast around. Family-run and you'll feel like family while you are here. Mon through Sat 7 a.m. to 3 p.m., Sun 8 a.m. to 2 p.m. $.

Pink Pig Restaurant. 824 Cherry Log St., Cherry Log, GA 30522; (706) 276-3311; www.budspinkpig.com. Halfway between Ellijay and Blue Ridge, the Pink Pig is worth those few extra miles. A rustic setting for fabulous barbeque. $.

Sue's Log Cabin. 2693 Tails Creek; (706) 635-5500. Sue's is the closest you'll ever come to a good, Southern home-cooked meal. A favorite with the locals, you'll see the same people eating lunch there every day. Mon through Fri 11 a.m. to 3 p.m. Closed Sat and Sun. $.

where to stay

The Hearthstone Lodge. 2755 GA 282; (706) 695-0920; www.thehearthstonelodge.com. This pine log mountain lodge offers 3 beautiful rooms in a wonderful setting. Sit by the fire or out on the deck. The grounds are gorgeous and include a waterfall. $$.

The Overlook Inn. 9420 GA 52; (706) 517-8810; www.theoverlookinn.com. The Overlook is appropriately named: The inn is on the ridge of Fort Mountain and has a breathtaking view of the Chattahoochee National Forest and the Blue Ridge Mountains. With 6 well-decorated and comfortable rooms, you'll want to stay a while. Most rooms have private entrances. $$–$$$.

blue ridge

You've heard so much about the railroads in Georgia, and now here is a chance to experience one firsthand: the Blue Ridge Scenic Railroad. The railway keeps alive the town's railroad history and takes you on a nostalgic journey to neighboring McCaysville. It's a journey worth taking for the scenery alone.

The little mountain town of Blue Ridge came into being in 1886 because of the Marietta and North Georgia Railroad. It evolved into an elite health resort, drawing people from near and far to take its pure mineral waters. Over the years, the resort faded, but the beauty of the area continues to lure visitors. Even if you don't ride the rails, Blue Ridge is a wonderful place to spend a few hours wandering the streets and enjoying the antiques shops, galleries, and restaurants.

getting there

Blue Ridge is just 16 miles north of Ellijay. Follow GA 5 out of Ellijay until it becomes US 76. You'll pass through the small town of Cherry Log along the way. If you are coming from Atlanta, take I-75 North to I-575. I-575 will turn into GA 5 which will take you into Blue Ridge.

where to go

Blue Ridge Welcome Center. 152 Orvin Lance Dr.; (706) 632-5680 or (800) 899-MTNS (6867); http://blueridgemountains.com. Since Blue Ridge is the gateway to the Blue Ridge Mountains themselves, this is the perfect place to stop for information and guidance. There are several self-guided tours available including a Historic Walking Tour guide for the town of Blue Ridge.

Baugh House. 411 W. 1st St.; (706) 258-2645. Built in 1890 by pioneer John Baugh for his son James, this home gives a sense of life in the developing Blue Ridge of the 1800s. Baugh was a brick mason, and the bricks used here were made out of clay from the backyard. The home houses a great deal of information about geology of the area. Fri and Sat 10 a.m. to 3 p.m. Free.

The Blue Ridge Depot. 241 Depot St.; (706) 632-TRAIN (8724); www.brscenic.com. This 1906 depot (the first one burned) is at the center of Blue Ridge and has been the focus point of the town's activities for more than 150 years. In its heyday, the train would take 4 hours to get to Atlanta. These days, the depot is operated by the Northeast Georgia Railroad and is home to the Blue Ridge Scenic Railway.

Blue Ridge Mountains Arts Center. 420 W. Main St.; (706) 632-2144; http://blueridgearts.net. Housed in the 1937 Fannin County Courthouse, this arts center has an impressive gallery of works by local artists. Be sure to tour the courthouse and see the restored courtroom, too. Tues through Thurs 10 a.m. to 4 p.m., Fri and Sat 10 a.m. to 6 p.m. Free.

Blue Ridge Scenic Railway. 241 Depot St.; (706) 632-TRAIN (8724); www.brscenic.com. The Scenic Railway is truly that. Operating between Blue Ridge and McCaysville, 10 miles away, it travels through rolling hills along the Toccoa River. The views are constantly changing with the seasons. Fall is a particularly popular time to ride, but you can enjoy the dogwoods and wildflowers in spring or the rhododendron and mountain laurel in summer. The railroad operates with the help of more than 200 local volunteers. $$$.

Mercier Apple Orchards. GA 5 North; (706) 632-3411; www.mercier-orchards.com. Mercier has been growing and selling apples for more than 60 years. Still family owned and operated, the orchard has a bake shop and store. Daily 7 a.m. to 8 p.m.

Swan Drive-In Theater. 651 Summit St.; (706) 632-5235. Take a trip into the past by simply driving your car to this drive-in. In operation since 1955, the Swan is 1 of only 4 drive-in theaters in the state of Georgia still operating. Movies nightly at 9 and 11 p.m. $$.

where to eat

Blue Ridge Brewery. 187 Depot St.; (706) 632-6611; www.w.blueridgebrewery.com. Great gastro pub fare in an unexpected place. Creative items on the menu and a wide selection of beers on tap. Wed through Sat 11 a.m. to 9 p.m. $$.

Bumblebee Cafe. 5850 Appalachian Hwy.; (706) 946-2337. A local favorite, you'll love the yellow and black decor. Bumblebee serves breakfast all day and offers great Southern-style lunches. Daily 7 a.m. to 2 p.m. $.

Danielle's Great Eats Deli. 611 E. Main St.; (706) 632-3094. Wonderful and creative sandwiches and subs. Also try the salads. Mon through Sat 11 a.m. to 4 p.m. $.

Harvest on Main. 576 E. Main St.; (706) 946-6164; http://harvestonmain.com. Harvest showcases local, sustainable produce and regional, artisanal flavors. The menu is always fresh and creative. Wed 11 a.m. to 5 p.m., Thurs through Sat 11 a.m. to 9 p.m., Sun noon to 8 p.m. $–$$.

L & L Beanery. 260 W. Main St.; (706) 632-3242. Blue Ridge's favorite coffee shop and breakfast place, L.L. was a 1926 bank building; the original vault is still there. Breakfast and lunch daily. $.

Toccoa Riverside Restaurant. Aska River Rd.; (706) 632-7891; www.toccoariverside restaurant.com. Fabulous views on the Toccoa River and great food to go with it. Mountain trout, steaks, seafood, and ribs along with an extensive salad bar. Wed through Mon 11:30 a.m. to 9 p.m., closed Tues. $$.

The Village Restaurant. 4131 E. 1st St.; (706) 632-2277. The Village is a staple here in Blue Ridge. It offers a great breakfast buffet and lunch and dinner of good old Southern-style cooking. Daily. $.

where to stay

Aska Lodge Bed and Breakfast. 178 Calen Dr.; (706) 632-0178; www.askalodge.net. Aska Lodge B&B offers 4 rooms in the 2-story lodge. You'll feel very pampered here, and the views are amazing. $$.

Bear Rock Ridge Bed and Breakfast. Big Creek Rd.; (706) 273-6222; www.bearrock ridge.com. This mountaintop lodge offers 3 large rooms in a spacious lodge setting. Sit on the deck or hike nearby trails. Bear Rock Ridge is a true retreat. $$.

whitewater fun

From April to October, Atlantans do their own day tripping to take on whitewater rafting on the Ocoee River. No rafting experience? No problem! There are no Class V rapids, but it's great fun. A full day is about 7 hours (and includes lunch) while a half day runs 3 hours. The full day includes the upper Ocoee, which was the location of the 1996 Atlanta Summer Olympics kayak competition. Most rafting companies are located out of Copperhill, TN, just a few miles outside of McCaysville, GA. Prices average about $35 to $45 for a half day and $80 to $90 for a full day. Among the best-known companies are:

Ocoee Rafting: *www.ocoeerafting.com or call (800) 251-4800*

Raft1: *www.raft1.com or call (888) 723-8663*

Ocoee Adventure Center: *www.ocoeeadventurecenter.com or call (888) 723-8622*

Adventures Unlimited: *www.adventuresunlimited.net or call (800) 662-0667*

Outdoor Adventure Rafting: *www.raft.com or call (800) 627-7636*

Quest Expeditions: *www.questexpeditions.com or call (800) 277-4537*

Carolina Ocoee Outfitters: *www.ocoeeriverwhitewaterrafting.com or call (800) 468-7238*

Wildwater Ocoee: *www.wildwaterrafting.com or call (866) 319-8870*

Blue Ridge Inn. 477 W. 1st St.; (706) 632-0222; www.blueridgeinnbandb.com. This 1890 Victorian home was first known as the Kincaid House. Beautifully restored, the 3-story house offers 7 guest rooms. The house itself has 14 rooms, 8 fireplaces, 12-foot ceilings, original carved woodwork, heartpine floors, and claw-foot tubs. $$.

worth more time

McCaysville. Take the Blue Ridge Scenic Railway over to McCaysville or drive yourself the 10 miles on GA 5 to this border town. McCaysville is right on the Tennessee line across from Copperhill, so named because of the copper mining in the region in 1843. McCaysville is a scenic little town on the Toccoa River with funky little shops and restaurants.

Southern Highroads Trail. The trail is a 360-mile scenic driving tour, starting here in the North Georgia mountains and traveling through 4 national forests, including the

Chattahoochee National Forest. A guide to the trail can be found at the Blue Ridge Welcome Center at 152 Orvin Lance Dr. in Blue Ridge or on the website, www.blueridge mountains.com. For more information call (706) 632-5680 or (800) 899-MTNS (6867).

blairsville

Scenic little Blairsville is probably the largest town you'll travel through today. Founded in 1835, its day-to-day life still revolves around the square in the center of town.

Blairsville has seen its share of changes in fate. It started as Cherokee lands and grew with the discovery of gold in the region. In fact, Blairsville was known to have the purest gold in the mountains. As the gold ran out, Blairsville settled into a sleepy community that continues to draw visitors because of its proximity to so many of the Blue Ridge Mountain attractions. There are several historical sites in town and numerous local craft shops.

getting there

From Blue Ridge, head east on US 76 for about 20 miles to Blairsville. If you are coming directly from Atlanta, you will still have to come through Blue Ridge, and the journey will take you about 2 hours. Take I-75 North to I-575, which turns into GA 5/US 76.

where to go

Blairsville Visitor's Center. 385 Welcome Center Ln.; (706) 745-5789 or (877) 745-5789; www.visitblairsvillega.com. The Welcome Center is just off US 76 as you enter town. Stop by for maps and advice. Mon through Fri 9 a.m. to 5 p.m., Sat 10 a.m. to 1 p.m. (May to Oct).

Enchanted Gardens Fairy House. 4339 Young Harris Hwy.; (706) 379-9622; www .miniature-gardens.com. Even if you don't have your own garden, you'll want to see this enchanted little garden center. Just 6 miles east of Blairsville, this nursery is owned by Arthur Millican, who was an artist and model maker for Disney. Kids love this place because many of the houses are just their size. Mon through Sat 9:30 a.m. to 4:30 p.m. Free.

Historic Courthouse. 1 Town Square; (706) 745-5493; www.unioncountyhistory.org. The Romanesque brick and granite old Union County Courthouse was built in 1899 right on the square. Recently restored, it now serves as a history museum, cultural center, and summertime concert hall. The displays in the museum are wide-ranging, many of them outlining notable figures in Union County history. The Union County Historical Society has its offices here. Museum hours for May through Oct are Wed through Sat 10 a.m. to 4 p.m. $.

Logan Turnpike Mill. US 19/129 South; (706) 745-5745; www.loganturnpikemill.com. If you want to know where flour and grits come from, here is your chance to see. This old mill grinds daily. An on-site store allows you to buy both the product and freshly baked goods.

Items available include pancake, muffin, and biscuit mix; flour; grits and porridge; and cornmeal. Tues through Sat 10 a.m. to 5 p.m.

Misty Mountain Model Railroad. 4381 Misty Mountain Ln. on Town Creek School Road; (706) 745-9819; www.mistymountainmodelrailroad.com. You'll be fascinated by just how much detail has gone into the creation of what is America's largest 0-gauge train display. Privately owned by train enthusiast Charles Griffin, this 3,400-square-foot layout features 14 0-gauge Lionel trains traveling on a mile of track over 12 bridges and 4 trestles and through 15 tunnels. Jan through Apr Wed and Sat, May though Dec Mon, Wed, Fri, Sat tours begin promptly at 2 p.m. $$.

Museum of Mountain Living. 99 School St.; www.unioncountyhistory.org. Sitting on 2 acres in the heart of town, this complex includes the 1906 Butt-Mock Home and the 1861 John Payne Cabin, the 1830 Duncan Cabin, and a late 1800s Corn Crib. The fully restored Butt-Mock house serves as the focal point to the complex and contains exhibits and a gift shop. The complex is designed to celebrate and preserve the history and folk traditions of this mountain community. The Historical Society is in the process of saving other structures that will form a circa 1880s small mountain farm.

Southern Tree Plantation. 2531 Owltown Rd.; (706) 745-0601; www.southerntreeplantation.com. This 60-acre working tree farm includes all sorts of family activities from pony and train rides to a petting zoo. Many activities like the pumpkin patch and hayride are seasonal, so check the schedule. Mon through Sat 10 a.m. to 6 p.m., Sun noon to 6 p.m. $$.

Sunrise Country Store. 7568 Gainesville Hwy.; (706) 745-5877; www.sunrisegrocery.com. Sunrise Grocery sits at the foot of Blood Mountain and has been serving the local folks since 1922. It started as Pure Oil gas station and evolved into a country grill and store. It even has a little moonshiner history thrown in there. These days Sunshine is a little country market offering local goods such as pottery, jams and jellies, honey, syrup, and local ground meal. There are also camping supplies, firewood, bait, and tackle.

Walasi-Yi Center. 9710 Gainesville Hwy.; (706) 745-6095; www.mountaincrossings.com. Even if you don't want to hike, this stone structure is worth a look. Listed on the National Register of Historic Places, the Walasi-Yi Center was built in 1937 by the Civilian Conservation Corps. It is the only place where the Appalachian Trail passes through a man-made structure on its entire 2,175-mile-long course. Walasi-Yi is now home to Mountain Crossings, a hiking outfitter as well as a hostel. It is currently the first mail-drop on the trail available to northbound hikers. By the way, Walasi-Yi is Cherokee for "Frog Town." Mon through Fri 9 a.m. to 5 p.m., Sat and Sun 8 a.m. to 6 p.m.

where to eat

Aviator Cafe. 417 E. Blue Ridge St.; (706) 781-1043. Quick and good, Aviator serves up hot and cold subs, wraps, salads, and soups. Mon through Sat 9 a.m. to 6 p.m. $.

Catfish Corner. 444 Blue Ridge St.; (706) 745-3180. As the name suggests, catfish is the specialty, but you'll find steak and chicken and everything else that comes with country-style cooking. Tues through Sat lunch and dinner. $$.

Comfort Cafe. 94 Town Square; (706) 745-8825. Comfort says it all. This is a comfortable place serving up comfort food such as mac and cheese and Southern specialties. Mon through Fri 11 a.m. 8 p.m., Sat 11 a.m. to 3 p.m. $.

Hole in the Wall. 90 Town Square; (706) 745-5888; www.holeinthewallga.com. As the sign says, "There ain't nothing like Home cooking," and the Hole in the Wall's version is the real deal. Around since 1921, Hole in the Wall is a landmark. It is known for its desserts, so save room if you can. Mon through Fri 7 a.m. to 3 p.m., Sat 7:30 a.m. to 3 p.m., Sun 7:30 a.m. to 2:30 p.m. $.

Mike's Seafood Market & Grill. 513 Murphy Hwy.; (706) 745-9519. Some of the freshest and best seafood dishes you'll find in the Blue Ridge. The restaurant has its own market, so it's busy with people picking up to take home, but the dine-in is creative and perfectly cooked. Mon through Sat 11 a.m. to 2 p.m., 5 to 9 p.m. $$.

Sawmill Place. 1150 Pat Haralson Memorial Dr.; (706) 745-1250. Another local favorite, the Sawmill is known for its Southern cooking and huge portions. You can't beat the biscuits and gravy. Breakfast and lunch daily. $.

where to stay

Misty Mountain Inn & Cottages. 55 Misty Mountain Ln.; (706) 745-4786; www.misty mountaininn.com. The inn part of Misty Mountain is a Victorian farmhouse renovated to provide 4 spacious guest rooms. Each room includes a private bath and fireplace. Three rooms have balconies. The property also includes 6 tin-roof self-catering cottages. Complimentary breakfast is available until noon for inn guests. $–$$.

Season's Inn. 16 Town Square; (706) 745-8490; www.seasons-inn.com. This modern inn is settled right on Blairsville's historic square. Family owned and operated, you'll find many guests come back again and again. $–$$.

Your Home in the Woods B&B. 2830 Timber Ln.; (706) 745-9337; www.yourhomeinthe woods.com. Nestled in the woods, this quiet retreat has 3 bedrooms available. It has front and back porches with gardens and hiking trails on the grounds. $–$$.

worth more time

Brasstown Bald. GA 180 Spur; (706) 745-6928 or (706) 896-2556 (visitors center); http://fs.usda.gov/conf. This is the highest spot in the state of Georgia and only a few miles east of Blairsville. Drive to the summit and the visitor center where you can get a 360-degree view of the mountains from the observation deck. The ambitious can make the climb to the tower for even better views. Brasstown Bald also includes the Trackrock Archeological Area, which is 2 acres featuring preserved petroglyphs of ancient native origin carved or pecked into soapstone boulders. Open daily Memorial Day through Oct., weekends only Apr through May. Call for fees.

Lake Nottely. US 19 North; www.lakenottelyblairsville.com. Lake Nottely is a Tennessee Valley Authority (TVA) reservoir that features 106 miles of shoreline. Built in 1941, it's a great place to picnic, boat, or swim.

Suches. This tiny little community is just south of Blairsville and is best known for its proximity to the trailhead of the Appalachian Trail. The Appalachian Trail starts at Springer Mountain and crosses GA 60 at the Woody Gap Recreational Area as it snakes its way over 2,000 miles to Maine. Suches is one of the highest-elevation communities in the state and calls itself "The Valley Above The Clouds." The area offers places to fish, hike, picnic, swim, or camp. Also near Suches is the Chattahoochee Forest National Fish Hatchery (4730 Rock Creek Rd.; 706-838-4723; http://southeast.fws.gov/chattahoocheeforest). The hatchery raises more than a million rainbow trout a year to stock the rivers, streams, and lakes of North Georgia. Bring your own bait and gear.

young harris

There is a reason they call the area around Young Harris the Enchanted Valley. It is breathtaking as you drive over the ridge and see this valley at the base of Brasstown Bald Mountain. The town of Young Harris centers around the college from which it gets its name.

Young Harris College was founded in 1886 by Methodist circuit minister Artemus Lester. Lester had wanted to guarantee a quality education for residents of the area and called the new place McTyerie after the local Methodist bishop. As the college grew, it was renamed for Judge Young Loftin Gerdine Harris of Athens.

The college remains the main reason for the town's existence, but the surrounding natural beauty affords a great deal to see. You'll often hear Young Harris and its neighboring town of Hiawassee in the same breath. They share a shoreline with the reservoir called Chatuge Lake, and it's easy to go back and forth from one to the other. There are several resorts in the area, so if golf and tennis appeal to you, there are ample opportunities.

getting there

From Blairsville, continue north on US 76/GA 5 for 9 miles to the town of Young Harris. Coming from Atlanta, take I-75 North to I-575, which becomes US 76/GA 5 and goes into Young Harris. The trip takes about 2 hours.

where to go

Towns County Chamber of Commerce and Welcome Center. 1411 Jack Dayton Circle; (706) 896-4966 or (800) 984-1543; www.mountaintopga.com. Stop in for maps and useful information about the area. Mon through Fri 9 a.m. to 5 p.m.

Crane Creek Vineyards. 916 Crane Creek Rd.; (706) 379-1236; www.cranecreekvineyards .com. Crane Creek is a perfect little haven in the Georgia mountains. The family-run winery offers wonderful quaffs and plays host to events and weddings. The setting is amazing. With the mountains as a backdrop, the grounds include a culinary garden, apple orchard, tasting room, and gift shop. Chickens and guinea hens roam free. Tasting room: Tues through Sat 11 a.m. to 5 p.m., Sun 1 to 5 p.m.

Destiny Alpacas. 1952 Gibson Rd.; (706) 379-2361; www.destinyalpacas.com. You'd think you were in the mountains of Peru instead of North Georgia when you visit Destiny Alpacas. On a scenic farm overlooking the mountains, visitors can interact with the alpacas and purchase alpaca products. Destiny sells not just the products, but the animals themselves, although we doubt you'd want to carry one home with you. Call for an appointment.

Rollins Planetarium. 1 College St.; (800) 241-3754; www.yhc.edu. Rollins Planetarium is the largest in Georgia. Situated on the campus of Young Harris College, Rollins has a seating capacity of 109 people under a 40-foot-diameter dome. It features a GOTO Chronos Space Simulator star projector that uses light guide technology to project a realistic and beautiful starry sky. The dome projection truly offers a "you-are-there" experience for the audience. The observatory is opened every Fri night at 8:45 p.m., and observing sessions end before 9:45 p.m. except in the summer.

where to eat

Bread of Life Family Restaurant. 871 Main St.; (706) 379-2136. You're part of the family when you come to this Southern restaurant. If it's not on the menu, ask and they will try to accommodate. Mon through Sat 7:30 a.m. to 8 p.m., Sun 7:30 a.m. to 3 p.m. $–$$.

Brother's at Willow Ranch. 6223 US 76 West; (706) 379-1272. A great place to take the family. Good food ranging from mountain trout to steaks and burgers. Tues through Thurs 11:30 a.m. to 8:30 p.m., Fri and Sat 11:30 a.m. to 9:30 p.m., Sun 11:30 a.m. to 8:30 p.m. $–$$.

Mary Ellen's Southern Grill. 1617 GA 17 North; (706) 896-1048. You will think you've died and gone to heaven. Everything here is good from the grilled and split homemade biscuits to the catfish and fried chicken. Bring your appetite. Tues through Sat 7 a.m. to 8 p.m. $$.

where to stay

Brasstown Valley Resort & Spa. 6321 US 76; (706) 379-9900; www.brasstownvalley.com. It's easy to see why this is considered one of the premier mountain resorts in the region. It has something for everyone from fine dining to a pub for food, golf, equestrian activities, and a full-service spa. $$$.

River Keepers Cottage. Crane Creek Vineyards, 916 Crane Creek Rd.; (706) 379-1236; www.cranecreekvineyards.com. The vineyards offer a guesthouse on-site. For trout fishermen, you'll find the Frogtown Creek branch of the Chestatee River, a certified Georgia trout stream, right outside its door. $$.

The Ridges Resort & Marina. 3499 US 76 West; (888) 834-4409; www.theridgesresort.com. The Ridges Resort & Marina is located right on the western shore of Lake Chatuge. The mountain and lake scenery is just gorgeous. Guests can enjoy lake activities or take in a round of golf on the championship course. Stay in the lodge or rent a villa ranging from 1 to 4 bedrooms. $$–$$$.

hiawassee

First, let's look at the name. "Hiawassee" is a Cherokee word meaning "meadow," so keep in mind the town got its name long before 7,000-acre Chatuge Lake straddling the Georgia-Tennessee border was created in the 1950s. The meadow is not as expansive as it once was, but still Hiawassee is as beautiful as its name.

Life here centers around the lake and mountain recreational activities. Many artists reside in this community, perhaps inspired by the beauty of the surrounding area.

getting there

Only 6 miles from Young Harris, take US 76 east to Hiawassee. From Atlanta, take I-75 North to I-575 which then becomes US 76.

where to go

ArtWorks Artisan Centre. 308 Big Sky Dr.; (706) 896-0932; www.mtnregartscraftsguild.org. If you are looking for locally made artwork, this is the place to stop. The guild consists of 87 of the finest artisans and artists in the area of North Georgia, Tennessee, and North Carolina. The center includes displays and workshops, but the highlight is the great gift shop. Mon through Sat 10 a.m. to 5 p.m.

Georgia Mountain Fairgrounds. 1311 Music Hall Rd.; (706) 896-4191; www.georgiamountainfairgrounds.com. On the shores of Lake Chatuge, the fairgrounds stay busy with special events, so check the schedule to see what's on while you are in the area. Unique venues include a pioneer village, complete with a 1-room schoolhouse, a general store, a blacksmith shop, a repair shop, and an "old mountain home." The Anderson Music Hall plays host to area concerts with big-name performers. Among the events taking place here are the Georgia Mountain Fair, the Georgia Mountain Roots & Music Festival, the Superstar Concert Series, the Georgia Mountain Fall Festival, and Georgia's Official State Fiddler's Convention.

Hamilton Rhododendron Gardens. 1311 Music Hall Rd.; (706) 896-4191. These gardens are beautiful at any point in the year, but try to time a visit during April and May when the 3,000 varieties of rhododendrons are in bloom. Hamilton boasts one of the largest collections of hybrid rhododendrons in the state of Georgia. The garden is on the grounds of the Georgia Mountain Fairgrounds and blankets a hillside sloping to Lake Chatuge. Pine bark trails will help you explore views filled with dogwoods, tulip magnolias, native azaleas, lady slippers, and trillium. Daily 8 a.m. to 7 p.m. $.

where to eat

Bear Meadows Grill. 715 N. Main St.; (706) 896-0520; www.bearmeadowsgrill.com. This fun little place with great views offers everything from wings to steaks. Mon through Thurs 11 a.m. to 8 p.m.; Fri and Sat 11 a.m. to 9 p.m. $–$$.

Madison Anne's Kitchen. 75 Main St.; (706) 896-4171. A local favorite for homemade soups, salads, sandwiches, and desserts. Tues through Sat 11 a.m. to 5 p.m. $.

Michaelee's Chocolate Caffe. 142 N. Main St.; (706) 896-2752; www.michaelees.com. Offering one of the best selections of food in town, ranging from paninis to creative salads and steaks. Mon through Thurs 11 a.m. to 8 p.m., Fri and Sat 11 a.m. to 9 p.m. $$–$$$.

Smoke Rings Barbecue. 325 Big Sky Dr.; (706) 896-6467. Not your typical barbeque place. Dry rub ribs and great pulled pork or the peach baked beans. And you can't beat the views! Tues through Thurs 11 a.m. to 3 p.m., Fri and Sat 11 a.m. to 8 p.m., Sun 11 a.m. to 3 p.m. $–$$.

where to stay

Chancey Hill Inn Bed & Breakfast. 385 Chancey Dr.; (706) 896-8424; www.chanceyhillinn.com. Every one of this modern inn's 5 rooms has views of the mountain. On a terraced hilltop overlooking Lake Chatuge. $$.

Laurel Mountain Cabin Rental Resort. Laurel Mountain Rd.; (706) 896-8015 or (888) 859-6018; www.laurel-mountain-cabins.com. The resort is on 12 acres on Laurel Mountain within the Chattahoochee National Forest. All cabins have fully equipped kitchens, Jacuzzis, stone fireplaces, covered porches, barbecue grills, and mountain views. $$–$$$.

day trip 04

north

helen back:
cleveland, helen, sautee nacoochee

The Alps and North Georgia collide in today's day trip as we travel to an area that is awash with natural beauty and a little man-made as well. Just to the north of Atlanta is the alpine village of Helen, which is a favorite day trip that allows you to not just escape Atlanta, but feel as if you have fled the US entirely! You'll swear you have been transported to a Bavarian village when you drive into this scenic little mountain town. The entire region follows that alpine motif, complete with much of the local restaurants and their cuisine.

Getting there takes you away from crowded Atlanta and into the scenic Appalachian foothills. We'll pass through the tiny town of Cleveland, which is famous in its own right for a phenomenon that hit the toy industry in the 1970s: Cabbage Patch Kids.

The neighboring community of Sautee Nacoochee will enthrall you with is dedication to the arts, and you'll wonder how someplace so small can have so much going for it.

But you will soon recognize as you drive from place to place that the real reason people come here is because of the surrounding beauty, and there are some amazing parks to visit and enjoy.

So come along to a little slice of Georgia heaven as we take you to Helen, and back.

cleveland

In fairness to Cleveland, the quaint little town generally plays second fiddle to Helen because there is so much to do in the other big-name city of White County. But as the county seat,

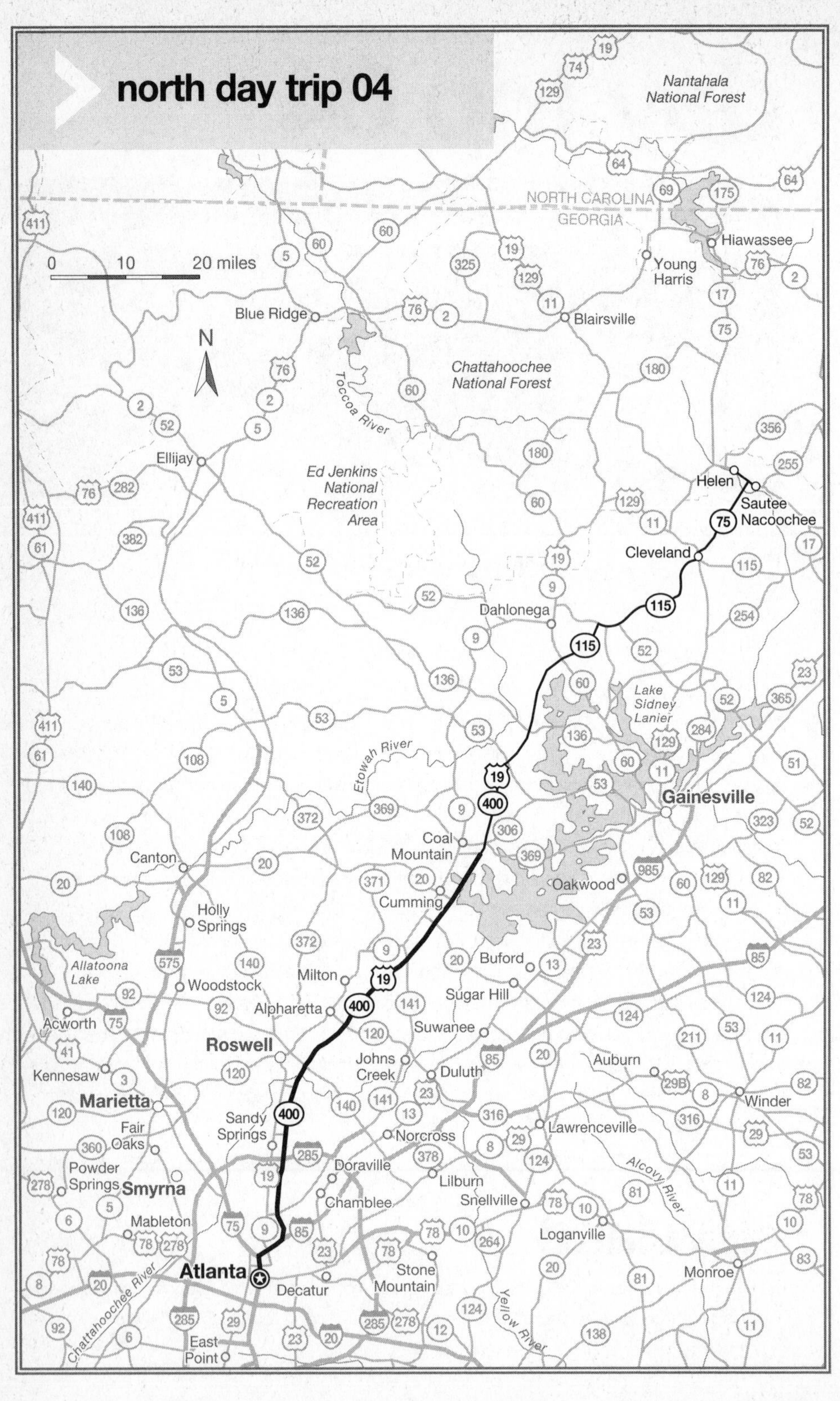

north day trip 04
Nantahala
National Forest
NORTH CAROLINA
GEORGIA
Hiawassee
Young
Harris
0
10
20 miles
Blue Ridge
Blairsville
N
Chattahoochee
National Forest
Toccoa River
Ellijay
Ed Jenkins
National
Recreation
Area
Helen
Sautee
Nacoochee
Cleveland
Dahlonega
Lake
Sidney
Lanier
Etowah River
Gainesville
Coal
Mountain
Canton
Oakwood
Cumming
Holly
Springs
Allatoona
Lake
Woodstock
Milton
Buford
Sugar Hill
Alpharetta
Acworth
Suwanee
Roswell
Johns
Creek
Duluth
Auburn
Kennesaw
Marietta
Winder
Sandy
Springs
Lawrenceville
Fair
Oaks
Norcross
Powder
Springs
Smyrna
Doraville
Chamblee
Alcovy River
Lilburn
Snellville
Mableton
Loganville
Stone
Mountain
Monroe
Atlanta
Decatur
Chattahoochee River
Yellow River
East
Point

Cleveland does have a lot to offer, so you should plan on making a few stops here on your day trip.

The town square is busy with shops and restaurants, and there are always activities taking place there. Most famously, Cleveland is the home to the world-famous Cabbage Patch Kids dolls. Take a step into the past at the old courthouse museum, and then venture over to BabyLand General Hospital. It's an experience you truly have to witness to appreciate.

getting there

Cleveland is 90 minutes from downtown Atlanta. Take I-85 to GA 400 North until it ends. Go 5 miles to the traffic light and turn right on to GA 52/115. It's 13 miles to Cleveland.

where to go

White County Chamber of Commerce. 122 Main St.; (706) 865-5356; www.whitecountychamber.org. Stop here for local maps and coupons. Mon through Fri 8 a.m. to 4:30 p.m.

BabyLand General Hospital. 300 NOK Dr.; (706) 865-2171; www.cabbagepatchkids.com. This place is mecca for Cabbage Patch fans, but is something to behold for just about anyone. The 70,000-square-foot complex sits on a 100-acre spread, the brainchild of Cabbage Patch Kid creator, artist Xavier Roberts. There are all sorts of Babies and Kids exclusive to this location. A museum-like setting shows vignettes of Kids dating back to 1977. The hospital includes a nursery and the cabbage patch planted beneath the Magic Crystal Tree. Mother Cabbage gives birth here, and it is the only place you can find "hand-stitched to birth" soft-sculpture Original Cabbage Patch Kids®. Mon through Sat 9 a.m. to 5 p.m., Sun 10 a.m. to 5 p.m.

Gold N' Gem Grubbin. 75 Gold Nugget Ln.; (706) 865-5454; www.goldngem.com. Try your hand at panning for gold and gemstones at this fun little stop. You can pan in the sluice or go basic and head down to the creek. Grubbin will help evaluate all finds. Custom jewelry making on-site. Daily 9 a.m. to 5 p.m. $$.

North Georgia Zoo and Petting Farm. 2912 Paradise Valley Rd.; (706) 348-7279; www.northgeorgiazoo.com. North Georgia's only zoo has a wide range of animals from the exotic (alligators, monkeys, kangaroos, wildcats, zebras) to the domestic. There is a petting zoo that is sure to bring a smile to your face. The North Georgia Zoo also has a program called "Wildlife Wonders," which brings some of the more docile animals from the zoo to you. Fri 10 a.m. to 4 p.m., Sat 9 a.m. to 6 p.m., Sun 10 a.m. to 6 p.m. $$.

White County Historical Society and Museum. Cleveland Square; (706) 865-3225; www.whitecountyhistoricalsociety.com. The brick White County Courthouse was constructed between 1859 and 1860 and is a living history museum on the town square listed on the National Register of Historic Places. The museum contains artifacts predating

Cleveland itself and includes geological exhibits, a Civil War exhibit, old documents, and works by the local clay legend, Meaders Pottery. It also has a small gift shop. Thurs through Sat 10 a.m. to 3 p.m. $.

where to eat

Creekside Deli. 16 Old Nacoochee Rd.; (706) 865-3666. Sit creekside and enjoy great sandwiches, salads, and soups in a relaxing atmosphere. Mon through Wed 11 a.m. to 3 p.m., Thurs through Sun 11 a.m. to 8 p.m. $.

Glenda's. 286 S. Main St.; (706) 865-7850. Good Southern food with great meat-and-three veggie combinations. Mon through Sat lunch and dinner. $–$$.

The Soda Fountain Cafe. Cleveland Pharmacy & Gifts, 19 E. Jarrard St.; (706) 865-1212. The Soda Fountain Cafe has changed little since it opened in the 1950s. An old-fashioned diner, you can get great sandwiches, soups, and blue-plate specials and well as great ice-cream concoctions. Mon through Fri 9:30 a.m. to 6 p.m., Sat 9:30 a.m. to 3 p.m. $.

where to stay

The Lodge at Windy Acres. 16 Windy Acres Rd.; (800) 435-5032 or (706) 865-6635; www.thelodgeatwindyacres.com. This country lodge has 5 rooms in a relaxing atmosphere. Halfway between Cleveland and Helen. $–$$.

Town Creek Bed and Breakfast. 811 Hooper Rd.; (706) 865-0410. Four rooms are available in this great bed-and-breakfast on Town Creek. Owner Steve LaTorre will happily give you gold-panning lessons on the creek. $$.

helen

When you drive into Helen, you'll simply shake your head in wonder. Yes, it looks just like a Bavarian village complete with cobblestone streets and painted facades. And no matter how many times people tell you about it, the full extent of it can't be grasped until you actually visit.

Strangely, Helen had no real connection to Germany until the 1960s when a group of businessmen cooked up the theme as a way to revitalize their town. A local artist who had been stationed in Germany helped them draw up the plans, and in 1969, the transformation began. The plan worked, and Helen is one of the hottest tourist spots in North Georgia. In fact, each fall Helen plays host to the longest and largest Oktoberfest celebration in the US.

Some would argue it has been an odd look for a town that was first made a center of activity by Cherokees until the 1800s. They were pushed out from this area in the infamous Trail of Tears, and the discovery of gold in the region brought prospectors and then timber merchants to the valley.

A visit today offers not just a chance to explore the village, but numerous natural wonders around Helen that have remained unchanged over time. Waterfalls, streams, and hiking trails abound here.

getting there

From Cleveland, take US 129 North to GA 75 and follow it for 9 miles to Helen. From Atlanta, it's about a 90-minute drive (follow the directions from Atlanta to Cleveland, above).

where to go

Helen Chamber of Commerce. 726 Brucken Strasse; (706) 878-2181; www.helenchamber.com. You may not know where to start when you arrive in town, so it's best just to start here. This is a town designed to be explored. Mon through Sat 9 a.m. to 5 p.m., Sun 10 a.m. to 4 p.m.

Anna Ruby Falls. 3455 Anna Ruby Falls Rd., GA 356; (706) 878-1448; http://fs.usda.gov/conf. If you want to see waterfalls, Anna Ruby are some of the most scenic in Georgia, and they are easy to get to. Located in the heart of the Chattahoochee National Forest, Anna Ruby Falls are actually twin cascading falls which mark the junction of Curtis and York Creeks. These falls include a popular interpretive trail for the blind and visually impaired called "The Lion's Eye Trail," which features Braille signs regarding area features. Walking is easy to moderate, and the trail will take approximately 30 minutes to complete, while ambitious hikers can make it to Unicoi State Park (see "Worth More Time"). Picnicking is available in the area. Daily 9 a.m. to 7 p.m. $.

Dukes Creek Gold and Ruby Mines. 6145 Helen Hwy.; (706) 878-2625; www.dukescreek.com. Try your hand at finding gems or just come in and learn about the history of mining in the area. Dukes Creek Gold is an operating gold and gem mine and was formerly a productive part of America's first gold rush. These days guests can try to share in the wealth by scouring buckets of rocks for a special find. Dukes has a little bit of everything from demonstrations on stone polishing to guidance on how to identify gemstones. Daily 10 a.m. to 5 p.m.

Habersham Winery. 7025 S. Main; (706) 878-9463; www.habershamwinery.com. Habersham is one of Georgia's oldest and largest wineries, having been producing wine in North Georgia since 1983. The tasting room allows you to see for yourself why their wines have won more than 150 awards. Tours of the production can be arranged by calling ahead. Mon through Sat 10 a.m. to 6 p.m., Sun 12:30 to 6 p.m.

Helen Arts and Heritage Center. (706) 878-3933; www.helenarts.com. Located in the heart of town in Old City Hall, this center provides a lot of things to see and do. First, it houses a museum that traces the unique history of Helen back to its days as a Cherokee center. It also houses a wonderful gallery of works by local artists, as well as offering art classes. There are shows and events, so check the schedule to see what might be happening. Thurs through Mon noon to 4 p.m.

Live Tarantulas Museum. 8660 N. Main St.; (706) 348-7279; www.livetarantulasgallery.com. Not for the faint of heart. This unusual museum features 25 different big hairy spiders, scorpions, lizards, bearded dragons, iguanas, and also a 12-foot-long albino Burmese python. Guests can even interact with some of its denizens if they dare. The museum also offers programs to help educate people about their creatures. Mon through Fri noon to 6 p.m., Sat noon to 8 p.m., Sun noon to 7 p.m.

Nora Mill Granary. 7107 S. Main St.; (800) 927-2375; www.noramill.com. This gristmill and country store has been right here on the banks of the Chattahoochee River since 1876. Fully operational, it is listed on the National Register of Historic Places. The mill was built by a gold miner and later purchased by Dr. Lamartine Martin, who named it after his sister Nora. Standing 4 stories tall, the mill has 1,500-pound French burr mill stones, a 100-foot wooden raceway, and a water turbine rather than a waterwheel. The store sells a variety of products including local jams, jellies, and more. Mon through Sat 9 a.m. to 5 p.m., Sun 10 a.m. to 5 p.m.

where to shop

There are more than 200 specialty shops in downtown Helen ranging from authentic German crafts to authentic Georgian crafts, clothes, antiques, and more. The visitor center provides maps for area shopping and some discount coupons.

where to eat

Bigg Daddy's American Tavern. 807 Edelweisse Strasse; (706) 878-2739; www.biggdaddys.com. Bigg Daddy's is known for its food, its beer, and its music. The menu ranges from sushi to pasta and pizza. Mon through Thurs 5 p.m. to midnight, Thurs and Fri noon to 1 a.m., Sun 1 p.m. to midnight. $$.

Cafe International. 8546 Main St.; (706) 878-3102. Living up to its name, Cafe International draws its menu from a host of countries. They are known for their Weiner schnitzel, but sandwiches and pastas are great as well. Sun through Thurs 11 a.m. to 9 p.m., Fri and Sat 11 a.m. to 10 p.m. $$.

Goats on the Roof. Ridge Road; (706) 782-2784; www.goats-on-the-roof.com. This fabulous deli has something for everyone from big, meaty sandwiches to homemade pimento cheese. Daily 11 a.m. to 3 p.m. $.

Helen's Country Cafe. 8988 N. Main St.; (706) 878-4603; http://helenscountrycafe.vpweb.com. As the name says, this is country cooking and country cooking done well. A popular spot for breakfast and lunch. Fresh baked biscuits and homemade daily specials. Daily 7 a.m. to 3 p.m. $.

Hofer's Bakery & Cafe. 8758 N. Main St.; (706) 878-8200; www.hofers.com. One of Helen's best German restaurants, serving breakfast and lunch daily. German cakes, pastries, and bread are prepared on the premises. Sun through Tues 8 a.m. to 5 p.m., Thurs and Fri 8 a.m. to 5 p.m., Sat 8 a.m. to 6 p.m. $$.

King Ludwig's Biergarten. 8660-1 N. Main St.; (706) 878-0191. This is as typical a German biergarten as you will find. Sit outside, have "ein Mass" (a liter), and enjoy a pretzel. 11 a.m. to 11 p.m. $.

Nacoochee Grill. 7277 S. Main St.; (706) 878-8020; www.nacoocheevillage.com. Fine dining in Helen and some of the best food in North Georgia. Steaks, duck, and seafood all from a wood-fired grill. Mon through Thurs 4 to 9 p.m., Fri 4 to 10 p.m., Sat and Sun 11 a.m. to 10 p.m. $$.

Troll Tavern. 8590B N. Main St.; (706) 865-5710; www.trolltavern.com. Under the bridge and over the river in downtown Helen, Troll Tavern serves German, American, and even Mexican food. Sun through Thurs 11 a.m. to 11 p.m., until midnight Fri and Sat. $$.

where to stay

Alpine Hilltop Haus. 362 Chattahoochee St.; (706) 878-2388; www.alpinehilltop.com. This traditional bed-and-breakfast has 4 rooms and 1 suite available. Comfortable and affordable in downtown. $$.

Black Forest Bed & Breakfast & Vacation Rentals. 8902 N. Main St.; (706) 878-3995; www.blackforestvacationrentals.com. Catering to couples, this conveniently located inn offers 4 themed rooms and 3 suites in the main house. They also rent 6 cabins for couples only. $$–$$$.

Smithgall Woods. 61 Tsalaki Trail; (706) 878-3087; http://gastateparks.org/Smithgall Woods. This is a unique mountain retreat experience. On one of the state's best-known trout streams, Dukes Creek, Smithgall features 5 cabins which can be rented separately or reserved as a group. Covering 5,600 acres, the park is known for its abundant wildlife, and hikers can explore 4 miles of trails and 18 miles of roads. Trout fishing and shuttle service are offered only on certain days of the week, so visitors should call for a current schedule and to make reservations. Van tours are offered daily at 12:30 p.m. Cabin rates include accommodations, meals, and activities. $$$.

Unicoi Lodge. Unicoi State Park, 1788 GA 356; (800) 573-9659 or (706) 878-2201; www.unicoilodge.com. In the heart of the popular Unicoi State Park, this lodge has more than 100 rooms available. Guests have all of the features of the park right at their front door, including 12 miles of nature and hiking trails, lake and trout stream fishing, 4 lighted tennis courts, softball and volleyball areas, and picnic facilities. The Unicoi Restaurant is open year-round and serves buffet meals for breakfast, lunch, and dinner. The lodge gift shop specializes in handmade quilts and pottery. $$.

worth more time

Unicoi State Park. 1788 GA 356; (800) 573-9659 or (706) 878-2201; www.gastateparks.org/Unicoi. Just 2 miles from Helen, Unicoi is one of Georgia's favorite parks. The 1,050-acre park features programs throughout the year to highlight the unique natural wonders of the area. The park has a 53-acre lake in its midst, and trails here lead both to Anna Ruby Falls nearby and down to Helen itself. Mountain biking is also available in the park. In addition to the Unicoi Lodge, there are cabins available for rent as well as camping sites.

sautee nacoochee

Sautee Nacoochee is barely a crossroads, but there is so much here to see and experience that you'll quickly recognize why it is ranked among the "100 Best Small Arts Towns in America." This small hamlet is filled with the creative arts: music, dancing, art, food, and much more.

Just the name alone lets you know this was an area that was important to Native Americans. The Nachoochee Indian Mound outside of town is a testament that they considered this place sacred. Those who followed agreed it was a special place, and efforts have been made to preserve it.

A group of citizens formed the Sautee-Nacoochee Community Association (SNCA) in the 1970s to protect what they have and to promote arts in the region. They succeeded in having the entire Sautee Valley added to the National Register of Historic Places and followed up that success by creating the Sautee Nacoochee Center to make sure others could share.

getting there

Sautee Nacoochee is 4 miles from Helen on GA 17. From Atlanta, the trip will take you about 90 minutes. Follow the directions to Helen from Cleveland, but you will turn right off of US 75 onto GA 17 just before reaching Helen.

where to go

Folk Pottery Museum. 283 GA 255 North; (706) 878-3300; www.folkpotterymuseum.com. The Folk Pottery Museum is part of the Sautee Nacoochee Center and celebrates the region's 200-year history in clay. The museum recognizes and celebrates pottery as the

South's premier grassroots art form while exploring its historical importance in Southern life. Mon through Sat 10 a.m. to 5 p.m., Sun 1 to 5 p.m. $.

The Gourd Place International Gourd Museum. 2319 Duncan Bridge Rd.; (706) 865-4048; www.gourdplace.com. Call this "all things gourd." Starting in 1976, this museum has featured more than 200 gourds in all shapes, forms, and uses from 23 countries. There is also a retail shop where you can, of course, buy gourds. Open daily Apr through Dec 23 and by appointment Jan through Mar. Call for hours. Free.

Nacoochee Indian Mound. GA 17 and 75. Located 3 miles from Sautee on the way to Helen, the Nacoochee Indian Mound was originally the center of the ancient Cherokee town of Gauxule and is believed to date back to AD 700 and the time of the Native Americans known as the Mound Builders. Excavations of the mound in 1915 revealed graves at several levels as well as ceremonial fire pits. The mound measures 190 feet long, 150 feet wide, and 20 feet high and is listed on the National Register of Historic Places. Roadside. Free.

Old Sautee Store and Museum. 2315 GA 17; (706) 878-2281 or (888) 463-9853; www.oldsauteestore.com. The Old Sautee Store and Museum is one of those fun places that just begs you to stop. Built in 1872, it still functions as a store but also has a museum section commemorating the years it has been here and the changes it has seen in the area. In the store you will find old-fashioned toys and candies as well as cheeses and other time-tested merchandise such as Carhartt, Life is good, Manual Weavers, and Royal Robbins. Fresh baked goods are also available. Mon through Sat 10 a.m. to 5:30 p.m., Sun noon to 5:30 p.m. Free.

Sautee Nacoochee Center. 283 GA 255 North; (706) 878-3300; www.snca.org. On the grounds of an old school, the Sautee Nacoochee Center is a thriving center for art and history and is operated by the Sautee-Nacoochee Community Association (SNCA). The center is home to a museum, a gift store, a 100-seat theater, an art gallery, and an African-American heritage exhibition. Among the displays in the African-American section is the only known slave cabin still existing in the Northeast Georgia mountains. Built in the 1850s, it has been painstakingly restored. Exhibits at the gallery change regularly and showcase local artists. Mon through Sat 10 a.m. to 5 p.m., Sun 1 to 5 p.m. Free.

Sautee Nacoochee Vineyards. 98 Nacoochee Way; (706) 878-0542; www.sauteenacoocheevineyards.com. This little vineyard prides itself on selling wines from 100 percent Georgia grapes. Sautee Nacoochee Vineyards started in 2009 and encompasses 6 acres on 2 vineyards in the Sautee and Nacoochee Valleys. In addition to its tasting room, it also hosts events and weddings. Fri through Sun noon to 5 p.m.

Stovall Mill Covered Bridge. GA 255; (706) 878-2181. This small covered bridge just east of Sautee off GA 255 has the distinction of having the shortest clear span of any covered bridge in Georgia. The bridge across Chickamauga Creek is 36.8 feet long with queen-post truss. It was built by Fred Stovall Sr. in 1895 to replace a bridge that had burned. Stovall also had a gristmill, sawmill, and shingle mill on the creek. The bridge is all that remains. It has a parking area, picnic area, and historic marker on-site. Daily. Free.

Yonah Mountain Vineyards. 2454-B GA 17; (706) 878-5522; www.yonahmountainvineyards.com. On an old 197-acre family farm, the vineyards take their name from nearby Yonah Mountain. "Yonah" is the Cherokee word for "bear." The vineyard started slowly with just 5 acres of grapes and has grown in the years since. Its tasting room has become a destination for many, and the vineyards plays host to events and weddings. Mon and Thurs noon to 5 p.m., Fri noon to 6 p.m., Sat 11 a.m. to 6 p.m., Sun 12:30 to 6 p.m.

where to eat and stay

Bernies Restaurant at Nacoochee Valley Guest House. 2220 GA 17; (706) 878-3830; www.letsgotobernies.com. This 1920s cottage is a quiet haven for both diners and those who choose to stay overnight in one of the 4 comfortable guest rooms. The owners are a mother-daughter team. Bernie's daughter Monda operates the restaurant and is a graduate of the Culinary Institute of America. The restaurant's reputation draws diners from throughout the region. $$.

The Stovall House Country Inn & Restaurant. 1526 GA 255 North; (706) 878-3355; www.stovallhouse.com. Located on 26 acres out in the country, this 1837 inn offers a great backdrop for an escape. There are 4 rooms available upstairs with views overlooking the Sautee Valley. The restaurant features regional cuisine in a relaxed country setting. $$.

day trip 05

gorge-ous!

toccoa, tallulah falls

As we head up toward the North Carolina border in this last day trip north, we will go off the beaten path to some gorgeous scenery. In fact, we call this trip Gorge-ous because we are going up to Tallulah Falls and the gorge that runs beneath it.

Passing through Toccoa on the way to Tallulah, you will feel that you are on a winding journey through lush and still rocky terrain. These areas have long drawn tourists to the region, and they are filled with nostalgic stops along the way—old inns and old stores that harken back to a bygone era.

You'll feel like you have traveled a world away from the big city, but all of this is still only an hour and a half outside of Atlanta.

toccoa

The name "Toccoa" comes from the Cherokee word for "beautiful," and it's easy to see why that term was chosen for this area when the town was founded back in 1873. It's a place of spectacular waterfalls, rugged mountains, and historic homes.

There is plenty to see on a day trip here. The old downtown is filled with shops and restaurants. The railroad cuts through the heart of town, so it's easy to get your bearings and you'll soon be charmed by it all.

Toccoa sits in the shadow Currahee Mountain, which is the last mountain in the Blue Ridge chain. The rugged peak was the site of the legendary Camp Toccoa paratrooper

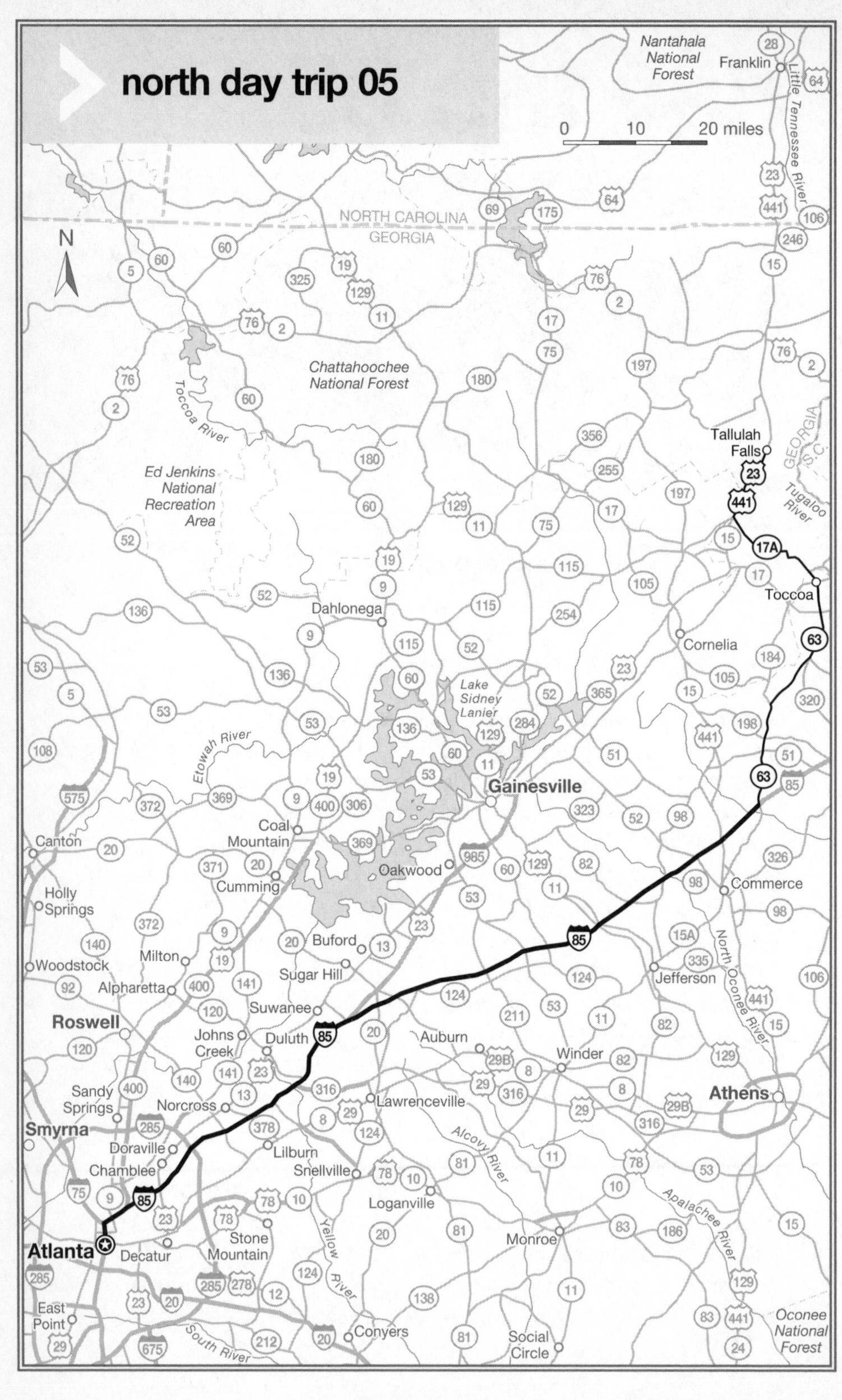
north day trip 05
0 10 20 miles
N
Nantahala National Forest
Franklin
Little Tennessee River
NORTH CAROLINA
GEORGIA
Chattahoochee National Forest
Toccoa River
Ed Jenkins National Recreation Area
Tallulah Falls
GEORGIA
S.C.
Tugaloo River
Toccoa
Dahlonega
Cornelia
Lake Sidney Lanier
Etowah River
Gainesville
Canton
Coal Mountain
Oakwood
Cumming
Holly Springs
Commerce
Buford
Milton
Woodstock
Sugar Hill
Jefferson
North Oconee River
Alpharetta
Suwanee
Roswell
Johns Creek
Duluth
Auburn
Winder
Sandy Springs
Norcross
Lawrenceville
Athens
Smyrna
Doraville
Lilburn
Alcovy River
Chamblee
Snellville
Loganville
Apalachee River
Stone Mountain
Atlanta
Decatur
Yellow River
Monroe
East Point
Conyers
Social Circle
South River
Oconee National Forest

training facility during WWII. Located at its base is the Toccoa Falls College, the site of one of the tallest free-fall waterfalls in the eastern US.

Yes, there is plenty to do here, so let's get started.

getting there

The journey to Toccoa will take about an hour and a half. Take I-85 north from Atlanta to exit 154, GA 63/Martin Bridge Road. Go left on the exit and follow GA 63 to Toccoa.

where to go

Toccoa–Stephens County Chamber of Commerce and Welcome Center. 160 N. Alexander St.; (706) 886-2132; www.toccoagachamber.com. The Welcome Center is in the old rail depot along with the town's 2 museums. As a former resort town, the whole downtown area is filled with history, cute shops, and things to see. Visit the Welcome Center to get a perspective on where to go first, and don't be surprised if trains pass by while you are there. Mon through Fri 8:30 a.m. to 5 p.m., Sat 8:30 a.m. to 4 p.m.

Currahee Mountain. GA 17 and GA 365; (706) 886-2132; www.toccoagachamber.com. The 900-foot Currahee is the last mountain in the Blue Ridge chain. Its name appropriately means "stand alone" in Cherokee. It was featured in battles during both the Indian Wars of the early 1900s and the Civil War. During World War II, the Camp Toccoa paratrooper facility was established here. The stories of the men who trained at the camp have been made famous through movies such as *Band of Brothers*, *Saving Private Ryan*, and *The Dirty Dozen*. Several monuments stand at the entrance of the old base to honor the troopers. The mountain is now used for strictly recreational purposes. Hiking and biking trails available. Daily. Free.

Schaefer Center for the Performing Arts. 125 W. Doyle St.; (706) 886-2132. In downtown Toccoa in the refurbished Ritz Theater, this venue is home to the Toccoa-Stephens County Community Theatre and the Currahee Arts Council. Musicals and nonmusical productions have included *Fiddler on the Roof*, *Guys and Dolls*, *Raisin in the Sun*, *Leader of the Pack*, and *The Sound of Music* to mention just a few. The Currahee Artists Guild, also formed in the '70s, sponsors arts shows featuring visual artists in the area. Call for a schedule of events.

Stephens County Courthouse. 90 N. Alexander St.; (706) 886-2828. Constructed in a Classical Revival style, the old courthouse was completed in 1905 and features a clock tower above the second floor. It has been completely restored and is still in use. It is listed on the National Register of Historic Places.

Stephens County Historical Museum and the Currahee Military Museum. 160 N. Alexander St.; (706) 282-5055; www.toccoahistory.com. Both museums are in the historic railroad depot in the heart of town. The Currahee Military Museum is devoted to the men of the World War II military training camp called Camp Toccoa as well as local veterans. The museum particularly focuses on the 506th Paratrooper Infantry Regiment, known more commonly as the Band of Brothers, made famous by the namesake HBO miniseries based on the book by historian Stephen Ambrose. The County Museum houses numerous artifacts tracing local history back to the time when Native Americans occupied the region. Mon through Sat 10 a.m. to 4 p.m., Sun 1 to 4 p.m. $.

Toccoa Falls. GA Alt 17; (706) 886-6831, ext. 5215; www.tfc.edu. This beautiful 186-foot-high waterfall is one of the highest free-falling waterfalls east of the Mississippi. At 186 feet, Toccoa Falls is 26 feet taller than Niagara Falls. At its base, the meandering stream flows through the lower part of the 1,000-acre wooded campus of Toccoa Falls College. Enter the falls area through the Gate Cottage Gift Shop which carries items from local craftsmen. The shop is operated by TFC. $.

Toccoa Falls College. 17 Rainwater Dr.; (706) 886-6831; www.tfc.edu. Toccoa Falls College is a fully accredited Christian college founded in 1907 by Dr. Richard A. Forest. On a 1,000-acre wooded campus, TFC currently has 21 majors and 34 minors in 9 different schools: Arts & Sciences, Bible & Theology, Business Administration, Christian Education, Communication, Counseling, Music, Teacher Education, and World Missions.

Traveler's Rest Historic Site. 4339 Riverdale Rd.; (706) 886-2256; www.gastateparks.org/TravelersRest. This 1815 home was built by James Wylie to serve as an inn and stagecoach stop. He strategically built it near the newly constructed Unicoi Turnpike, a busy highway over the Appalachian Mountains. In 1833, he sold it to Devereaux Jarrett, the "richest man in the Tugaloo Valley." Jarrett more than doubled its size so it could serve as home for his more than 14,000-acre plantation. Now a state park, visitors can sit on the 90-foot porch or tour the inn which has antique and hand-numbered rafters. 1st and 3rd Sat each month and 3rd Fri each month 9 a.m. to 5 p.m. $.

where to shop

Whistle Stop Cornerstone Antique Mall. 202 N. Sage St.; (706) 282-1386; www.whistlestopmall.com. The Whistle Stop Cornerstone Antique Mall takes up a good chunk of downtown Toccoa. It features 14 retail stores and 60,000 square feet of antiques as well as 17,000 square feet devoted to artisans and restaurants. You'll find fine antiques, old cars, collectibles, and artwork for sale. Mon through Sat 10 a.m. to 5:30 p.m., Sun 1 to 5:30 p.m.

where to eat

The Cornerstone. 27 Doyle St.; (706) 282-7771. Casual fine Southern dining among great antiques shopping. The shrimp and grits are a must! Mon through Sat 7 a.m. to 9 p.m., Sun 7 a.m. to 2 p.m. $$.

Gregory's at the Bus Stop. 99 Railroad St.; (706) 886-2874. At the old Greyhound bus stop, Gregory's serves wonderful homemade Italian dishes along with steaks, seafood, and chicken. Mon through Sat 11 a.m. to 2 p.m., 5 to 10 p.m. $$.

Rebel Cafe. 66 Doyle St.; (706) 886-5801. Best breakfast in town and awesome burgers for lunch. Mon and Wed through Sat 6 a.m. to 3 p.m., Tue 6:30 a.m. to 3 p.m. $.

Shirley's Soul Food. 212 W. Currahee St.; (706) 297-7739. Shirley's is the most popular place in town. Owner and head cook Shirley Combs is known for her great Southern cooking, her Southern hospitality, and her big heart. When she closes down her restaurant in the afternoon, she feeds the homeless from her kitchen. Mon through Sat 11:30 a.m. to 2 p.m., Thurs and Fri 5 to 8 p.m. $.

where to stay

Simmons-Bond Inn. 74 W. Tugalo St.; (706) 282-5183; www.simmons-bond.com. This beautifully restored 1903 Victorian mansion in downtown Toccoa features 5 beautifully decorated rooms with private baths. The architectural detailing in the home is just amazing, and most rooms feature working fireplaces. Fabulous gourmet breakfasts. $–$$.

tallulah falls

The name Tallulah is attached to a lot of things here. A town, a state park, a gorge, a waterfall, a lake. It is easy to see why they all want to be associated because they are all things of beauty.

In the late 1800s, Tallulah Gorge was the state of Georgia's first real tourist attraction, bringing sightseers from across the US. It rivaled Niagara Falls for visitors, and the town of Tallulah Falls became a bustling resort. A train line was built just to bring people in, and at one time 17 inns dotted the area.

All of that came to an end in the early 1900s when Georgia Power decided the rushing waters through the gorge were perfect for a dam, and when the waters dried up, so did the tourism. These days the only reminders of those days are the old train depot and the gorge itself.

The waterfall may not be as spectacular as it was, but the gorge remains a gorgeous place to visit. Several movies have been shot here, most notably the 1971 movie *Deliverance*.

getting there

Take GA 17 Alt North from Toccoa for 6 miles to US 441. Take a right and follow this 8 miles to Tallulah Falls.

where to go

Tallulah Falls Gallery. Tallulah Gorge Scenic Loop, Old US 441; (706) 754-6020; www.tallulahgallery.biz. The gallery promotes the works of local artists and features a wide variety of art including original paintings, pottery, raku, folk art, sculpture, fiber art, jewelry, furniture, photography, books, and prints. Proceeds go to the Tallulah Falls School, a coeducational boarding school located near the falls.

Tallulah Falls School Museum. 150 Willet Dr. (off School Rd.); (706) 754-0400, ext. 3530; www.tallulahfalls.org. Tallulah Falls School is a coed boarding school that overlooks the gorge. The museum displays photos, paintings, and artifacts that reflect the history of Tallulah Falls School. Call for hours. Free.

Tallulah Gorge State Park. 338 Jane Hurt Yarn Dr.; (706) 754-7970 or (706) 754-7979 (camping); www.georgiastateparks.org. This park affords one of the most beautiful sights in this part of Georgia. Tallulah Gorge is 2 miles long and nearly 1,000 feet deep and contains not one, but a series of 6 waterfalls cascading down through it. Visitors can hike rim trails to several overlooks, but the park puts a limit on how many people can actually go down to the gorge floor each day (100). Permits are free, but you have to sign up for them. If you aren't afraid of heights, there is a suspension bridge that sways 80 feet above the rocky bottom, providing spectacular views of the river and waterfalls. Exhibits in the park's Jane Hurt Yarn Interpretive Center tell the story of the area in its heyday as a Victorian resort town, as well as give geological explanations for the rugged terrain and fragile ecosystem of the area. Daily 8 a.m. to dark. $5 parking.

Tallulah Point Overlook. 940 Tallulah Gorge Scenic Loop; (706) 754-4318; www.tallulahpoint.com. This roadside store has been here on the side of the gorge since 1912, and it is the only roadside view of Tallulah Gorge. The general store provides a bit of everything from tacky souvenirs to books to handcrafted works of art or handcrafted soaps. Sip an RC Cola and have a MoonPie while enjoying the views. Daily 9 a.m. to 6 p.m.

Tallulah Station. 105 Moss St.; (706) 839-1906; www.tallulahstation.com. Built in 1914, this historic train station is the last reminder of Tallulah Falls' days in the early 1900s as a top tourist destination. It is now home to 3 shops: Idyllwood Gallery (local art), Depot Delights (sweets), and Wild Wood Works (rustic, handmade furniture). The depot is listed on the National Register of Historic Places. Idyllwood Gallery: Thurs through Mon 10 a.m. to 6 p.m., Sun noon to 6 p.m.; Depot Delights: Thurs through Mon noon to 6 p.m.; Wild Wood Works Studio: by appointment.

where to eat

Louie's on the Lake. 1659 Lake Rabun Rd., Lakemont, GA 30552; (706) 782-3276. Rustic and charming and right on the lake. Great pizzas and sandwiches in a beautiful setting. $.

Tallulah Gorge Grill. 110 Main St.; (706) 754-9149. Just across US 441 from the falls, the restaurant features gourmet sandwiches and wonderful sides. As they put it, "Familiar Foods with a Twist." Daily lunch and dinner. $–$$.

where to stay

Lake Rabun Hotel. 35 Andrea Ln., Lakemont, GA 30552; (706) 782-4946; www.lake rabunhotel.com. This inn has been charming visitors since 1922. There are 3 rooms with fireplaces. Sit out on the deck and have a glass of wine or enjoy their friendly restaurant. $$.

The Lodge at Tallulah Falls. US 441 North at Scenic Loop Rd.; (706) 754-9400. Clean and quiet with an incredible location. Modern rooms and conveniences with a friendly staff. $$.

Lodging on the Lake. Terrora Circle; (706) 754-3474 or (706) 490-3456; www.lodgingon thelake.com. Right on Tallulah Lake within minutes of Tallulah Gorge, the lodge features 1 bedroom cabin for nightly or weekly rental. $–$$.

worth more time

Lakemont/Lake Rabun. Just a few miles north of the falls on US 441 is the town of Lakemont on scenic Lake Rabun. Lakemont is a rustic little mountain town with some inviting places to visit like Annie's at Alley's—a grocery and deli that serves up fantastic lunches, fine wines, and groceries; the Lakemont Gallery, which sells art from various local artists; the Corner Cupboard antiques and gift store; and the wonderful spa, Mind Body Haven. Lake Rabun itself is an 835-acre lake on the Tallulah River and part of a chain of lakes owned and operated by Georgia Power.

northeast

day trip 01

northeast

otp:

norcross, duluth

OTP is an Atlanta insider's comment. It means Outside the Perimeter, or Outside I-286. This little trip will take you just OTP to the northeast of Atlanta into the little towns of Norcross and Duluth. Considered suburbs of Atlanta, they really are towns in their own right.

Norcross and Duluth are well known and frequented by Metro residents, but you'll be surprised at the historic and laid-back atmosphere in the heart of the towns themselves. Some of Atlanta's premier event venues are here, and you'll find Atlantans themselves venturing OTP to shop, dine, and relax. The best part of it all is that you are literally minutes from downtown when you make this little day trip, and you can easily come back as often as you like during an Atlanta stay.

norcoss

Just a few minutes outside I-85, Norcross grew up as a resort community in the 1800s—a place for Atlantans to get away from it all, but still be nearby. This is a habit many of them continue today; only they live here and commute to Atlanta to work.

Norcross is Gwinnett County's second oldest city, sitting along the Continental Divide. It developed in the 1800s as a stop between two frontier forts built for the War of 1812—Fort Daniel (at Hog Mountain) and Peachtree Fort (in Atlanta). That road between them eventually evolved to become Atlanta's famous Peachtree Road.

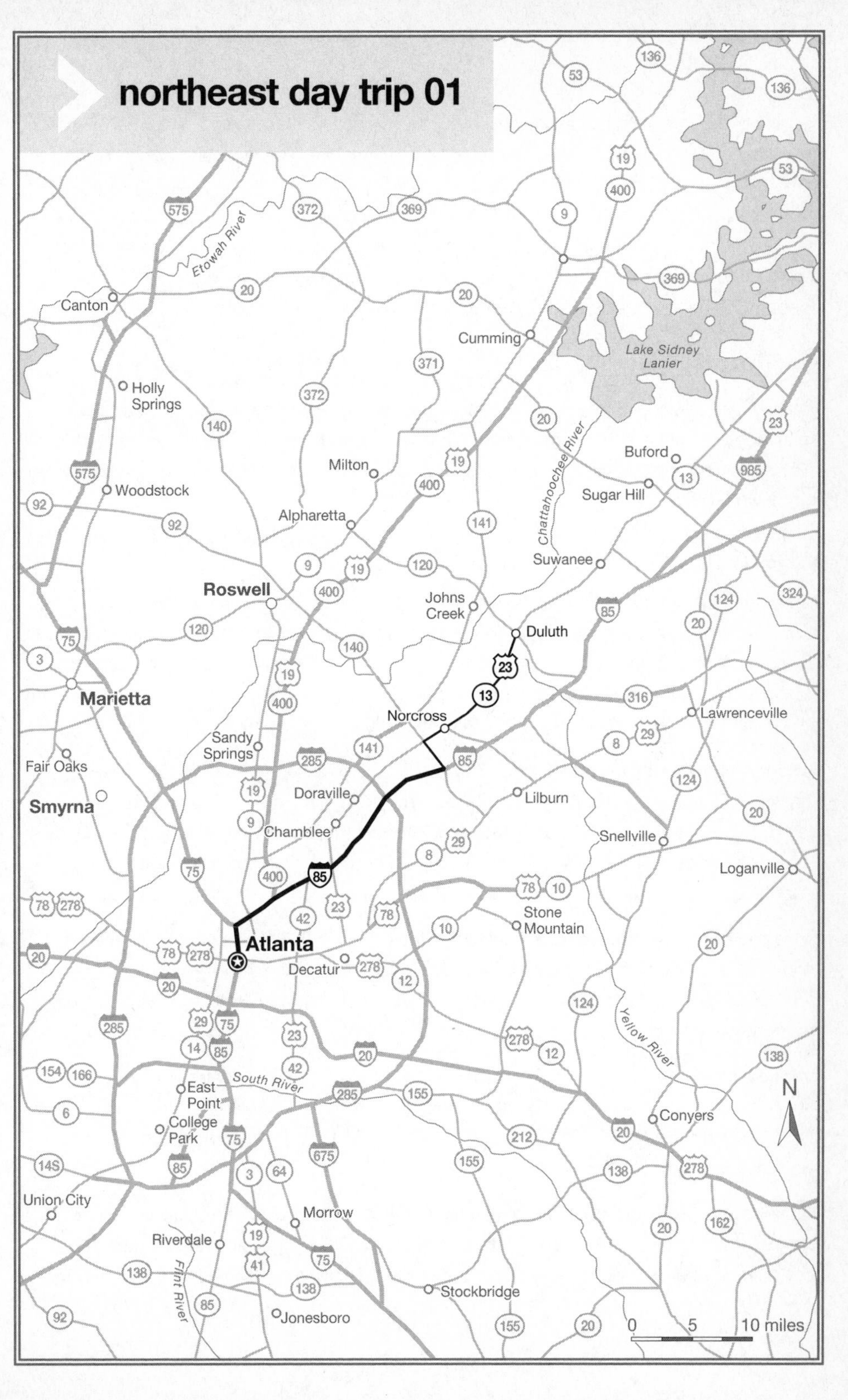

northeast day trip 01
Etowah River
Canton
Cumming
Lake Sidney Lanier
Holly Springs
Woodstock
Milton
Alpharetta
Buford
Sugar Hill
Chattahoochee River
Suwanee
Roswell
Johns Creek
Duluth
Marietta
Norcross
Lawrenceville
Sandy Springs
Fair Oaks
Smyrna
Doraville
Lilburn
Chamblee
Snellville
Loganville
Stone Mountain
Atlanta
Decatur
Yellow River
South River
East Point
College Park
Conyers
N
Union City
Morrow
Riverdale
Flint River
Stockbridge
Jonesboro
0
5
10 miles

When former Atlanta mayor John Norcross proposed the building of a railroad to improve that connection, the new stop was named after him. The terminal was completed in 1889.

Norcross had its heyday until the early 1900s when the town was bypassed by the incipient interstates. While this hurt the downtown area at the time, it helped preserve the region for today. These days, the historic downtown capitalizes on its vintage look and is bustling with new shops and fun restaurants.

getting there

From Atlanta, it's less than 30 minutes to Norcross. Go north on I-85 to just outside the Perimeter and take exit 99/Jimmy Carter Boulevard. Go left or west toward Norcross. In 2 miles, take a right on Buford Highway, and in less than a mile lake a left on Cemetery Street into downtown Norcross.

where to go

Norcross Welcome Center. 189 Lawrenceville St.; (678) 421-2049. In the heart of downtown, the welcome center can provide useful information including maps for self-guided tours. Inside the center is a museum which traces the early settlements which became Norcross. It's also a starting point for the very entertaining Norcross Ghost Tour, which is held nightly at 8 p.m. Center hours: Mon through Fri 9 a.m. to 5 p.m.

American Elm. Betty Mauldin Park; (678) 421-2025; www.norcrossga.net. The towering "American Elm" in Betty Mauldin Park is the second tallest of its kind in Georgia. While many trees were devastated by Dutch elm disease, this one has survived and is recorded as having a crown spread of 105 feet and a height of 79 feet. There is an entire illustrated walking tour of Norcross's estimated 1,123 trees available at the Norcross Welcome Center.

Downtown Historic Norcross. S. Peachtree Street; (770) 448-2122; www.aplacetoimagine.com. Historic Norcross bills itself as "A place to imagine." The whole of downtown is a destination. With its brick sidewalks and great parks, shops, and restaurants, just come here and make a day of it.

Lionheart Theatre. 10 College St.; (770) 885-0425; www.lionhearttheatre.org. This community theater is housed in one of the oldest churches in Norcross: the old Methodist church built around 1875 and completely renovated in 2011. It is now a part of the Cultural Arts and Community Center.

Train Depot. 6655 Crescent Dr., Norcross; (770) 416-6490; www.norcrossstation.com. This historic depot is now home to the Norcross Station Cafe. The station was built in 1909 for Southern Railway (later Norfolk Southern) by John Pettyjohn & Company. It was a hub of activity throughout the early 1900s. The depot was then donated to the city of Norcross by Norfolk Southern in 1983. The cafe opened in 1993 and is decorated with railroad memorabilia.

where to eat

Alligator Blues Cafe. 15 Jones St.; (678) 969-0295; www.somelikeithotfoods.com. This cozy little cafe in the historic district serves up authentic and delicious Cajun cuisine. Mon through Sat 11 a.m. to 2 p.m. and 5 to 10 p.m., Sun brunch 10 a.m. to 3 p.m. $$.

Bleu House Cafe. 108 N. Cemetery St.; (770) 209-0016; www.bleuhousecafe.com. This little cottage is a great place for sandwiches, soups, salads, and desserts. Patio seating available. Mon through Fri 11 a.m. to 3 p.m. $.

Dominick's. 95 S. Peachtree St.; (770) 449-1611; www.dominicksitalian.com. People come from all over to dine at this family-style Italian restaurant. Dominick's serves platters of every kind of pasta, seafood, chicken, and veal in an old-world atmosphere. Mon through Fri 11 a.m. to 4 p.m., Mon through Sat 5 to 10 p.m., Sun 5 to 9 p.m. $$.

Iron Horse Tavern. 29 Jones St. Northwest; (678) 291-9220. The Iron Horse is a local favorite. A traditional English pub, the food is good and the beer is cold. There are pool tables and darts. It also has a cozy fireplace as well as an outdoor patio. Mon through Thurs 11 a.m. to midnight, Fri 11 a.m. to 2 a.m., Sat noon to 2 a.m., Sun. noon to 10 p.m. $–$$.

Mojito's Cuban-American Bistro. 35 S. Peachtree St.; (770) 441-2599; www.mojitos bistro.com. Authentic Cuban, serving up sandwiches and plates of shredded brisket. Try the lamb lollypops. Mon through Thurs 11 a.m. to 9 p.m.; Fri and Sat 11 a.m. to 10 p.m.; Sun 1 to 9 p.m. $–$$.

Norcross Station Cafe. 6655 Crescent Dr.; (770) 416-6490; www.norcrossstation.com. You'll get a lot of sightseers as you dine in this popular restaurant which was built in 1909 for Southern Railway. The trains still roll by but they don't stop, and the place is filled with train memorabilia. The cafe serves made-from-scratch food. Mon through Sat 11 a.m. to 9:30 p.m. $–$$.

Pickles Neighborhood Grill. 5450 Peachtree Pkwy.; (770) 447-5997. Serving up a wide selection of great sandwiches—of course, with pickles on the side. Mon through Sat lunch only. $.

where to stay

Holiday Inn Express. 7035 Jimmy Carter Blvd.; (770) 409-0004; www.hiexpress.com. Great location with easy access to Norcross and the interstate. Friendly staff. $.

Hyatt Place Norcross. 5600 Peachtree Pkwy.; (770) 416-7655 or (866) 599-6674. Friendly, comfortable, and clean. Convenient to Norcross and I-85. $.

duluth

Downtown Duluth has maintained its small-town atmosphere while the land around it has simply exploded. The heart of the town is just a few miles off I-85, which is lined with shopping and entertainment venues such as Gwinnett Place Mall and the Gwinnett Arena.

This old community was also erected along the early Peachtree Road that snaked through Indian territory. It developed as a town when Evan Howell constructed a road connecting his cotton gin at the Chattahoochee River with Old Peachtree Road. Howell's Cross Roads was born, but that name would change when the railroad came through in 1871 and the area was connected to another Duluth, one over a thousand miles away in Minnesota.

getting there

Driving from Norcross, simply take Buford Highway/US 23/GA 13 north 6 miles into Duluth. From Atlanta, head north on I-85 and take exit 103, Steve Reynolds Boulevard. Go left a mile and then make another left onto Pleasant Hill Road. At Buford Highway, make a right and follow the signs to Buford.

where to go

Gwinnett Convention and Visitors Bureau. 6500 Sugarloaf Pkwy., Ste. 200; (770) 623-3600 or (888) 494-6638; www.gcvb.org. The CVB handles Duluth, Lawrenceville, Buford, Norcross, Suwanee, Lilburn, Sugar Hill, Stone Mountain, and Snellville, so that's why it is not in the heart of downtown, but stop here on your way in for maps and suggestions. Mon through Fri 8 a.m. to 5 p.m.

The Arena at Gwinnett Center. 6400 Sugarloaf Pkwy.; (770) 813-7500, www.gwinnettcenter.com. This is Metro Atlanta's premier indoor venue. There is a constant schedule of concerts and sporting events. The arena is the home of the ECHL Gwinnett Gladiators hockey team and the Georgia Force Arena Football team. Check a schedule for events and pricing.

Duluth History Museum. 2956 Buford Hwy.; (770) 232-7854; www.duluthhistorical.org. You could call this a museum within a museum. Located in a historic 1898 home built by Henry and Alice Strickland, the building was Duluth's first hospital. Alice was also Georgia's first female mayor. Exhibits trace Duluth from its time as Creek and Cherokee territory to its founder, Evan Howell, and the history of those who have followed. Fri and Sat noon to 3 p.m.

Jacqueline Casey Hudgens Center for the Arts. 6400 Sugarloaf Pkwy.; (770) 623-6002; http://thehudgens.org. The Hudgens Center was created as a place where children could play and learn. The original more than 35,000-square-foot center includes gallery space, the Weeks Sculpture Garden, and a Children's Art Museum. Special exhibits in the Children's Art Museum include a do-it-yourself puppet theater, a magic kaleidoscope, an 8-foot-tall harp whose strings play chords when plucked, and a foot-powered giant keyboard set up on the floor that allows children to dance on it to create original melodies. Tues through Sat 10 a.m. to 5 p.m. $.

Landers-Cain House. Club Drive at Cruse Road; (770) 441-1645. Eli Linson Landers was a Confederate soldier from Gwinnett County whose moving letters were memorialized in the book *Weep Not for Me, Dear Mother*. He was born in this home, which has been moved from its original location 2 blocks away to be adjacent to the Sweetwater Cemetery. The Landers family helped found the church. The home itself was built around 1824 and is closed to the public.

McDaniel Farm Park. 3251 McDaniel Rd.; (770) 814-4920. McDaniel Farm has been restored to depict a typical 1930s farm in Gwinnett County and features interactive exhibits and paved trails. Tour packages include a self-guided tour; weekly preservation farm guided tours ($3 per person); weekly wildlife tours ($3); and school group tours and outreach programs.

Red Clay Theatre. 3116 Main St.; (678) 407-0772; http://redclaytheateronline.com. This variety playhouse on Main Street was once a church. Parts of the building have been rebuilt to include state-of-the-art sound, lighting, and multimedia projection technology. The theater features stadium-style seating with a capacity of 280 and is used for both theatrical production as well as corporate events and presentations. Check the schedule for performances.

Southeastern Railway Museum. 3595 Peachtree Rd.; (770) 476-2013; www.srmduluth.org. Train buffs flock to this museum which features 90 items of rolling stock including historic Pullman cars, classic steam locomotives, and even the private car *Superb* once used by President Warren G. Harding. Check the website for hours. $.

Sweetwater Primitive Baptist Church and Cemetery. Pleasant Hill Road. The whitewashed wooden structure of Sweetwater Primitive Baptist Church was built in 1902, replacing the first building which dated back to 1824. The cemetery is relatively well maintained, and you'll find the graves of more than 30 Confederate and Revolutionary soldiers, as well as slave grave sites.

Town Green. 3142 Hill St.; (770) 476-3434; www.duluthga.net. In the heart of town, the Town Green features a Victorian-age amphitheater which can seat 10,000, the Festival Center, and an interactive fountain that kids can play in. The Green is surrounded by the back of the Main Street stores, new condominiums, Taylor Park, and the City Hall. In the summer, the amphitheater is used for a host of performances, include the symphony on the green.

Towne Park Place. Downtown; (678) 957-1777. This mixed-use development across from Town Green is a constant hub of activity. Homes and condos have been mixed in with an office campus, professional services, dining, and shops. Mon through Sat 11 a.m. to 6 p.m. and Sun 1 to 5 p.m.

where to eat

Abaee Noodle. 2476 Pleasant Hill Rd.; (770) 817-0906. Asian food lovers will enjoy Abaee's full range of simple Korean noodle dishes. $–$$.

Arena Tavern. 2000 Satellite Blvd.; (770) 623-4585; www.thearenatavern.com. This sports-themed tavern is very near the Gwinnett Place Arena. Food ranges from basic tavern fare to bacon-wrapped filets and lobster. Great beer selection. Mon through Sat 11 a.m. to 2 a.m., Sun 11 a.m. to midnight. $–$$$.

Armando's Caribe. 3170 Peachtree Industrial Blvd.; (770) 232-9848. Escape to the Caribbean with a trip to Armando's Caribe, a Latin-American bistro in Duluth. Large portions of paella, Cuban sandwiches, burritos, and quesadillas. $–$$.

Boudreaux's Cajun Seafood Market and Restaurant. 3067 Main St.; (770) 814-8388; www.boudreauxscajun.com. One of downtown Duluth's hidden jewels, Boudreaux combines a seafood market with a cafe so you know the food is fresh. They offer a Cajun seafood buffet of blue crabs, crawfish, jambalaya with sausage, shrimp, and gumbo. Live music on Saturday nights. Wed and Thurs 10 a.m. to 2 p.m., Fri and Sat 10 a.m. to 8:30 p.m. $–$$.

Chocolate Perks. 3160 Main St.; (770) 342-0037; www.chocolateperks.com. The term "Chocolate" in the name will draw you in, but you'll stay for all else Chocolate Perks offers, including sandwiches, soups, pastries, truffles, cupcakes, and other desserts. Mon, Wed, and Thurs 7 a.m. to 9 p.m.; Tue 6:30 a.m. to 9 p.m.; Fri 7 a.m. to 10 p.m.; Sat 8 a.m. to 9 p.m.; Sun noon to 6 p.m. $.

Marlow's Tavern. 1950 Satellite Blvd., Ste. 300; (770) 622-2033; www.marlowstavern.com. Marlow's has a great neighborhood tavern feel and is popular with the after-work crowd. The food is American pub fare and good. Live music Wednesday through Sunday! Mon through Thurs, Sun 11:30 a.m. to midnight; Fri through Sat 11:30 a.m. to 1 a.m. $–$$.

Park Cafe. (770) 476-2989; www.parkcafeduluth.net. Located in a beautiful 106-year-old house in historic downtown Duluth, the Park Cafe is known for its excellent Southern cuisine. Dine inside or on their large outdoor patio overlooking the Town Green. Reservations suggested but not required. Tues through Sun 11 a.m. to 3 p.m., 5 to 9 p.m.; Sat 5 to 10 p.m. $$.

where to stay

Atlanta Marriott Gwinnett Place. 1775 Pleasant Hill Rd.; (770) 923-1775. Convenient to the Gwinnett Place Mall for shopping, this property is clean and the staff professional. $–$$.

Atlanta Wingate by Wyndham. 3450 Venture Pkwy.; (770) 622-7277 or (800) 228-1000; www.wingateinnduluth.com. Rooms are large, clean, and comfortable. Convenient location. $.

Candlewood Suites. 3665 Shackleford Rd.; (678) 380-0414; www.candlewoodsuites.com. The property is designed for extended stays, so each room is a suite allowing for extra space. $.

day trip 02

up by the lake:
buford, gainesville

There are two huge lakes north of Atlanta, Lake Allatoona to the northwest and Lake Sidney Lanier, or simply Lake Lanier, to the northeast. But when someone says, "I'm headed up to the Lake," you can bet they mean Lanier. With 692 miles of shoreline, it is one of the top recreational sites in the entire state of Georgia, and lucky for us, it's only an hour from Atlanta.

Lanier is the result of a dam built by the Army Corps of Engineers in the early 1950s near the town of Buford. The 912-foot dam restricted the flow of the Chattahoochee River, creating a 38,000-acre reservoir which provides both power and water to the Metro Atlanta area.

Today's trip will take you up to Lanier to visit the two cities on its shoreline and to enjoy a bit of the lake itself. Both Buford and Gainesville were around long before anyone ever dreamed up a lake, but they have flourished on its shores and have much to offer in a day trip without necessarily involving water.

buford

Buford grew up with the nickname "The Leather City," a nod to its origins as a center for tanneries making everything from shoes and belts to horse saddles. These days the tanneries are long gone, but the factories they left behind have been transformed. The Buford of today has become a destination for those wanting to explore a growing antiques district and artist colony that is now housed in the old structures around Main Street.

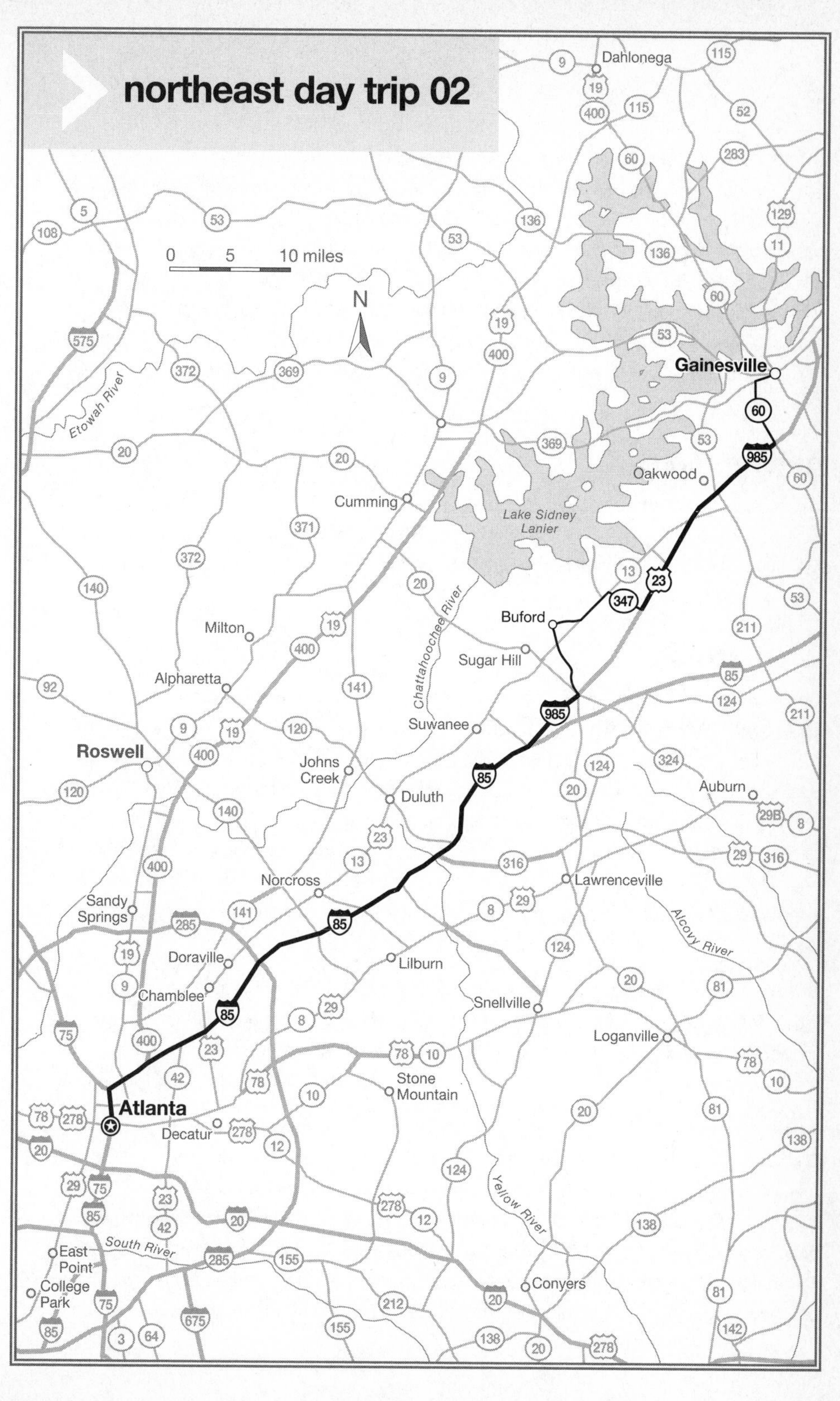

northeast day trip 02
0 5 10 miles
N
Dahlonega
Gainesville
Oakwood
Lake Sidney Lanier
Cumming
Buford
Sugar Hill
Milton
Alpharetta
Roswell
Suwanee
Johns Creek
Duluth
Auburn
Lawrenceville
Norcross
Sandy Springs
Doraville
Chamblee
Lilburn
Snellville
Loganville
Stone Mountain
Atlanta
Decatur
East Point
College Park
Conyers
Etowah River
Chattahoochee River
Alcovy River
Yellow River
South River

Like so many North Georgia towns, Buford owes its existence to the railroad. This picturesque little city wasn't much more than a railroad depot when it was officially chartered in 1872. At that point, the leather industry was in its infancy, founded by Robert Allen and then expanded by his brother Bonaparte "Bona" Allen. The arrival of the railroad meant their business could ship products easily, and that expansion drew other businesses to the region.

In the early 1900s, Buford was called "The New York of Gwinnett" because of its industries. The Depression took its toll, though, and the town never quite recovered. The creation of Lake Lanier in the 1950s breathed new life into the town, which has since developed a well-earned reputation for its hospitality, something you will notice right away when you visit this charming little city.

getting there

Only 45 minutes from downtown Atlanta, take I-85 north 28 miles to outside the Perimeter and then head north on I-985. Take exit 4 toward Buford/Cumming and follow GA 20 2 miles into Buford, taking a right onto S. Lee Street and then another right on W. Main Street to take you into the heart of town.

where to go

Bona Allen Mansion. 395 E. Main St.; (770) 271-7637; www.bonaallenmansion.com. This stately 1911 home was built by Bona Allen, who spared no expense in its construction. Allen was one of the founders of Buford's tannery industry and wanted his home to be a showcase. While the house now sits on one-sixth of its original 1,700 acres, it is still a masterpiece and a popular venue for events such as weddings. The main house is known for its 2-story entryway with a mural of an Italian villa. It has 17 rooms, 12-foot ceilings, original carved wood paneling, intricate moldings, stained glass windows, and 7 fireplaces. The manicured grounds include gardens with 5 original outbuildings. Tues through Thurs 10 a.m. to 2 p.m., Fri 10 a.m. to 5 p.m. Call for tours.

Buford Variety Theater. 170 W. Main St.; (770) 271-7878; www.bufordvarietytheater.com. The Variety Theater is as much a social gathering spot as it is an entertainment venue. Inside what was the sanctuary of a 1920s Presbyterian church, there are regular comedy performances each week, and you can order food at "Uncle Pearle's Tavern" on-site. Check the calendar or call for schedules.

Gwinnett Environmental & Heritage Center. 2020 Clean Water Dr.; (770) 904-3500; www.gwinnettehc.org. This unusual museum and center combines conservation with history in a unique way and makes both interesting. GEHC is a hands-on facility which allows visitors to explore water and natural resource conservation and sustainability combined with Cherokee and Creek American Indian culture. Learn how water has been used over time, and how it has shaped our way of life. Mon through Sat 9 a.m. to 4 p.m. $.

Lake Lanier. (770) 945-9531; http://lanier.sam.usace.army.mil. Enjoy 690 miles of shoreline and more than 100 small islands offering fishing, camping, boating, picnicking, and swimming. Open daily.

Lake Lanier Islands Beach & Waterpark. 7000 Holiday Rd., Lake Lanier; (770) 536-5209. Lake Lanier Islands is a destination unto itself, featuring a beach, water park, golf course, and restaurants. You could certainly spend a whole day here. It has water features ranging from the Kiddie Lagoon and the Wiggle Waves child-size pool to Georgia's largest wave pool, "Wild Waves," and the interactive, 3-story water attraction, the Fun Dunker. There are sandy beaches on the lake itself where you can rent boats, tubes, or Jet Skis. The Legacy on Lanier Golf Club was created by renowned designer Billy Fuller and features 12 scenic holes on the water. There are also 7 restaurants in which to dine ranging from beachfront snack bars to an Italian bistro. $$$.

Lanier Project Management Office/Visitor Center. 1050 Buford Dam Rd.; (770) 945-9531 or (770) 945-9531. Get an up-close look at the dam that is behind, or should we say in front of, Lake Lanier. The visitor center includes a small museum and glimpses of the dam operation. You may also notice a small herd of goats in Lower Pool Park near the powerhouse entrance. The goats have been a tradition here for more than 3 decades as a way to maintain hard-to-reach places above the dam.

Lanier Sailing Academy. 6920 Holiday Rd.; (770) 945-8810 or (800) 684-9463; www.laniersail.com. Learn to sail at this accredited school or simply rent a boat. Daily 9 a.m. to 6 p.m.

Museum of Buford. 95-B E. Main St.; (770) 616-6318; www.museumofbuford.com. The Museum of Buford is a treasure trove of the history of this town. Stop here and pick up a walking guide to the downtown area which will point out the historic significance of the buildings and grand homes you see. There is also a small museum store. Call for hours.

Stonehenge. 406 E. Shadburn Ave. Now a private home, this house is worth a walk by and is included on the walking tour. Kate Allen Shadburn and Wylie Burl Shadburn built Stonehedge between 1903 and 1904. Kate was Mr. Bona Allen's only daughter. Stonehedge gets its name from the low stone wall that runs along Shadburn Avenue and 5th Street. The mansion is stunning and has incredible architectural features. The grounds boast beautiful gardens with perennial flower beds and rose arbors. There are two state champion trees on the property, recorded by the forestry service as the largest of their kind in Georgia.

where to shop

Buford Antiques and Arts District. Main Street. Buford's Historic Main Street is an antiques lover's dream. It sits in the midst of 13 acres of the Buford Antiques and Arts district featuring shops, galleries, and restaurants. The most notable complex in that district is Tannery Row.

Mall of Georgia. 3333 Buford Dr.; www.mallofgeorgia.com. The Mall of Georgia is the largest in North Georgia, featuring more than 2 million square feet of shopping and entertainment, including an IMAX theater.

Tannery Row Artist Colony. 554 W. Main St., Bldg. C; (770) 904-0572; www.tanneryrowartistcolony.com. Once the home of the Bona Allen Shoe and Horse Collar Factory, Tannery Row is a creative center for more than 30 Buford artists. Four buildings make up the complex and surround a landscaped courtyard. Visitors can browse the galleries and watch the artists work on their pieces. There are also shops and restaurants to add to your experience. A little trivia about Bona Allen: It was one of the most popular makers of Hollywood saddles during the Western movie era. In the 1940s, singing cowboy Roy Rogers and his horse Trigger took a private train to Buford so the famous horse could be fitted. Tues through Sat noon to 5 p.m.

where to eat

Aqua Terra Bistro. 55 E. Main St.; (770) 271-3000. Aqua Terra is an eclectic bistro where traditional Southern foods get an international twist. Try the egg roll–enrobed potatoes or the country-fried chicken with peach chutney. People drive from miles around just to buy their bread dipping sauce. Mon through Sat 11 a.m. to 2:30 p.m., daily 5 to 10 p.m. $$.

Bona Allen Mansion. 395 E. Main St.; (770) 271-7637; www.bonaallenmansion.com. If you only have one chance to have Sunday brunch, make it at this historic home in downtown Buford. It offers full-blown Southern gourmet dishes, featuring things like 3-cheese grits, brown sugar bacon, cucumber salad, and toasted pecan chicken. Reservations are required. See website for brunch dates and times. $$–$$$.

Firesalt Tavern. 33 Buford Village Way; (770) 963-6284; www.firesalttavern.com. A local favorite, Firesalt's extensive menu covers just about every craving. They are known for their killer steaks. Live music every Fri and Sat. Mon through Thurs 11 a.m. to 2:30 p.m. and 5 to 10 p.m., Fri and Sat 11 a.m. to midnight, Sun 10 a.m. to 9 p.m. $$.

Mimi's Cafe. 1880 Mall of Georgia Blvd.; (770) 614-0554; www.mimiscafe.com. Mimi's will make you feel like you are in New Orleans. Elegant and family-friendly, the food draws from home-style, French, and New Orleans influences. Favorites include 3-berry stuffed French toast, pasta jambalaya, and creamy chicken potpie. Open for breakfast, lunch, and dinner daily 7 a.m. to 11 p.m. $$.

Old McDonald's Real Pit BBQ. 5774 Holiday Rd.; (770) 945-8608. It's not much more than a shack, but Old McDonald's has been a fixture along the road to Lake Lanier since the '70s. Fans claim it's "the best BBQ on earth." Mon 8 a.m. to 3 p.m., Tues through Thurs 8 a.m. to 5 p.m., Fri through Sun 8 a.m. to 9 p.m. $–$$.

37 Main—A Rock Cafe. 37 E. Main St.; (678) 288-2030; www.37main.com. For a little place, this cafe has big-city attitude, and you certainly wouldn't expect such in historic Buford. The cafe features a bar menu and specialty drinks. Live music or events almost every night. Tues through Thurs 5 to 11 p.m.; Fri and Sat 5 p.m. to 12:30 a.m.; also open Sun.

where to stay

Country Inn & Suites Mall of Georgia. 1395 Mall of Georgia Blvd.; (770) 271-1441. Clean, comfortable, and good value. $.

Holiday Inn Express & Suites Buford/Mall of Georgia. 2499 Satellite Blvd.; (678) 318-1080. Near Buford and the mall, the Holiday Inn Express also features a business center. $–$$.

Whitworth Inn B&B. 6593 McEver Rd., Flowery Branch; (770) 967-2386; www.whitworth inn.com. This country inn features 10 rooms on a beautiful property near Lake Lanier. Clean and quiet. $.

gainesville

The Gainesville of today is a far cry from its beginnings under the catchy name of Mule Camp Springs. These days it goes by two other monikers: "Poultry Capital of the World" or "Queen City of the Mountains." You will likely experience more of the latter than the former, although chicken farming remains a major industry here.

The historic town on the shore of Lake Lanier is now a center for trade, industry, medicine, culture, and recreation. While its normal population is about 35,000, it swells daily to more than 100,0000 when including those who commute in to work.

What you will find on your visit is a historic core town flanked by modern building and industry and, of course, that all-important lake.

getting there

From Buford, get back on I-985 and go 10 miles to exit 20, GA 53/60 toward Gainesville, staying with 60 (right) when these two state highways split. From Atlanta, it will take you just over an hour. Take I-85 north and exit on I-985 North. Travel 20 miles to exit 20.

where to go

Gainesville Tourism & Trade. 117 Jesse Jewell Pkwy.; (770) 531-6598; http://visitgainesville ga.com. Stop by for maps and information and even discounts to some area attractions. You can also get a map to the popular "Walking Tour of Our Solar System." The 2-mile trek starts in Gainesville's downtown square and ends at Lake Lanier and features a solar system scale model with component monuments along the way (770-536-5209; http://northgeorgiaastronomers.org). Tourism offices: Mon through Fri 8 a.m. to 5 p.m.

Alta Vista Cemetery and Walking Tour. (770) 535-6883. The 75-acre Alta Vista is perched on a rolling hill overlooking Gainesville. Founded more than 140 years ago, Alta Vista is filled with historical and interesting graves and monuments. A walking guide of the cemetery will lead you to graves of veterans of the Revolutionary War and more than 100 graves of Civil War veterans; the most famous and most visited grave is that of Lt. Gen. James Longstreet. The cemetery is also the final resting place for two former Georgia governors, one son of a former Georgia governor, an astronaut, a rocket scientist, former mayors, fire chiefs, sheriffs, police chiefs, and even a circus performer. Dawn to dusk. Free.

Beulah Rucker Museum. 2301 Athens Hwy.; (404) 401-6589. This museum memorializes Beulah Rucker, who was a longtime educator and community leader. Born of sharecroppers, Rucker knew education was important, and she founded a school for African-American children in Gainesville in the early 1900s, which became known as the Beulah Rucker Industrial School. The wooded property includes a historic residence, Ms. Rucker's grave, and an educational center. The museum is open by appointment only.

Brenau University Galleries Permanent Art Collection. 500 Washington St. Southeast; (770) 534-6263; brenau.edu. On the Gainesville campus of Brenau University, these galleries feature more than 1,000 pieces of original art, including sculpture and paintings in a variety of media. Call for hours. Free.

Chief White Path's Cabin. 403 Brenau Ave.; (770) 536-0889. Chief White Path was the leader of the Cherokee at the time of the Trail of Tears. This cabin was built in 1780 near present-day Ellijay and was moved here and fully restored to depict a Cherokee farmstead circa 1835, with authentic furnishings, vegetable gardens, and herb gardens typical just prior to the removal.

Elachee Nature Science Center. 2125 Elachee Dr.; (770) 535-1976; www.elachee.org. Located in a 1,500-acre forest nature preserve with 13 miles of hiking trails, Elachee serves as a plant and animal sanctuary and an ideal outdoor classroom. There is an interactive museum on-site as well as live animal displays. Mon through Sat 10 a.m. to 5 p.m. $.

Historic Piedmont Hotel. 827 Maple St.; www.longstreet.org/piedmont.html. This restored historic property is what remains of what was one of Gainesville's premier hotels of the 1800s. The Piedmont was built in 1873 and owned and managed by Confederate Lt. Gen. James Longstreet for almost 20 years following the Civil War. Among the notables who stayed here were Union general and New York congressman Daniel Sickles, Confederate general Joseph Johnston, newspaperman Henry Grady, writer Joel Chandler Harris, and a young Woodrow and Ellen Axson Wilson. Their second daughter, Jessie Woodrow, was born here on August 28, 1887, in a still-existing room. The majority of the hotel building was demolished in 1918, but in 1994, the hotel was revitalized and serves as headquartered to the Longstreet Society, dedicated to preserving Longstreet's memory.

Interactive Neighborhood for Kids (I.N.K.). 999 Chestnut St.; (770) 536-1900; www.inkfun.org. Children will love the Interactive Neighborhood for Kids, or I.N.K., which gives them the opportunity to interact while role-playing various careers such as bankers and dentists. Visit Buddy and the Healthy Body Exhibit. Good fun for ages 2 to 102. Mon through Sat 10 a.m. to 5 p.m., $8; Sun. 1 to 5 to p.m., $6. Group discounts by phone.

Logan Turnpike Mill. 4494 Gainesville Hwy.; (706) 745-5735 or 800-84-GRITS; www.loganturnpikemill.com. This family-run antique mill makes fresh-ground grains on-site, and visitors can see the process. There is also a bakery on the grounds so you can sample the difference the fresh process makes in your cooking. Tues through Sat 10 a.m. to 5 p.m. Bakery open Thurs through Sat.

Northeast Georgia History Center. Academy Street Northeast; (770) 297-5900; www.negahc.org. The History Center is dedicated not just to Gainesville's story but to that of all North Georgia. At Brenau University, its exhibits include the American Freedom Garden and Chief White Path's log cabin. Tues through Sat 10 a.m. to 4 p.m. $.

Quinlan Visual Arts Center. 514 Green St. Northeast; (770) 536- 2575; http://quinlanartscenter.org. Come view the world-class art exhibits here at this regional center or perhaps look in and even take a workshop. Mon through Fri 9 a.m. to 5 p.m., Sat 10 a.m. to 4 p.m. Free.

Smithgall Arts Center. 331 Spring St.; (706) 534-2787; www.theartscouncil.net. The Smithgall Arts Center is housed in the 2-story former Gainesville train depot, built in 1914 for the Gainesville Midland Railroad. Fully renovated, its official name is now the Arts Council Depot to the Arts Council Smithgall Arts Center. Its grand interior features beveled glass windows and a crystal chandelier and plays host to events and concerts. Smithgall sits on 2.5 acres which include an outdoor theater and arts sculpture garden. Mon through Fri 8 a.m. to 5 p.m.

where to eat

Collegiate Grill. 220 Main St. Southwest; (770) 297-6554. Operating since 1947, this old-fashioned diner is known for its burgers. It's always busy and for good reason. Mon through Fri 11 a.m. to 7 p.m., Sat 11 a.m. to 3 p.m. $.

The Hickory Pig. 3605 Thompson Bridge Rd.; (770) 532-6036. Follow your nose to the Hickory Pig, offering a "true barbecue experience," and you'll want to gorge yourself. Tues and Wed 10 a.m. to 2 p.m., Thurs through Sat 10 a.m. to 6 p.m. $.

Longstreet Cafe. 1043 Riverside Ter.; (770) 287-0820; http://longstreetcafe.com. They claim to have put the "home" in home cooking, and if you look around at the crowded tables, you'll see customers agree. Longstreet also offers drive-through pickup. Open daily for breakfast, lunch, and dinner. $–$$.

Luna's Restaurant. Hunt Tower, 200 Main St. Southwest; (770) 531-0848; www.lunas.com. Luna's goes out of the way to make you feel at home with great food, a good wine selection, and a fun piano bar. Lunch and dinner daily. $$.

The Monkey Barrel. 115 Washington St. Southeast; (770) 297-0116. The Monkey Barrel cooks up great pizzas and calzones. Live music on weekends. Mon through Wed 3 to 11 p.m.; Thurs and Fri 3 p.m. to 1:30 a.m.; Sat noon to 1:30 a.m.; also open Sun.

Re-cess Southern Gastro Pub. 118 Bradford St. Northwest; (678) 450-0444; www.recesspub.com. A creative menu in a great atmosphere. Locals love this place. Tues through Thurs 11:30 a.m. to 10 p.m.; Fri and Sat 11:30 a.m. to 11 p.m. $$.

where to stay

Comfort Suites. 1755 Browns Bridge Rd.; (678) 971-4670; http://choicehotels.com. Excellent staff, and rooms are comfortable and clean. Pool on-site. $.

Country Hearth Inn & Suites. 766 Jesse Jewell Pkwy.; (770) 287-3205; http://countryhearthgainesville.com. Clean and friendly, there is a free continental breakfast and children stay free. $.

Days Inn. 520 Queen City Pkwy.; (770) 535-8100 or (800) DAYSINN; www.daysinn.com. Great place for families, clean and friendly. $.

Hilton Garden Inn Gainesville. 1735 Browns Bridge Rd.; (770) 532-3396 or (866) 599-6674; www.hilton.com. Clean and convenient to everything in Gainesville. $–$$.

worth more time

Chateau Elan. www.chateauelan.com. Less than 10 miles from Gainesville and along I-85 is Chateau Elan. Built to resemble a French country estate, the chateau sits on 3,500 acres of rolling hills with beautiful views of the North Georgia foothills. The grounds include a vineyard, a spa, and championship golf. It has become a favorite corporate and private retreat for many.

day trip 03

musical dawgs:
athens

If you're headed to Athens, Georgia, you'd better know your Dawgs, and you'd better know your music. And yes, that is Dawgs, as in the University of Georgia Bulldogs. But of course, if you are in the know, you have to pronounce it "Dawgs."

Athens is both a historic and a cosmopolitan town. Home to UGA since the 1700s, the city seems to reinvent itself with each new class that comes through. A hub of education and research, Athens is also known for its evolving music scene. Internationally acclaimed bands such as R.E.M. and the B-52s got their start here.

Its tree-lined streets are bursting with history and history in the making. A day trip here will make you feel a part of both.

athens

Don't let the historic, sleepy look of the town fool you. If you start paying attention, you will see that Athens is a hopping little city. It grew up around the University of Georgia, which was founded here in 1785. While the school was responsible for its initial growth, Athens took off on its own a long time ago.

Mills built in the 1800s earned it the nickname "Manchester of the South" after the English mill town by that name. Following the Civil War, the city's focus shifted to the railroad, and growth has been steady ever since.

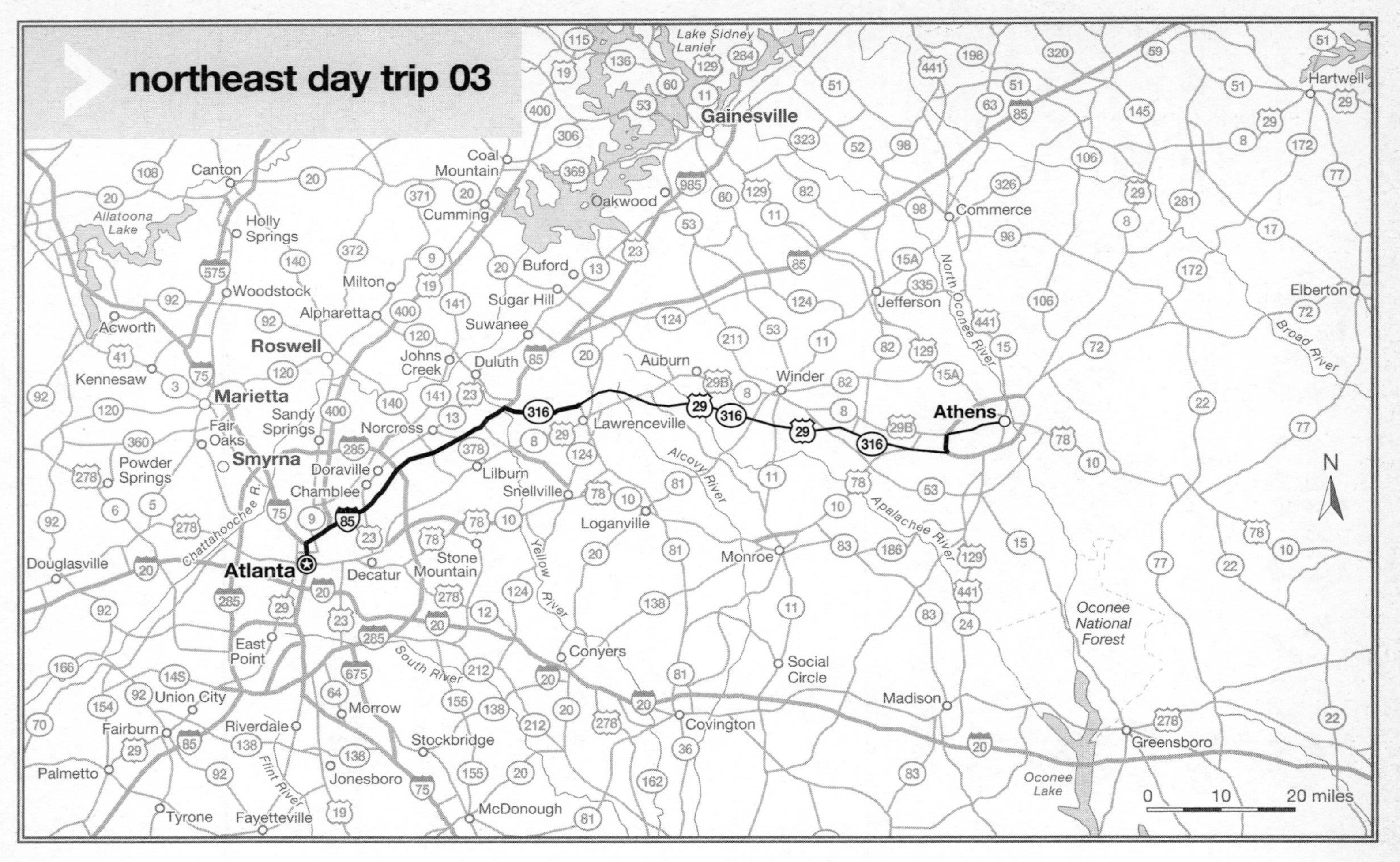

northeast day trip 03
Lake Sidney Lanier
Gainesville
Hartwell
Canton
Coal Mountain
Cumming
Oakwood
Commerce
Allatoona Lake
Holly Springs
Buford
Woodstock
Milton
Sugar Hill
Jefferson
North Oconee River
Elberton
Acworth
Alpharetta
Suwanee
Broad River
Roswell
Johns Creek
Duluth
Auburn
Kennesaw
Winder
Marietta
Sandy Springs
Norcross
Lawrenceville
Athens
Fair Oaks
Smyrna
Powder Springs
Doraville
Chamblee
Lilburn
Snellville
Alcovy River
Apalachee River
Chattahoochee R.
Loganville
Douglasville
Atlanta
Decatur
Stone Mountain
Yellow River
Monroe
Oconee National Forest
East Point
Conyers
Social Circle
South River
Union City
Madison
Morrow
Fairburn
Riverdale
Covington
Stockbridge
Greensboro
Palmetto
Flint River
Jonesboro
Oconee Lake
Tyrone
Fayetteville
McDonough
N
0
10
20 miles

Today you will find an incredible mixture of Victorian architecture and beautiful gardens juxtaposed against a trendy downtown with hip shops and galleries and vibrant music clubs.

getting there

It will take about 90 minutes to get to Athens from downtown Atlanta. Take I-85 north 20 miles to exit 105 toward Lawrenceville/Athens. Follow US 29/GA 316 or University Parkway until you get to US 78/GA 10, then take this to the heart of Athens.

where to go

Athens Visitors Bureau. 300 N. Thomas St.; (706) 357-4430 or (800) 653-0603; www.visitathensga.com. Make the most of your time in Athens with maps, coupons, and suggestions from the visitor center. They are equipped to handle whatever your interest and can give you guides for the music scene, the art scene, and even the garden scene. Mon through Fri 8 a.m. to 5 p.m.

Athens Welcome Center/Classic City Tours. 280 E. Dougherty St.; (706) 353-1820 or (866) 455-1820; http://athenswelcomecenter.com. The Welcome Center is affiliated with the visitors bureau listed above, but this center is located in the Church-Waddel-Brumby House and is a starting point for many tours including the self-guided Music History Tour. The Church-Waddel-Brumby House is believed to be the oldest residence in Athens. It was moved to its current location in 1967 and is being restored to its 1820–29 glory. The effort to save this house is what started the preservation movement for all of downtown Athens. Mon through Sat 10 a.m. to 5 p.m., Sun noon to 5 p.m.

Butts-Mehre Heritage Hall. 1 Selig Circle; (706) 542-9036; www.georgiadogs.com. The athletic complex and museum for the University of Georgia, it is named for 2 longtime coaches, Wally Butts and Harry Mehre. The Heritage Museum is on the third floor of this 4-story building, offering up history, facts, sports bios, athletic information, and memorabilia of football and other sports. Call for hours and tours.

40 Watt Club. 285 W. Washington St.; (706) 549-7871; www.40watt.com. Originally known as the Georgia Theater, this club has launched countless acts including R.E.M. and the B-52s. 40 Watt is only open Fri and Sat. Check the schedule for band listings.

Founders Memorial Garden. 425 S. Lumpkin St.; (706) 542-4948; www.uga.edu/gardenclub/foundersgarden.html. This intricate garden is laid out on the grounds of an 1857 antebellum home in the heart of Athens. It was created in 1936 as a tribute to the 12 founders of the Ladies' Garden Club of Athens, the first garden club in America, organized in 1891.

Garden Club of Georgia. 2450 S. Milledge Ave.; (706) 227-5369; www.uga.edu/gardenclub. There are 12,000 members of the Garden Club of Georgia, so you can imagine what their headquarters looks like. Come see for yourself. Tours by appointment. $.

Georgia Museum of Art. 90 Carlton St.; (706) 542-4662; http://georgiamuseum.org. Although it is on the UGA campus, this is the State of Georgia's official art museum. As home to more than 10,000 holdings, the museum organizes its own exhibitions in-house, creates traveling exhibitions for other museums and galleries, and plays host to traveling exhibitions from around the country and the globe. Tues and Wed 10 a.m. to 5 p.m., Thurs 10 a.m. to 9 p.m., Fri and Sat 10 a.m. to 5 p.m., Sun 1 to 5 p.m. Free, but suggested donation $3.

ITA Collegiate Tennis Hall of Fame. 518 Brooks Dr.; (706) 542-8064; www.georgiadogs.com. The International Tennis Association's Collegiate Tennis Hall of Fame is also on UGA's campus. It has inducted more than 170 players, coaches, and contributors, including Arthur Ashe and Jimmy Connors. Call for hours and guided tours. Free.

The Melting Point. 295 E. Dougherty St.; (706) 254-6909; www.meltingpointathens.com. In the Foundry Park Inn and Spa, the Melting Point is a unique concert setting that hosts nationally and internationally known music acts. The rustic interior with its exposed brick walls makes for a great backdrop and amazing sound. Box office: Mon through Fri 9 a.m. to 5 p.m. Check schedule for performances.

The Morton Theatre. 195 W. Washington St.; (706) 613-3770; www.mortontheatre.com. Built in 1910, the Morton was one of the first vaudeville theaters in the US to be owned by African Americans and is the only one that still survives. In those early days, the Morton Theatre hosted such legendary acts as classical pianist Alice Carter Simmons, Butterbeans and Susie, Blind Willie McTell, Curley Weaver, and Roy Dunn. Listed on the National Register of Historic Places, the fully restored Morton is a rental facility that hosts a wide range of performances and special events. Local bands such as R.E.M. and the B-52s have used the Morton for rehearsals. Box office: Mon through Fri 10 a.m. to 1 p.m., 3 to 5 p.m. Check website for show schedules.

The State Botanical Garden of Georgia. 2450 S. Milledge Ave.; (706) 542-1244; www.uga.edu/botgarden. The garden is sited on 313 acres along the Middle Oconee River and features extensive display beds and 5 miles of nature trails. Operated by UGA, it functions as a "living laboratory" for university students and faculty. For the visiting public, however, the garden affords beauty, knowledge, and solitude in a lush setting. The 3-story visitor center and conservatory also house a gift shop and cafe. Call for hours. Guided tours by reservation. Donations accepted.

Taylor-Grady House. 634 Prince Ave.; (706) 549-8688; www.taylorgradyhouse.com. This Greek Revival home was built in 1844 by successful Irish immigrant Robert Taylor, but is best known as journalist Henry W. Grady's summer retreat. Grady is credited with establishing the view of the New South after the Civil War. Now a house museum dedicated to his writings, it is open for tours and use as a venue. Mon through Fri 9 a.m. to 1 p.m., 2 to 5 p.m. $$.

that dawg

The University of Georgia's celebrated mascot ***Uga*** *(get it? U-GA) comes from a long line of English bulldogs owned by Georgia alumnus Frank W. "Sonny" Seiler. The dogs live with the Seiler family in Savannah but travel to all the football games. The tradition dates back to Uga I, who reigned from 1956 through 1966. Each subsequent dog is a descendent of the original Uga and goes by a birth name until the death of its predecessor, at which time it is bestowed the "Uga" designation. All of the deceased dogs have been interred in a mausoleum at the entrance to UGA's Sanford football stadium.*

Terrapin Beer Co. Tour. 265 Newton Bridge Rd.; (706) 549-3377; http://terrapinbeer.com. Home to Athens's favorite local brew, a tour shows how the beers are crafted and allows tasting of their full line of beers ("Hopsecutioner," anyone?). Live music most nights. Tours Wed through Sat 5:30 to 7:30 p.m.

T.R.R. Cobb House. 175 Hill St.; (706) 369-3513; http://trrcobbhouse.org. Thomas Reade Rootes Cobb, or T.R.R. Cobb, was a UGA graduate and chief author of the Confederate constitution. His restored antebellum home now houses a Civil War museum. The Confederate constitution which he drafted is housed at the University of Georgia's Hargrett Rare Book and Manuscript Library. Tues through Sat 10 a.m. to 4 p.m. Free.

University of Georgia Visitors Center. Four Towers Building, 405 College Station Rd.; (706) 542-0842; http://visit.uga.edu. In the heart of Athens, you can't miss UGA. Founded in 1785, it was the first state-chartered university in the country. There is a lot to learn about this sprawling campus, and the visitor center will help orient you. Free guided tours are available daily, but reservations are recommended. Mon through Fri 8 a.m. to 5 p.m., Sat 9 a.m. to 5 p.m.

We Let the Dawgs Out. Downtown Athens; (800) 653-0603; http://weletthedawgsout.jinglesatfivepoints.com. You don't have to go far to see this public art exhibit. Athens is festooned with 3 dozen larger-than-life bulldogs painted by local artists according to themes like "Dawg Fan" or "Caesar Dawgustus." Go online or pick up a self-guided tour map to see where to find the dawgs.

where to eat

Allen's Bar and Grill. 810 Hawthorne Ave.; (706) 355-6244; www.allensbarandgrill.com. Despite a brief closing around 2003, Allen's is the oldest operating bar and grill in Athens.

The rustic restaurant serves up some fabulous burgers and steaks. Its motto is "No Frills, Just Damn Good Food!" Locally owned and operated. Lunch and dinner daily. $.

Broad Street Bar & Grill. 311 E. Broad St.; (706) 548-5187. A bit of a dive, but the sort of dive you'll love. A local favorite, there are TVs to watch sports and great blue-plate specials. Mon through Sat 11 a.m. to 2 a.m. $–$$.

Farm 255. 255 W. Washington St.; (706) 549-4660; www.farm255.com. Farm 255 is a uniquely fresh experience. The owners grow their own crops at Full Moon Farms and raise most of their own livestock. The restaurant supplements its harvest by supporting other local family growers and ranchers. The menu changes with the season, according to what is fresh. Farm Cart on Patio: Mon 11:30 a.m. to 2:30 p.m., Tues 11:30 a.m. to 1:30 p.m., Thurs and Fri 11:30 a.m. to 2:30 p.m., Fri and Sat 5:30 to 10:30 p.m. $$.

The Globe. 199 N. Lumpkin St.; (706) 353-4721.Consistently ranked as one of the best bars in the US, the Globe also serves up some pretty good food. Daily 11 a.m. until 2 a.m. $$.

The Grit. 199 Prince Ave.; (706) 543-6592. Near downtown, the is one of Athens's top vegan restaurants. The Grit is in a century-old brick storefront and looks like no big deal, but one taste and you'll beg to differ. Lunch and dinner daily. $$.

Last Resort Grill. 174-184 W. Clayton St.; (706) 549-0810; www.lastresortgrill.com. Last Resort started as a music venue, but now makes its name as one of Athens's favorite restaurants. Comfortable and welcoming, the food is as good as the music. Quesadillas, salads, seafood, steaks, or try the Asian-style pulled pork. It's all good. Mon through Thurs, Sun 11 a.m. to 3 p.m., 5 to 10 p.m.; Fri and Sat 11 a.m. to 3 p.m., 5 to 11 p.m. $$.

The Varsity. 1000 W. Broad St.; (706) 548-6325; www.varsity.com. The Varsity has been a fixture in Athens since 1934, serving up hot dogs and hamburgers and their famous Frozen Orange (F.O.) drink. We sure know how to respond when the order taker shouts "What'll ya have?" The main Varsity is the one in Atlanta, but this branch does Atlanta proud. 10 a.m. to 10 p.m. daily. $.

Weaver D's Delicious Fine Foods. 1016 E. Broad St.; (706) 353-7797. With some of the best soul food around, they take the term "delicious" in their name seriously. Weaver D's was the inspiration for the title of R.E.M.'s song "Automatic for the People." Mon through Sat 7:30 a.m. to 6 p.m. $.

where to stay

Best Western, Colonial Inn. 170 N. Milledge Ave.; (706) 546-7311 or (800) 592-9401; www.bestwestern.com. Near the heart of downtown with clean and comfortable rooms. $$.

Days Inn, Athens. 230 N. Finley St.; (706) 543-6511 or (800) DAYSINN; www.daysinn athens.com. Clean, friendly, and convenient. Kids stay free. $$.

Foundry Park Inn & Spa. 295 E. Dougherty St.; (706) 549-7020 or (866) 9ATHENS; www .foundryparkinn.com. This inn and spa is on the grounds of an old foundry building and parts of it date back to 1850. The watchwords today, though, are ultramodern and ultra-comfortable. $$$.

Hotel Indigo. 500 College Ave.; (706) 546-0430 or (888) 9ATHENS; www.athensdowntown hotel.com. A boutique hotel that prides itself on being eco-friendly. Decorated to reflect the eclectic art and music scene of Athens. $$–$$$.

The University of Georgia Center for Continuing Education Conference Center and Hotel. 1197 S. Lumpkin St.; (706) 548-1311 or (800) 884-1381; www.georgiacenter.uga .edu. This large conference center caters to businesspeople and those attending conferences. $$.

worth more time

Watson Mill Bridge State Park. 650 Watson Mill Rd., Comer; (706) 783-5349; www.ga stateparks.org/info/watson. Just 30 minutes northeast of Athens on GA 72 is one of the most picturesque state parks in Georgia: Watson Mill Bridge. This park contains the longest covered bridge in the state, spanning 229 feet across the South Fork River. It's pretty amazing to look at the work that went into the bridge when it was built in 1885. The bridge is supported by a town lattice truss system held firmly together with wooden pins. Its architect was Washington (W.W.) King, son of freed slave and famous covered-bridge builder Horace King. The two men are credited with having constructed more than 100 wooden bridges around the state of Georgia. They are buried in Columbus on the opposite side of the state (Southwest Day Trip 05). This is one of just 20 covered bridges still standing in Georgia. At one time, there were more than 200. Watson Mill Bridge State Park is picture-perfect with a thick forest along the river near the bridge. Hiking and picnicking are available as well as some overnight camping. $.

day trip 04

bridges & lakes:
hartwell, elberton

Let's make a run for the border one last time on this day trip to the northeast. Georgia and South Carolina are separated to the northeast by water and lots of it. The Savannah River, which is the natural border between the two states, has been dammed up in several locations for power and flood control in this area, and the results are known as Lake Hartwell, followed farther downstream by Russell Lake then Clarks Hill Lake.

Lake Hartwell gets its name from the tiny town located on its shores, and today we'll venture to that Hartwell and to the nearby town of Elberton. Vermont may be the Granite State, but it has nothing on this place.

hartwell

This town has been around since 1856, but its real claim to fame lies on its front door: Lake Hartwell. Established in 1955, this beautiful reservoir contains 55,900 acres of water and has 962 miles of shoreline, of which the town of Hartwell shares 222. The Army Corps of Engineers named the lake after the town where they built their dam largely because of where the town got its name—Nancy Hart.

Miss Nancy, as some people call her, was a Revolutionary War hero from these parts who was known for her shooting skills and the fact that she captured some British spies back in the day. There are several Revolutionary War sites in town as well as Native

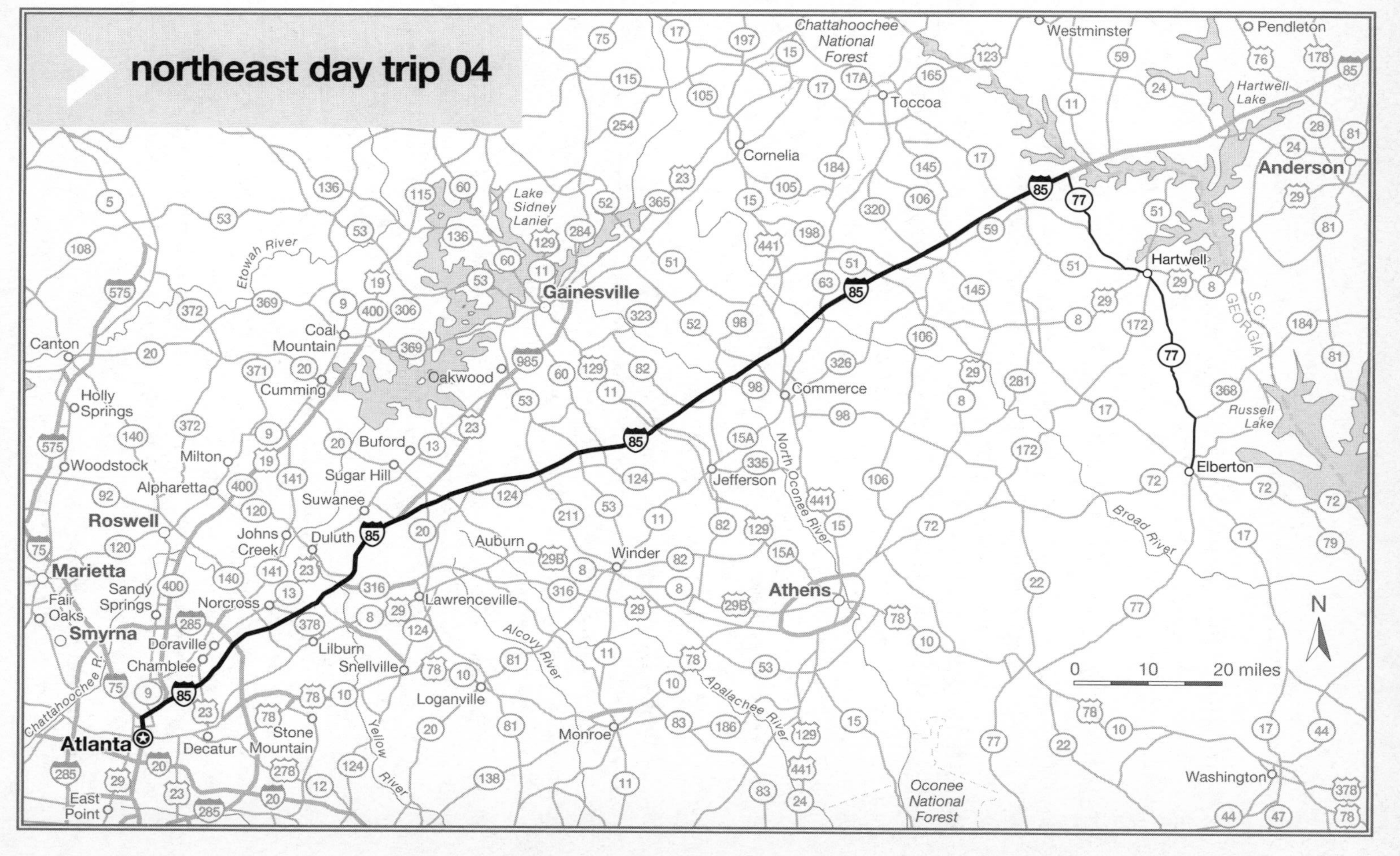
northeast day trip 04
Westminster
Pendleton
Chattahoochee National Forest
Toccoa
Hartwell Lake
Anderson
Cornelia
Lake Sidney Lanier
Etowah River
Gainesville
Hartwell
S.C.
GEORGIA
Canton
Coal Mountain
Cumming
Oakwood
Commerce
Holly Springs
Russell Lake
Buford
Woodstock
Milton
Sugar Hill
Jefferson
North Oconee River
Elberton
Alpharetta
Suwanee
Roswell
Johns Creek
Duluth
Auburn
Winder
Broad River
Marietta
Sandy Springs
Fair Oaks
Norcross
Lawrenceville
Athens
Smyrna
Doraville
Alcovy River
Lilburn
Chamblee
Snellville
Chattahoochee R.
Loganville
Apalachee River
Atlanta
Decatur
Stone Mountain
Yellow River
Monroe
East Point
Oconee National Forest
Washington
N
0
10
20 miles

American sites as the proximity to the Savannah River made this a key trading area for the Cherokee.

Historic Hartwell is a hopping-off point for those who want to enjoy all the lake has to offer in the way of water sports. For those who prefer to stay dry, there are plenty of shops, restaurants, and historical sites here to visit along the beautiful tree-lined streets.

getting there

From Atlanta the trip is under 2 hours. Head straight up I-85 for 90 minutes to exit 177 and GA 77 toward Hartwell and Elberton. Follow GA 77 through Lavonia 10 miles to Hartwell.

where to go

Hart County Chamber of Commerce. 31 E. Howell; (706) 376-8590; www.hart-chamber.org. The visitor center is in the 1880 Victorian-style Teasley-Holland House which is also home to the Hall County Historical Museum and the Hall County Historical Society. The museum is a great resource for understanding Hartwell's history and the development both before and after the creation of the lake. Stop by for a map of the historic downtown area and advice on the best walking tours, lake access, restaurants, and shops. Hartwell has several historic districts and numerous places listed on the National Historic Register. Mon through Fri 8:30 a.m. to 5 p.m. The museum and information are free.

The Art Center. 338 E. Howell St.; (706) 377-2040; http://hartregionalartscouncil.org. There is always something going on at the Art Center from exhibits to classes, so check their schedule. The renovated building on the town square is used to display the best of regional and national arts and crafts. Thurs through Sat 1 to 5 p.m. and by appointment. Free ($1 donation suggested).

Bluegrass Express. 57 Depot St.; (706) 376-3551. Every Saturday night this old cotton warehouse is hopping with live bluegrass music. There is a house band always on call, but they are joined by a constant array of nationally known bluegrass and gospel artists. Music starts at 7 p.m. and a radio broadcast joins in at 8 p.m. Come and listen or get up and dance! Call for a schedule.

Cateechee Golf Club. 140 Cateechee Trail; (706) 856-4653; www.cateechee.com. We haven't included many golf courses in this guide, but Cateechee is worth noting because of its location and the unusual layout of the course. It is an Audobon Signature Course and spans 380 acres out in the middle of nature: no homes, no highways, nobody but you and the ball. There is, however, the 19th hole, a 40,000-square-foot clubhouse and conference center that has a friendly bar and an excellent restaurant called the Waterfall Grille. Cateechee Golf Club is semiprivate.

Center of the World Monument. US 29, 3 miles south of Hartwell; (706) 376-8590. Yes, this monument confirms that Hartwell is the Center of the World. Well, at least it was for the

Cherokee. The Native Americans referred to this spot as "Ah-Yek-A-Li-A-Lo-Hee," which in Cherokee means "Center of the World." They came here for tribal councils and to trade with other natives as well as the white men. This is just a historical marker here, but it is worth noting because the monument pays tribute to Native American contributions to the region.

The Hart County Community Theatre. 338 E. Howell St.; (706) 377-2040; www.hartcountycommunitytheatre.com. This theater group has been around since the 1970s but came together under one roof at this venue in 1987. The community theater produces four plays and an annual holiday program each year for the citizens of Hartwell. Check schedule for performances.

Hartwell Lake and Dam. 5625 Anderson Hwy.; (706) 856-0300 or (888) 893-0678; www.sas.usace.army.mil/lakes/hartwell. Take a drive up to the dam that is behind, or as we say, in front of the lake. The visitor center offers information about the Savannah River, the dam, its construction, and the power plant. The 1,900-foot-long dam was started in 1955, and the reservoir was filled between 1961 and 1962. The power plant is on the Georgia side, but there are no public tours available. Limited group tours may be arranged in advance for educational/school groups and civic organizations. There are hiking trails on both sides of the dam. On the Georgia side, the trail starts at the Big Oaks Recreation Area off of US 29 about a mile from the state line. The trail follows the shoreline of Hartwell Lake from Big Oaks up to the concrete portion of the dam on the Georgia side for a total of 2.75 miles round-trip (or 1.37 miles one-way). Visitor center: Mon through Fri 8 a.m. to 4:30 p.m. Call for fees and weekend hours.

Hartwell Outdoor Recreation Area. 330 Hart Park Rd.; (706) 213-2405; www.georgiastateparks.org/hart. Just north of the downtown area is the official Hartwell Outdoor Recreation Area managed by the state of Georgia. The park sits on a peninsula that stretches out into the lake and offers swimming, hiking, camping, and fishing. It's also a nice place to just take your shoes off and go stick your toes in the cool water. Daily 7 a.m. to 10 p.m. $.

where to eat

Backstreet BBQ. 290 W. Franklin St.; (706) 377-6465. Perfect location for chicken, ribs, wings, and burgers. Lunch and dinner daily. $–$$.

The Depot in Hartwell. 90 Depot St.; (707) 376-3688. This restaurant makes the most of its historic setting in the century-old train depot. Good food from soups, sandwiches, and salads to light fare. Live music on the weekends. Lunch and dinner daily. $–$$.

Dockside Seafood. 100 W. Howell St.; (706) 376-1571. Fresh seafood right on the water at Lake Hartwell. A wide array of dishes from which to choose and a choice of fried or broil. Tasty catfish available. Daily 11 a.m. to 8 p.m. $–$$.

Korner Kitchen. 185 Chandler St.; (706) 376-2885. The Korner Kitchen serves up Southern-style breakfasts all day long. Try the daily specials. Sun through Wed 5 a.m. to 2 p.m., Thurs and Fri 5 a.m. to 8 p.m. Closed Sat. $.

Siblings Restaurant. 21 Vickery St.; (706) 377-5555; www.siblingsrestaurant.com. In a historic home in downtown Hartwell, Siblings is a family-run favorite. From soups, salads, and sandwiches to fresh seafood and hand-cut steaks, you'll feel right at home in this old home. Lunch Mon through Sun from 11:30 a.m., dinner Mon through Sat from 5 p.m. $–$$$.

Swamp Guinea. 1615 Reed Creek Hwy.; (706) 376-5105. A local favorite, Swamp Guinea is right on Lake Hartwell and features a broad menu with a great deal of seafood dishes. Wed through Sat 4 to 9 p.m. $–$$.

where to stay

The Skelton House. 97 Benson St.; (706) 376-7969 or (877) 556-3790; www.theskelton house.com. This beautiful 1896 Victorian home and garden will make you feel right at home. Each room is given the name of a person who used to live here. Right in the historic district. $–$$.

elberton

Most people haven't heard of this little town, but anyone in the granite industry knows all about it. Elberton is considered the "Granite Capital of the World." This town produces more granite-related products a year than any other city in the world, and granite has given the town a solid(!) basis for industry since the first commercial quarry was opened here in 1886.

The entire region is steeped in history including that of Native Americans and the Revolutionary War, and a visit here will yield some surprisingly old locations to visit including the home of Revolutionary War heroine Nancy Hart.

And if you enjoyed your visit to Lake Hartwell, you may want to also check out Lake Richard B. Russell which is right next door.

getting there

From Hartwell, take GA 77 south 18 miles to Elberton. If you are coming directly from Atlanta, you may want to consider cutting through Athens and taking GA 72. That route will take you about 1 hour and 45 minutes.

where to go

Elbert County Courthouse. 58 Oliver St.; (706) 283-2020. Some say this 1894 courthouse looks like a wedding cake, even more so in the past when it was actually painted white. When it was restored in the early 2000s, the exterior brick was repainted red to resemble the original appearance. The interior features a sweeping double staircase, and courtrooms are located on the second floor. Mon through Fri 8:30 a.m. to 5 p.m.

The Bicentennial Memorial Fountain. Town Square; (706) 283-5651. This tall monument with its eagle on top and surrounding fountain was contributed by the granite industry in 1976. If you wander over to the corner of the town square to have a look, you'll see it commemorates major events in local history. They are laid out on 13 panels in honor of the 13 original colonies.

Elbert County Chamber and Welcome Center. 104 Heard St.; (706) 283-5651; www.elbertga.com. Just a half block from the town square, the visitor center has friendly volunteers who are happy to share their town's unusual history. Make sure to grab a walking map. Mon through Fri 9 a.m. to 5 p.m.

The Elbert Theatre. 100 S. Oliver St.; (706) 283-1049; www.elberttheatre.org. Originally opened in 1940 as a movie theater, the art-deco-style Elbert has been fully restored to a new life as a performing arts facility. The theater has the total look of a bygone era. Check the schedule to see what performances might be taking place while you are in town. Box office: Mon through Fri 8 a.m. to 5 p.m.

Elberton Granite Museum. 1 Granite Plaza Northwest; (706) 283-2551; www.egaonline.com/egaassociation/museum. This museum pays tribute to Elberton's status as the "Granite Capital of the World." It features 3 tiers of self-guided exhibits which include historical exhibits, artifacts, and educational displays. Visitors see unique granite products as well as antique granite-working tools used in the quarrying, sawing, polishing, cutting, and sandblasting of granite cemetery memorials. Mon through Sat 2 to 5 p.m. Free.

Georgia Guidestones. 1065 Guidestones Rd., Nuberg; (706) 283-5651; www.elbertga.com. These mysterious granite stones sit high on the tallest hill in Elberton. Known as "The Stonehenge of America," no one can confirm the identity of a group of sponsors who paid to have them erected in 1979. There are four 19-foot-tall stones with a common capstone and carved in the sides on the slabs are 10 Guides, or commandments engraved in 8 different languages which hold a philosophical message providing guides for the preservation of mankind. Free.

Nancy Hart's Cabin. Off GA 17, south of Elberton; (706) 283-5651; www.stateparks.com/nancy_hart.html. This one-room log cabin is a replica of the home of Revolutionary War heroine Nancy Hart. A staunch patriot, she was reportedly also a deadly shot and a skilled doctor. A spy for the Colonists, she is credited with capturing several British Tories. The cabin was built here in 1932 on the site of the original structure. The stones from the fireplace and chimney of Benjamin and Nancy Hart's early home were used to re-create the cabin in its original state.

Old Dan Tucker's Grave. Heardmont Rd.; (706) 283-5651. Old Dan Tucker's Grave is found in a wooded area overlooking Lake Richard B. Russell and marks the burial site of Reverend Daniel Tucker. Tucker made his way into American folk music through a song written by slaves in admiration of him. Tucker was a Methodist minister who came to Elbert County to take up a land grant. He cared deeply for the plight of slaves and spent much of his time teaching them and praying with them. Rev. Tucker died April 7, 1818.

Richard B. Russell State Park. 2950 Russell State Park Dr.; (800) 864-7275; www.georgiastateparks.org/RichardBRussell. Richard B. Russell State Park is just a few miles outside of Elberton on the 26,500-acre lake by the same name. The Richard B. Russell Lake is the next dam lake down from Lake Hartwell on the Savannah River. This 2,508-acre park features hiking, fishing, swimming, and the 18-hole Arrowhead Pointe Golf Course. Cabins are available to rent here; some of them are right on the water. Daily 7 a.m. to 10 p.m. $.

where to eat

Granite City Restaurant. 225 College Ave.; (706) 283-6928. Good old-fashioned cookin'. Breakfast is served all day, but the daily lunch specials will make your mouth water. Whole fried catfish, country steak, and of course, homemade desserts. Mon through Fri 5:30 a.m. to 2 p.m., Sat 6:30 a.m. to 12:30 p.m. $–$$.

Th' Shanty. 132 N. Oliver St.; (706) 213-7555. This tiny little place serves up big flavor. It brags about having home cooking and is true to its claims. Daily specials with a good choice of vegetables. Lunch Mon through Sat. $.

Time Square Sandwich Cafe. 103 Heard St.; (706) 283-1235. A good place to stop for a quick bite. They have more than great sandwiches and are known for their soups and desserts. Lunch Mon to Sat. $.

where to stay

Rainbow Manor. 217 Heard St.; (706) 213-0314; www.rainbowmanor.com. This grand Southern manor was built in 1882 by local businessman Drury P. Oglesby. The historic bed-and-breakfast features 5 rooms decorated in different themes. This is a place you'll want to return to. $–$$.

east

day trip 01

a stone's throw away:
stone mountain park, stone mountain village

For those who don't want to venture far from Atlanta but want a taste of both Georgia's natural wonders and history, visiting Stone Mountain, both the park and the village, is the day trip for you. Not only is the park itself full of activities ranging from leisurely to strenuous, the neighboring Stone Mountain Village will give you a sense of historic small-town Georgia.

If you fly into Atlanta from any direction, you will likely see this amazing rock jutting out of the landscape like some huge bald spot on the horizon. But Stone Mountain is about much more than the protuberance itself. The area surrounding it is lush and offers a microcosm of the best of North Georgia's nature. The history of the region dates back to Native Americans who were no doubt drawn to the area because of its unique terrain and the fact that you can see for miles from atop the mountain.

Exploring the park and village can give you a peek at why this part of the US has continued to be an important destination throughout the centuries. And for those who aren't interested in history? Well, there is plenty for you here as well.

stone mountain park

Stone Mountain has existed as a park for 50 years, but the area surrounding this giant outcropping has been drawing tourists for centuries. After the Civil War, the area was purchased by brothers Samuel and William Venable, who, in addition to quarrying granite from

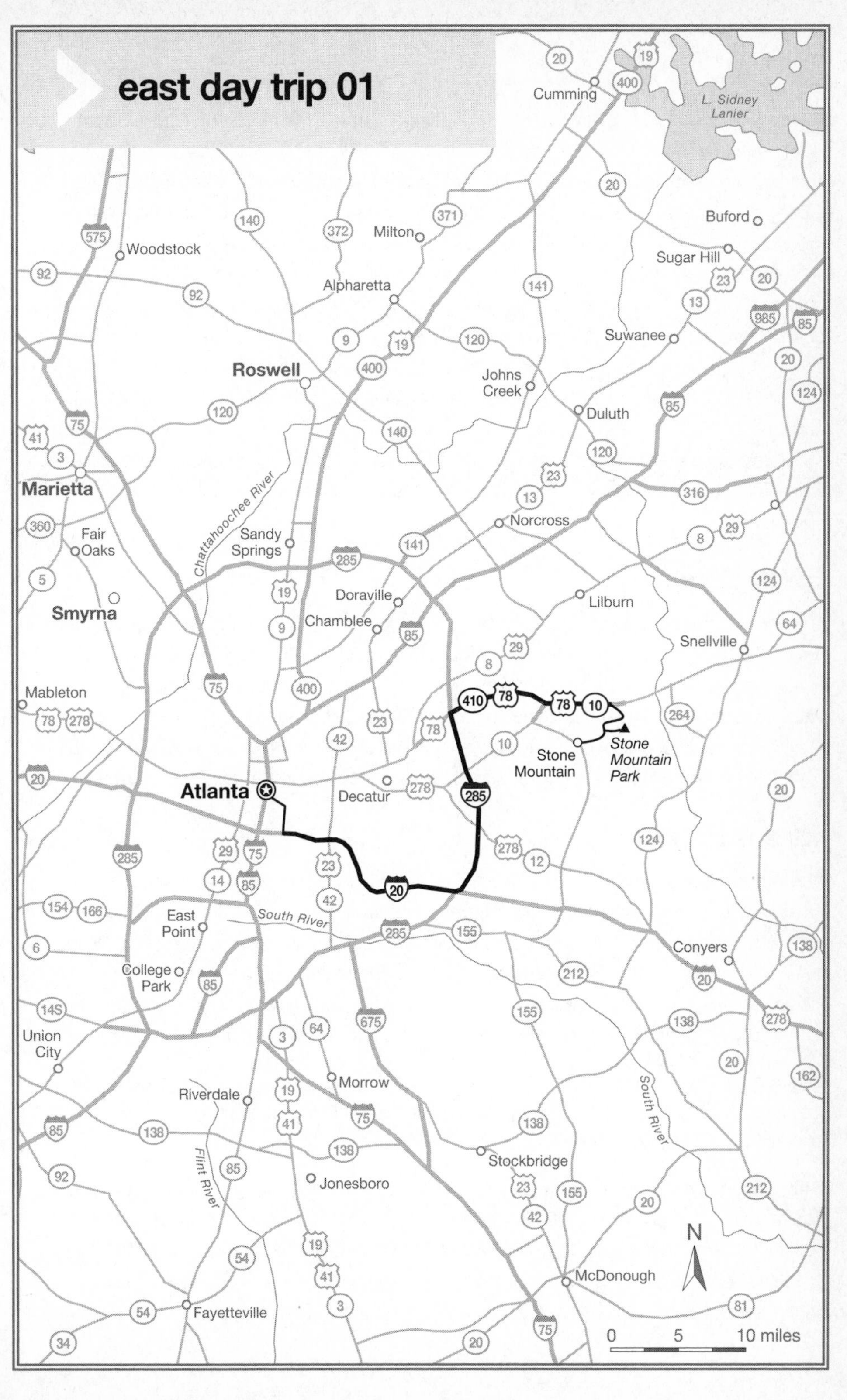
east day trip 01
Cumming
L. Sidney Lanier
Buford
Sugar Hill
Milton
Woodstock
Alpharetta
Suwanee
Roswell
Johns Creek
Duluth
Marietta
Chattahoochee River
Norcross
Fair Oaks
Sandy Springs
Doraville
Smyrna
Lilburn
Chamblee
Snellville
Mableton
Stone Mountain
Stone Mountain Park
Atlanta
Decatur
East Point
South River
Conyers
College Park
Union City
Morrow
Riverdale
South River
Stockbridge
Flint River
Jonesboro
N
McDonough
Fayetteville
0
5
10 miles

the area, decided to carve a relief on the side of the mountain memorializing three Confederate generals (Robert E. Lee, Stonewall Jackson, and Jefferson Davis).

Disputes over the carving led to it taking more than 50 years to complete, ultimately ending with the Venables turning the park over to the Stone Mountain Confederate Memorial, Inc., which in turn sold it to the state of Georgia, which owns it today.

The finished relief is the largest in the world. While most literature you read about Stone Mountain will say it is the largest outcropping of granite in the world, it actually consists of quartz monzonite, granite, and granodiorite. It rises 825 feet above the surrounding landscape and also extends 8 miles below the earth's surface. Its base is more than 5 miles around. Thus, in addition to hiking trails, there is a host of other activities in which to take part.

Park gates are open 10 a.m. to 8 p.m., but you are allowed to stay inside the park well after the admission booth closes (www.stonemountainpark.com; 770-498-5690 or 800-401-2407; $$).

getting there

The entrance to Stone Mountain Park is off US 78, less than 8 miles outside of I-285. From downtown, take I-20 East to I-285 North. Once on I-285 North, take exit 39B, the US 78 East (Snellville/Athens) exit. Travel 7.7 miles and take exit 8, the Stone Mountain Park main entrance. Follow the exit ramp to the east gate entrance of Stone Mountain Park.

Or, if you are in Midtown, you could simply get on Ponce de Leon Avenue and head east, taking care to follow the US 78 signs to the left after the fork in the road in Decatur.

where to go

The Antebellum Plantation. This collection of buildings was built between 1783 and 1875 in various areas of the state of Georgia. Each was then moved from its original site and restored to preserve its authenticity. The resulting assembly gives visitors a sense of life for 18th- and 19th-century Georgia residents. You not only experience everyday life, but in the kitchen area, you can enjoy culinary traditions of the South. The farmyard is particularly fun for the kids. Included in the One-Day Adventure Pass to the park or $$.

Carillon. Sitting on the edge of Stone Mountain Lake, the 732-bell carillon was donated to the park by Coca-Cola after its being exhibited in the 1964 World's Fair in New York City. Free concerts are Mon through Sat noon and 4 p.m., Sun 1 p.m., 3 p.m., 5 p.m.

Confederate Hall. Located at the base of the trail on the back side of the mountain opposite the carving, Confederate Hall is designed to educate visitors about the geology and ecology of Stone Mountain. The 5,400-square-foot hall contains a theater, a gallery, and interactive exhibits as well as state-of-the-art classrooms. The theater is set in a cave and shows a video about the origins of the mountain. There is also a video about the carving of the relief and information about the Civil War. Free with park entrance, Mon through Fri 9 a.m. to 5 p.m., Sat 10 a.m. to 5 p.m., Sun noon to 5 p.m.

Crossroads. This amusement area is set up just to the east of the lawn in front of the Stone Mountain carving. It is a great place to let kids spend some energy and includes dining areas as well as the Great Barn (an indoor amusement area with slides, trampoline floors, and games), the Great Locomotive Chase Mini-Golf, Yogi Bear 3-D Adventure Theater, and the Scenic Railroad Stop. Free to wander, but amusements $$.

Discovering Stone Mountain Museum. Memorial Hall. The self-guided tour traces the history of Stone Mountain from the Native Americans to its earliest European settlers, the Civil War, and finally the carving of the relief. The museum contains artifacts and photographs. Included in the One-Day Adventure Pass to the park or $$.

Grist Mill. Located on the east side of Stone Mountain on Robert E. Lee Boulevard. The gristmill was originally located in Ellijay in North Georgia and was moved to this site in 1965. While it is no longer used to grind grain, the process is described in the display area. Free with park entrance.

Hike the Mountain. The 1.3-mile hike up the back side of the mountain can truly give you your exercise for the day. The well-worn trail passes stone walls built centuries ago by Native Americans and centuries-old carvings in the stone itself. The trail starts at a gradual slope and then gets pretty steep past the midway mark. But the view at the top is worth the climb. On a clear day, you can see for more than 60 miles. Besides the trail to the top, there are more than 16 miles of other trails throughout the park. Free with park entrance.

Laser Light Show. The laser light show extravaganza is held nightly throughout the summer on the face of the mountain. The audience brings blankets and chairs or just sits on the lawn. There is food available, but you can bring picnics, too. Music, lights, and fireworks—it's a Stone Mountain tradition. There are VIP tickets which include dinner; otherwise the laser show is free with park entrance.

Paddle Wheel. The *Scarlett O'Hara* paddle wheel boat takes guests on a 20-minute ride across Stone Mountain Lake. The side-wheeler excursion is a relaxing journey with often just the sound of the whoosh-whoosh-whoosh of the turning wheel. The boat holds 150 passengers. Included in the One-Day Adventure Pass to the park or $$.

Pedal Boats. This is a fun way to get out on Stone Mountain Lake on your own and get a little exercise. These 2-seater boats rely on you to propel them. Boats are rented by the half hour. Included in the One-Day Adventure Pass to the park or $$.

Quarry Exhibit. On the east side of the mountain next to the Grist Mill. Long before it was a park, Stone Mountain was used as a quarry. This outdoor display describes the process of granite quarrying at Stone Mountain and the changes in technology over time. It is open daily from dawn until dusk. Free with park entrance.

Ride the Ducks. The Duck vehicles in question are 1940s Army DUKWs, equipped to travel on land and water. They have been converted into open-air vehicles which take you out onto Stone Mountain Lake for a different tour of the park. Included in the One-Day Adventure Pass to the park or $$.

The Scenic Railroad. The railroad will take you entirely around the 5-mile base of the mountain aboard an open-air car. Trains depart every 40 to 45 minutes and the journey lasts 25 to 30 minutes. The first train departs at 11 a.m. with the last departing at closing time. Included in the One-Day Adventure Pass to the park or $$.

Sky Hike. This suspending hiking area will take you up to 40 feet in the air on wooden bridges and ropes. Safety harnesses will make sure you don't fall, but this is a real confidence builder for those not afraid of heights. Included in the One-Day Adventure Pass to the park or $$ separately.

Song Bird Habitat. On the back side of the mountain off of Stonewall Jackson Drive, the habitat sits on the site of the former 1996 Summer Olympic Games venue for archery and cycling. Winding for a mile through both woodland and meadow trails, it allows visitors to see such birds as the eastern bluebird, white-breasted nuthatch, and northern cardinal. Free with park entrance.

Summit Skyride. This is the easy way to see the top of the rock. Take the Swiss cable car–style gondola up the face of the mountain. The 3-minute journey up gives you as close a look as you will get to the carving on the mountain's side. You can stay as long as you want or even choose to hike down the other side. Park entrance fee and $$.

where to eat

Big Rock Cafe. A great place to get a quick cheap bite to eat. The cafe features 7-inch cheese or pepperoni pizzas, salads, hot dogs, and nachos. At Skyride Plaza. $.

The Commons. Ranging from salads to burgers, you'll enjoy your food in the setting here on Stone Mountain Lake. Golf Course Clubhouse. $–$$.

Granite Chicken Cafe. The Granite Chicken is a place where you can sit and relax and enjoy Southern fare including fried chicken with fresh biscuits, chicken and dumplings, green beans, macaroni and cheese, and mashed potatoes with gravy. Chicken tenders and salads are also available. Make sure to leave room for the fresh peach cobbler for dessert. Memorial Hall. $.

Marketplace at Stone Mountain Park. If you would rather take it with you, this market area provides a great selection from pizza and deli sandwiches to salads or hamburgers. You can also get fresh fruit and bakery goods or candy and granola. Crossroads. $$.

Miss Katie's Sideboard. Open for lunch and dinner in a boardinghouse atmosphere amid the Crossroads section, you'll feel right at home with the heaping portions of fried chicken or chicken and dumplings. Desserts are a must, so try the peach cobbler or pecan pie. Crossroads. $$.

Mountain View. This Southern-style buffet offers a great view of the carving along with good home-style cooking. Stone Mountain Inn. $$.

Waterside. Open for all meals, this restaurant is one of the nicer offerings in the park. It features specialty buffets in a lakeside setting. Right on Stone Mountain Lake at Evergreen Marriott Conference Resort. $$.

where to stay

Evergreen Marriott Resort & Conference Center. www.marriott.com. Within the park itself, the Evergreen Marriott Resort and Conference Center offers spectacular views of the mountain and the lake throughout. Guests will have access to the amenities of the park as well as a spa, 2 championship golf courses, indoor and outdoor swimming pools, conference facilities, and 2 restaurants. $$–$$$.

Stone Mountain Campground. Stone Mountain Park has its own campground which has 431 campsites for tents as well as room for RVs. There are 202 hookups and 191 partial hookups. $$.

stone mountain village

Incorporated in 1839 under the name New Gibraltar, Stone Mountain Village grew up around a post office, an inn, and a general store that were built to handle the numerous people passing through the area or coming to visit the mountain. The name "Stone Mountain Village" came from the Georgia State Legislature in 1849. The village was all but destroyed during the Civil War, so most of the buildings seen today were built in the ensuing years.

The streets of downtown are now lined with quaint shops and restaurants, and while the village itself has grown, the downtown area has maintained that distinctive small-town feel. Stone Mountain prides itself on that atmosphere and plans a great deal of community activities to nurture the feel. Of course, with Southern hospitality as a key, visitors are more than welcome to be a part.

getting there

Stone Mountain Village is right outside the west gate of Stone Mountain Park. Simply exit the gate off Robert E. Lee Boulevard near the walk-up trail and go straight into downtown. If coming from Atlanta, the journey will take you less than 30 minutes. Take I-20 East to I-285 North. Once on I-285 North, take exit 39B, the US 78 East (Snellville/Athens) exit. Travel 5 miles and take exit 5 South, Memorial Drive/GA 10. Travel a quarter-mile and make a left on Ponce de Leon Avenue into downtown.

where to go

Stone Mountain Visitor's Center. 922 Main St.; (770) 879-4971; www.stonemountaincity.org. In a vintage railroad caboose, the visitor center will fill you in on how much there is to do in this historic town. Be sure to pick up a walking map of the downtown area. Mon through Fri 9 a.m. to 6 p.m., Sat and Sun 10 a.m. to 7 p.m.

ART Station. 5384 Manor Dr.; (770) 469-1105; www.artstation.org. In the historic trolley barn of Stone Mountain, ART features art galleries and a theater and hosts a steady array of events, camps, and activities. Make sure to check their calendar so as not to miss something. Gift shop: Tues through Fri 10 a.m. to 5 p.m., Sat 10 a.m. to 3 p.m.

Bollywood Cinema. 5157 Memorial Dr.; (770) 438-6464. The only theater in Atlanta to show Bollywood movies. There are 2 different theaters which usually show 2 different movies. Some of these can be a hoot to watch. Call for listings. Admission is dependent on the film. Sun through Thurs 8 p.m., Fri 9:30 p.m., Sat 6 p.m. and 9:30 p.m. $.

Stone Mountain Depot. 922 Main St.; (770) 498-7334; www.stonemountainvillage.com. Mostly burned during Gen. Sherman's march, the 1857 train depot has been fully restored and now serves as the Stone Mountain Village City Hall and Police Station. Weekdays 8 a.m. to 9 p.m., Sat 9 a.m. to 9 p.m., Sun 11 a.m. to 6 p.m.

Tupac Amaru Shakur Center for the Arts. 5616 Memorial Dr.; (404) 298-4222; www.tasf.org. Built in memory of the late rapper Tupac Shakur, the center helps students interested in the arts further their studies. The visitor center contains a gallery with works from artists from across the globe. There is also a Peace Garden with fountains, pavilions, and a statue honoring Tupac. Mon through Fri 10 a.m. to 5 p.m., Sat noon to 6 p.m., closed Sun. Free.

where to eat

Bev's Place. 1054 Main St.; (770) 469-7877. This gastro pub has a distinctive neighborhood feel, and you'll be treated as a local. With its horseshoe-shaped bar, you'll sense right away that this is not a typical bar. The food is called "American fare," but none of it is typical.

Try the daily special: it won't disappoint. Mon through Fri 11 a.m. to 2 a.m., Sat 11 a.m. to midnight, Sun 12:30 p.m. to 2 a.m. $–$$.

Continental Park Cafe. 941 Main St. #A; (770) 413-6448. In the heart of it all, you can hang out on the balcony and watch the world walk by. Casual fare with salads, burgers, etc. Good food, good location, good atmosphere. Mon through Fri and Sun 11 a.m. to 3 p.m., Thurs and Fri 5 to 9 p.m. $.

Crazy Ron's Hot Off the Grill. 6187 E. Ponce De Leon Ave.; (770) 413-5900. Great barbeque in a down-home atmosphere. A little more than a shack because the effort goes into the "Q." The ribs are to die for. Sun noon to 4 p.m., Wed through Sat 11 a.m. to 8 p.m. $–$$.

Creative Celebrations. 923 Main St.; (770) 469-5889. This cafe and bakery is a great place to grab a quick bite or to pick up something to take with you. Daily 7 a.m. to 10 p.m. $.

Geraldine's Fish and Grits. 971 N. Hairston Rd., Ste. 1-B; (770) 498-3660. Open only for breakfast and lunch, you could never imagine fish prepared so many different ways. Cheese grits and grilled trout for breakfast? But of course! Tues through Sun 7 a.m. to 3 p.m. $–$$.

Mamma Nem's. 6049 Memorial Dr.; (770) 469-0000. Not just Mamma, it's the whole family greeting you as you walk in the doors. A great place for down-home cooking. From fried chicken to turnip greens, this is the place to eat your fill. Daily 11:30 a.m. to 9 p.m. $.

Metro Cafe. 1905 Rockbridge Rd.; (770) 879-0101; www.metrocafediner.com. A local favorite, this diner is just a few blocks from downtown. Serving up American and Greek cuisine, it's also known for its awesome desserts. Open 24/7. $–$$.

Michael David's at Magnolia Cottage and Gardens. 5459 E. Mountain St.; (770) 879-6282; www.michaeldavidsevents.com. In a historic home amid gardens in downtown Stone Mountain, the food is as good as the atmosphere is quaint. A popular location for events, Michael David's serves up Southern cuisine with flair. Weekdays 11 a.m. to 2:30 p.m., Sun 10:30 a.m. to 3:30 p.m. $–$$.

Nice Mon. 663 S. Stone Mountain Lithonia Rd.; (678) 476-0013. Authentic Jamaican cuisine in the heart of Georgia. Known for its breads and beef patties, this small restaurant stays hopping because of the food and the price. Mon through Sat 11 a.m. to 10 p.m. Closed Sun. $.

The Sycamore Grill. 5329 Mimosa Dr.; (770) 465-6789. The Sycamore Grill capitalizes on its location in a Civil War–era home to serve up elegant Southern food. Consistently good, the atmosphere will also win you over. If you can't make dinner, try their brunch. Tues through Thurs 11:30 a.m. to 9 p.m., Fri and Sat 11:30 a.m. to 10 p.m., Sat and Sun brunch 10 a.m. to 3 p.m. $$–$$$.

Village Cafe. 6670 James B. Rivers Memorial Dr., #500; (770) 879-6599; www.villagecafellc.com. You'll feel right at home in this family-oriented restaurant. They serve up good Southern fare with a friendly atmosphere. Fried chicken, ribs, and the typical "meat-and-three" mantra of Southerners. Tues through Thurs 11 a.m. to 7 p.m., Fri and Sat 11 a.m. to 8 p.m., Sun 1 to 5 p.m. Closed Mon. $–$$.

where to stay

Hampton Inn. 1737 Mountain Industrial Blvd.; (770) 934-0004; www.hamptoninn.hilton.com. Convenient to the park and the village, this inn features a business center and breakfast area. $$.

Village Inn Bed and Breakfast. 992 Ridge Ave.; (770) 469-3459; www.villageinnbb.com. Within walking distance to all of downtown Stone Mountain, this inn is in one of the oldest surviving buildings in the village itself. The inn was built as such in the 1820s and has a rich history. It has 6 individual rooms with private baths included. $$–$$$.

day trip 02

east

historic heartland:
conyers, covington, social circle

This little adventure, while still very close to Atlanta, allows you to escape the big city and venture into what they refer to as the Heartland of Georgia. Conyers, Covington, and Social Circle are all considered suburbs of Atlanta by many, but you'll come to understand why so many people are willing to brave the traffic of a commute to live here and work in Atlanta.

These communities still adhere to small-town values, and generation after generation continue to raise their families here. All of these towns' histories date back to the early settlements of the state of Georgia, and in some cases, there are colorful stories to tell.

conyers

Conyers had its beginnings centuries ago as part of the "Great Indian Road," later called the "Hightower Trail." Creek and Cherokee Indians shared this area before the European settlers came inland. As with most successful towns in Georgia, the advent of the railroad helped spark Conyers's growth. The town's history includes an active mill community and, of course, a role in the Civil War.

These days, the area around the old city center has developed into a sprawl of shopping centers and industriousness with I-20 zipping by, but if you venture into Olde Town Conyers, you'll find a charming community worth exploring. Great effort has been made to restore and preserve the area. Many of the homes are listed on the National

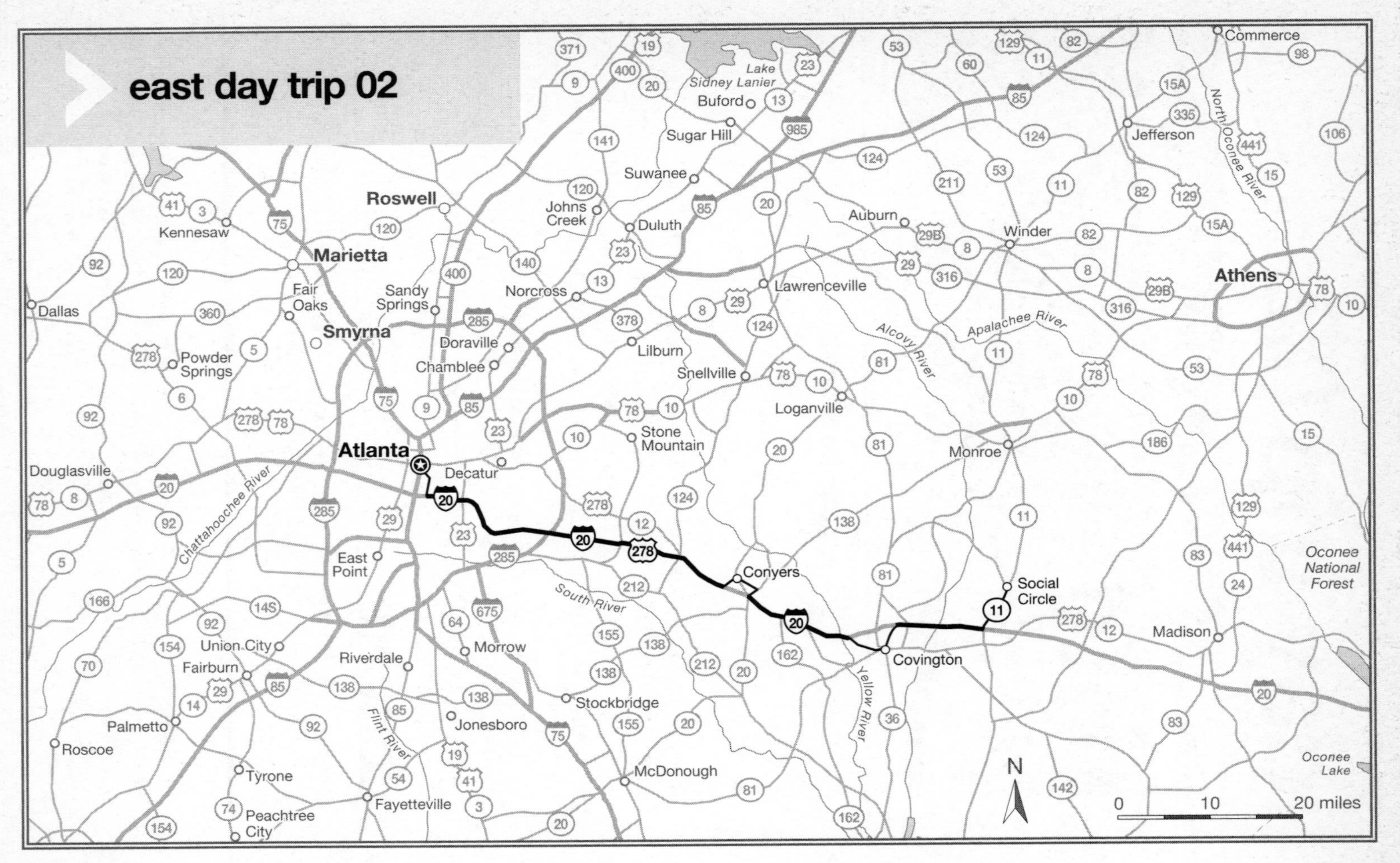
east day trip 02
Commerce
Lake Sidney Lanier
Buford
Sugar Hill
Jefferson
North Oconee River
Suwanee
Roswell
Johns Creek
Duluth
Auburn
Winder
Kennesaw
Marietta
Athens
Fair Oaks
Sandy Springs
Norcross
Lawrenceville
Dallas
Smyrna
Doraville
Apalachee River
Alcovy River
Powder Springs
Chamblee
Lilburn
Snellville
Loganville
Stone Mountain
Atlanta
Monroe
Douglasville
Decatur
Chattahoochee River
East Point
Conyers
Social Circle
Oconee National Forest
South River
Madison
Union City
Riverdale
Morrow
Covington
Fairburn
Palmetto
Jonesboro
Stockbridge
Yellow River
Flint River
Roscoe
Tyrone
McDonough
Oconee Lake
Fayetteville
Peachtree City
N
0
10
20 miles

Historic Register. Quaint shops, a historic residential area, and great little restaurants deserve a look.

getting there

Just 25 miles east of downtown Atlanta, all you have to do is hop on I-20 East and take exit 82 North on West Avenue into downtown.

where to go

Conyers Welcome Center. 901 Railroad St.; (770) 602-2606; http://visitconyersga.com. In a 1890s rail depot, the visitor center is in the heart of the old town section of Conyers. The depot was a working station until 1972. Completely restored, the building serves as an event/function facility as well as a visitor center. Come here for discount coupons, maps, and walking guides. Mon through Fri 8 a.m. to 5 p.m. Closed weekends.

Big Haynes Creek Nature Center. Georgia International Horse Park, 1996 Centennial Olympic Pkwy.; (770) 860-4190. If your want to get out and enjoy a combination of woodlands, meadows, and wetlands, take in the Big Haynes Creek Nature Center. Big Haynes is actually on 170 acres of protected land within the Georgia International Horse Park. The nature center has interpretive signs throughout its hiking trails, which take you across Stone Mountain–like terrain and granite outcroppings, as well as through the marshes. There is a canoe intake as well as a pavilion overlooking the wetlands. Daily dawn to dusk. Free.

Georgia International Horse Park. 1996 Centennial Olympic Pkwy.; (770) 860-4190. This 1,400-acre multipurpose facility was originally built for the 1996 Atlanta Olympic Games. Since then, the equestrian facilities continue to be used, but the park itself has become an event location hosting everything from festivals to car races to rodeos. Make sure to check the schedule online as hours vary.

Haralson Mill Covered Bridge. In Panola Mountain State Conservation Park on Haralson Mill Road off of Bethel Road. The bridge is open to traffic, but there are areas to park and take photographs on either side. The 150-foot-long wooden bridge is actually new, having been built in 1997, but it was designed in look like the bridges that used to dot the region. It is just north of the Haralson Mill historic district, which includes Haralson Mill House, a general store, the old mill site, and blacksmith shop.

Milstead 104 "Dinky" Steam Locomotive. Commercial and Railroad Streets. A 1905 Rogers steam locomotive is permanently located here in the center of town and is free to explore. The historic engine is 1 of only 3 left in the world and once ran rail service between Conyers to the neighboring mill town of Milstead along 3.5 miles of rail. The engine and tender car were used to haul cotton bales from the main line to the textile mill that operated along the banks of the Yellow River.

The Monastery of the Holy Spirit. 2625 GA 212 Southwest; (770) 483-8705; www.trappist.net. Founded in 1944, this community of 40 monks is the first native-born Trappist foundation in the US. The monastery itself is on a wooded property complete with a lake and trails. Visitors are welcome to come visit for the day, attend services, or participate in a retreat. The monks have a gift shop where they sell religious materials as well as their homemade breads and bonsai trees. Check their website for the various schedules.

Old Jail Museum. 967 Milstead Ave. The old jail was built in 1897 and includes a "hanging room." You'll need to time your visit to get inside to see the room and all the jail has to offer. The Rockdale County Historical Society offers free tours of the jail the second Sat of each month from 10 a.m. to 2 p.m.

Panola Mountain State Park. 2600 GA 155, Stockbridge; (770) 389-7801; www.gastateparks.org/PanolaMountain. If you don't want to climb Stone Mountain, hiking through Panola Mountain State Park will certainly give you a sense of what it is like to walk on granite. Encompassing 100 acres, Panola Mountain is home to many rare plants of the Piedmont region. The park is minimally developed, and visitors are allowed to explore the granite outcropping and watershed area on their own. Daily 8:30 a.m. to 5 p.m.

The Shrine of Our Loving Mother. 2324 White Rd.; (770) 922-8885; www.conyers.org. This farm and grounds has become a pilgrimage site for many ever since the Virgin Mother was reported to have started making appearances in 1991. Millions have made their way to this farm for the monthly visits by the apparition and to receive blessings. While the appearances stopped in 1998, the farm remains open for those who want to come, pray, and meditate. Donations are suggested, and a schedule of activities is posted on their website.

Walk of Heroes–Veterans Memorial Park. 3001 Black Shoals Rd.; (770) 278-7000; www.walkofheroes.org. The Walk of Heroes–Veterans War Memorial opened in 2010 and is still being expanded while honoring those who have sacrificed to fight for their country. The memorial is on Black Shoals reservoir and includes an amphitheater, a brick walkway of heroes, and various statuary commemorating battles and wars. Thurs through Tues 7 a.m. to 9 p.m. Free.

where to eat

Borage Grill. 914 Commercial St.; (770) 929-8885; www.boragegrill.com. A small hole in the wall, but with incredible authentic Middle Eastern cuisine of pizzas, salads, grilled seafood, and kabobs. There are also theme nights, so make sure to check. Mon through Thurs 11 a.m. to 10 p.m.; Fri 11 a.m. to 11 p.m.; Sat 9 a.m. to 11 p.m.; Sun 9 a.m. to 9:30 p.m. $–$$.

Celtic Tavern. 918 Commercial St.; (770) 785-7001; http://conyersceltictavern.com. Every town needs a good local Irish bar, and this is it for Conyers. Serving traditional Irish fare with lots of Guinness, the Celtic Tavern is known best for its stews and live music. Tues through Sun 11:30 a.m. to midnight. $–$$.

Evans Pharmacy. 933 Center St. Northeast; (770) 483-7211. This old-fashioned pharmacy has an old soda fountain and sandwich shop area that is as good as it is nostalgic. Great sandwiches and wonderful milkshakes! Mon through Sat 9 a.m. to 4 p.m. $.

Mamie's Kitchen & Biscuits. 1294 Main St.; (770) 922-0131. Heaven for biscuit lovers. Expect them every way imaginable with just about anything possible on them. Mon through Sat 5 a.m. to 2 p.m. $.

Oakes Family Diner. 1040 Flat Shoals Rd.; (678) 413-1597. Not in the downtown area, but worth the drive. This traditional diner has great home-cooked meals at great prices. Make sure to check the daily blue-plate specials. Mon through Fri 6 a.m. to 9 p.m., Sat 6 a.m. to 10 p.m., Sun 6 a.m. to 9 p.m. $–$$.

Sugar Baker's. 939 Bank St.; (770) 761-9922; http://sugarbakers2.com. While the bakery's hours are a bit longer, lunch is only served midday. Great soups, sandwiches, and of course, desserts. There are daily specials, so check them out because they are always good. Mon through Fri 10:30 a.m. to 2:30 p.m.

Whistle Post Tavern. 935 Railroad St.; (770) 785-5008; www.whistleposttavern.com. A local favorite, the Whistle Post has a creative menu with Southern flair. It's right next to the tracks, so if you are in the bar and a train goes by—free shots! Live music on the weekends. Mon through Thurs 8:30 a.m. to midnight, Fri 8:30 a.m. to 2:30 a.m., Sat 8 a.m. to 1 a.m., Sun 10 a.m. to midnight.

where to stay

Hampton Inn. 1340 Dogwood Dr.; (770) 483-8838; www.hamptoninn.com. Clean and comfy and convenient to I-20. Continental breakfast included. $–$$.

Lakeside Inn Bed and Breakfast. 3051 N. Tower; (770) 922-7269. There are 2 private rooms available in this home, which is very near the Georgia International Horse Park. Quiet setting with a private dock on the lake. $$.

Ramada. 1351 Dogwood Dr.; (770) 483-3220; www.ramada.com. Convenient to I-20, the Ramada features a pool and fitness center as well as a conference center. $–$$.

covington

Picturesque Covington is another of those little treasures that many people may miss if they don't have it pointed out to them. Built around the town square, you'll still find a great deal of activity centered here. Concerts, festivals, and social events take place regularly.

The community has an active Choral Guild and Community Band, which are often found performing together.

Stroll around a bit, and you'll understand why Hollywood is enamored with this place and has used it as a backdrop for movies and television shows. Covington's nickname is the "Hollywood of the South." It has three distinct historic districts which each deserve attention. In addition to the Downtown Historic District, there is the Floyd Street District east of downtown and Covington Mills and Mill Village Historic District just to the north of downtown. The churches, parks, and mansions will make you want to set down roots of your own in this small town.

getting there

It's easiest to just get back on I-20 from Conyers and head east 15 miles to Covington. From Atlanta, the drive is only about 30 to 35 minutes. Take exit 90 south into town.

where to go

Newton County Welcome Center. 2101 Clark St.; (770) 787-3868; www.gocovington.com. Stop by here to get the latest on events taking place in town as well as a maps and brochures. There are self-guided walking and driving maps, or they can help you arrange a tour. Mon through Fri 10 a.m. to 5 p.m., Sat 10 a.m. to 4 p.m.

First United Methodist Church of Covington. 1113 Conyers St. Southwest; (770) 786-7305. Built in 1854, this beautiful old Greek Revival church is one of the city's oldest. During the Civil War, it was used as an infirmary. Among its inside features is a Czech crystal chandelier that is considered priceless. The weight of the chandelier forced the church to undergo some renovations to make sure it could maintain the 1,100-pound piece of art.

Newton County Courthouse. Courthouse Square. Built in 1884, this beautiful brick structure is probably one of the best-known historic courthouses in all of Georgia. The building has been used in numerous television shows and movies. It stands as symbol of not just Covington, but all of Newton County after its predecessor burned. The courthouse is still in use, but the judicial functions take place in a newer structure next door. Mon through Fri 8:30 a.m. to 5 p.m.

where to eat

Freeman's Low Country Fish Camp. 2123 Usher St.; (678) 658-7828; www.freemanslowcountry.com. Specializing in seafood, the extra somethings on the menu come from the South Carolina low country. Think shrimp and grits and a low country seafood boil. Mon through Sat 11 a.m. to 9 p.m. $$.

Hard Luck Cafe. 2123 Pace St. #A; (770) 787-0421; http://hardluckconyers.com. The menu here is simple with basic hamburgers, sandwiches, and subs, but the best wings you'll ever try. Mon through Thurs 11 a.m. to 9:30 p.m., Fri and Sat 11:30 a.m. to 10:30 p.m., Sun noon to 9 p.m. $.

R L's Off the Square. 1113 Floyd St. Northeast; (770) 385-5045. In the heart of town, this restaurant is consistently good with a Louisiana-style menu featuring gumbo, barbeque shrimp, and jambalaya with a good selection of beers and wine. Sun and Mon noon to midnight, Tues through Thurs 5 to 9 p.m., Fri and Sat 5 to 10 p.m. $–$$.

Thomas Country Buffet. 4122 Emory St. Northwest; (678) 212-0186. This country buffet open for lunch and dinner will tempt you to spend the whole day. Great cooking and great prices will keep you going back for more. Mon through Sat 9 a.m. to 8 p.m. $–$$.

Townhouse Cafe. 1145 Southwest Washington St.; (770) 787-2788. This place hasn't changed in decades, and that's a good thing. Good home-cooking and reasonable prices make the Townhouse Cafe a staple in the Covington area. Mon through Fri 7:30 a.m. to 5 p.m., Sat 7:30 a.m. to 4:30 p.m. $–$$.

where to stay

Baymont Inn & Suites. 10111 Alcovy Rd.; (770) 787-4900; www.baymontinns.com. The Baymont features an outdoor pool and breakfast. Easy access to I-20. $–$$.

Days Inn. 10166 Alcovy Rd.; (770) 788-8919; www.daysinn.com. Offering an outdoor pool and a guest laundry, the Days Inn is clean, comfortable, and convenient to the interstate as well as downtown Covington. $–$$.

Hampton Inn. 14460 Paras Dr.; (678) 212-2500; www.hamptoninn.hilton.com. Right at the I-20 exit, this hotel offers spacious rooms and a business center. $–$$.

worth more time

The Brick Store. 12931 US 278 (10 miles east of downtown). This was Newton County's first brick structure. Built in 1821, it was a general store, stagecoach stop, and housed Newton County's first court session. It was refurbished in 2010, but is a historical site to see, not necessarily visit.

social circle

Social Circle bills itself as "Georgia's Greatest Little Town," and you'll understand why when you make a visit to the heart of this quaint little community. The town has its origins in the 1820s with a Georgia Land Lottery drawing. Incorporated in 1832, Social Circle quickly became a place where people sought to build a new life and businesses.

There are homes dating back to that time. In fact, there are more than 50 buildings on the National Register of Historic Places ranging from Greek Revival mansions and

Neoclassical and Victorian architecture to the old mill and mill village cottages. Social Circle may not be very big, but there is plenty to see in the walkable downtown area with its quaint shops and restaurants.

getting there

From Atlanta, Social Circle is just 50 miles away. Take I-20 to exit 98. Go north on GA 11. The town of Social Circle is approximately 4 miles north of I-20.

where to go

Social Circle Visitor Center. 129 E. Hightower Trail; (770) 464-1866; www.socialcircle georgia.citymax.com. Social Circle Visitor Center is a great place to start because it also houses a museum that will help you understand more about this community's beginnings and why it remains such a popular place to visit. The actual visitor information portion calls itself "The Better Hometown Office" and will give you plenty of information about upcoming events, festivals, and concerts. The Visitor Center also houses an artist co-op gallery. Mon through Fri 8:30 a.m. to 5 p.m.

City Hall. 166 N. Cherokee Rd.; (770) 464-2380. City Hall is located in an antebellum house known as the Hester House. Built in 1840, the home has been completely restored. Mon through Fri 8:30 a.m. to 5 p.m.

Fox Vineyards. 225 GA 11 South; (770) 787-5402; www.foxvineyardswinery.com. Fox Vineyards is one of the more-established vineyards in this neck of the woods, and it's easy to see why. The vintner here knows how to make good wine! Using California grapes, they work with riesling, pinot grigio, grenach rose, pinot noir, zinfandel, merlot, cabernet sauvignon, and have created a nice blend called Hot Flash, which dumps together petite syrah, malbec, and shiraz. They have also started working with Georgia muscadines and scuppernongs. Stop by the tasting room, and by all means taste. Wed through Sat 10 a.m. to 6 p.m., Sun 1 to 6 p.m.

Georgia Railroad Depot. 200 S. Dogwood Ave.; (770) 464-3365. Built in 1913, this red-brick depot has been in constant use since that time. It is now the Social Circle base of the CSX line and is still worth checking out.

Great Walton Railroad. 1096 N. Cherokee Rd.; (770) 464-0761; www.greatwaltonrailroad .com. With so many of these Georgia towns associated with railroads, here is a chance to see one in operation. The Great Walton is a short line railroad company operating a 10-mile line between Monroe and Social Circle since 1987. Originally constructed in 1880 as the Walton Railroad, it now operates several short lines including the Hartwell Railroad and the former Norfolk Southern line between Toccoa and Elberton (built as the Elberton Air-Line Railroad).

where to eat

Blue Willow Inn. 294 N. Cherokee Rd.; (770) 464-2133; www.bluewillowinn.com. The Blue Willow has long been a place that is its own destination for many because of its food. For that reason, you may want to consider reservations. Known for its Southern hospitality and an endless buffet of Southern dishes, guests will simply love the setting in the old antebellum home. Mon through Sat 11 a.m. to 2:30 p.m., Mon through Thurs 5 to 8 p.m., Fri 5 to 9 p.m., Sat 4:30 to 9 p.m., Sun 11 a.m. to 8 p.m. $$.

Buckeye's Restaurant. 170 S. Cherokee Rd.; (770) 464-1464; www.buckeyesplantation.com/Lunch. Buckeye's is open for breakfast, lunch, and dinner, serving up home cooking including the traditional meat-and-three. Portions are generous. Mon through Sat 6 a.m. to 2 p.m., Fri and Sat 6 to 9 p.m. $–$$.

Butcher Block Grill. 1299-A N. Cherokee Rd.; (770) 267-9132. Butcher Block is a traditional burger grill serving up sandwiches, fries, and salads as well as a wide variety of "dawgs." Mon 11 a.m. to 3 p.m., Tues through Sat 11 a.m. to 9 p.m. $.

Debbie's Cherokee Grill. 125 S. Cherokee Rd.; (770) 464-9902. A new favorite, Debbie's offers freshly made soups, salads, sandwiches, vegetables, and dinner entrees. Open for both lunch and dinner daily. $–$$.

Lou's Soda Fountain & Grille. 208 Village Circle; (770) 464-1020. Lou's is like a blast from the past. An old-fashioned soda fountain and grill right behind the Blue Willow Inn, Lou's serves up burgers, sandwiches, milkshakes, and malts. It's owned by the same people as the Blue Willow Inn, so you know the food is good. $.

Social Circle Wing Factory. 1008 N. Cherokee Rd.; (770) 464-4400. All you can eat, and you will indeed. The Wing Factory serves wings in a wide variety of flavors from barbeque to teriyaki to buffalo style. Lunch and dinner daily. $$.

where to stay

Welcome Inn Motel. 184 S. Cherokee Rd.; (678) 465-9051. In the heart of town, the Welcome Inn provides a haven if you decide to stay over in Social Circle. $.

day trip 03

treasure trail:
rutledge, madison, greensboro, crawfordville

This could easily be one of our favorite trips in this book. Venture a little farther out I-20, and you will find some true treasures, literally and figuratively. There is a string of well-preserved Southern towns stretching almost to Augusta along US 12, which parallels the interstate. They are historical treasures and offer an amazing array of shopping opportunities if that is what you enjoy.

We've tried to group the towns in this outing because of their commonalities regarding both their past and their present. These four centuries-old towns—Rutledge, Madison, Greensboro, and Crawfordville—are known for their beautiful historic buildings, laid-back lifestyle, welcoming atmosphere—and their antiques. Antiques malls and shops abound. Each town also has restaurants which draw Atlantans in-the-know to come partake.

Each of these towns could easily be a destination on its own, and while you can see them all in a day, you could and perhaps should plan several days on this day trip alone. Even traveling between the towns is like a trip through time if you stay on US 12 and pass through the rural farmlands. You'll be sure to find yourself stopping and taking photos along the way.

rutledge

Rutledge is probably one of the smallest towns listed in this book and is a nice little diversion off the busy interstate. Its motto is "Small but Special," and just spend some time here

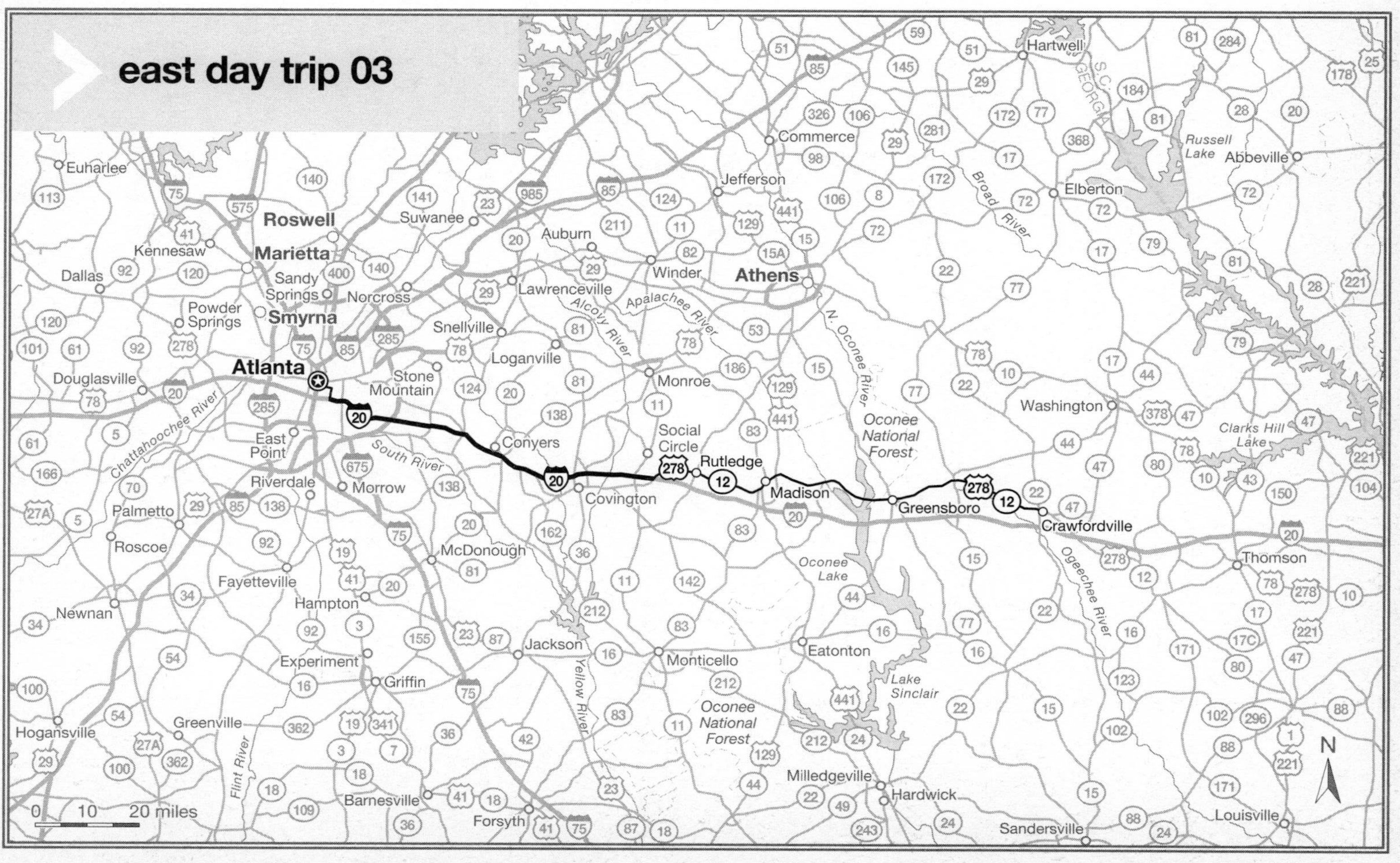

east day trip 03
Euharlee
Roswell
Suwanee
Kennesaw
Marietta
Dallas
Sandy Springs
Norcross
Powder Springs
Smyrna
Atlanta
Douglasville
Stone Mountain
East Point
Riverdale
Morrow
Palmetto
Roscoe
Newnan
Fayetteville
Hampton
Experiment
Griffin
Hogansville
Greenville
Barnesville
Forsyth
McDonough
Jackson
Conyers
Covington
Snellville
Loganville
Lawrenceville
Auburn
Winder
Monroe
Social Circle
Rutledge
Madison
Greensboro
Crawfordville
Athens
Jefferson
Commerce
Hartwell
Elberton
Abbeville
Washington
Thomson
Monticello
Eatonton
Milledgeville
Hardwick
Sandersville
Louisville
Chattahoochee River
South River
Alcovy River
Apalachee River
N. Oconee River
Broad River
Ogeechee River
Yellow River
Flint River
Russell Lake
Clarks Hill Lake
Oconee Lake
Lake Sinclair
Oconee National Forest
S.C.
GEORGIA
N
0 10 20 miles

and you will agree. Founded in 1871, the town enjoyed a heyday as a favorite railroad stop between Atlanta and Augusta.

Despite its popularity, Rutledge stayed small and has changed very little in appearance since that time. The historic district stretches only a few blocks off of its green square, and there are almost a dozen historical markers around town commemorating everything from the railroad to the crash of a B25-C in 1945. There is always something going on in the park, from music to exhibits. Rutledge has a reputation now as an artists' community.

getting there

Located just 3 miles off of I-20 and less than an hour from Atlanta, take exit 101, US 287/GA 12 North. You'll have to cross the railroad tracks to actually get into the heart of the town.

where to go

Hard Labor Creek State Park. (706) 557-3001; www.gastateparks.org/info/hardlabor creek. One of Georgia's largest state parks, Hard Labor is best known for its golf course, but there is a host of other activities available in this more than 5,800-acre park. There are more than 24 miles of trails available for hiking and horseback riding. Swimming and camping are also options. Daily 7 a.m. to 10 p.m., Golf $$ (call 706-557-3006 for golf reservations).

Rutledge Hardware. 116 Fairplay St.; (706) 557-1770. This place is amazing. It's a store to visit even if you aren't shopping, and that's why it is listed here. Continuously operated since the 1800s, stepping into Rutledge Hardware is like stepping back in time. This vintage hardware store has all of its original fixtures, with floor-to-ceiling shelves and rolling ladders to find what is needed. It serves the hardware and gardening needs of the town but has wonderful curios to check out as well. It is such an unusual place, it has even garnered a mention in *Smithsonian Magazine*. Mon through Fri 8 a.m. to 5 p.m., Sat 8 a.m. to 3 p.m.

Sunflower Farm. 1430 Durden; (706) 557-2870; www.sunflowerfarmfestival.com. This 15-acre sunflower farm is best visited in June and July when you can actually cut your own flowers. It is also home to the yearly Sunflower Festival. The center of the farm is an 1811 home, and the farm itself is still worth a stop any time of the year.

where to shop

Crossroads Antiques. 124 Fairplay St.; (706) 557-9119. Another gem for strolling and antiquing, it's the relative newcomer of the group, but has an eclectic selection of antiques, advertising, collectibles, and signed sports memorabilia. Tues through Sat 10 a.m. to 5 p.m. Closed Sun and Mon.

D'Antiques. 106 E. Main St.; (706) 557-2599. Specializing in primitive antiques, this is a great shop to browse and explore in. Tues through Sat 10 a.m. to 5 p.m. Closed Sun and Mon.

Red Doors Studio. 104 W. Main St.; (706) 557-9020; www.reddoorsstudio.com. A working studio, Red Doors is best known for its hand-painted floor clothes. Artist Molly Lesnikowski is generally at work, so the studio alone is worth a drop in. Mon through Fri 10 a.m. to 5 p.m., Sat 10 a.m. to 4 p.m.

where to eat

The Caboose. 102 W. Main St.; (706) 557-9021. This great little food stop is set up in the last railroad car to serve Rutledge. Serving up sandwiches and homemade fudge, ice cream, and root beer, the Caboose has a great nostalgic feel. Mon and Tue 10 a.m. to 5 p.m., Wed and Thurs 10 a.m. to 6 p.m., Fri and Sat 10 a.m. to 7 p.m., Sun 11 a.m. to 5 p.m. $.

Yesterday's Cafe. 120 Fairplay St.; (706) 557-9337; http://yesterdayscaferutledge.com. This cafe is in an old pharmacy which displays historic photographs of Rutledge. Dine on Southern fare while looking at the vintage pictures, including those of the old pharmacy itself. Great breakfasts and lunches, or stick around for their family dinners. Daily 8 a.m. to 2 p.m., Fri and Sat also 5 to 9 p.m. $–$$.

where to stay

Rutledge Inn. 189 W. Main St.; (706) 557-7762; www.therutledgeinn.com. This bed-and-breakfast was built as a farmhouse in the 1850s and, while only a few blocks from the square, backs up to cotton fields. It has just 3 rooms, but this charming inn is a great way to allow yourself extra time in a quintessential tiny Southern town. With a chef on the premises, breakfasts are amazing, and dinner can be prepared upon request. $$.

madison

Madison is known as Georgia's "Antebellum Showcase." As the one town in the state that Gen. Sherman agreed not to burn during the Civil War, it still holds example after example of spectacular historic mansions, cottages, and buildings to explore on driving and walking tours.

The entire town is a testament to the days when cotton was king in the South. The majority of the historic section of Madison was built between 1830 and 1860. For this reason, don't be surprised if you run into a movie crew. Madison is a popular location for both period and modern movies about the South.

Bear in mind that because the historic district is so large, many of the homes are private and not open to visitors. Public buildings are designated as such.

getting there

Coming from Rutledge, just continue east on US 278/GA 12 for 25 miles. If you are coming from Atlanta, it will take you less than an hour. Take I-20 East. Exits 113 (Monticello Raod) and 114 (Eatonton Road) will get you there, but 114 to GA 24 is a better choice.

where to go

Madison-Morgan County Chamber of Commerce. 115 E. Jefferson St.; (706) 342-4454 or (800) 709-7406; www.madisonga.org. It is highly recommended that you make this your first stop. There are more than 4 dozen historical structures listed on the tours of Madison, and the visitor center at the Chamber can help you make the most of your time. The center itself is in a 2-story brick building that has served as both the City Hall and a fire station. Open daily 8 a.m. to 6 p.m.

Bruce Weiner Microcar Museum. 2950 Eatonton Rd.; (706) 343-9937; www.microcar museum.com. You certainly wouldn't expect to find the largest collection of microcars in the world in a place like Madison, but yet, here it is. Microcars were first developed in Europe following World War II. You'll find every shape and color of these small "bubble" cars in this collection, which concentrates on cars built up to the early 1960s. Bruce Weiner was an executive of Dubble Bubble and began collecting these as a hobby. Mon through Sat 10 a.m. to 5 p.m. $.

Heritage Hall. 277 S. Main St.; (706) 342-9627; www.friendsofheritagehall.org. This 1811 home was originally part of an in-town farm of 4 acres. A private residence until 1977, it is best known for its architecture. It's the only house in town where 4 columns are flanked by 4 square pillars. In addition to tours, it is available for private events. The home has been carefully restored and is furnished with period antiques. Mon through Sat 10 a.m. to 4:30 p.m., Sun 1:30 to 4:30 p.m. Free.

Hunter House. 580 S. Main St. Hunter House is probably Madison's most photographed home. The Queen Anne–style house, built in 1883, looks like a fairy-tale house. As a private residence, you will be restricted to just viewing the incredible exterior, but you'll understand why it is a "must" for a walk or drive-by.

Madison Artists Guild. Cottage Gallery at Town Park, 48 W. Jefferson St.; (706) 342-5200; www.madisonartistsguild.org. The guild started as a group of local artists who wanted to get together and socialize and share ideas. The result is a 150-member guild which now operates a great gallery where you can see not only their art, but that of guest artists. Wed through Sat 11 a.m. to 4:30 p.m., Sun 1 to 5 p.m.

Madison County Courthouse. 149 E. Jefferson St.; (706) 343-6500. Built in 1905 for a whopping $18,314, this Neoclassical building stands out at the center of town. Listed on the National Register of Historic Places, the courthouse recently underwent an entire renovation. The courts themselves have been moved to a new complex, but this building remains in use as government offices. Mon through Fri 8:30 a.m. to 6 p.m.

Madison-Morgan Cultural Center. 434 S. Main St.; (706) 342-4643; www.mmcc-arts.org. Housed in an 1895 school, the center is a keeper of Madison history. Featuring galleries and a museum, this is a great place to explore and get some context for what you'll see as you roam the town. The gorgeous 397-seat theater hosts numerous world-class artists, so be sure to check the schedule while you are in town. Tues through Sun 9 a.m. to 5 p.m. Closed Mon. Free.

Morgan County African-American Museum. 156 Academy St.; (706) 342-9191; www.mcaam.org. This museum is designed to promote the numerous contributions of African Americans throughout the South. It includes 4 galleries as well as a wealth of research material. Tues through Sat 10 a.m. to 4 p.m. $.

The Rogers House & Rose Cottage. 179 E. Jefferson St.; (706) 342-9627. These antebellum homes can be found just off the square. The Rogers House was built in 1809 by Reuben Rogers and has been carefully restored. It's considered one of the finest examples of the Piedmont Plain–style architecture in the US. The Rose Cottage was built in 1891 by former slave Adeline Rose and was moved to this location in 1966. Miss Rose spent most of her life working for the mother of comedian Oliver Hardy. Mon through Sat 10 a.m. to 4:30 p.m., Sun 1:30 to 4:30 p.m. Free.

where to shop

Downtown Historic Madison. (800) 709-7406; www.madisonga.org. It would be impossible to pick a favorite here. Downtown has more than 45 retailers and 150 antiques dealers. The visitor center has an updated map.

where to eat

Adrian's Place. 342 W. Washington St.; (706) 342-1600. Family-style Southern cooking served up just like mom used to make. Great fried chicken to go along with classic American favorites. Daily 11 a.m. to 9 p.m. $–$$.

Amici Cafe. 113 S. Main St.; (706) 342-0000; www.amici-cafe.com. Offering pizza and pasta, this locally owned chain now has 5 locations in the region. Good food at good prices and a favorite among the locals. Daily 11 a.m. 10 p.m. $–$$.

Chop House Grille. 202 S. Main St.; (706) 342-9009. You'll want to come back here again for the laid-back atmosphere and wide selection on the menu from steaks, seafood, and prime rib to ample-size sandwiches and salads. Daily 11 a.m. to 9:30 p.m. $–$$.

Ice House Restaurant. 271 Washington St.; (706) 343-0040; www.icehouserest.com. Great food in the heart of Madison, "serving up grits and grilled," as they say. Steaks and Philly cheesesteaks with Southern sides. Tues through Thurs 5 to 11 p.m., Fri and Sat 5 p.m. to midnight. $–$$.

Perk Avenue Cafe. 111 W. Jefferson St.; (706) 342-2562; www.perkave.com/links.html. The coffee is great, but so are the baked goods. Open for breakfast, lunch, and early dinner, Perk Avenue offers a full breakfast menu with fabulous French toast. For lunch or dinner, they have homemade soups, salads, and sandwiches. Mon through Thurs 7 a.m. to 5 p.m., Fri 7 a.m. to 9 p.m., Sat 8 a.m. to 9 p.m., Sun 9 a.m. to 5 p.m. $–$$.

Tequila Express. 270 W. Washington St.; (706) 342-0729; www.tequilaexpresscafe.com/2401.html. As they say, they are not just chips and salsa. Tequila Express has a great atmosphere, serving up Mediterranean-style dishes as well as pasta, salads, and sandwiches. Mon through Sat 11 a.m. to 3 p.m., 5 to 9 p.m., closed Sun. $–$$.

Town 220 Restaurant & Catering. 220 W. Washington St.; (706) 752-1445; www.town220.com. A touch of elegant dining in Madison. Lunch includes gourmet burgers and some unusual pairing, while evenings have scrumptious steaks and seafood. Tues through Sat 11 a.m. to 2:30 p.m., Tues through Thurs 5 to 9 p.m., Fri and Sat 5 to10 p.m., closed Sun. $$.

Ye Old Colonial Restaurant. 108 E. Washington St.; (706) 342-2211. This cafeteria-style restaurant is a staple in downtown Madison. You'll find everything Southern from ribs to fried chicken to sweet potatoes and mac and cheese. Open for breakfast, lunch, and dinner. Mon through Sat 5:30 a.m. to 8:30 p.m. $–$$.

where to stay

The Brady Inn. 250 N. 2nd St.; (706) 342-4400 or (866) 770-0773; www.bradyinn.com. Two Victorian bungalows make up this quiet inn located in the heart of the historic district. It features 9 comfortable rooms and is within walking distance of many of the sites of Madison. You'll feel right at home as guests of Karen and Peter Wimbell, who grew up in the area. $$–$$$.

The Farmhouse Inn. 1051 Meadow Ln.; (706) 342-7933; www.thefarmhouseinn.com. Just outside of town at Hundred Acre Farm, the Farmhouse Inn is a true escape. This bed-and-breakfast includes 5 private guest rooms, a 2-bedroom cottage, and a 4-bedroom farmhouse, and the entire place can be reserved as a family or corporate retreat. The farm includes a fish pond, hiking trails, and a vegetable garden. $$–$$$.

The James Madison Inn. 260 W. Washington St.; (706) 342-7040; www.jamesmadisoninn.com. A boutique hotel just across the street from Madison's Town Square, the James Madison is a touch of luxury. It features 17 individually themed rooms, each with a fireplace as well as an outdoor porch. Walk to just about anywhere. $$–$$$.

Madison Oaks Inn. 766 East Ave.; (706) 343-9990; www.madisonoaksinn.com. Only half a mile from the town square, Madison Oaks Inn and Gardens is a beautifully restored 1905 Neoclassical Revival mansion. Guests have 4 rooms from which to choose and are treated as any guest in a classic Southern mansion would be. Take a dip in the pool or explore the 6-acre estate. Madison Oaks Inn also has a reputation as a wedding and events venue. $$$.

Reese-Bourgeois Cottage. 444 N. Main St.; (706) 342-4603; www.reesebourgeoiscottage.com. You'll have the place to yourself. The cottage rents just 1 guest room at the back of this 1850s home. It has its own entrance overlooking the perennial gardens and back lawn. The large, quiet room features a king-size bed and a sitting area, as well as a screened-in porch where you can sit and relax. $$.

Southern Cross Guest Ranch. 1670 Bethany Church Rd.; (706) 342-8027; www.southcross.com. For a different experience, try out Southern Cross Guest Ranch. This year-round guest ranch, horse farm, and bed-and-breakfast is just 10 minutes from downtown Madison. Home to well over 150 quality paint and quarter horses, the ranch includes a hands-on horseback riding program, as well as unguided riding opportunities. In addition to breakfast, dinner options are available. $$$.

worth more time

Lake Oconee. Lake Oconee is the reservoir that you will cross as you travel between Madison and Greensboro. A favorite recreational area, it is the fourth largest lake in the state, spanning 4 counties. There are numerous private boat ramps and several resorts on its shore.

Rock Eagle. US 441 south of Madison. This is one of those unusual sites that people are still trying to figure out. Now within a 1,500-acre 4-H Center, Rock Eagle is just that, a formation of an eagle made out of rocks. The mound, with its 102-foot wingspan, is believed to date back 1,000 to 3,000 years. Access to the effigy is permitted throughout the year and is free.

greensboro

Greensboro calls itself Lake Oconee's hometown, but it has been here far longer than the lake. Founded in 1803, it grew up as the largest retail district between Atlanta and Augusta. People came from miles around to shop here, and today the tradition continues.

These days, Greensboro is an antiques lover's dream, and scattered among the antiques shops are creative retail stores and numerous artisans. Shop 'til you drop, and take in the historic sites in the small, but well-laid-out downtown area. You'll really be surprised by the diversity you will experience. You'll find shops with imports from around the world and restaurants that will rival any European five-star offering.

getting there

Greensboro is just 19 miles east of Madison on US 278/GA 12, which will take you across part of Lake Oconee. If you are coming directly from Atlanta, take I-20 due east to exit 130, GA 44. The trip from Atlanta will take about 90 minutes.

where to go

Greene County Chamber of Commerce. 111 N. Main St.; (706) 453-7592; www.greeneccoc.org. Stop by here to get information on the history and sites of Greensboro. These guys are literally the keepers of the keys in some cases. Because this is a small town, visiting hours can be a suggestion rather than a rule, and sometimes the visitor center staff has to go with you to open the doors to some of the locations. Mon through Fri 9 a.m. to 5 p.m., Sat 9 a.m. to 3 p.m.

"The Big Store," J.H. McCommons Company. 103 S. Main St. Built in 1856, the building looks much the same as it did when it was constructed. In those days, it was the largest retail store between Atlanta and Augusta and sold everything imaginable. At one point, there was even a blacksmith shop and stable in the rear of the store. Although originally built by Charles Alfred Davis Sr., it has been owned by 4 generations of McCommons. Their motto was "from the cradle to the grave," and the store literally housed a funeral home on the upper floors and everything else in between. It now houses the Antique Mall. Opened daily.

Greene County African-American Cultural Museum (Barber House Museum). 1415 N. East St.; www.gcaacm.org. This Craftsman bungalow was the home of Dr. Calvin M. Barber, the second African-American doctor in Greene County, and now houses a museum and cultural center which seeks to preserve the history of blacks in Greene County. Tues through Fri 9 a.m. to 4 p.m., Sat on request. $.

Greene County Historical Society Museum. 201 E. Greene St.; (706) 453-7592. This museum traces the more than 200-year history of Greene County. It pays homage to notable residents and outlines the building of Lake Oconee in the 1970s. Mon through Fri 9 a.m. to 5 p.m., Sat 11 a.m. to 2 p.m. $.

Greensboro Cemetery. N. East Street. With graves dating back to the 18th century, there are soldiers here from the Revolutionary War and the Civil War as well. A little off the beaten path, it shelters some of Greene County's most prominent citizens. The chamber can give walking guides. Open daily.

Historic Mill Studio. 206 N. West St.; (770) 957-5023; www.historicmillstudio.com. The Mary-Leila Cotton Mill is the oldest mill remaining in Greensboro and is now the home of an artist retreat. Artists of all levels come from around the world to take part in workshops here.

L.L. Wyatt Museum. N. East St.; (706) 453-7592. This museum is housed in the current sheriff's office and contains artifacts dating back to the days of the gaol next door. You'll find everything from modes of restraint to centuries-old arrest warrants to moonshine stills that were seized. Call for an appointment. $.

The Old Gaol. E. Greene St.; (706) 453-7592 or (800) 866-LAKE. You'd expect to see this more in Europe than in Greensboro. Complete with ramparts, this stone structure is the old Greene County Jail. Built in 1807, it was used until 1895 when a new jail was built next door. Once inside, it doesn't take much imagination to see what conditions a prisoner might endure, given the 2-foot-thick walls and lack of amenities. Mon through Fri 9 a.m. to 5 p.m., Sat 9 a.m. to 3 p.m. Free, but you will need to get the key at the Chamber of Commerce. $.

Scull Shoals Mill Village Archaeological Site. Macedonia Church Road, Oconee National Forest; (706) 453-7592. Scull Shoals is a Historic Recreation Area in the Oconee National Forest. It was home to Georgia's first paper mill, water-powered sawmill, gristmill, and textile mills, and remnants of those buildings still remain. Call for hours. Free.

where to shop

Downtown Greensboro is one whole shopping district. Main Street between East Greene Street and South Street is lined with antiques stores and quaint shops.

Genuine Georgia Artisan Marketplace. 101 N. Main St.; (706) 453-1440; www.genuinegeorgia.com. The artisan marketplace is actually within the Big Store. It offers a wide array of handcrafted items from pottery to jewelry, glassworks to folk art. If you are looking for a unique item from Georgia, this is the place to shop. Mon through Sat 10 a.m. to 5 p.m., Sun 1 to 5 p.m.

Greensboro Antique Mall. 101 S. Main St.; (706) 453-9100; http://greensboroantiquemall.com. Within part of the Big Store, the antique mall houses more than 50 dealers in 11,000 square feet of retail space. There are some amazing finds to be had here. Mon through Sat 10 a.m. to 5 p.m., Sun 1 to 5 p.m.

Ripe Thing Market. 112 W. Broad St.; (706) 454-2155. This little roadside market will astound you with what all it contains. Not only is there locally grown produce and milk and cheeses from local dairies, but they have imported herbs, lotions, and products from all over the world. Daily 8 a.m. to 6 p.m.

where to eat

Grand Oaks Restaurant. 102 N. Laurel Ave.; (706) 453-0008; www.grand-oaks.com. This elegant old Southern home is a great setting for fine dining. The house was built in 1910 and has been fully restored and furnished with antiques and artwork. The food is exceptional. You have your choice of 2 dining rooms and a full-service bar downstairs and 3 dining rooms upstairs. Thurs through Sun 5 to 10 p.m., Sun 11 a.m. to 2 p.m. $$–$$$.

Holcomb's Barbeque. 404 W. Broad St.; (706) 453-2577. This is the real deal when it comes to down-home barbeque. In an old service station, you can smell the smoky goodness when you drive up. The pulled pork is great; the stew is even better. Thurs, Fri, and Sat 11 a.m. to 7 p.m. $–$$.

Los Torres Mexican Grill. 117 E. Broad St.; (706) 453-0092. This simple restaurant is a local favorite because of its authentic dishes and great margaritas. A favorite hangout during happy hour. Daily 11:30 a.m. to 9 p.m. $.

Washington Grass Inn. 2281 Fuller Rd.; (706) 467-2520; www.washingtongrass.com. Built in 1852, this beautiful inn is known for its elegant brunches, lunches, and dinners. Its setting on 16 acres also makes it a favorite for weddings and events. Daily, 9 a.m. to 9 p.m. $$.

The Yesterday Cafe. 114 N. Main St.; (706) 453-0800; www.theyesterdaycafe.com. Home-style cooking with generous portions, the cafe will also charm you with its setting. Featuring vintage photographs of Greensboro, you can dine on fried chicken, ribs, or grilled salmon while taking a trip back in time. Mon and Tues 11 a.m. to 3 p.m., Wed through Sat 11 a.m. to 9 p.m. $–$$.

where to stay

Goodwin Manor Bed & Breakfast. 306 S. Main St.; (706) 817-1372; www.goodwinmanor.com. Still owned by the family whose ancestors built the mansion more than a century ago, this great B&B is in the heart of downtown Greensboro. There are 5 private rooms in the mansion and a "gathering area" for those who want to socialize with other guests. Breakfasts are full-on Southern style. $$.

Jameson Inn. 2252 S. Main St.; (706) 453-9135 or (800) 527-3766. This contemporary inn was built to fit in with the historic community. It features a swimming pool as well as a business center. Breakfast is included. $–$$.

Lewis Creek Lodge. Washington Grass Inn, 2281 Fuller Rd.; (706) 467-2520; www.washingtongrass.com. The lodge is rented through the Washington Grass Inn and includes the lodge and Aunt Maddie's Cabin. This is the sort of place that you would want to come to as a group. The lodge and the cabin are self-catering, so you can come make yourself at home. $$$.

The Ritz-Carlton Lodge, Reynolds Plantation. 1 Lake Oconee Trail, Greensboro; (706) 467-0600. This luxury 5-diamond resort includes tennis, spectacular golf, and one of the best-known spas in the area. If you don't stay here, at least roam the grounds and see what you're missing. $$$.

worth more time

Iron Horse. GA 15, 11 miles north toward Watkinsville. Worth a small detour, there is a massive iron sculpture of a horse sitting in a cornfield just after you cross the Oconee River. The sculpture by Abbot Patterson was originally erected on the University of Georgia campus in Athens in 1954, but it became the subject of constant student pranks. Agriculture professor L.C. Curtis finally moved it to his farm where it still sits. In the summer, it is sometimes hard to see because of the height of the corn. (Drive by only.)

crawfordville

Crawfordville is county seat of Taliaferro County and is one of those sleepy Southern towns that is just more than a crossroads, but still worth a visit. It was founded in 1878 and named for William H. Crawford, who held a long list of offices, including US senator, US minister to France, Secretary of War, and Secretary of the Treasury. But the town is best known for another son, Alexander H. Crawford, who served as the vice president of the Confederacy. (He was also a US congressman and the governor of Georgia.) Because of this, Crawfordville is part of the Civil War Heartland Trail of Georgia.

If the town looks familiar, it is because Crawfordville was used for scenes in the movie *Sweet Home Alabama*, starring Reese Witherspoon. You may have seen her strolling up Main Street, watching the town's fireworks and visiting the courthouse.

getting there

Either continue following US 278/GA 12 or get off I-20 and take GA 22 North to the four-way stop and make a right on US 278/GA 12. The highway becomes Broad Street just a few hundred yards from the stop sign, and you enter the little town of Crawfordville.

where to go

A. H. Stephens State Historic Park. 456 Alexander St. Southwest; (706) 456-2602; www.gastateparks.org/AHStephens. The A. H. Stephens State Historic Park is adjacent to the homestead and is best known for its equestrian facilities and campground. There are 12 miles of trails for horseback riders to explore, and they can even overnight in a primitive campground. Other activities include geocaching, fishing and boating in the park's 2 lakes, a junior Olympic-size swimming pool, picnic areas, and a children's playgrounds. Park hours: 7 a.m. to 10 p.m.; office hours: 8 a.m. to 5 p.m. $.

Confederate Museum. Alexander Street; (706) 456-2602. Sitting next to Liberty Hall, the Confederate Museum is filled with rare artifacts. This is a hidden treasure for history lovers, no matter what your sentiments are on the Civil War. The exhibit includes a recount of the "Road to War," and traces a soldier's life from his home to battlefield. Artifacts include firearms, uniforms, historic documents, and a great deal more. It's operated by the Georgia State Parks and Historic Sites. Tues through Sat 9 a.m. to 5 p.m.; Sun 2 to 5 p.m. $.

Crawfordville Baptist Church. 1125 Memorial Dr.; (706) 456-2878. The church is literally right across the street from Liberty Hall, and you may end up parking in its lot. Established in 1802, this was the first Christian church in the area and predates the town itself. The picturesque wooden structure was originally called Bethel Church and has been a gathering point for more than two centuries. Sun 10 a.m. to 1 p.m., and events. Call for access.

Crawfordville Cemetery. 1125 Memorial Dr., just behind the Baptist Church; (706) 456-2878. Explore this old cemetery, and you will truly discover Central Georgia history. Some stones are very intricate, and if you like old cemeteries, you will love this one.

Liberty Hall. 456 Alexander St. Southwest; (706) 456-2602; www.gastateparks.org/AHStephens. If you turn left at the courthouse on Monument Street, you will see the A. H. Stephens home directly in front of you a few blocks up. Called Liberty Hall, the renovated and fully furnished antebellum home is preserved as a museum. Tours of the home and its outbuildings go into great depth about Stephens's scholarly works. Stephens and his half brother, Linton Stephens, are both buried in front of the home. Wed through Sun 9 a.m. to 5 p.m.; closed Mon (except holidays), Tues, Thanksgiving, Christmas, and New Year's Day. Last tour at 4 p.m. $.

The Taliaferro County Courthouse. GA 12 and Monument Street; (706) 456-2176; http://taliaferrocounty.georgia.gov. Built in 1902, this is only the county's second courthouse. The first was erected in 1828 and torn down in 1901 to make way for the present courthouse. It was designed by Lewis F. Goodrich in the High Victorian style and is on the National Register of Historic Places. The friendly staff will gladly let you look around as long as you aren't interrupting any official business. Mon through Fri 8:30 a.m. to 5 p.m. Free.

where to eat

County Cafe. 114 Monument St. Southeast; (706) 456-1067. Just across the street from the courthouse, County Cafe serves up home-style breakfast, lunch, and dinner. A local standout. Mon through Sat 7 a.m. to 8 p.m. $–$$.

Heavy's Barbeque. 2288 Sparta Rd. Southeast; (706) 456-2445. Tucked away in an old homestead, it's worth hunting down. Known for its "stews and Ques," Heavy's has been around since 1970. Check out the butt-kicking machine by the door. $.

where to stay

A. H. Stephens State Historic Park. 456 Alexander St. Southwest; (706) 456-2602; www.gastateparks.org/AHStephens. The 1,177-acre Georgia State Park includes 4 cottages along with trailer, RV, and tent campsites. There are a junior Olympic-size pool, 2 lakes, and equestrian facilities on-site. $.

Higdon Inn and Gardens. 301 W. Greene St.; (706) 453-2511; www.higdonhouseinn.com. In a Victorian home built in 1810, the inn sits on 2 acres of landscaped gardens. A favorite wedding venue because of the setting, the inn has 5 private bedrooms as well as an outdoor pool and exercise room. $$.

day trip 04

river city, ga:
augusta

Venture due east from Atlanta along I-20 and you'll run into one of Georgia's classic Southern cities, Augusta. Known as the "Garden City" because of the numerous gardens associated with its homes, most people recognize the name because of the Augusta National, home of the Masters Golf Championship. But Augusta is so much more than its well-manicured golf courses.

Augusta grew up on the banks of the Savannah River, which was a major thoroughfare for sending goods to and from the coast. The August Canal system of the mid-1800s was influential in making the entire area grow. A visit here is not just a walk through history, but an opportunity to enjoy the riverfront setting, explore the historic neighborhoods, or enjoy a growing art scene.

The drive is an easy one and worth the 2.5-hour journey. Along the way you will pass the exits for many of the names listed in the earlier day trips of this chapter. Feel free to stop and make this sojourn from Atlanta a bit more than a day trip. You won't be sorry. Augusta offers the perfect vacation from your vacation.

augusta

A combination of a modern lifestyle in a historic setting, Augusta likes to call itself "the best kept secret on the Savannah River." Its colorful history includes Native American settlements, Civil War skirmishes, strides in industry, and recognition for music, most notably

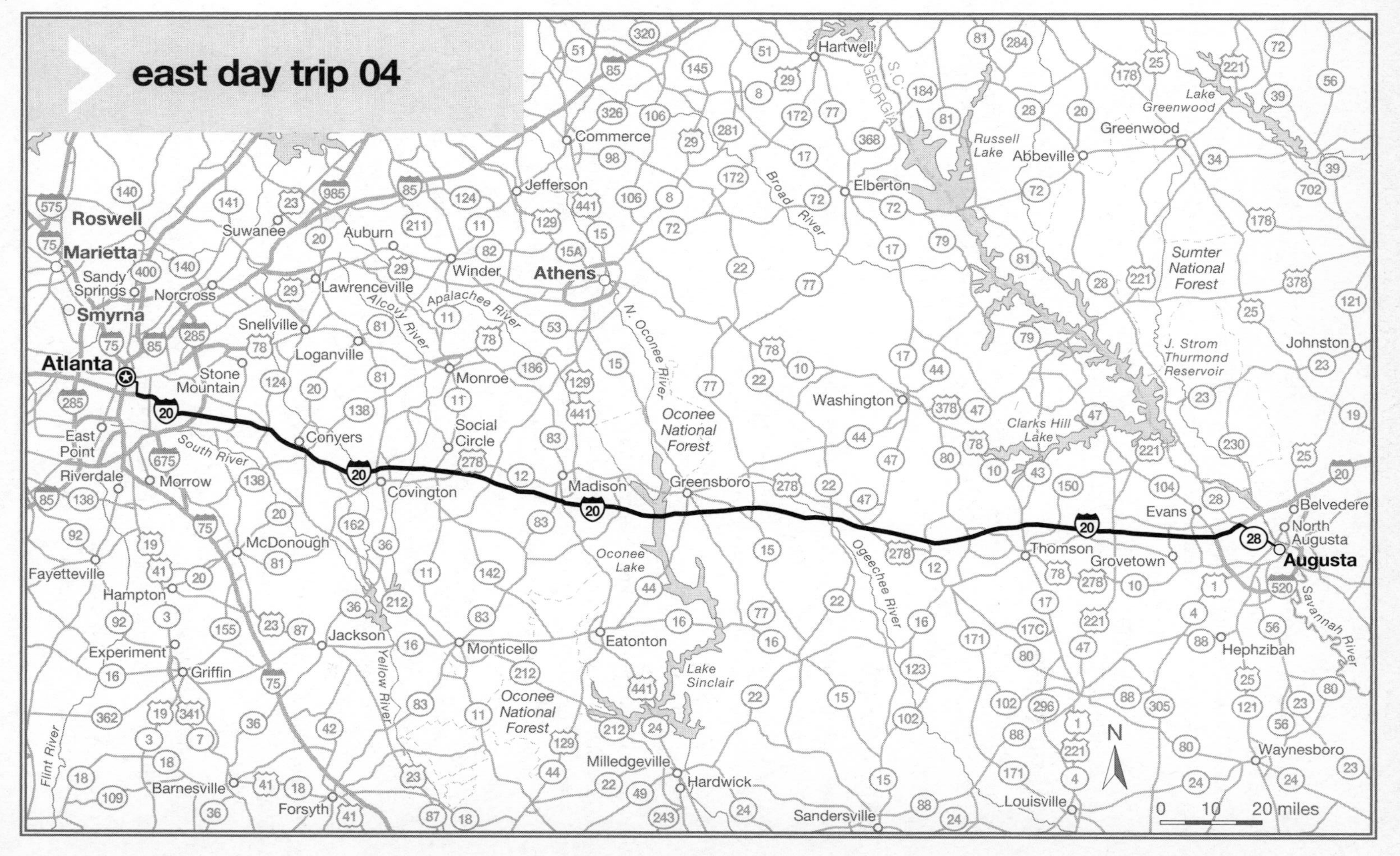
east day trip 04
Roswell
Marietta
Sandy Springs
Smyrna
Atlanta
Norcross
Suwanee
Auburn
Winder
Athens
Jefferson
Commerce
Lawrenceville
Snellville
Loganville
Stone Mountain
Monroe
Conyers
Social Circle
Covington
Madison
Greensboro
Washington
Hartwell
Elberton
Abbeville
Greenwood
Johnston
Evans
Belvedere
North Augusta
Augusta
Thomson
Grovetown
Hephzibah
Waynesboro
Louisville
Sandersville
Hardwick
Milledgeville
Eatonton
Monticello
Jackson
McDonough
East Point
Riverdale
Morrow
Fayetteville
Hampton
Experiment
Griffin
Barnesville
Forsyth
S.C.
GEORGIA
Russell Lake
Lake Greenwood
Sumter National Forest
J. Strom Thurmond Reservoir
Clarks Hill Lake
Oconee National Forest
Oconee Lake
Lake Sinclair
Broad River
Apalachee River
Alcovy River
N. Oconee River
South River
Yellow River
Ogeechee River
Savannah River
Flint River
N
0 10 20 miles

being the inspiration for the legendary late James Brown. In homage to him, the city's current slogan is "We feel good."

Augusta was founded in 1736 and boasts a large number of buildings on the National Historic Register. Exploring the downtown area will take the bulk of your day, and you will be surprised by just how much there is to do. Visit the river, stroll tree-lined streets, listen to music, or explore the galleries and museums. You'll be impressed by the Southern charm of the city and the Southern hospitality of its inhabitants.

getting there

Take I-20 east from downtown Atlanta. Augusta is 140 miles east of Atlanta, and it will take you about 2.5 hours to get there. Get off I-20 at exit 199, Washington Road/GA 28 and follow signs to downtown.

where to go

Augusta Visitor Information Center/Augusta Museum of History. 560 Reynolds St.; (706) 722-8454; www.augustaga.org or www.augustamuseum.org. The visitor center is in the lobby of the history museum and is a good start to help you get oriented for the area's attractions. It can also offer discounts to some locations. The museum provides an overview of Augusta's story dating from prehistoric times to the present day. Make sure to take time for the movie *Augusta's Story*.

Augusta Canal Heritage Site. Enterprise Mill, 1450 Greene St.; (888) 659-8926 or (706) 823-0440; www.augustacanal.com. This unusual site was Georgia's first National Heritage Site and encompasses both the man-made canal and the natural area surrounding it. Associated with the National Park Service, the Augusta Canal Site allows visitors to experience part of what is the nation's only industrial power canal (built in 1845) still in use for its original purpose. There is an interpretive center, and tours are offered, or you can explore on your own on foot or by bicycle, canoe, or kayak. You may even choose to take a trip on a replica canal cargo boat which is particularly nice at sunset. Tours take up to 3 hours. Interpretive center: Mon through Sat 9:30 a.m. to 5:30 p.m. (8:30 a.m. in July and Aug), Sun 1 to 5:30 p.m. $.

Augusta Cotton Exchange. 32 8th St.; (706) 432-3332. Built in 1866, this huge brick structure was once the second largest cotton exchange in the world, processing more than 200,000 bales of cotton a year. The building housed offices for the brokers as well as the trading floor. Women were not allowed inside the Exchange, and it was known as being a "man's getaway" where they held after-hours cockfights and other gaming activities. It is now the downtown branch of Georgia Bank and Trust. Mon through Fri 9 a.m. to 4 p.m.

Augusta National Golf Course. 2604 Washington Rd.; (706) 729-9190; www.augusta.com. Well, we knew you'd want to see it, but don't count on getting in. The Augusta

National is a private club, so you can't just drive up to the clubhouse, but they are used to people taking photos near the sign.

Boyhood Home of President Woodrow Wilson. 419 7th St.; (706) 722-9828; www.wilsonboyhoodhome.org. This fully restored home in the heart of Augusta's historic garden area was where Wilson lived during the Civil War and witnessed Reconstruction. Built in 1859, in this house the president was known as "Tommy." The grounds of the brick structure include a service building which houses a 1860s kitchen, a laundry room, a wood storage room, and 2 servant's rooms. Across the backyard was a carriage house. Tues through Sat 10 a.m. to 5 p.m. $.

Ft. Gordon Signal Corps Museum. Building 29807, Fort Gordon; (706) 791-2818; www.signal.army.mil/ocos/museum. Fort Gordon is the home of the US Army's Signal Corps, and this museum contains an extensive collection of communication artifacts from all the major wars. The museum provides training and education to the soldiers, military dependents at Fort Gordon, and the general public on all aspects of the history of the Signal Corps, the development of Fort Gordon and vicinity, and the US Army. Tues through Fri 8 a.m. to 4 p.m.

Lake Omstead Stadium. 78 Milledge Rd.; (706) 736-7889; http://web.minorleaguebaseball.com. This 4,322-seat stadium opened its doors in 1995 and is home to Augusta's level A minor league baseball team, the Greenjackets (the Southeastern division of the San Francisco Giants). The Greenjackets play from March through September so check their schedule for games and seat pricing. When the team isn't playing, the stadium also gets plenty of use hosting high school baseball games, concerts, and community events.

The Lucy Craft Laney Museum of Black History. 1116 Phillips St.; (706) 724-3576; www.lucycraftlaneymuseum.com. In Ms. Laney's former home, this museum seeks to promote and preserve black history. Lucy Craft Laney was considered one of Georgia's most influential black educators. She founded Augusta's first black kindergarten, the Lamar

that green jacket

Ever wonder why the winner of the prestigious Masters Golf Tournament dons a ***green jacket*** *as he's awarded his trophy? Members of Augusta National Golf Club began wearing the jackets with the club emblem on the pocket during the 1937 Masters so visitors would know who to go to if they had questions. When Sam Snead won the tournament in 1949, he was presented a jacket, a tradition which has continued to this day. There are only about 300 members of Augusta National, all there by invitation only.*

Nursing School for black women, and the Haines Normal and Industrial Institute, where the Lucy Laney Comprehensive High School is now located. The museum's exhibits are designed to show the history of blacks in the Central Savannah River Area. Tues through Fri 9 a.m. to 5 p.m., Sat 10 a.m. to 4 p.m., Sun by appointment, closed Mon.

Meadow Garden. 1320 Independence Dr.; (706) 724-4174; www.historicmeadowgarden.org. One of Georgia's oldest homes, Meadow Garden was built prior to 1791 by the youngest signer of the Declaration of Independence, George Walton. The home has been beautifully restored and houses period furniture that gives you a sense of life back in that time period. The grounds also encompass a 1700 medicinal herb garden, kitchen garden, and weaver's garden. The museum shop has some fun souvenirs of the era. Mon through Fri 10 a.m. to 4 p.m. $.

Morris Museum of Art. 1 10th St.; (706) 724-7501; www.themorris.org. This museum is dedicated to promoting Southern artists and the Southern heritage. In addition to its galleries, the Morris offers public programs such as storytelling sessions, readings, concerts, lectures, conversations with artists, and art-making workshops. Tues through Sat 10 a.m. to 5 p.m., Sun noon to 5 p.m. Closed Mon and major holidays

Phinizy Swamp Nature Park. 1858 Lock & Dam Rd.; (706) 796-7801; www.phinizyswamp.org. If you have never visited a swamp, this 1,150-acre preserve just 7 miles south of downtown is a great place to start. Wildlife spotted here includes herons, red-tailed hawks, alligators, and even bobcats. The park is also home to the Southeastern Natural Sciences Academy, which promotes environmental stewardship through education, research, and public outreach.

Riverwalk. 4 8th St. The 2-tiered walkway along the Savannah River begins at the visitor center and runs for 3 blocks but is at the center of historic downtown Augusta. There are 2 museums, the Jessye Norman Amphitheater (named for the local-born opera star), and numerous restaurants nearby. Historical markers along the walk call attention to relevant events and people, including William Bartram, America's first naturalist, who explored Georgia during the time of the American Revolution. This is also the site of many cultural activities, including free jazz concerts in the amphitheater during summer months.

Sacred Heart Cultural Center. 1301 Greene St.; (706) 826.4700; www.sacredheartaugusta.org. Sacred Heart Cultural Center is a former Catholic church built in 1900. Services ended here in 1971, but this beautiful structure is definitely worthy of a visit. Now on the National Register of Historic Places, it continues to be home to various cultural activities including choral concerts, art exhibits, and holiday events. Guided tours are available as well as a gift shop featuring artwork by local artisans. The former rectory is now home to the business offices of 7 arts groups: the Art Factory, Augusta Ballet, the Augusta Children's Chorale, the Augusta Choral Society, the Augusta Players, the Augusta Symphony, and the Greater Augusta Arts Council. Sacred Heart Cultural Center serves individuals from across the Central Savannah River Area and visitors from throughout the nation and beyond. Mon through Fri 9 a.m. to 5 p.m. Free.

Sibley Mill and Confederate Powder Works Chimney. 1717 Goodrich St.; (706) 823-0440; www.nps.gov/nr/travel/augusta/sibleymill.html. The tower is the only remaining structure of the Confederate Powder Works, which operated in Augusta to service the Confederate Army. Built on the Augusta Canal, the Powder Works themselves were destroyed after the war and the land confiscated. Bricks from the demolished powder works were used in the construction of the Sibley Mill between 1880 and 1882. Accessible any time free of charge.

Springfield Baptist Church. 14 12th St.; (706) 724-1056; www.historicspringfieldbaptist church.org. Founded in 1787, Springfield is the oldest independently formed black Christian church in the US still holding regular services on its original site. The old clapboard sanctuary, constructed in 1801 for St. John United Methodist Church, was purchased by Springfield in 1844 and is Augusta's oldest church structure. A second structure on the site was built in 1897 to help house the expanding congregation. Mon through Fri 10 a.m. to 4 p.m. Free, but guided tours available for small fee.

St. Paul's Episcopal Church. 605 Reynolds St.; (706) 724-2485; www.saintpauls.org. This old church sits on the spot where Fort Augusta once stood, and there are markers in the cemetery commemorating it. The church itself was established in 1750, but several buildings have stood on the site. The building today was built in 1919. Explore the church and its historic graveyard. Services are Sun at 8 a.m. and 10 a.m. and Wed at noon.

where to eat

The Bee's Knees. 211 10th St.; (706) 828-3600; www.beeskneestapas.com. The tasty tapas menu allows you to sample a wide variety of flavors. Items vary from omelets to cheese plates, tuna tartare, and stuffed portobello mushrooms. The Bee's Knees also features a great outdoor patio, making it a fine place for drinks and a snack, as well as lunch or dinner. Tues through Thurs 5 to 11 p.m., Fri through Sun 5 p.m. to midnight, Sun brunch 11:30 a.m. to 3:30 p.m. $–$$.

Blue Sky Kitchen. 990 Broad St.; (706) 821-3988. Blue Sky stands for the blue skies of the Caribbean. Their eclectic menu ranges from spicy black bean soup to Cuban sandwiches and more. Lunch only daily 10 a.m. to 2 p.m. and then dinner on the first Fri of the month from 5 to 10 p.m. $–$$.

Boll Weevil Cafe. 10 9th St.; (706) 722-7772; thebollweevil.com. Located in an old cotton warehouse near Riverwalk, the Boll Weevil serves up Southern cuisine like fried green tomatoes and shrimp and grits. The desserts are to die for, and there are more than 30 from which to choose. $–$$.

Calvert's. 475 Highland Ave., Surrey Center; (706) 738-4514; www.calvertsrestaurant.com. Named for owner/chef Craig Calvert, Calvert's is a longtime favorite in Augusta. Seafood and steaks are the mainstay, but you've never had either like this. Tues through Sat 5 to 10 p.m. $$–$$$.

French Market Grille. 425 Highland Ave., Surrey Center; (706) 737-4865; www.thefrenchmarketgrille.com. Locally owned, this casual restaurant will make you think you are in New Orleans with its distinctive Cajun menu. Jambalaya, she-crab soup, and red beans and rice will fill you up. The bar scene here can be hopping, especially when there is live music. $–$$.

Joe's Underground Cafe. 144 8th St.; (706) 724-9457. A quirky little dive bar, Joe's really is located underground, beneath a former bank. Its large menu includes sandwiches, wraps, salads, and great pizza. They also feature live music most nights. Smoking is allowed at Joe's, but kids are not. Mon through Fri 11:30 a.m. to 2:30 a.m.; Sat 5 p.m. to 1:30 a.m.; also open Sun. $–$$.

La Maison on Telfair. 404 Telfair St.; (706) 722-4805; www.lamaisonontelfair.com. Fine international cuisine in the heart of Dixie. La Maison is actually an 1853 Southern mansion that exudes the elegance of the period. The food is inventive and includes German, French, and Italian influences. It has one of the best-stocked wine cellars in Augusta. If you are not up for the formality of the main restaurant, you may choose the more casual Veritas Wine and Tapas Lounge where smaller bites are available. Mon through Sat 5 p.m. to midnight, closed Sun. $$–$$$.

Luigi's. 590 Broad St.; (706) 722-4056; www.luigisinc.com. Luigi's first opened its doors in 1949, and the family still runs this local favorite. Serving up generous portions of Italian and Greek cuisine, you'll find people who make dining here a weekly routine. Mon through Thurs and Sat 5 to 11 p.m.; Fri 11:30 a.m. to 2 p.m., 5 to 11 p.m. $–$$.

Nacho Mama's. 976 Broad St.; (706) 724-0501; www.nachomamasaugusta.com. Fast, cheap, and good, Nacho Mama's has built a well-earned reputation in Augusta for heaping plates of nachos and massive burritos. Mon through Sat 11:30 a.m. to 10 p.m. $–$$.

1102 Downtown Bar and Grill. 1102 Broad St.; (706) 364-4075; www.1102augusta.com. This downtown bar has a wide menu ranging from burgers and salads to ribs and steaks. It's also been voted as one of downtown's best bars. A smoking establishment, you must be 18 to enter. Sun through Thurs 11 a.m. to midnight, Fri and Sat 11 a.m. to 1 a.m. $–$$.

Ruth's Family Restaurant. 3843 Washington Rd.; (706) 863-5616. Ruth's has been serving up breakfast and lunch since 1965, and while it may look like a dive, it's some of the best Southern food you'll come across. She also tries a few new ones out, like her red velvet pancakes. Ample portions for low prices. Mon through Sat 6 a.m. to 2:30 p.m., Sun 7 a.m. to 2:30 p.m. $.

Sunshine Bakery. 1209 Broad St.; (706) 724-2302. Hefty sandwiches and homemade soups are the staples here. The food is good and inexpensive, and if you are on the move with your tour of Augusta, it's a great place to swing by. Don't forget the desserts! Mon through Sat 9:30 a.m. to 3:30 p.m. $.

where to stay

Azalea Inn. 312 Greene St.; (706) 724-3454. This restored Victorian bed-and-breakfast is situated in the heart of historic Olde Town within walking distance of the business district. The quiet location has 21 rooms with private baths. Some include fireplaces and kitchens. $$.

Country Suites. Riverwalk, 3 9th St.; (706) 736-8988. Located in the heart of the historic Riverfront area, the Country Suites provides a home away from home. Close to area shopping, restaurants, and attractions, there are 136 suites available. Amenities include an indoor pool and fitness center as well as coffeemakers, hair dryers, and microwave ovens in the rooms. $$.

Partridge Inn. 2110 Walton Way; (800) 476-6888 or (706) 737-8888; www.partridgeinn.com. Known as "the Grand Hotel of the Classic South," this 120-year-old landmark is a great romantic getaway. The old 2-story building is completely modernized and has balconies with wonderful views of Augusta. The spacious comfy rooms will make you want to stay. The P.I. Bar and Grill which is located on-site is alone worth the visit. $$–$$$.

Perrin Guest House Inn. 208 Lafayette Dr.; (706) 737-9444; http://perringuesthouse.com. Once a cotton plantation, this antebellum-style bed-and-breakfast sits on 3 beautiful acres just west of downtown. There are 10 rooms from which to choose with period antique furniture, fireplaces, and Jacuzzis. There is also a business center on-site, and a continental breakfast and afternoon wine and tea are included with your room. Stroll the grounds or just sit on the porch in a rocker and enjoy. $$–$$$.

south

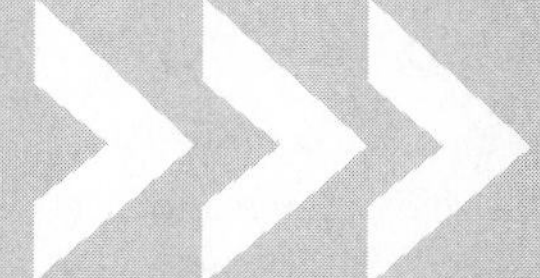

day trip 01

south

trailing miss scarlett:
jonesboro, mcdonough

While most people consider Atlanta the mecca for *Gone with the Wind,* most of the book (and movie) took place in areas south of the city. Specifically? The towns found on this day trip. Best of all, Jonesboro and McDonough are both close.

Those who live here know the story by heart, and most will happily share their take on Scarlett, Rhett, and of course, "The" War. Even if the book is not your thing, you'll enjoy the great mix of old and new found in these towns, who, while proud of their past, are not lost in it.

Start in Jonesboro where you'll discover a museum dedicated to Tara. To end the day, you will take the road to McDonough, just as Rhett and Scarlett did.

jonesboro

Long before the railroad reached Atlanta, Jonesboro was the end of the line, making it an important place to be. The budding city grew as the county seat when Clayton County was formed in 1858 and was the heart of Georgia for several years. The Battle of Jonesboro was a turning point during the Civil War because it resulted in the fall of Atlanta and thousands of deaths on both sides.

Jonesboro rebuilt itself following the war, and when you stop at the visitor center and the Road to Tara Museum, make sure you take time to explore the historic downtown area. These days many consider Jonesboro an Atlanta suburb.

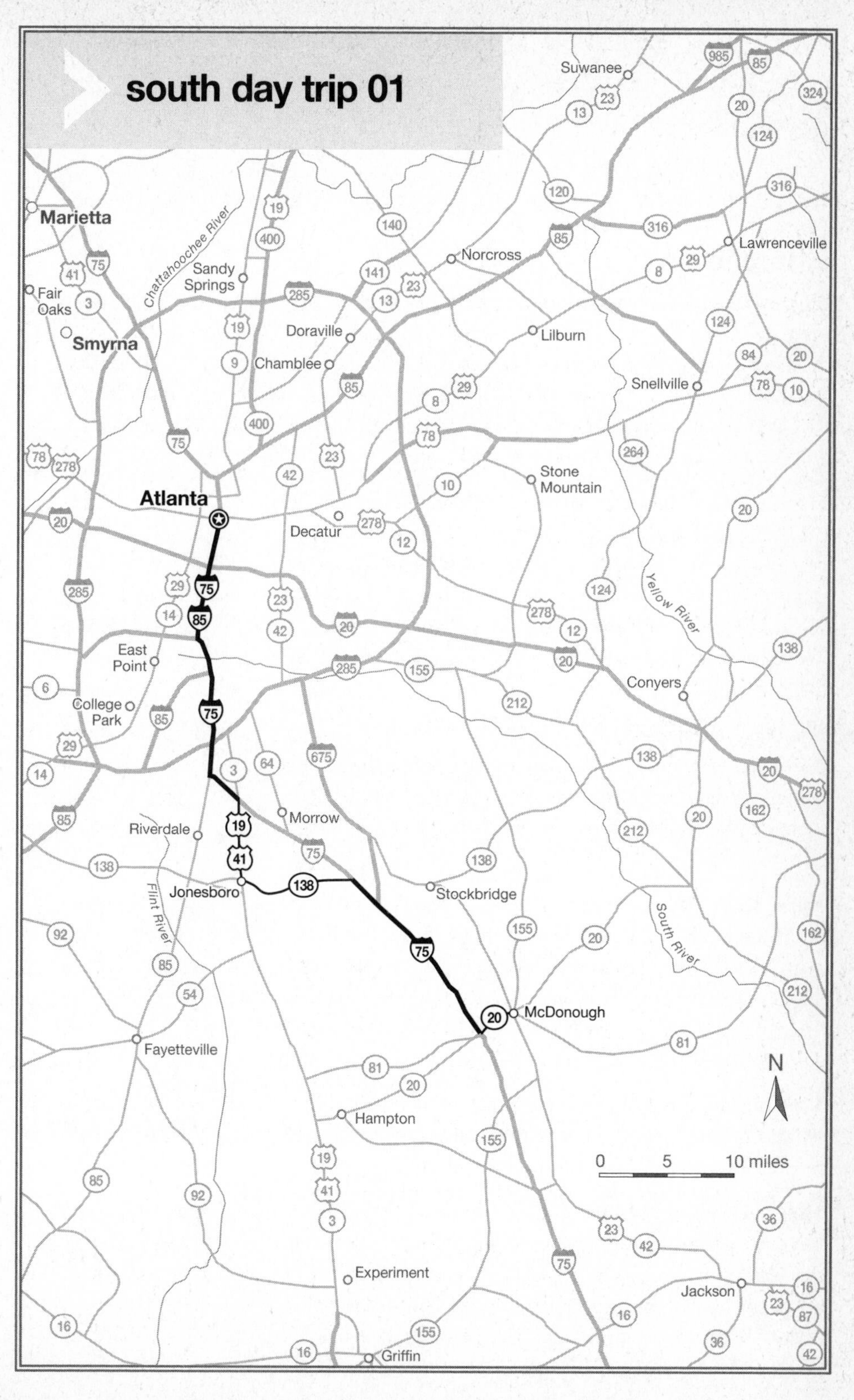

south day trip 01
Suwanee
Marietta
Fair Oaks
Smyrna
Sandy Springs
Chattahoochee River
Norcross
Lawrenceville
Doraville
Chamblee
Lilburn
Snellville
Stone Mountain
Atlanta
Decatur
Yellow River
East Point
College Park
Conyers
Riverdale
Morrow
Jonesboro
Flint River
Stockbridge
South River
McDonough
Fayetteville
Hampton
Experiment
Jackson
Griffin
N
0
5
10 miles

getting there

Jonesboro is just 25 minutes from the heart of Atlanta. Take I-75 South to exit 235, US 19 Griffin/US 41 which merges into Tara Boulevard which will take you toward downtown.

where to go

Clayton County Convention and Visitors Bureau. 104 N. Main St.; (770) 478-4800; www.visitscarlett.com. Clayton County is the legendary home of *Gone with the Wind,* and the visitor center will happily point you in the direction of anything related to the classic book and movie, as well as countless other activities and sites. The visitor center can be found in the Old Rail Depot. Constructed of granite, the building was erected in 1867. Mon through Fri 8:30 a.m. to 5:30 p.m., Sat 10 a.m. to 4 p.m.

Antique Funeral Museum/Margaret Mitchell Playhouse. 168 N. McDonough St. Morbidly fascinating and you don't even have to leave your car for what is likely the world's only drive-by Funeral Museum. Pull up behind the Pope Dickson and Son Funeral Home and a large window will open to display a collection which includes a small Civil War–issue iron casket and a horse-drawn hearse. Opposite the funeral home is the Margaret Mitchell Playhouse, where the future author of *Gone with the Wind* played as a child. Daily 9 a.m. to 5 p.m. Free.

Arts Clayton Gallery. 137 S. Main St.; (770) 473-5457; www.artsclayton.org. In a restored building not far from the visitor center, this gallery is part of a community arts program. It features monthly exhibitions by emerging and established Georgia artists, and the gallery store is a great place to shop for handcrafted gifts. Mon through Fri 9 a.m. to 5 p.m., Sat 10 a.m. to 4 p.m.

Ashley Oaks Mansion. 144 College St.; (770) 478-8986. Built in 1879 by the then-sheriff of Clayton County, Leander Hutchenson, this place was made to last. It's constructed of more than 1 million handmade bricks, and the walls are more than a foot thick. Each of the 4 large rooms downstairs stands on its own independent foundation. Ashley Oaks has been fully restored. Lunch is included with tours. Tues through Fri at 11 a.m., noon, and 1 p.m. $$.

1869 Clayton County Jail. 125 King St.; (770) 473-0197. This old building is open seasonally through the Historical Clayton society. The 2-story jail has living quarters on the lower floor and cells on the upper.

1869 Courthouse/Masonic Lodge. 146 McDonough St.; www.jonesborolodge87.com. Jonesboro Masonic Lodge #87 dates back to 1847, before the town itself was founded, and Masons have met in this building since 1869. When the Masons built their first lodge at Main and Mill Streets, the Clayton County Court held sessions in their building until they could construct their own. The two shared space again after the buildings were destroyed during the Civil War. The Masons took full ownership when the courts moved to a new building in 1898. The lodge is only open for meetings and Masonic functions.

1898 Clayton County Courthouse. 121 S. McDonough St. The old town clock is the distinguishing feature of this building which served as county seat until 2000. It was here that Margaret Mitchell sifted through historical records while doing her research for *Gone with the Wind.* The 2-story redbrick structure has been fully restored.

Patrick Cleburne Memorial Confederate Cemetery. Corner of Johnson and McDonough Streets; (770) 478-4800. This small cemetery is near the site of the Battle of Jonesboro and shelters more than 1,000 unidentified Confederate soldiers who died in that encounter. The headstones are arranged to form the shape of the Confederate battle flag. Open daily from dawn to dusk. Free.

Road to Tara Museum. 104 N. Main St.; (770) 478-4800; www.visitscarlett.com/roadtotaramuseum.html. Inside the Welcome Center, the Road to Tara Museum is a compilation of all things *Gone with the Wind.* Many of the items are from the private collection of Herb Bridges, who was the largest private collector of GWTW memorabilia. The museum exhibits costumes, scripts, photographs, as well as Civil War artifacts. Mon through Fri 8:30 a.m. to 4:30 p.m. $.

Stately Oaks Plantation. 100 Carriage Ln.; (770) 473-0197; www.historicaljonesboro.org. This Greek Revival home overlooks the site of the Battle of Jonesboro. On the grounds you will find the main house, a country store, an old schoolhouse, a cookhouse, and much more. Tours are conducted by costumed tours guides so expect a "fiddle-de-dee" or two. The plantation is also home to the Historical Jonesboro/Clayton Society. Mon through Fri 10 a.m. to 4 p.m.

scott antiques

Forget Antiques Road Show, *you'll be in awe of Scott's! While barely outside of Atlanta on the south side, there are antique lovers who plan their whole trip to Atlanta around Scott Antique weekends. Billed as the World's Largest Antique exposition, Scott's takes place in the Atlanta Exposition Center on the second weekend of each month. With 366,000 square feet of displays, you can find everything from furniture and rugs to jewelry, books, glassware, and collectables. It takes a tough customer to go home empty handed. I've actually gone shopping here with a U-Haul in anticipation of my finds. www.scottantiquemarket.com, 3650 Jonesboro Rd. Southeast, Atlanta, (404) 363-0909.*

where to eat

Butch's Chicken House. 192 Jonesboro Rd.; (770) 478-2586. Family-owned and family-run. This is a barbeque joint that prides itself on its chicken. Try the chicken melt, and you'll come back for more. Mon through Fri 6:30 a.m. to 8:30 p.m., Sat 6:30 a.m. to 2 p.m. $.

Cuban Cafe. 7929 N. Main St.; (770) 478-8676; www.cubancafe.webs.com. Authentic Cuban food in good-size portions. They even offer some traditional Cuban soft drinks and desserts. Fri and Sat 11 a.m. to 9 p.m., Sun 11 a.m. to 6 p.m. $–$$.

Dean's Barbeque. 9480 S. Main St.; (770) 471-0138. Any place this basic has got to be good. This little barbeque shack has been serving up its slow-cooked 'que since 1947, and after one taste you'll understand why it is still here. It's small, so you may have to wait, but the crowd moves quickly. For tea, you have your choice of Sweet, Mason-Dixon, or Yankee, with Yankee being the unsweetened version. Mason-Dixon is half and half. Mon through Fri 6:30 a.m. to 8:30 p.m., Sat 6:30 a.m. to 6 p.m. $–$$.

Divine Flavor Jamaican. 532 Flint River Rd.; (770) 473-4232. A local favorite, this place offers a true taste of Jamaica. Authentic food with rich spices. Ask about the daily specials. Mon through Thurs 11 a.m. to 8 p.m., Fri and Sat 11 a.m. to 9 p.m. $–$$.

Rooster's Southern Style Chicken House. 10249 Tara Blvd. The name pretty much says it all: nothing fancy, but plenty good. Mon through Thurs 11 a.m. to 9 p.m., Fri and Sat 11 a.m. to 10 p.m. $–$$.

Willie Mae's Kitchen. 7929 N. Main St.; (770) 210-6262; www.williemaeskitchenga.com. This small Cajun restaurant rivals anything this side of New Orleans. The gumbo is perfection. Tues through Thurs 6 a.m. to 8 p.m.; Fri and Sat 6 a.m. to 10 p.m.; Sun 8 a.m. to 7 p.m. $–$$.

where to stay

The Jonesboro Greenhouse (Looney-Hanes-Smith House). 139 College St.; (770) 477-1084. This bed-and-breakfast was built in 1880 by then-president of Middle Georgia College, G.C. Looney, who used it to house his family as well as students. These days, the 10-room house, with its gardens and wraparound porch, makes an inviting retreat for guests. It is also open for tours by appointment. $$.

worth more time

Atlanta Motor Speedway. 1500 Tara Place, Hampton, GA 30228; (770) 946-4211; www.atlantamotorspeedway.com. Home to NASCAR racing in Georgia, the Atlanta Motor Speedway is actually in Hampton, just south of Lovejoy. In addition to the big races, there is always something going on here like drag and stock car races. Thursday night races during the summer as well as concerts.

Lovejoy. Ten miles south on US 19 from Jonesboro. The name Lovejoy may spark some romantic reasons for the name, but it actually comes from one of the town's fathers, Frank Lovejoy. This little town had its beginnings as an agricultural center in the early 1800s, and the town is still centered around farming. It even had a working cotton gin until 1932. When you visit, you'll notice the town is divided down the middle by the railroad tracks. They are still active, but not like they used to be. Most of the buildings in town are more than 100 years old, and the community maintains its friendly, rural atmosphere.

mcdonough

McDonough is very close to Atlanta, but it could not be more different. The small town grew up around the courthouse square at the heart of town and remains the center of today's activities. The seat of Henry County, McDonough was founded in 1823 and named for Commodore Thomas MacDonough, who was a hero during the Battle of Lake Champlain during the War of 1812.

The whole downtown area looks like you've taken a step back in time and is a perfect place to spend a day exploring local history as well as some of unusual shops and restaurants. McDonough has received national recognition for its focus on maintaining its downtown area, and within a few minutes of arriving, you will understand why.

getting there

Traveling from Jonesboro, take GA 138 back to I-75 South (unless you want to travel to Lovejoy first, then you can take GA 81 east for 10 miles to McDonough). Take exit 218 toward McDonough on GA 20. McDonough is 45 minutes south of Atlanta.

where to go

McDonough Welcome Center. 5 Griffin St.; (770) 898-9311 or (866) 380-6154; www.tourmcdonough.com. This welcome center is, well, welcoming. In a 1920s-prototype Standard Oil Station, the McDonough Welcome Center is filled with ideas of things to do in the area. They can even help you get tickets to events taking place in town. Mon through Fri 8 a.m. to 5 p.m., Sat 10 a.m. to 4 p.m.

Brown House Hotel. 136 Keys Ferry Rd.; (770) 954-1456; www.tourmcdonough.com. Now home to the Henry County Historical Society, the Brown House Hotel is one of the oldest buildings in Henry County. Built in 1826, the structure was originally the home of Revolutionary War veteran Andrew McBride. It was converted to the Brown House Hotel after it was expanded in 1874. Since then it has again served as a private home before being turned over to the Historical Society and used as a base for its genealogical research.

Courthouse Square. 1 Courthouse Square; (770) 898-9311; www.mainstreetmcdonough.com. The historic Courthouse Square at the heart of McDonough looks like a movie set, and indeed, it has been on several occasions. Beautifully manicured, the square itself is overlooked by the beautiful old 3-story 1897 Henry County Courthouse with its clock tower. At the square's center is a Confederate Monument. You should make sure to take some time to walk around the shops and restaurants. There are always events and activities taking place here, so be sure and check with the visitor center about what is on the schedule.

Heritage Park. 101 Lake Dow Rd.; (770) 288-7300. This 129-acre park houses a historic village that includes a covered bridge, a community garden, an 1827 settler's log cabin, the original 2-room schoolhouse, a cookhouse, the first library building in Henry County, and a 1934 steam engine locomotive. You'll also find playgrounds, concession stands, a walking/jogging track, a senior center, softball fields, and a library. Daily 8 a.m. to 10 p.m. Free.

Historical Military Museum of McDonough at Heritage Park. 101 Lake Dow Rd.; (770) 288-7300. The museum is easy to spot. In a red barn, the Historical Military Museum contains artifacts dating back to World War I. It houses a wide selection of uniforms, rations, equipment, and supplies, most of which were donated by local residents. Also in the park you will find the Veterans Wall of Honor, an 80-foot-long granite monument depicting battle scenes. Open Mon, Wed, and Fri 10 a.m. to 3 p.m.

McDonough City Cemetery. 456 Macon St. Graves in the city cemetery date back to 1846, and among the almost 3,000 people buried there you'll find veterans of the American Revolution, the Civil War, both world wars, and the Korean War. There are also graves of many of the victims of what is known as the Great Train Wreck of 1900 in which 39 people died. You will also find a good selection of funerary art.

Southern Belle Farm. 1658 Turner Church Rd.; (770) 898-0999; www.southernbellefarm.com. Southern Belle Farm is a 200-acre working farm which allows visitors to gain an understanding of what "farm fresh" means. It includes a dairy barn exhibit, berry picking, a cornfield maze, and hayrides.

where to eat

Catfish Mahoney's. 119 Old Griffin Rd.; (770) 320-9313. Southern food cooked up like mom used to make. Mon through Sat 11 a.m. to 8 p.m. $.

Chevy's Diner and Pub. 45 Macon St.; (678) 583-8777. Some of the best burgers in town and many would argue the best outside of Atlanta. This '50s-themed restaurant serves up malts and shakes as well as local microbrews. Tues through Thurs 11 a.m. to 9 p.m., Fri and Sat 11 a.m. to 10 p.m., Sun 11 a.m. to 3 p.m. $–$$.

Cruizers Cafe. 430 Racetrack Rd.; (770) 954-1744. This restaurant and bar is very much a locals' place. The food is good and cheap, and people tend to linger. The menu features everything from burgers to salmon and fresh oysters. Daily 11 a.m. to 2 a.m. $.

Dawgs-N-Jackets. 13 Hampton St.; (770) 954-3434; http://dawgznjacketz.com. Dawgs-N-Jackets serves up far more than dawgs. In fact, they serve up everything from grilled steak to spaghetti, boasting more than 150 menu items. The catch is it's all good. Mon through Thurs 8 a.m. to 9 p.m., Fri 8:30 a.m. to 9 p.m., Sat 7:30 a.m. to 9 p.m., Sun 10 a.m. to 5 p.m. $.

Gritz Family Restaurant. 14 Macon St.; (770) 914-0448. Gritz has been on the square longer than any other restaurant, and you'll understand why it's a favorite. They bill themselves as seriously Southern in their cooking and certainly deliver. Daily specials augment the awesome fried chicken and a variety of vegetables like okra and collards. Order breakfast all day long. Mon through Sat 7 a.m. to 3 p.m., Sun 8:30 a.m. to 3 p.m. $.

OBs BBQ. 725 Industrial Blvd.; (770) 954-1234; www.obs-bbq.com. A bit away from downtown, but well worth the drive. OBs packs them in with fried catfish and pit-cooked barbeque to die for. If you've never tried fried pickles, do so here. Mon through Sat 11 a.m. to 9 p.m., Sun 11 a.m. to 8 p.m. $.

Pippins Barbecue. 40 Sims St.; (770) 957-2539; www.pippinsbarbecue.com. Slow-cooked pit barbeque that will set your mouth watering. Near the square in a small strip mall, take the effort to find it and try the stew. Tues through Sat 10 a.m. to 7 p.m. $.

PJs Cafe. 30 Macon St.; (770) 898-5373; www.pjscafemcdonough.com. Hang out on the square in this great little corner cafe. Decorated in hand-painted murals, the sandwiches and entrees are as welcoming as the atmosphere. If you've brought your pet, the dog-friendly patio is complete with places to hook leashes and water bowls for doggy refreshment. This longtime local favorite even made an appearance in the old movie *Smokey and the Bandit*. Tues through Thurs 11 a.m. to 9 p.m., Fri and Sat 11 a.m. to 10 p.m., Sun 11 a.m. to 3 p.m. $–$$.

where to stay

Best Western. 805 Industrial Blvd.; (770) 898-1006; www.bestwestern.com. This hotel features all suite rooms, an indoor pool, and a free continental breakfast each morning. $.

Hilton Garden Inn. 95 GA 81 West; (678) 827-7200; www.hiltongardeninn1.hilton.com. Clean, comfortable, and spacious, the Hilton Garden Inn is convenient to I-75 and includes a pool, fitness room, and full business center. Restaurant on-site. $–$$.

day trip 02

capital "m"s:

monticello, milledgeville

This capital "M" day trip takes you to special towns to the southeast of Atlanta. Both the tiny town of Monticello and the former state capital of Milledgeville have well-earned reputations for their historic architecture, and getting to either are drives that you will remember for their beauty.

Monticello is one of those towns that has been a crossroads dating back to the Native Americans and the remnants of history are everywhere. Surprisingly it has not sprawled into some metropolis, but those who live there seem happy that they have been able to keep their small-town charm and you will be too.

Milledgeville was once the capital of Georgia and even though Atlanta claims that title now, the buildings of the town remain significant.

monticello

Monticello is one of those almost picture-perfect Southern towns. The county seat for Jasper County, the entire Historic District is listed in the National Register of Historic Places, and it is probably one of the best-laid-out towns in the state. At the heart is the historic Jasper County Courthouse Square with six of the town's main roads converging there. All roads lead to Monticello!

Within the city you will find a surprising array of architectural styles including Greek Revival, Gothic Revival, Italianate, Queen Anne, Second Empire, Colonial, Neoclassical,

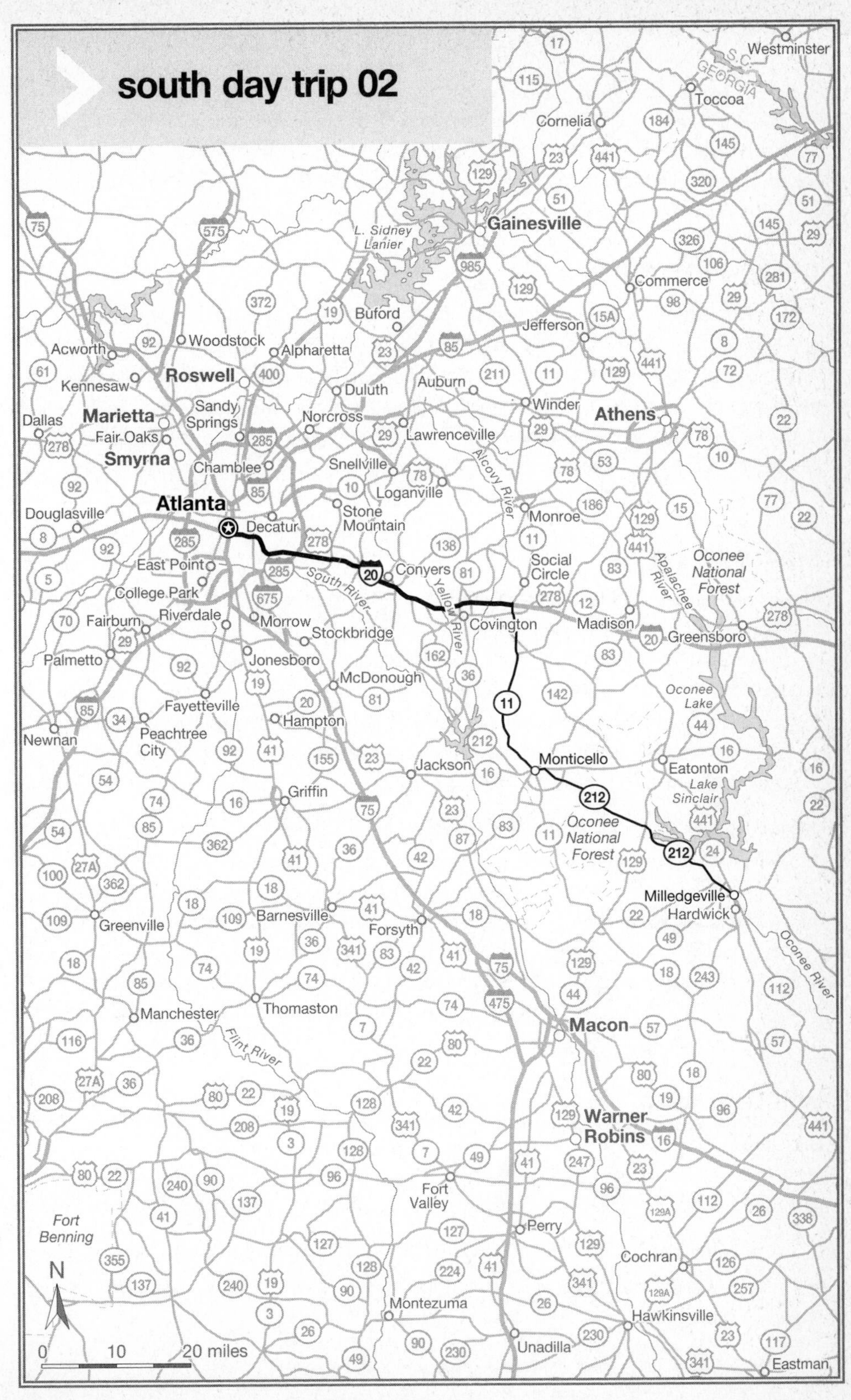
south day trip 02
Westminster
S.C.
GEORGIA
Toccoa
Cornelia
Gainesville
L. Sidney Lanier
Commerce
Buford
Jefferson
Acworth
Woodstock
Alpharetta
Kennesaw
Roswell
Duluth
Auburn
Winder
Dallas
Marietta
Sandy Springs
Norcross
Athens
Fair Oaks
Lawrenceville
Smyrna
Chamblee
Snellville
Alcovy River
Loganville
Atlanta
Douglasville
Decatur
Stone Mountain
Monroe
East Point
Conyers
Social Circle
Oconee National Forest
College Park
South River
Yellow River
Apalachee River
Fairburn
Riverdale
Morrow
Covington
Madison
Greensboro
Stockbridge
Palmetto
Jonesboro
McDonough
Oconee Lake
Fayetteville
Hampton
Newnan
Peachtree City
Monticello
Eatonton
Jackson
Lake Sinclair
Griffin
Oconee National Forest
Milledgeville
Hardwick
Greenville
Barnesville
Forsyth
Oconee River
Manchester
Thomaston
Macon
Flint River
Warner Robins
Fort Valley
Fort Benning
Perry
Cochran
N
Montezuma
Hawkinsville
0
10
20 miles
Unadilla
Eastman

English Tudor, and Craftsman. Part of that variety can be attributed to the fact that this town's rich history dates back to the 1600s! Explore the square and wander the streets to see the almost countless stately homes. Make sure you stop by the Chamber of Commerce and get a copy of the driving tour so you can see all of the homes listed.

getting there

A little more than an hour from Atlanta, Monticello is located virtually midway between I-20 and I-75. We recommend that you take I-20 East and get off at the Social Circle exit 98 and take GA 11 South. This will take you along part of what is called the **Monticello Scenic Byway.** GA 11 and GA 83, which runs roughly parallel to it, were routes once used by Native Americans as well as evangelical Methodist circuit riders as they crossed the state. (GA 83 was also part of the Seven Island Stage Coach Road that ran from Augusta to New Orleans and the Natchez Trace.) GA 11 will take you right into Monticello.

where to go

Monticello-Jasper Chamber of Commerce. 119 Washington St.; (706) 468-8994; www.historicmonticello.com. Right on the square in what used to be an old general store, the chamber staff will provide maps (including the Monticello Historic District Driving Tour) and suggestions for places to visit during your stay. The building also serves as the trailhead for the Monticello Scenic Byway, which runs along GA 11 and GA 83 North beginning at the square. If you followed our suggestion, you would have come in on the GA 11 portion. Mon through Fri 10 a.m. to 6 p.m., Sat 10 a.m. to 1 p.m.

Jasper County Courthouse. 126 W. Green St. on the Square; (706) 468-4932. If this courthouse looks familiar, it is because it was the one used in the 1991 movie *My Cousin Vinnie*. Built in 1907 of Georgia marble and brick, it features a hexagonal cupola clock tower and front portico held up by 4 massive Corinthian columns. Take the time to go inside and see the beautiful stained woodwork and cast-iron staircase leading to the upstairs courtroom. There is a stained-glass skylight in the dome that can be seen from the main floor foyer. This is still a working courthouse, so expect security. Mon through Fri 8:30 a.m. to 5 p.m.

where to eat

Big Chic. 229 W. Greene St.; (706) 468-8576. Southern fried chicken is their specialty, and they do it up right. Mon through Thurs 10 a.m. to 8 p.m., Fri 10 a.m. to 9 p.m., Sat 10 a.m. to 8 p.m. $.

D & D's Continental Cafe. 107 W. Washington St.; (706) 468-2587. A tasty little pizza and pasta place right on the square. Wed through Sat 11 a.m. to 9 p.m., Sun 10 a.m. to 2 p.m. $.

Dave's Barbeque. 114 Frobel St.; (706) 468-0213. Not just some of the best barbeque in town but a great selection of soul food. Mon through Thurs 7 a.m. to 8 p.m., Fri and Sat 7 a.m. to 9 p.m. $.

Red Clay Gallery & Cafe. 139 W. Washington St.; (706) 468-8090. Dine on Southern fare while enjoying the works of local artists. Tues through Sun 6 a.m. to 2:30 p.m. $.

Tillman House. 247 W. Washington St.; (706) 468-6952. Home cooking served up buffet style, this is a longtime favorite. Tillman's also serves breakfast all day long. Mon through Fri 6 a.m. to 2 p.m. $.

where to stay

The Warren House. 380 Persons St.; (706) 468-8205. In the downtown historic district, this home has 3 rooms available. You can rent individual rooms or even reserve the whole house. $$.

milledgeville

There is not enough room to put down everything that needs to be said about Milledgeville, which gives itself the subheading of "capitals, columns, and culture." At the very center of the state, the town served as Georgia's capital from 1802 to 1868. As such, it boasts all the things you'd expect in a capital city—grand homes, impressive buildings, and even an arboretum.

Prosperous and a seat of power, Milledgeville was known throughout the South for its culture. Then the Civil War brought that to a crashing halt. During Reconstruction, the capital moved to Atlanta, and Milledgeville moved forward, reinventing itself by building schools. Middle Georgia Military and Agricultural College (later Georgia Military College) was erected on the statehouse square, and the Georgia Normal and Industrial College (later Georgia College & State University) was constructed where the state penitentiary once stood.

Through these institutions, the city was able to maintain some of its earlier prominence. Take a trolley ride and explore some of this incredible town, and by all means, bring your camera. This is considered a top stop on the Antebellum Trail.

getting there

From Monticello, Milledgeville is a straight shot, taking you about 40 miles. You'll take GA 212 the entire way. If you come from Atlanta, it's about 90 minutes. Take I-20 east 56 miles to exit 114 and then take US 129/441 and GA 24 toward Eatonton. It will be about 40 miles off the interstate, and you will pass through Eatonton.

where to go

Milledgeville Convention and Visitor's Bureau. 200 W. Hancock St.; (800) 653-1804 or (478) 452-4687; www.visitmilledgeville.org. The folks at the visitor center take obvious pride in their town, and you'll find more than enough information to help you find your way around. A "must do" is the trolley ride, which starts here and operates at 10 a.m. Mon through Fri and 2 p.m. on Sat ($$).

Andalusia Farm. 4 miles north of Milledgeville on the west side of US 441; (478) 454-4029; www.andalusiafarm.org. This 544-acre estate was the home of acclaimed Southern writer Flannery O'Connor. She spent much of her teenage years here and then returned for the 14 years before her death. She was known for the peacocks she raised, and they still wander the estate. Tours are self-guided and in addition to the main house and the grounds, there is a gift shop which of course sells the O'Connor novels. Open Mon, Tues, Thurs, Fri, and Sat 10 a.m. to 4 p.m.

Central State Hospital Museum. Broad Street, on the grounds of Central State Hospital; (478) 445-4878. The Central State Hospital was Georgia's first mental hospital. On its grounds is a small museum dedicated to its history as well as the treatments used in its almost 2 centuries of existence. The hospital first went under the dubious name of the Georgia Lunatic Asylum when it opened in 1842, to take care of "lunatics, idiots and epileptics." At one point, it had more than 100 buildings and housed 1,100 patients. The museum is on Broad Street in an 1891 train depot across from the CSH Auditorium. Call for an appointment.

Lockerly Hall. 1534 Irwinton Rd.; (478) 452-2112; www.lockerlyarboretum.org. This beautiful 50-acre public garden and educational facility dates to the 1800s. Lockerly Hall was built in 1849 on the site of another mansion that had been named Rose Hall because of the numerous Cherokee roses on the property. The arboretum is a nonprofit dedicated to the natural environment, history, and conservation of the middle Georgia region. Mon through Fri 8:30 a.m. to 4:30 p.m.; Sat 9 a.m. to 1 p.m.; closed Sun. Lockerly Hall tours are conducted Mon, Tues, and Wed. Grounds are free to the public.

Marlor House. 200 N. Wayne St.; (478) 452-3950; www.milledgevillealliedarts.com. This impressive complex of 3 historic homes was built by local architect John Marlor and now house the Milledgeville-Baldwin County Allied Arts Center. The original home is the most prominent and was built in 1830 as a wedding gift to Marlor's wife. Gallery hours: Mon through Fri 9 a.m. to 4:30 p.m. Free.

Memory Hill Cemetery. Liberty and Franklin Streets; www.friendsofcems.org/MemoryHill. You could virtually trace Georgia's history through the tombstones found here. Established in 1809 as a Methodist cemetery, it quickly became Milledgeville's main burial ground. Here you can find the graves of a wide variety of people from state legislators and authors like Flannery O'Connor to slaves and patients from the state lunatic asylum. The grounds are well maintained, and there is some beautiful funerary art.

Old Capital Building. 201 E. Greene St.; www.gmc.cc.ga.us or www.oldcapitalmuseum.org. Sitting in the middle of the Georgia Military College campus, the Old Capital Building still commands with its presence. When it was built in 1804, it was the highest point in town, befitting its importance. The building's walls are 3 feet thick, and construction required 1,377,266 bricks, 65,000 shingles, 44 windows, and 200 feet of window glass. It is the oldest public building constructed in the Gothic style in the US. The ground floor houses a museum dedicated to regional and local history and archives. Exhibits encompass prehistoric times, early settlements, the Civil War, and the present day. Tues through Fri 10 a.m. to 4 p.m., Sat noon to 4 p.m. $$.

Old Governor's Mansion. 120 Clark St.; (478) 445-4545; www.gcsu.edu/mansion. This was Georgia's executive mansion from 1839 to 1868 when the state capital moved to Atlanta. Gen. Sherman claimed the mansion as his "prize" during his March to the Sea. Painstakingly restored, it is considered one of the finest examples of High Greek style in the US. The Old Governor's Mansion is dedicated to the history of its occupants both free and enslaved, as well as antebellum society in Georgia. Tues through Sat 10 a.m. to 4 p.m., Sun 2 to 4 p.m.

Stetson-Sanford House. 601 W. Hancock; (478) 453-1803; www.visitmilledgeville.org. This home was built in 1825 for George T. Brown by John Marlor. The clapboard house was constructed in what is called the "Milledgeville Federal" style. Characteristics include a Palladium double portico. The home first served as the state capital before being turned into a hotel for the many visiting legislators who came to the area. The spiral staircase inside is a Marlor trademark. Open by appointment and on the Historic Trolley Tour Thurs, Fri, and Sat 10 a.m. to 5 p.m.

where to eat

Aubri Lanes. 114 S. Wayne St.; (478) 454-4181; www.aubrilanes.com. Southern cooking with flair. They serve up whole catfish, crab hush puppies, fried shrimp, and oysters along with local produce. Tues through Fri 11 a.m. to 2:30 p.m., Tues through Sat 5 to 10 p.m. $–$$.

Barberitos. 146 W. Hancock St.; (478) 451-4717. All natural southwestern-style Mexican food with a good choice of burritos, tacos, salads, and quesadillas. $.

BoJo's. 3021 N. Columbia St.; (478) 453-3234. Known for their steaks and seafood, you can also get sandwiches. Mon through Sat 4 to 10 p.m. $$–$$$.

The Brick. 136 W. Hancock St.; (478) 452-0089; www.thebrick.info. Great brick-oven pizza and tasty sandwiches. Fast and friendly. Mon through Sat 11 a.m. to 11 p.m. $.

Buffington's. 120 W. Hancock St.; (478) 414-1975; www.eatinthebuff.com. Creative sandwiches with a wide variety of quesadillas available. Good and affordable. Weekdays 11 a.m. to 2 a.m., Sat 11 a.m. to 1:30 a.m., Sun 11 a.m. to 10 p.m. $.

Country Buffet. 1465 S. Jefferson St.; (478) 453-0434. This place will make you want to strap on the feed bag. It's an all-you-can-eat country buffet, so be sure to bring your appetite. Mon through Fri 11 a.m. to 5 p.m. $.

Jackson's on Sinclair. 3065 N. Columbia St.; (478) 453-9744. Jackson's is on Lake Sinclair, and while it caters a lot to the boat crowd during the summer, it's always a great place to relax on the water. The food is simple—burgers, salads, and tacos—but always good. Wed and Thurs 4:30 p.m. to midnight, Fri and Sat 4:30 p.m. to 1:30 a.m. $.

Pickle Barrel Cafe. 1888 N. Columbia St.; (478) 452-1960; www.picklebarrelcafe.com. This local sports bar is known for its baskets and its nachos. It has a large menu which includes salads and wraps to wings. Mon through Fri 11 a.m. to 2 a.m., Sat 11 a.m. to 1:30 a.m., Sun 11 a.m. to 10 p.m. $.

Pig in a Pit Barbeque. 116 W. Hancock St.; (478) 414-1744. You can smell this slow-cooking barbeque from across the square. Great sweet sauces. Mon through Thurs 11 a.m. to 9 p.m., Fri and Sat 11 a.m. to 10 p.m. $.

where to stay

Antebellum Inn. 200 N. Columbia St.; (478) 453-3993; www.antebelluminn.com. In one of Milledgeville's stately historic manors, the Antebellum Inn has 6 distinctive rooms, including a pool cottage. Each has its own private bath and is furnished with antiques. Breakfast is included with your stay. $$–$$$.

Fairfield Inn and Suites. 2631A N. Columbia St.; (478) 452-5202; www.marriott.com. All rooms are suites with a continental breakfast included. Pool and fitness center on-site. $$.

Lake Sinclair Villages. 1000 Marigold Rd.; (478) 453-2068. This time-share development on Lake Sinclair offers units to rent for vacation. They come as 1- or 2-bedroom fully furnished condominiums. $$–$$$.

day trip 03

it's the little things:

senoia, gay, thomaston

These little towns are close to Atlanta, but truly a world away. Get outside the big city and into Senoia, Gay, and Thomaston, and you'll find some of the most unique and interesting small towns in the state.

In Senoia, time has stood still, and these days, the residents are making sure to keep it that way. As a favorite backdrop for movies, the city has made a concerted effort to make sure even the new buildings look old.

You'll have to pass through Gay to get to Thomaston, and Gay truly is as small as it gets. But if you can schedule your visit around the Cotton Festival each May and October, do! It's a true Southern celebration. Oh, and Gay does have a stoplight!

As for Thomaston, it has received national acclaim as a "storybook small town" and has been listed among the 100 Greatest Small Towns in America. Take the hour drive, and you'll see why.

senoia

It's all about "location" with Senoia, and in fact, this historic little town's first name was "Location," changing to Senoia in 1860. There were two railroads here, perfect for shipping peaches and cotton. While agriculture is still important to Senoia, another meaning of "location" reigns here: movie location.

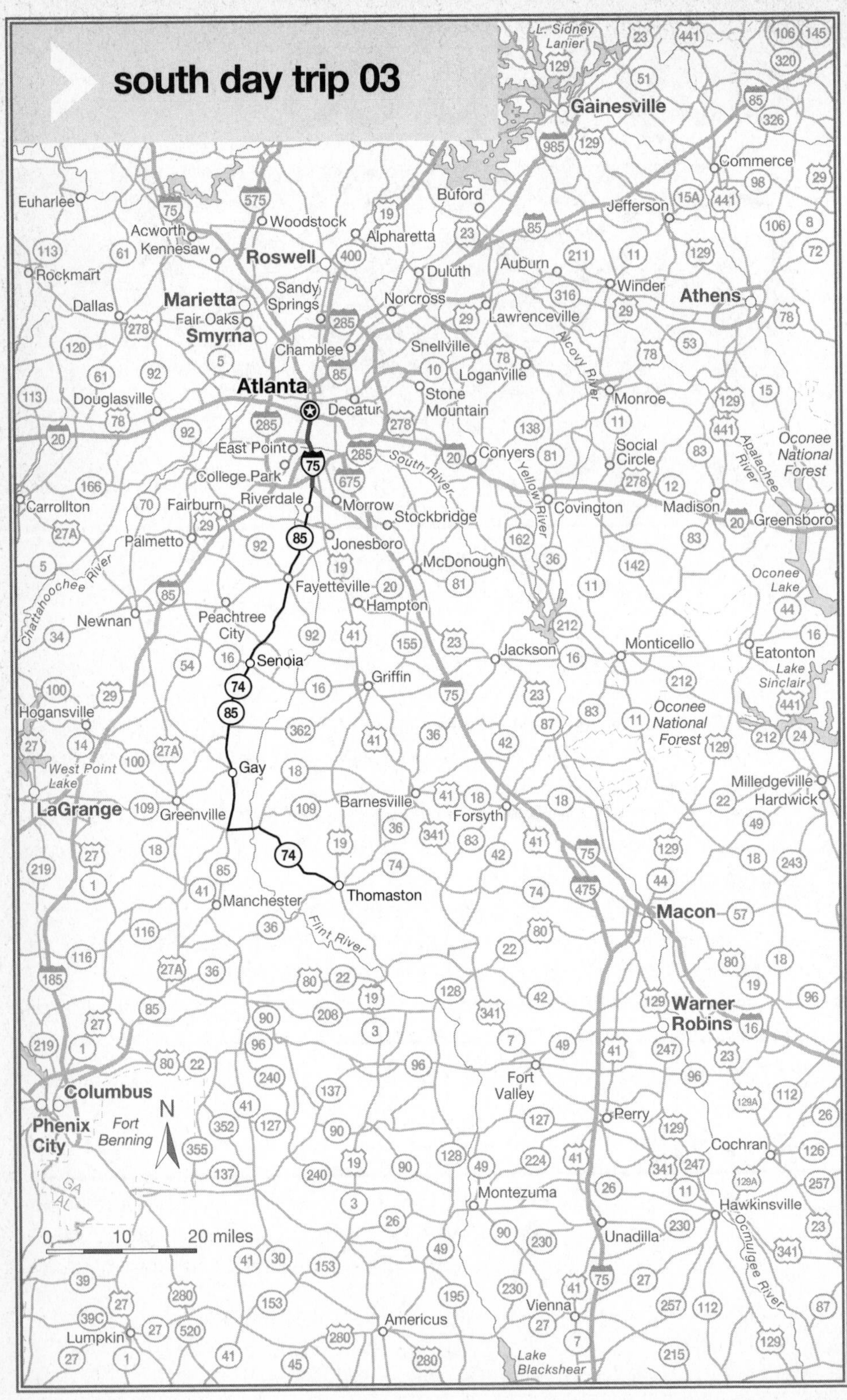
south day trip 03
L. Sidney Lanier
Gainesville
Commerce
Jefferson
Buford
Euharlee
Woodstock
Alpharetta
Acworth
Kennesaw
Roswell
Duluth
Auburn
Winder
Rockmart
Sandy Springs
Norcross
Lawrenceville
Athens
Dallas
Marietta
Fair Oaks
Smyrna
Chamblee
Snellville
Loganville
Alcovy River
Douglasville
Atlanta
Stone Mountain
Monroe
Decatur
East Point
College Park
Conyers
Social Circle
Oconee National Forest
Apalachee River
South River
Yellow River
Carrollton
Fairburn
Riverdale
Morrow
Stockbridge
Covington
Madison
Greensboro
Palmetto
Jonesboro
McDonough
Chattahoochee River
Fayetteville
Hampton
Oconee Lake
Newnan
Peachtree City
Senoia
Griffin
Jackson
Monticello
Eatonton
Lake Sinclair
Hogansville
Oconee National Forest
West Point Lake
Gay
Milledgeville
Hardwick
LaGrange
Greenville
Barnesville
Forsyth
Thomaston
Manchester
Flint River
Macon
Warner Robins
Fort Valley
Columbus
Phenix City
Fort Benning
N
Perry
Cochran
GA
AL
Montezuma
Hawkinsville
Ocmulgee River
0
10
20 miles
Unadilla
Vienna
Americus
Lumpkin
Lake Blackshear

The town is just 4 square miles in size, but you'll find over 113 sites on the National Historic Register. The fact that Senoia has been somewhat frozen in time means it is consistently used as a backdrop for films. Among them: *Fried Green Tomatoes*, *Pet Cemetery II*, *Christmas Memories*, *Mama Flora's Family*, and *Fighting Temptations*.

A movie studio (Raleigh Studios Atlanta) has even set up shop in town to keep the industry going. They were instrumental in pushing to help preserve the local "look" through something called "Project Senoia." Under the project's guidelines, vacant lots in the historic district are being bought up and structures built that will blend in with the 1800–1900 architecture. The true old buildings are generally marked by plaques so make sure to check and see if you have the real deal in front of you.

getting there

The drive from Atlanta will take less than an hour. Take I-75 south and get off at the Riverdale exit (237A), which is right at I-285. Follow GA 85 south for 26 miles to Senoia.

where to go

Buggy Museum. 72 Main St.; (770) 253-1018. See what 6 generations of a family and a town growing together looks like in this museum on the historic downtown Senoia square. The museum, complete with its weathered wood exterior, takes the viewer back to the days when the livery stable was a town fixture. The sign proudly displayed on the wall states "Proprietor W.R. Baggarly, Est. 1890." The Buggy Museum holds a nostalgic collection of items circa 1890–1930. The treasures this museum exhibits vary from antique buggies and cars, Coca-Cola memorabilia, tools, machinery, and player pianos to many other curiosities. Thurs through Sun 1 to 5 p.m., Apr through Oct. Free but donations are appreciated.

New Senoia Raceway. 171 Brown Rd.; (770) 599-6161; www.newsenoiaraceway.com. Visit the fastest 3/8-mile high-banked paved oval in Georgia for great racing! Do visit the New Senoia Raceway website, but we hope that the redesign will make it easier for both racers and spectators to find information about the events. Check back often as they add to the schedule, photos, and other areas of the site.

Raleigh Studios Atlanta. 600 Chestlehurst Dr.; (770) 599-4000; www.raleighstudiosatlanta.com. Raleigh Studios is a full-fledged Hollywood production facility. In fact, it's the East Coast offices of a California-based company that fell in love with Senoia while shooting movies like *Fried Green Tomatoes* nearby. Raleigh has been instrumental in preserving downtown Senoia by building new buildings that fit in with the look of existing structures. Call about tours.

Senoia Area Historical Society Museum. 6 Couch St. In an 1870 cottage, the Historical Society can give you context for many of the homes and businesses in Senoia. Many of their exhibits were donated by local residents to help preserve the history of their own families. Fri and Sat 1 to 4 p.m. Free.

Senoia Driving Tour of Homes. (800) 826-9382; call this number to get the map. The driving tour is offered through the Senoia Area Historical Society and Coweta County Convention and Visitor's Bureau and will take you throughout the 4-square-mile town. Because Senoia was named for the mother of William McIntosh Jr., chief of the Lower Creek Indians who officially founded as a town in 1860, the Senoia Historical Society uses an Indian princess as the symbol of its organization. Their interpretation of Princess Senoia appears on the front cover of the driving tour map.

Senoia United Methodist Church. 229 Bridge St.; (770) 599-3245; www.senoiaumc.org. Built in 1898, this beautiful building is considered one of the finest examples of Queen Anne architecture in Georgia. The exterior is stunning with its two towers, but if you have the opportunity to go inside, do. The rustic interior with its stained-glass window and balcony is simply beautiful. The congregation itself was founded in 1861 and was Senoia's first official church.

where to shop

Hollberg's Fine Furniture Store. 33 Main St.; (770) 599-3443; www.hollbergs.com. This place is a destination of its own. The first Hollberg store was founded in 1890 as a jewelry store. When furniture was added, the focus shifted, and 4 generations of Hollbergs have carried on the tradition. They have an amazing selection, and it is worth wandering the showrooms even if you think you aren't buying. Many directions in Senoia are started by saying, "Go to Hollberg's and turn."

where to eat

Country Cooking Buffet. 8116 Wells St.; (770) 599-3652. Southern food with a country buffet. A great choice of meats and fresh vegetables. Mon through Sat 11 a.m. to 7 p.m. $$.

Founders Restaurant and Bar. 20 Main St.; (770) 599-4144; www.foundersrestaurant.com. Called Founders because it is owned by descendants of Senoia's founder, Francis Warren Baggarly, the restaurant has made its own mark on the town. It serves up classic Southern food in a historic atmosphere. Tues through Sat 11 a.m. to 4 p.m. and Sun 11 a.m. to 4 p.m. $–$$.

Maguire's Irish Pub. 42 Main St.; (770) 727-3020; www.maguiresirishpub.com. There is a reason they call this Maguire's Family & Friends Restaurant. Owned by two brothers, you are likely to see their family and friends there. Known for their pub food, they have great burgers and a nice selection of wines to go along with the Guinness. Sun through Thurs 11:30 a.m. to 9 p.m., Fri and Sat 11:30 to 10 p.m. Bar open until last call. $–$$.

Redneck Gourmet. 42 Main St.; (678) 723-0235; www.redneckgourmet.com. Family-operated since 1991, the Redneck serves up sandwiches and barbeque with homemade desserts. The original is in nearby Newnan. Mon through Sat 7 a.m. to 9 p.m. $.

Senoia Coffee Company. 1 Main St.; (770) 599-8000; www.senoiacoffeeandcafe.com. Not just for coffee, you'll find biscuits and muffins for breakfast and sandwiches and salads for lunch and dinner as well as ice cream and desserts. Live Music on Fri. Mon, Tues, and Thurs 6:30 a.m. to 6:30 p.m., Wed 6:30 a.m. to 5:30 p.m., Fri 6:30 a.m. to 9 p.m., Sat and Sun 7:30 a.m. to 5 p.m. $.

Southern Country Steakhouse. 34 Chestlehurst Rd.; (770) 599-9616. Family-owned, this isn't just a good place to eat, it's a fun place to be. Steaks and burgers cooked to perfection, but there are billiards, live music, and sometimes karaoke as well. Mon through Thurs 4:30 to 9:30 p.m., Fri and Sat 4:30 to 10 p.m. $$.

where to stay

Culpepper Bed and Breakfast. 35 Broad St.; (770) 599-8182; www.culpepperhouse.com. Built in 1871 by a returning Confederate soldier, Dr. John Addy, this Victorian-era home is easily one of Senoia's most recognizable structures. And of course, it is on the National Register of Historic Places. With is manicured gardens and wraparound porch, the Culpepper is picture perfect. Three rooms are available, and each includes a private bath. $.

The Veranda Inn. 252 Seavy St.; (866) 598-3905 or (770) 599-3905; www.verandabandbinn.com. Listed on the National Register of Historic Places, this 8,000-square-foot 1906 Greek Revival mansion was originally the Holberg Hotel. Staying here, you are in good company. It was here that Margaret Mitchell interviewed Confederate veterans for *Gone with the Wind,* and William Jennings Bryan stayed at the Holberg in 1908 while running for president. The inn maintains all of its original features such as heartpine floors and chandeliers in each room. There are 9 guest rooms, but numerous other rooms to explore like the library or the parlor. $$–$$$.

gay

Gay is less than 1 mile squared in either direction, but this quiet little farming community is worth a stop. The town dates back to the early 1800s, and the downtown, while not "bustling," does have a few old buildings and businesses to explore.

The community is most active during its Cotton Pickin' Fair and accompanying Shady Days Arts and Crafts Fair in the spring and fall held at 18830 GA 85.

getting there

From Senoia, head south on GA 85 for 18 miles. It's 2-lane roads most of the way and will take you about 20 minutes. If you are coming directly from Atlanta, you will follow the same route through Senoia, and it will take about an hour.

where to go

Big Red Oak Plantation. 8428 GA 85; (706) 538-6870; www.bigredoakplantation.com. If you want to try your hand at target practice, here's your opportunity. This 3,500-acre working farm has sporting clays, skeet shooting, trapshooting, five stand, and other clay targets and all the equipment you need available for rent or purchase. A sportsman's paradise, arrangements can also be made for quail, deer, turkey, and pheasant hunting. A lodge is available on-site for hunters who would like to stay. Summer: Fri and Sat 9 a.m. to 6:30 p.m., Sun 1 to 6:30 p.m., Mon through Thurs by appointment only; the rest of the year: Fri and Sat 9 a.m. to 5:30 p.m., Sun 1 to 5 p.m. $$.

Historic Downtown Gay. GA 85 and Greenville Street. Less than a square mile, just browse the storefronts and shops.

where to eat

Kings Pizza Barn. 19470 GA 85; (706) 538-1303. Fresh pizzas and oven-baked sandwiches. Daily. $.

Ragsdales. 19470 GA 85: (706) 538-1300. This is *the* place in Gay. Basic Southern fare with friendly folks. Mon through Sat 7 a.m. to 6 p.m. $.

worth more time

Red Oak Creek Bridge. Just 10 minutes south of Gay. Take GA 85 south 5 miles and turn left on CO 281, called Covered Bridge Road. The Red Oak Creek Bridge is the longest covered bridge in Georgia and the oldest. It was built by freed slave Horace King in the 1840s and stands 391 feet in length. The bridge is still in use today so feel free to drive through like countless others have before you.

thomaston

Thomaston just oozes small-town charm, and even though it's constantly getting national recognition for being such a great place to visit, it's been able to maintain that feeling despite all the attention. As you walk around the historic square, you will still find the streets lined with local businesses such as the local bank and barber shop. You'll find some great locally owned stores in which to browse. No big chains here! Everyone pretty much knows everyone else, and they will welcome you like you belong.

The town was founded in 1825 and named for General Jett Thomas, an Indian fighter in the War of 1812. Just about every building in the downtown area has history attached to it. Walk or drive around, and you will see some incredible sites.

getting there

If you are coming from Gay, take GA 85 south to Woodbury where GA 74 splits off to the left, go east and follow the signs 20 miles to Thomaston. From I-75 South in Atlanta, take exit 77 to US 19/41 to Griffin, Zebulon, and Thomaston. The drive will take about an hour and 20 minutes.

where to go

African-American Museum. 460 Cedar Row; (706) 646-2437. This 3-room shotgun house was moved to this location to help establish a museum chronicling the lives of African Americans in Upson County. The home was originally owned by Frances Walker, who lived here for 70 years, raising a son, grandson, and great grandchildren. It contains furniture and artifacts. Apr through Oct, Sat and Sun 1 p.m.; otherwise opened by arrangement. Free.

Auchumpkee Creek Covered Bridge. Adjacent to Allen Road at US 19. The original bridge was built in 1892 and underwent reconstruction in 1997. No longer open to traffic, the 96-foot-long bridge crosses the Auchumpkee Creek and has a distinguishable town lattice truss on its side. There is a parking and picnic area at the bridge.

Central Georgia Railroad Depot. 218 N. Center St.; (404) 300-9519; http://bluebird market.wordpress.com. Thomaston's Central Georgia Railroad Depot was built in 1920, replacing an earlier frame structure. Back then, it served both passengers and freight. These days, it's home to the Bluebird Market. Open daily year-round starting at 8 a.m.

Fincher Building. 201-203 S. Center St. Dating from 1873, this is the oldest existing building in downtown Thomaston. Always containing 2 store spaces on the first floor, the second floor was originally hotel rooms before being converted to offices in the early 20th century. Present home of the Thomaston-Upson Chamber of Commerce and Thomaston-Upson Arts Council.

Glenwood Cemetery. Lee Street. With graves dating back to 1832, this is the oldest burial ground in the city of Thomaston. Still operational, restoration is under way on many of the tombstones.

Harp House. 206 Barnesville St.; (800) 218-9125. Now operated as a photography studio, this Queen Anne building was constructed in 1880 for a prominent local merchant named W.A. Harp. This is one of the two finest examples of Queen Anne architecture existing in Thomaston. Listed on the National Register of Historic Places, it is currently a photo business. Mon through Fri 10 a.m. to 5 p.m., Sat 10 a.m. to 4 p.m.

Ritz Theatre. 112-114 S. Church St.; (706) 647-5372. Still in operation as a theater and event venue, the Ritz was built in 1927. The original Mission-style facade was altered in the 1930s to its present Art Deco design. The building also houses a cafe, 2 stores, and offices on the second floor. The interior has recently been refurbished for moviegoers' comfort. Call for details.

St. Mary's AME Church. 605 N. Hightower St.; (706) 647-3826. St. Mary's houses the oldest black Methodist congregation in Thomaston. While the congregation was founded in 1867, this church was constructed in 1905. It is distinctive for its rounded corner steeple.

Thomaston Mills and East Thomaston. Barnesville Street; (706) 646-3300; www.thomastonmills.com. Founded in 1899 as Thomaston Cotton Mills, this mill is still in operation today. It remains a top employer in Upson County, producing cotton products. No tours, but the building is historically significant.

Thomaston-Upson Archives. 301 S. Center St.; (706) 646-2437. These archives help trace the history and genealogy of Thomaston and Upson County. It holds historic records and microfilm and is a fully operational research facility. It is located in the former R.E. Lee Institute Library which was chartered in 1875 as the Thomaston High School. Mon through Fri 9 a.m. to 5 p.m.

Upson County Courthouse. Courthouse Square, Main St.; (706) 647-9686. Completed in 1908 for the whopping price of $68,000, this is the third courthouse to stand on the site. Although no longer used as such, it has been renovated as county offices. Legend has it that the county commissioners placed a $10 bill in one of the columns during construction so that the county would never be broke. On the southwest corner of the courthouse lawn you'll see a cannonball that is reputed to be the first fired at Fort Sumter during the Civil War, sent here by Confederate war correspondent P.W. Alexander. Mon through Fri 8:30 a.m. to 5 p.m. Free.

Weaver House. 205 S. Bethel St. This is believed to be the oldest house in Thomaston. The first portion of the house was a log cabin constructed in the 1820s. It was added on to twice, and in 1840, Judge T.A.D. Weaver purchased the property, finishing the house essentially as it stands today. The design is influenced by the Classical Revival and Federal styles popular in that era. It is a private residence, and no tours are allowed.

where to eat

Geneva's. 419 N. Bethel St., Thomaston; (706) 646-3853. Get here early. This soul food outlet is popular with the locals because of the authentic taste and healthy portions. Mon through Sat 10:30 a.m. to 2 p.m. $.

Justin's Place. 1441 US 19 North; (706) 646 -5171. Nothing fancy, but great down-home food in a friendly atmosphere. Good burgers, sandwiches, and salads. If Justin is there, he's sure to stop by. Mon through Sat lunch and dinner. $–$$.

Peachtree Cafe. 99 Jeff Davis Rd.; (706) 647-1659. Family-owned, this Southern-style buffet restaurant serves up some of the best fried chicken in town. Friendly and family-oriented, just make yourself at home. Mon through Fri 10:45 a.m. to 7 p.m., Sat 10:45 a.m. to 3 p.m. $.

Riverbend. 202 Riverbend Rd.; (706) 647-9738. Get here early because people come for the view and the catfish. If you don't? Well, it's worth the wait. Mon through Sat 4 to 10 p.m. $.

South City Grill. 111 W. Gordon St., Thomaston; (706) 646-3333. A quaint little restaurant just off the south side of the square serving up fresh foods. The menu has a New Orleans slant to it. The po'boys are great and oysters fresh. Weekend nights, enjoy some jazz. Ask about the daily specials. Tues through Sat lunch and dinner. $–$$.

Sweet Georgia Cafe. 200 N. Bethel St.; (706) 646-2007. Open for coffee, sandwiches, and pastries. Mon through Fri 7 a.m. to 7 p.m., Sat 8 a.m. to 6 p.m. $.

where to stay

Great Harvest Farms. 315 Hunt Rd.; (706) 646-2252; www.greatharvestfarms.com. Only 3 miles from the heart of town, Great Harvest is on 25 acres of landscaped grounds. The rooms are country chic with pine walls and floors. There is a separate cottage for those who want more privacy. The grounds themselves are just stunning. There is also a pool on the property. $$.

Woodall House. 324 W. Main St.; (706) 647-7044. Just 2 blocks from the Ritz Theatre in downtown, this charming old house with its wraparound porch will be your home away from home. $$.

worth more time

The Rock Ranch. 5020 Barnesville Hwy., The Rock, GA 30285; (706) 647-6374; www.therockranch.com. You may be familiar with the fast-food chain Chick-Fil-A. Founder Truett Cathey may make a living off of chicken, but his Rock Ranch is a 1,250-acre working cattle farm with a lot of fun thrown in. Cathey designed Rock Ranch to help promote what he calls "agritainment." There is no end to the activities here which can best be described as "wholesome," such as cane fishing, paddle boating, train riding, jumping pillows, cattle feeding, etc. Rock Ranch is available for field trips and groups. Each Saturday has a theme. Open seasonably and by reservation, the Rock Ranch does not operate on Sunday.

day trip 04

tomatoes & cherries:

juliette, macon

This is another one of those fun trips that will make you want to stay more than a day. It contrasts a very small town with a very large one, and there is so much to see and experience along the way.

We start in the tiny burg of Juliette which would have likely faded into the past if not for a movie called *Fried Green Tomatoes* which quickly started bringing folks in to check out the town depicted. We end with a city that could never be forgotten—Macon. This is a place that has not just played a role in Georgia's history but in that of the US. It has also given us legendary musicians and bands.

juliette

This tiny town would likely go unnoticed if it weren't for Hollywood. The 1991 movie *Fried Green Tomatoes* took over the town and turned it into a destination. But despite the Hollywood panache, Juliette remains a simple crossroads of a community that just oozes Southern charm.

Juliette grew with the coming of the railroad in 1882 and was named after Juliette McCrackin, who was the daughter of one of the engineers who built that railroad. It grew into a thriving mill town after two gristmills were constructed on the Ocmulgee River. When they ceased operations in 1959, the town slowly became a virtual ghost town until its rustic looks captured the attention of movie scouts. Two lesser known movies (*Born to Kill,* 1974,

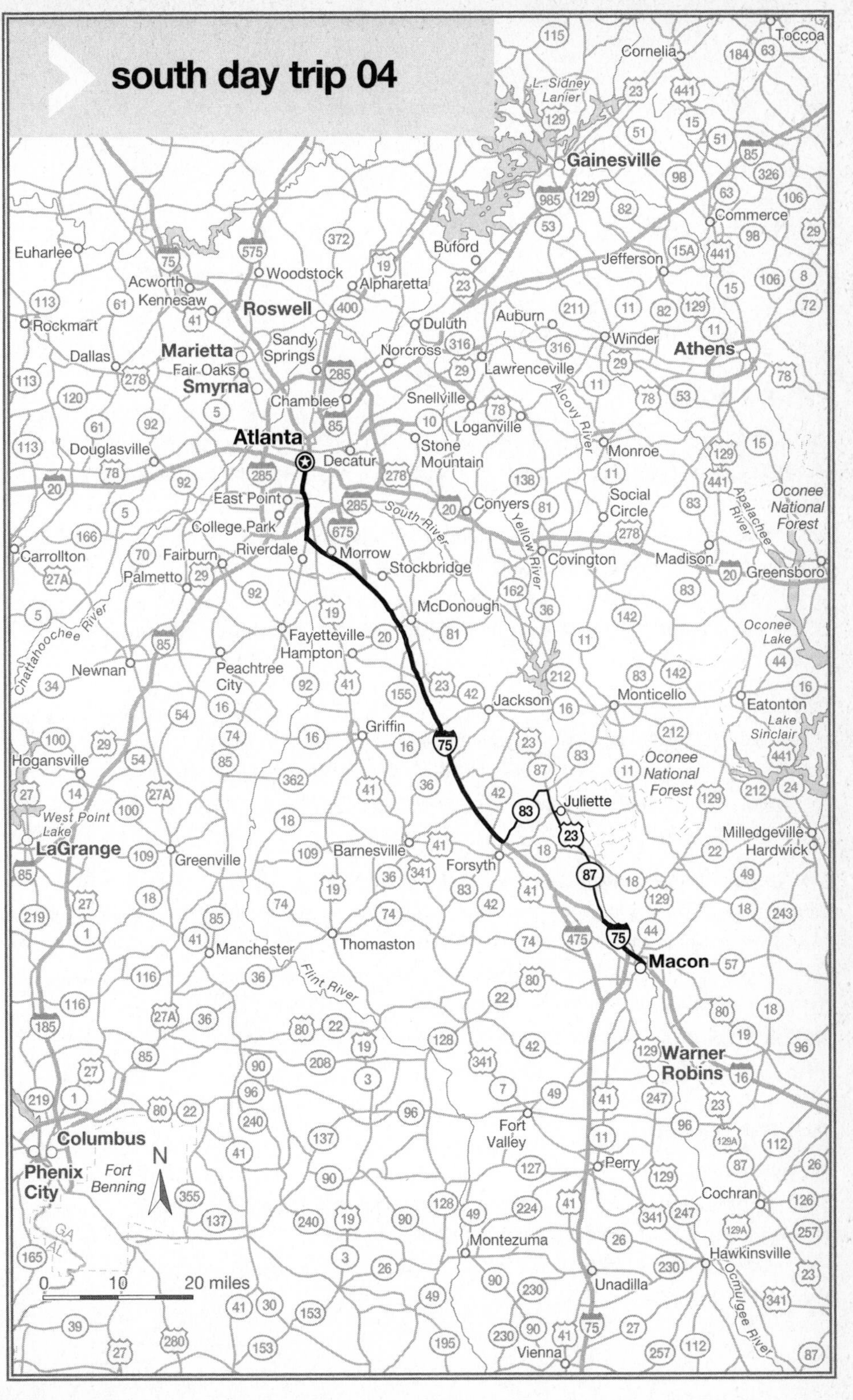
south day trip 04
Atlanta
Macon
Gainesville
Athens
Roswell
Marietta
Smyrna
Decatur
Forsyth
Juliette
Warner Robins
Columbus
Phenix City
LaGrange
0
10
20 miles

and *Return to Macon County,* 1975) were filmed in Juliette before the popular *Fried Green Tomatoes* came to town. Now Juliette has a modest tourism industry and promotes itself through festivals and activities.

getting there

From Atlanta, it will take you a little more than an hour to get to Juliette. Take I-75 south to exit 187 for Forsyth. You'll take GA 83 north 11 miles to Berner and make a right and head south on US 23/GA 87 for 4 miles to Juliette.

where to go

Jarrell Plantation. 711 Jarrell Plantation Rd.; (478) 986-5172; www.gastateparks.org/JarrellPlantation. If you want the sense of what a real cotton plantation looked like, visit the Jarrell Plantation. Now a state park, it was owned by the Jarrell family for more than 140 years. The 1,000-acre farm includes a heartpine home built by John Fitz Jarrell in 1860. Many of the furnishings were also handmade. The grounds look much the way they did when the plantation was in operation and include a sawmill, cotton gin, gristmill, shingle mill, planer, sugarcane press, syrup evaporator, workshop, barn, and other outbuildings. Open daily 8 a.m. to 5 p.m.

Old Mill Motorcycle Museum. Old Juliette Grist Mill; (478) 992-9931; www.oldmillmuseum.com. Owner Les White has converted this mill into a museum for his motorcycle collection. The vintage pieces date back to the 1930s, and he keeps them in pristine operating order. The museum also houses the shop where White works on his restorations. Sat and Sun noon to 5 p.m. $$.

The Original Whistle Stop Cafe. 443 McCrackin St.; (478) 992-8886; www.thewhistlestopcafe.com. Yes, this is a restaurant, but you can't come to Juliette and not go here. The building housing the cafe was built in 1937 as the local mercantile. It served as many things until the filming of the 1991 movie *Fried Green Tomatoes*. Following that movie's success, the owner decided to open the store as a cafe similar to one in the movie. Today's cafe serves up great Southern-style food including, yes, fried green tomatoes (when in season). Daily 11 a.m. to 4 p.m.

where to eat

Riverview Cafe. 465 McCrackin St.; (478) 992-8858. This tin-roofed restaurant will make you feel right at home. Breakfast is the thing here, and while at lunch they offer up burgers, hot dogs, and such, feel free to try breakfast all day. They also offer daily specials. Don't want to dine in? They have a drive-up window for takeout. Mon through Fri 5 a.m. to 3 p.m., Sat and Sun 8 a.m. to 3 p.m.

where to stay

Jarrell 1920 House. 715 Jarrell Plantation Rd.; (478) 986-3972; www.jarrellhouse.com. The Jarrell House was an original family home associated with the Jarrell Plantation State Park next door. The hand-built 1850s plantation-style home was the third built on the family compound. It is in pristine original condition and still owned by a Jarrell family member. Two large bedrooms are available for rent and include a large breakfast buffet in the morning. $$.

Old Mill Cabins. Old Juliette Grist Mill; (478) 992-9931; www.oldmillmuseum.com/cabins .html. Adjacent to the Old Grist Mill and Motorcycle Museum are wonderful cabins that overlook the Ocmulgee River. There are 10 cabins from which to choose with 1 or 2 bedrooms. $–$$.

macon

In the heart of Georgia, Macon is a city that deserves a good long look. Its story dates back to Creeks and Cherokees as well as Spanish explorers. The town itself was founded on what was considered the frontier in 1822. Growing steadily over the decades, Macon was somehow bypassed by Gen. Sherman during the Civil War. Because of this, its houses and buildings have remained well preserved. There are 12 historic districts and more than 5,500 registered historical buildings in Macon.

For many, however, Macon is best known for its cherry trees. What started in 1952 as a cutting from the Yoshino cherry trees of Washington, DC, has now grown to more than 300,000 trees, making Macon the cherry tree capital of the world.

The city is vibrant with cultural performances and exhibits and there are countless outdoor activities available as well, so you may want to consider staying longer than a day.

getting there

It's a 20-minute drive to Macon from Juliette as you just continue down US 23/GA 87. You'll pass through some beautiful country, including driving by Lake Juliette. Coming from Atlanta, the straight drive will take a little more than an hour down I-75.

where to go

Macon Downtown Visitor's Center. 450 Martin Luther King Jr. Blvd.; (478) 743-3401 or (800) 768-3401; www.maconga.org. Stopping here is a must to make the most of your time in this city. In addition to all of the cultural and outdoor activities, there are 12 historic districts around town, and each has its own distinct features. These fine folks will happily provide you with maps and can advise you on ticket prices to some locations. Mon through Sat 9 a.m. to 5 p.m.

Amerson Water Works Park. N. Pierce Ave.; (478) 722-9909; www.ohtmacon.com. If you want to take a break and get back to nature, head to the Amerson Water Works Park. This was the site of the Macon Waterworks until a flood destroyed it in 1994. The city's loss was the people's gain, though, because it has been restored to its original condition and includes a prehistoric natural lake, miles of riverfront, a large open meadow, and wooded trails. There are picnic areas if you decide to bring your own food and an outdoor concert pavilion. The Water Works are part of the Ocmulgee Heritage Trail. Daily 9 a.m. to 5 p.m. $3 parking fee.

The Big House. 2321 Vineville Ave.; (478) 741-5551; http://thebighousemuseum.org. For Allman Brothers fans, this is a must. The Allman brothers, their band, and their roadies moved into this house in 1969 and used it as their base of operations for decades. Gregg Allman wrote "Please Call Home" about this place. Now the site of the world's largest collection of Allman Brothers memorabilia, visitors are invited to tour the place or simply sit on the front porch where Duane Allman and Berry Oakley spent countless hours together. Hours change with the seasons, so check the site or call ahead. Otherwise Thurs through Sun 11 a.m. to 6 p.m. $$.

Cannonball House. 856 Mulberry St.; (478) 745-5982; www.cannonballhouse.org. This gorgeous Greek Revival mansion gets its name from the dubious honor of being the only home damaged in 1864 during a Union attack. Yes, it was hit by a cannonball. Now the 1853 home is beautifully restored with period furnishings and houses a Civil War Museum. It is also home to the repositories of the world's first secret societies for women—the Adelphean (Alpha Delta Pi) and Philomathean (Phi Mu) societies. The sororities were founded at Wesleyan College in 1851 and 1852. Jan and Feb: Mon through Fri 11 a.m. to 4:30 p.m., Sat 10 a.m. to 5 p.m.; Mar through Dec: Mon through Sat 10 a.m. to 5 p.m., Sun by appointment only. $$.

Fort Hawkins. Maynard Street at Emery Highway; (478) 742-3003; www.forthawkins.com. Across the Ocmulgee River from the heart of present-day Macon, Fort Hawkins was where the town first started. It was established as a frontier outpost in 1806 by President Thomas Jefferson and Indian agent Col. Benjamin Hawkins. Its purpose was for trading and meeting with Native Americans of the area. Fort Hawkins was the base of military operations during the War of 1812. A replication of the southeast blockhouse now stands on the site, and there are plenty of reminders of the fort itself in the way of archaeological finds. Efforts are under way to reconstruct the entire stockade itself, which spanned across almost 1.5 acres.

The Garden Club Center. 730 College St.; (478) 742-0921; http://fgcmacon.org. You can tour and shop at the Garden Club Center in its beautiful 4-story, brick 1910 English Tudor home, which of course also has beautifully manicured grounds. The home was designed by renowned architect Neel Reid and became headquarters for the Federated Garden Clubs of Macon, Inc. in 1957. Tues through Fri 10 a.m. to 1 p.m.

Georgia Sports Hall of Fame. 301 Cherry St.; (478) 752-1585; http://gshf.org. With 43,000 square feet of exhibits, the Georgia Sports Hall of Fame is the largest state sports museum in the country. What makes it fun is that you aren't just learning about the more than 300 inductees, you actually get to try your hand at some of the sports. Shoot hoops, relive that once-in-a-lifetime play, or drive a NASCAR simulator. The museum houses more than 3,000 artifacts from the old-style ticket booths to memorabilia from the likes of Ty Cobb, Jackie Robinson, Bobby Jones, Evander Holyfield, and Nancy Lopez. Tues through Sat 9 a.m. to 5 p.m. $$.

The Grand Opera House. 651 Mulberry St.; (478) 301-5460; www.thegrandmacon.com. Built in 1884, this ornate opera house has been beautifully restored to its original splendor. It has 1,000 seats and remains the premier performing arts venue in Central Georgia. Check the schedule to be able to take in live performances ranging from concerts to touring Broadway productions.

Hay House. 934 Georgia Ave.; (478) 742-8155; www.georgiatrust.org/historic_sites/hay house. You may hear it called the Johnston-Felton-Hay House, but that is a mouthful. It's easy to see why it is called the "Palace of the South," though. Sitting high atop Coleman Hill, the views from the front steps of this Italian Renaissance Revival home are spectacular. Built between 1855 and 1859 by William Butler Johnston and his wife Anne Tracy Johnston, it had some amazing features for the time. Of the 20 rooms, 15 are connected with a speaker tube system so people could talk to one another or the servants. There is an elevator of sorts and hot and cold running water. A behind-the-scenes tour will even let you go up to the cupola on top of the house. $$$.

Historic Douglass Theatre. 355 Martin Luther King Jr. Blvd.; (478) 742-2000; www.douglasstheatre.org. Opened in 1921 by the son of a former slave, Charles Douglass, the Douglass Theatre was the premier movie house and vaudeville hall open to African-American citizens in the city. It was here in the 1950s that a young Otis Redding won the Saturday talent show week after week and set his career on the road. Bessie Smith, James Brown, Ma Rainey, and Little Richard all performed here. Newly renovated, the Douglass Theatre is carrying on its rich tradition by hosting multicultural events and films for all races and by holding educational performances for area schoolchildren. Enjoy a tour, film, or live performance. Open as available.

Macon Arts Alliance and Gallery. 486 1st St.; (478) 743-6940; www.maconarts.org. There is a constant array of cultural activities taking place at the Alliance, so make sure to check the schedule, but also be sure to stop by the gallery and see the latest exhibit. You can even pick up some great locally made pieces of art ranging from ceramics to sculptures, jewelry, pottery, and paintings. Mon through Fri 11 a.m. to 5 p.m., Sat 11 a.m. to 3 p.m. $.

Museum of Arts & Sciences. 4182 Forsyth Rd.; (478) 477-3232; www.masmacon.com. A whale in Georgia? Who knew? One of the highlights of this museum and planetarium is

Ziggy, the 40-million-year-old whale fossil unearthed near Macon. Exhibits range from the prehistoric to modern astronomy. There is even an in-house zoo featuring birds, reptiles, and small mammals. The museum shop has all sorts of fun items for young and old. Tues through Sat 10 a.m. to 5 p.m., Sun 1 to 5 p.m., last Fri of the month 10 a.m. to 8 p.m. $$.

The Ocmulgee Heritage Trail. Martin Luther King Jr. Boulevard at Riverside Drive; http://ocmulgeeheritagetrail.com. The OHT, as it is called, encompasses trails on both sides of the river and meanders from one end of Macon to the next. It is the only riverside trail and park system in Middle Georgia and provides a means to escape into nature while still being in the middle of the city. Highlights of the trail include the Ocmulgee National Monument, Historic Rose Hill Cemetery, and the Amerson Water Works Park. The trailhead is at Gateway Park, where you will also find a life-size statue of local legend and musician Otis Redding.

Ocmulgee National Monument. 1207 Emery Hwy.; (478) 752-8257; www.nps.gov/ocmu. The monument pays tribute to the temple mound found in this national preserve on the Ocmulgee River. Visitors can climb the mound or explore a reconstructed earth lodge, wander through trails of wetlands, or see prehistoric trenches and the site of a colonial British trading post. The visitor center helps trace 12,000 years of Native American history in the area. There is a gift shop as well. Daily 9 a.m. to 5 p.m. Free

Riverside Cemetery. 1301 Riverside Dr.; (478) 742-5328; www.riversidecemetery.com. This beautifully maintained cemetery was first founded in 1887 and is on the National Register of Historic Places. It is also still in use today. As the name suggests, it is on the banks of the Ocmulgee. More than 17,000 people, including soldiers from both sides of the Civil War, are interred here. In addition to the funerary art, you may want to take note of the gatehouse where the cemetery offices are located. Built in 1897, it is considered a unique example of Old English half-timbered construction. Self-guided tour maps available.

Rose Hill Cemetery. 1071 Riverside Dr.; (478) 751-9119; www.historicrosehillcemetery.org. Rose Hill should be noted because it remains one of the oldest surviving public cemetery parks in the US. Listed on the National Register of Historic Places, Rose Hills graves date back to 1840. It is the final resting place of Georgia governors, Civil War soldiers, and famous musicians, include Duane Allman and Berry Oakley.

Sidney Lanier Cottage. 935 High St.; (478) 743-3851; www.historicmacon.org. Lanier is a name you hear often in Georgia. Sidney Lanier was a famous poet and musician from the 1800s, and he was born in this cottage in 1842. On the National Historic Register, the restored home houses his writings, flute, and even his bride's wedding gown. Mon through Sat 10 a.m. to 4 p.m. $.

St. Joseph Catholic Church. 830 Poplar St.; (478) 745-1631; http://stjosephmacon.com. This beautiful twin-spired church will remind you of something you might see in Europe. The Neo-Gothic-style church is constructed of Georgian and Italian marble and contains

60 Bavarian stained-glass windows. Its interior is just breathtaking. When it was dedicated in 1903, the *Macon Telegraph* newspaper was so inspired, it reported, "If architecture may be fittingly described as frozen music, St. Joseph's Church, to be dedicated today, is a symphony." The side door is open to the public daily from 9 a.m. to 4 p.m.

Terminal Station. Foot of Cherry Street; (478) 722-9909; http://terminalstation.net. Now a city office building, this beautifully restored 1912 railroad station once handled hundreds of arrivals and departures a day. Designed in the Beaux Arts style by architect Alfred Fellheimer (1875–1959), it is considered Georgia's grandest surviving railroad station and is a downtown centerpiece. Be sure to note the 4 stone eagles that watch over the main entrance.

Tubman African American Museum. 340 Walnut St.; (478) 743-8544; www.tubmanmuseum.com. The Tubman African American Museum is the South's largest facility devoted solely to African-American art, history, and culture. The museum makes the journey from Africa to America and also looks at local African-American history and contributions. In addition, the Tubman has a gallery that exhibits both folk and fine art by nationally and internationally known Georgia-born and Georgia-based artists. Mon through Fri 9 a.m. to 5 p.m., Sat noon to 4 p.m. $$.

where to eat

Fish & Pig. 6420 Mosely Dixon Rd.; (478) 476-8837; www.fishnpig.com. Just outside of town on Lake Tobesofkee, the name says it all. Fish & Pig serves fresh seafood and hickory-smoked barbeque in a great setting overlooking the lake. Tues through Thurs 4:30 to 9:30 p.m., Fri and Sat 4:30 to 10:30 p.m. $–$$.

H & H. 807 Forsyth St.; (478) 742-9810; www.mamalouise.com. Serving up soul food in Macon since 1959 when it was started by Mama Louise Hudson, there are people who drive from Atlanta just to eat here. Try the sweet potato pie, fried chicken, baked ham, collard greens, or black-eyed peas; you won't be disappointed. Mon through Sat 6:30 a.m. to 4 p.m. $.

Jeneane's at Pinebrook. 4436 Forsyth Rd.; (478) 476-4642; http://jeneanes.com/home. A classic meat-and-three restaurant, Jeneane's serves up a selection of 6 meats and seasonable fresh vegetables. They are also known for their made-from-scratch biscuits and desserts. Mon through Fri and Sun 11 a.m. to 2 p.m., Mon through Fri 5 to 8 p.m. $–$$.

Jim Shaw's. 3040 Vineville Ave.; (478) 746-3697. With the freshest seafood in town, Jim Shaw's has been a favorite in Macon for more than 3 decades. Bartenders are friendly, and the food, tasty. Mon through Sat 5 to 11 p.m. $–$$.

Nu-way Weiners. www.nu-wayweiners.com. There are 7 locations around Macon, but this is the original and it hasn't changed much since it opened its doors in 1916. You can't beat their hotdogs and hamburgers. Stepping in here is like stepping back in time. Mon through Sat 6 a.m. to 7 p.m. $.

The Rookery. 543 Cherry St.; (478) 746-8658; www.rookerymacon.com. This place will remind you of the old show *Cheers* when you walk in and see the huge oak bar. Friendly, with great food, the Rookery is a landmark in downtown Macon. Famous for its burgers and homemade battered fries, it has a great selection of salads, sandwiches, and steaks as well. The Rookery hosts live music, Trivia Night, and a wide selection of events. Lunch and dinner daily. $–$$.

Satterfield's. 120 New St., Macon; (478) 742-0352; www.satterfieldscatering.com. This barbeque place right in the heart of downtown serves up mouthwatering hickory-smoked Que ranging from ribs to chopped pork. The iron skillet corn bread is to die for. Mon through Fri 10:30 a.m. to 3 p.m. $.

where to stay

1842 Inn. 353 College St.; (478) 741-1842; www.1842inn.com. This stately Greek Revival mansion was built as a private home in 1842, and you will feel right at home on its more than 2-acre grounds. The inn now consists of 19 guest rooms, hospitality parlors, and service facilities, as well as a courtyard and porches for entertaining. Guests have access to the Macon Health Club nearby. $$–$$$.

Macon Marriott City Center Hotel. 240 Coliseum Dr.; (478) 621-5300; www.marriott.com. A relatively new property, this Marriott has 217 rooms and 3 suites. Clean and comfortable with Wi-Fi in every room. $$–$$$.

Ramada Plaza. 108 1st St.; (478) 746-1461; www.ramada.com. Conveniently located in downtown, this hotel is clean and comfortable with a full exercise room for guests. $$–$$$.

day trip 05

the deep south:
andersonville, americus, plains

Heading straight south for this day trip will truly take you a world away from Atlanta. You'll discover an entirely different terrain as you get more toward the flatlands and learn about some incredible history, both good and bad.

Two of the towns on this trip have reputations that are known throughout the world, and the third has such spectacular architecture that it should be. The name Andersonville has become synonymous with the horrors of war, while the town of Plains has proven that someone from a tiny town can grow up to be president of the United States. Americus? Well, let's just say that this charming town alone is worth the drive.

andersonville

Andersonville was founded in the 1800s as a stop on the Southwestern Railroad. While the town of today is not much larger than it was then, its role in the Civil War has cemented its place in history. The Confederates built a POW camp near here called Camp Sumter, and Andersonville was the supply depot where the prisoners would arrive. More than 13,000 Union soldiers died at the camp from exposure, disease, and malnutrition in the course of only 14 months.

In recent years, Andersonville has learned to deal with its past and promote it as a way to learn about both the atrocities of war and the way of life back at the time of the war. The

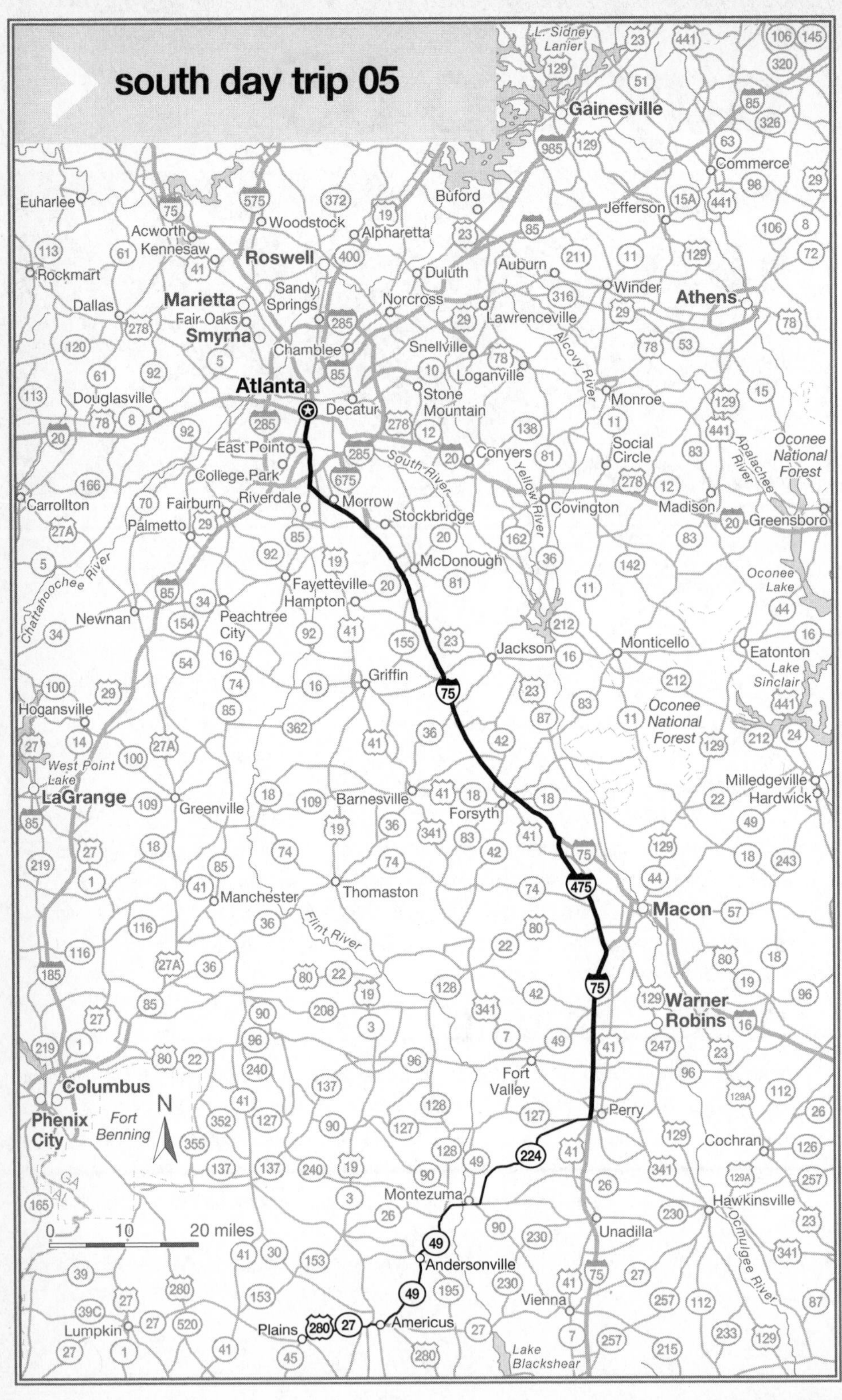
south day trip 05
L. Sidney Lanier
Gainesville
Commerce
Euharlee
Woodstock
Buford
Jefferson
Acworth
Alpharetta
Kennesaw
Roswell
Duluth
Auburn
Winder
Rockmart
Sandy Springs
Norcross
Athens
Dallas
Marietta
Lawrenceville
Fair Oaks
Smyrna
Chamblee
Snellville
Alcovy River
Loganville
Atlanta
Stone Mountain
Douglasville
Monroe
Decatur
East Point
Conyers
Social Circle
Oconee National Forest
South River
College Park
Apalachee River
Yellow River
Carrollton
Morrow
Riverdale
Fairburn
Covington
Madison
Greensboro
Palmetto
Stockbridge
McDonough
Chattahoochee River
Fayetteville
Oconee Lake
Hampton
Newnan
Peachtree City
Jackson
Monticello
Eatonton
Lake Sinclair
Griffin
Hogansville
Oconee National Forest
West Point Lake
Milledgeville
LaGrange
Greenville
Barnesville
Hardwick
Forsyth
Thomaston
Manchester
Macon
Flint River
Warner Robins
Fort Valley
Columbus
Phenix City
Fort Benning
N
Perry
Cochran
GA
AL
Montezuma
Hawkinsville
Unadilla
Ocmulgee River
0
10
20 miles
Andersonville
Vienna
Lumpkin
Americus
Plains
Lake Blackshear

town founded the Andersonville Guild, which continues to buy and refurbish buildings, going to great pains to restore the town and create a living history area.

getting there

From Atlanta, it will take you just over 2 hours. Take I-75 south to exit 135 (Perry). Head southwest on GA 224 from the interstate to Montezuma, approximately 20 miles. Just outside Montezuma, turn right on GA 26 and follow it to the intersection of GA 49. Turn left on GA 49 and head south approximately 6 miles to Andersonville. The park entrance will be on the left.

where to go

Andersonville Civil War Village Welcome Center. 114 Church St.; (229) 924-2558; www.andersonvillegeorgia.com. The town of Andersonville has turned back the clock to restore its historic downtown area to how it looked during the Civil War days. Living history exhibits take place daily. The town features battle reenactments, a restored town hall, post office, stores, railroad depot, and much, much more. Daily 9 a.m. to 5:30 p.m.

Andersonville National Cemetery and Historic Site. 496 Cemetery Rd.; (229) 924-0343; www.nps.gov/ande. The name Andersonville is synonymous with some of the atrocities of the Civil War. Called Camp Sumter at the time, Andersonville was one of the largest military prisons established by the Confederacy during the war. Though in existence for a mere 14 months, more than 45,000 Union soldiers were confined at the prison and almost a third of them died from exposure, disease, and malnutrition. The National Prisoner of War Museum at Andersonville pays tribute not just to them, but to all POWs from the time of the American Revolution to today. The cemetery has more than 20,000 graves and is still an active burial ground. The cemetery and park grounds are open daily 8 a.m. to 5 p.m.; the Visitors Center, 8:30 a.m. to 5 p.m. Free.

Drummer Boy Civil War Museum. 109 E. Church St.; (229) 924-2425; www.andersonvillegeorgia.com/Drummer_Boy_Museum.htm. This museum houses an unbelievable array of Civil War uniforms and artifacts. It's the sort of place that has folks from the Smithsonian drooling to get their hands on. Daily 9 a.m. to 2 p.m. $.

where to eat

Anderson Station. 107 Church St.; (229) 938-0316. This small restaurant in an old general store specializes in Southern cooking. The place is small, but the food is great and there is plenty of shopping to be done before and after you eat. Thurs through Sun 10 a.m. to 5 p.m. $.

where to stay

Traveler's Rest B&B. 318 N. Dooly St., Montezuma; (478) 472-0085; www.travelersrestbb.com. This beautiful 1898 Victorian home has 3 spacious rooms, each with its own private bathroom. There is also a self-contained apartment in a contemporary carriage house in the back garden of the main house for those wanting even more privacy, for longer stays. Breakfast included. $$.

americus

The entire downtown area of Americus is listed on the National Register of Historic Places, making it the sort of place where you find yourself taking pictures around every corner.

The town grew up in the early 1800s as the seat of the county and hinged its growth to agriculture. The arrival of the railroad in 1854 helped it develop into a center for the cotton trade. The prosperous little city continued to thrive after the Civil War, and that prosperity is apparent in the number of beautiful antebellum homes and historic buildings still standing.

getting there

Americus is about 2.5 hours south of Atlanta and only about 15 minutes from Andersonville. Just follow GA 49 south from Andersonville. If you are coming from Atlanta, follow the Andersonville directions and just continue through Andersonville to Americus.

where to go

Habitat for Humanity Global Village and Discovery Center. 721 W. Church St.; (800) 422-4828; www.habitat.org. Founded by Millard Fulmer, Habitat for Humanity builds homes in more than 83 countries across the world. Its global operations, however, remain where they started: right here in Americus. The headquarters are found in something called the Rylander Building, built in 1916. The Global Village and Discovery Center contains actual houses similar to ones built in areas around the world. Mon through Fri 9 a.m. to 5 p.m., Sat 10 a.m. to 2 p.m. (Mar through Nov). Closed holidays and Sun. Donations welcome.

Koinonia Farm. 1324 GA 49 South; (229) 924-0391 or (877) 738-1741; www.koinoniapartners.org. Koinonia Farm is a Christian commune that functions as a retreat for many. Founded in 1940, its teachings of racial equality and peace have made it a target of violence. Now the community raises organic fruits and sells baked goods while providing a peaceful haven for those who want to participate in their work, study, prayer, and service. Overnight stays are available. Mon through Sat 9 a.m. to 5 p.m., Sun 1 to 5 p.m. Donations accepted.

where to eat

The Fish House. 224 N. Jackson St.; (229) 924-5177. If you've never had catfish or frog legs, this is the place to try them. The Fish House also serves up a variety of other seafood as well as quail and other Southern foods. Mon through Sat 11 a.m. to 9 p.m. $–$$.

Forsyth 1889 Bar & Grill. 124 W. Forsyth St.; (229) 924-8193. A casual atmosphere with good food. A variety of sandwiches, pasta, steaks, seafood, appetizers, vegetarian dishes, and low-fat fare is on the menu of this casual dining restaurant that also offers an extensive wine and beer list to complement your meal. Tues through Thurs 11 a.m. to 9 p.m., Fri and Sat 5 to 10 p.m. Closed Sun and Mon. $–$$.

Gladys Kitchen. 1009 MLK Blvd.; (229) 928-1975. Good Southern-style soul food, complete with fried green tomatoes on Sun and Mon. Mon through Fri 11 a.m. to 3 p.m., Sun 11 a.m. to 4 p.m. $.

Granny's Kitchen. Intersection of US 19 South and GA 280 West; (229) 924-0028. More good home-style Southern cooking and fantastic breads. The fried chicken will fall off the bone, and you can't beat the lace bread and gravy. Mon through Sat 6 a.m. to 2 p.m. Closed Sun. $.

Pat's Place. 1526 S. Lee St.; (229) 924-0033; www.pats-place.com. In a building that dates back to 1885, this is one of those places worth driving for. The food is great and the atmosphere friendly, and the bar area is a local hangout. Their grilled sandwiches will fill you up, and the pizzas are all made with freshly thrown dough. Mon through Thurs 11 a.m. to 11 p.m., Fri and Sat 11 a.m. to midnight. $.

Ryan's Grill Buffet & Bakery. 1712 E. Lamar St.; (229) 924-4088. Good hearty fare for low prices. Ryan's offers up things like beef stew, fried chicken, and pot roast, along with low country boil and Brunswick stew. Mon through Fri 10:45 a.m. to 9 p.m., Sat 7:30 a.m. to 9 p.m., Sun 7:30 a.m. to 8:30 p.m. $–$$.

Sheppard House. 1608 E. Forsyth St., #H; (229) 924-8756. Down-home Southern cooking at its best. Sheppard House also specializes in barbeque pork. The noon buffet makes it popular with the locals. Mon through Fri and Sun 11 a.m. to 2:30 p.m. $.

Trellis Restaurant. 151 GA 27 East; (229) 924-1090; www.trellisamericus.com. A unique, casual fine-dining experience, Trellis offers great steaks and seafood with a Southern flair with an unusual combination of Filipino offerings. Their Sunday brunch is amazing. Tues through Sat 5 to 10 p.m., Sun 10 a.m. to 2 p.m. $$.

2 Dukes Barbeque. 500 Tripp St.; (229) 928-0049. You can smell the barbeque smoking when you drive into the lot. The chipped pork and baby back ribs are to die for. Considered a top lunch place in Americus. Tues through Fri 11 a.m. to 7 p.m., Sat 11 a.m. to 2 p.m. $.

where to stay

Americus Garden Inn B&B. 504 Rees Park; (229) 931-0122 or (888) 758-4749; www.americusgardeninn.com. The Americus Garden Inn gets its name from its grounds as well as its location near Rees Park. Built in 1847, you'll want to just park yourself in one of its rockers out on the porch. It offers 8 rooms with their own baths, some including a Jacuzzi. Fresh baked goods are available daily. The inn has been listed among the Top 10 "Best Bed & Breakfasts" in the US for several years, and in 2010 was named a Top 10 "Best Bed & Breakfast" in the world. $–$$.

The 1906 Pathway Inn. 501 S. Lee St.; (229) 928-2078 or (800) 889-1466; www.1906pathwayinn.com. Surrounded by porches, this beautiful B&B offers 5 comfortable rooms as well as a choice of a lakeside cottage. Consistently listed as one of the top B&Bs in the region. $–$$.

Windsor Hotel. 125 W. Lamar St.; (229) 924-1555; www.windsor-americus.com. There is a reason they call this Windsor Castle. Built in 1892 to attract visitors from the North, this beautifully restored Victorian inn comes complete with towers, turrets, and balconies. Now a Best Western Plus, the 5-story architectural masterpiece takes up an entire city block and is the site of numerous balls and celebrations. It was fully renovated and reopened in 2010. It has 53 individual guest rooms, 6 suites, and 2 tower suites, as well as a bridal suite and the Carter presidential suite, named in honor of local resident and our 39th president, Jimmy Carter. $–$$.

plains

The tiny town of Plains, Georgia, is one of those farming communities that most people would overlook in their tours, except for the fact that it has a famous native son: former president Jimmy Carter. Carter, his sister Ruth Carter Stapleton, and his brother Billy were all born in this town of fewer than 1,000, and Carter and his wife Rosalyn still call it home.

While Carter's presidency brought notoriety to the town, it remains an agriculturally based area with many of the residents a part of the peanut industry. The friendly downtown is fun to explore, and of course, everyone knows the Carters.

getting there

From Americus, head west on GA 49 and then follow US 280/GA 27 as it splits off to the right. Plains is just 10 miles.

If you are going directly from Atlanta, it will take you about 2.5 hours because there is no straight route. Go south on I-75 to Jonesboro and then take US 19 South for 73 miles through the town of Zebulon. Next take GA 153 for 6 miles, turning south on GA 45 toward Plains.

where to go

Jimmy Carter National Historic Site. www.nps.gov/jica/index.htm. The site encompasses much of the town of Plains, where the 39th president of the Unites States, Jimmy Carter, grew up. Included is the visitor center in what was the Plains High School at the time Carter attended. The 1988 Plains train depot was used as the Carter 1976 Presidential Campaign Headquarters and now functions as a museum commemorating the campaign and his presidency. And finally, there is the rural farm in nearby Archery where Carter spent his youth. The Carters still live in Plains, but their private residence and compound are not open to the public. Visitor center: 9 a.m. to 5 p.m. daily; train depot: 9 a.m. to 4:30 p.m. daily; Jimmy Carter boyhood farm: 10 a.m. to 5 p.m. daily. Free.

where to shop

Plain Peanuts. 128 Main St.; (229) 824-3462; www.plainpeanuts.com. It doesn't get more hometown than this. Plain Peanuts is housed in the old Carter Warehouse office, after being founded in a service station owned by President Carter's brother Billy. It's known for its wide variety of peanut candies as well as fried peanuts. If you don't want to carry the candy with you, they ship it! Mon through Sat 10 a.m. to 6 p.m., Sun noon to 4 p.m.

Plains Inn & Museum. 106 Main St.; (229) 824-4517; www.plainsinn.net. The street level of this old hotel has an antiques mall housing 25 booths with a wide variety of vendors. Mon through Sat 10 a.m. to 6 p.m., Sun 1 to 4 p.m.

where to eat

Daily Bread Sandwich Shop. 201 E. Church St.; (229) 824-5984. Daily Bread is in an old service station and puts a gourmet spin on its simple soups, salads, and sandwiches. They also offer up some pretty tasty pizzas—all made to order. Mon through Thurs 11 a.m. to 2 p.m., Fri and Sat 11 a.m. to 8 p.m. $.

Mom's Kitchen. 203 E. Church St.; (229) 824-5458. Almost a must in Plains. This is food like your mom used to make. Served up cafeteria style, you can expect anything from a Thanksgiving feast to fried chicken, catfish, and quail. Tues through Thurs 6 a.m. to 3 p.m., Fri and Sat 6 a.m. to 8 p.m., Sun 6:30 a.m. to 3 p.m. Closed Mon. $.

Old Bank Cafe. 118 Moon St.; (229) 824-4520. As the name suggests, this cafe is in an old bank. It serves up good and simple food. The sandwiches are substantial, and the homemade desserts are fabulous. Mon through Thurs 11 a.m. to 8 p.m., Fri and Sat 11 a.m. to 5 p.m. $–$$.

where to stay

Plains Historic Inn. 106 Main St.; (229) 824-4517; www.plainsinn.net. This quaint hotel is central to all things President Carter. It includes 5 large, comfortable period rooms, whose themes range from the 1920s to the 1980s. It also includes a presidential suite and a business suite. With its very friendly staff, you'll feel right at home. $.

worth more time

Southwest Georgia Excursion Train. (877) GA-RAILS (427-2457); http://samshortline.com. Operating between the towns of Archery, Plains, Americus, Leslie, the Georgia Veterans State Park, and the town of Cordele, this excursion train allows visitors to see these tiny towns in the air-conditioned comfort of a 1949 vintage train. The stops are all centralized and are a great way to spend some extra time in the area. Tickets can be ordered online or by calling.

southwest

day trip 01

calling coweta:

newnan, moreland, grantville

We take you less than an hour from Atlanta on this little jaunt to visit some sleepy communities and a vibrant historical town that is known for all of its historical homes.

Newnan is the largest of the stops on this day trip and the visitor center there knows what a jewel it has. They have even carefully laid out a driving map so you can see as much as possible. But not to be forgotten are the little towns of Moreland, Grantville, and even Sharpsburg. These tiny communities grew up as agricultural towns, and while they are no longer the bustling centers they once were, they deserve a detour off I-85.

newnan

Newnan is a beautiful Southern city that while steeped in history, marries its past with a vibrant present. Now considered almost a suburb of Atlanta, there was no such thing as Atlanta when Newnan was founded back in 1828.

The center of the town is the courthouse square and Newnan itself contains six districts which are listed on the National Register of Historic Places. Just walk around this pedestrian-friendly town and you'll understand why. It has some of Georgia's most beautiful homes and buildings and downtown is filled with locally owned shops and restaurants.

Hollywood has come calling more than once to take advantage of the small-town feel. Movies which filmed scenes here include *Sweet Home Alabama, Driving Miss Daisy,* and *Fried Green Tomatoes.*

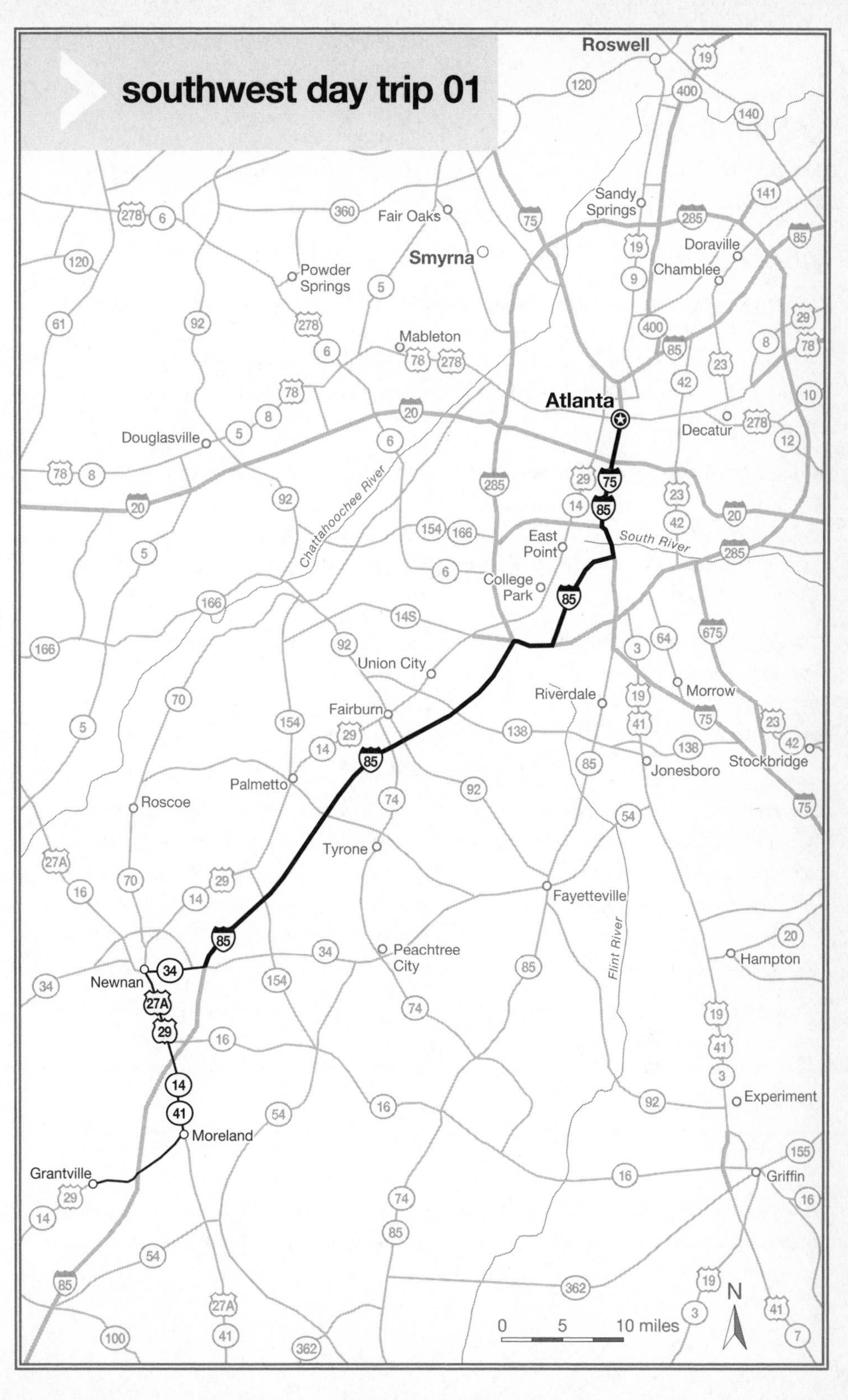
southwest day trip 01
Roswell
Sandy Springs
Fair Oaks
Smyrna
Doraville
Chamblee
Powder Springs
Mableton
Atlanta
Decatur
Douglasville
Chattahoochee River
East Point
South River
College Park
Union City
Riverdale
Morrow
Fairburn
Jonesboro
Stockbridge
Palmetto
Roscoe
Tyrone
Fayetteville
Flint River
Peachtree City
Hampton
Newnan
Experiment
Moreland
Grantville
Griffin
0 5 10 miles
N

getting there

Just 30 miles southwest of Atlanta, take I-85 south to exit 47 and take GA 24 west into downtown.

where to go

Coweta County Convention & Visitors Bureau. 200 Courthouse Sq.; (800) 8-COWETA or (770) 254-2627/2629; www.explorecoweta.com. Located in the historic courthouse, stop here to get a self-guided driving tour map that will help you see 52 of the best of the homes, which helped earn Newnan the name "City of Homes." Mon through Sat 9 a.m. to 5 p.m.

African-American Alliance Museum & Research Center. 92 Farmer St., (770) 683-7055; www.africanamericanalliance.net. This museum serves as a repository for the history of African Americans in Coweta County. Housed in a restored shotgun-style house, it features exhibits and artifacts as well as a genealogy workroom. It is located next to the Farmer Street Cemetery.

Carnegie Library. 1 LaGrange St.; (770) 683-1347; http://newnancarnegie.com. In 1903, Andrew Carnegie endowed $10,000 to build this library, the oldest Carnegie Library in the state of Georgia. It was Newnan's main library until 1987 and now serves as a reading room and gallery. Stop by to do research, use the computers, or read periodicals. There is also a children's reading room that hosts regular programs. Mon through Fri 9 a.m. to 5 p.m.

Coweta County Courthouse. The Coweta County Courthouse has a domed clock tower that rises 100 feet above the town square. Built in 1902, the courthouse combined classical architecture with an Italian influence. Copper covers the dome, the cornice, the pediment, and railings. It is considered unusual for the cornices to be made of copper instead of stone. Mon through Fri 9 a.m. to 5 p.m. Contact the Coweta County Convention & Visitors Bureau for information.

Farmer Street Cemetery. 92 Farmer St. This cemetery is thought to be the largest slave cemetery in the South. There are 269 grave depressions here but it is possible there are more. The last known burial in the cemetery was in 1869: a 3-month-old baby by the name of Charlie Burch.

Male Academy Museum. 30 College St.; (770) 251-0207; www.nchistoricalsociety.org. Located in a former private boys' school that dates back to 1883, this museum contains a wide variety of artifacts. Exhibits include period clothing, Civil War memorabilia, maps, early medical equipment, and photos. Exhibits change regularly. Tues through Sat 10 a.m. to noon and 1 to 3 p.m.

Newnan-Coweta History Center. 60 E. Broad St.; (770) 251-0207; www.nchistoricalsociety.org. Housed in the town's historic rail depot, the center displays memorabilia from throughout Newnan and the county. The depot was originally constructed in the 1850s as a freight and passenger depot for the Atlanta & West Point Railroad. It had its own brush with the Civil War when it became the site of a skirmish between Federal and Confederate forces in July 1864. By appointment only.

Oak Grove Plantation and Gardens. 4537 US 29 North; (770) 463-3010; www.oakgrovega.com. This beautiful 1835 plantation has 4 themed gardens which cover more than 20 acres. There is also an antiques shop on the grounds. Open daily 9 a.m. to 5 p.m.

Oak Hill Cemetery. 96 Bullsboro Dr.; (770) 253-3744. Dating back to 1828, the historic cemetery contains graves of Revolutionary War soldiers as well as 269 from the Civil War. Every state from the Confederacy is represented here. Georgia governors Ellis Arnall and William Atkinson, both native sons of Newnan, are also buried here.

where to eat

Christy's Cafe. 30 Perry St.; (770) 683-7512. This family-run restaurant serves up good home cooking. There are daily specials with everything from fried catfish to grilled chicken salad. Good food, good price, good people. Mon through Sat 7 a.m. to 2 p.m. $.

Classic Cafe Off the Square. 13 E. Broad St.; (770) 683-3231. Tucked away from the square, this small, family-owned cafe serves up hearty, awesome sandwiches. You may want to consider ordering only a half! Mon through Sat 10:30 a.m. 6 p.m. $.

Grille 1904. 9 E. Washington St.; (770) 683-3183; www.grille1904.com. Another family-owned restaurant, this place treats you like one of their own. There are nightly specials ranging from crab legs to fish tacos. There is even a martini night. Live music on weekends. Tues through Fri 11 a.m. to 2 p.m., Tues through Sat 5 p.m. until midnight. $–$$.

Mother's Kitchen. 33½ E. Broad St.; (770) 683-3033. A real institution in Newnan, Mother's is Southern cooking that will fill you up. Mother herself will take your order and keeps a watchful eye over the place. Everything is made from scratch. Come early because Mother's closes when she runs out of food. Mon through Sat 11 a.m. to 3 p.m. $.

Redneck Gourmet. 11 N. Court Sq.; www.redneckgourmet.com. Family operated since 1991, Redneck serves up sandwiches and barbeque with homemade desserts. They have a second location in Senoia. Mon through Sat 7 a.m. to 9 p.m. $.

Shirley's Country Kitchen Too. 1485 GA 34 East; (770) 253-8914. Shirley's serves up Southern food buffet style. All you can eat, but save room for the peach cobbler. Mon through Sat 11 a.m. to 3 p.m. $.

Sprayberry's Barbeque. 229 Jackson St.; (770) 253-4421; www.sprayberrysbbq.com. Sprayberry's has been serving up barbeque since 1929 and is now run by the fourth generation of the family. What started out as serving barbeque sandwiches out of the back of a gas station is now a landmark in Newnan. The do serve other food, and are good at it, but you simply have to have the ribs or chopped pork. Mon through Sat 10:30 a.m. to 9 p.m. $–$$.

where to stay

Casa Bella Bed and Breakfast. 51 Temple Ave.; (770) 755-6750; www.girondascasa bella.com. Located in the heart of Newnan, Casa Bella has taken care to make sure its rooms are comfy havens for its guests. The grounds are beautiful and include a saltwater pool. $$.

Oak Grove Plantation and Gardens. 4537 N. US 29; (770) 841-0789; www.oakgrovega .com. Oak Grove is a vacation spot unto itself. Located on 20 acres of the grounds of an 1820 plantation, guests can make themselves at home in antique furnished rooms of the carriage house or guest cottage. Oak Grove's acclaimed gardens and home are open for tours. A hearty breakfast accompanies each room. $$$.

worth more time

Serenbe. 9055 Selborne Ln., Chattahoochee Hills; (770) 463-9997; www.serenbe.com. Serenbe is a 900-acre self-sustaining community that includes restaurants, a farm, a bed-and-breakfast, and now homes. It started as a simple bed-and-breakfast community and its organic, healthy lifestyle has helped it to evolve into an entire community. There are 3 restaurants serving up organic food and a farm shop is available if you want to purchase your own. Shops in the Serenbe complex include a spa and galleries. Come for a visit or stay a few days.

Sharpsburg. Just 8 miles east of Newnan on GA 34, Sharpsburg is one of the smallest towns in Georgia, with a population of just over 300. If you are going to spend some time in Newnan, then it is worth your while to take the 10-minute drive over to this little town.

Downtown is little more than a crossroads now, but in the early 1900s, this was a thriving agricultural community. Founded in 1825, Sharpsburg was named for a Judge Elias Sharp who built the first house here. Cotton was definitely king but the town was hit hard by the Depression and never recovered. Walk down Main Street and it doesn't take long to realize what a jewel this was during its heyday.

moreland

Moreland is less than 1 square mile, but it packs a lot into that space. It is constantly referred to as Coweta County's Mayberry and you will see why. With a population of only about 400, it has 3 museums, 4 churches, and 2 cemeteries.

The town was founded in 1903 as an agricultural community and has maintained that community atmosphere. Downtown is made up of a handful of quaint old buildings, some of which are used as galleries and shops.

What's most notable about Moreland are its native sons, Erskine Caldwell and Lewis Grizzard. That fact makes Moreland a stop on the Southern Literary Trail. Both men are celebrated here and there are museums to honor them.

getting there

From Newnan or Atlanta, take I-85 south to exit 41 and go south on US 27. It is 3 miles from the interstate. It will take you 10 minutes from Newnan and 45 minutes from Atlanta.

where to go

Erskine Caldwell Museum. E. Camp Street; (770) 251-4438. Literary giant Erskine Caldwell grew from these humble beginnings. The simple 1800s-era wooden house was his birthplace and contains both US and foreign versions of his works, such as *Tobacco Road* and *God's Little Acre,* as well as numerous artifacts. Call for hours.

Lewis Grizzard Museum. 2769 US 29 South; (770) 254-2627; www.lewisgrizzard.com/museum.htm. Lewis Grizzard was a Southern humorist and syndicated newspaper columnist who was raised in the tiny town of Moreland, an experience that helped shape his writing. This little museum was organized by his friends and family and contains memorabilia, including family photos and manuscripts. You can also buy copies of his books.

Old Mill Museum. E. Camp Street. Located on the square on the site of the Moreland Knitting Mills (1900–1945), the museum contains artifacts from the mill's ledgers to artifacts from local stores and residents. It also has a reconstructed vintage medical office from the early 1900s. The mill is home to the town offices and the Moreland Community Historical Society. If you are in Moreland, stop by because there is no phone to call. Thurs through Sat 10 a.m. to 3 p.m.

where to eat

D P & T Fast Food. 188 Ball St.; (770) 251-5556. This is really the only place in town to grab a bite to eat, but that's OK. It's good and it's fast. Sandwiches, barbeque, and fried fish. That's all you need. Mon through Sat 7 a.m. to 4 p.m. $.

grantville

Grantville is another one of those tiny towns that is worth driving through and having a look-see. Incorporated in 1852, it was originally called Calico Corners. It was renamed after a railroad engineer by the name of Colonel L.P. Grant. At one point there were two cotton mills operating here and Grantville was a bustling mill village. Remnants of the mills are still standing in downtown. These days historic Grantville is a nice place to spend a few hours and wander.

getting there

Continue down I-85 from Moreland one exit to Grantville. Take exit 35 and make a right on US 29. If you come down I-85 from Atlanta, it is 50 minutes.

where to go

First United Methodist Church. 127 Church St.; (770) 583-3113. This beautiful old red-brick church from the 1800s is the reason Church Street has its name. One of the largest buildings in Grantville, you'll find a bell on the lawn directly in front of the church which was used to call people to service.

Grantville Train Depots. 5 W. Broad St.; (770) 583-9013; www.ccgsinc.org. There are actually two train depots here. One was passenger and the other freight. The freight depot was the original and was built in 1852 to handle both freight and passengers. The second depot on the opposite side of the tracks on Broad Street was built in the early 1900s so passengers would have a separate place to wait. The passenger depot is home to the Coweta County Genealogical Society. The freight depot houses a small museum for the Newnan-Coweta Historical Society. Call for hours for both.

John C. Meadows Log Cabin. Post Road, Coweta County Recreation Park. This log cabin was built in 1828 by Grantville settler John C. Meadows. The cabin was set for destruction when I-85 was being built, but it was purchased and moved to its present site in the 1970s by the Coweta County commissioners. It is now used for events.

where to eat

Historic Grill. 13 Church St.; (770) 583-3332. This small-town diner serves up Southern fare. Chicken and dumplings are a must, but feel free to attempt the "trash plate," which is macaroni salad, fries, a hot dog, and chili. Mon through Sat 6:30 a.m. to 8 p.m. $.

Mi Pueblito. 6454 US 29 South; (770) 583-3944. Authentic Mexican food at great prices. Mon through Sat 11 a.m. to 8 p.m. $.

Nick's Pizzaria. 17 LaGrange St.; (770) 583-2240; www.nickspizzastop.com. Hand-tossed pizza, homemade pasta. Great stuff for a small-town pizzeria. Tues through Thurs 5 to 9 p.m., Fri and Sat 5 to 10 p.m. $.

where to stay

Bonnie Castle. 2 Post St.; (770) 683-3090; www.bonnie-castle.com/grantville.htm. Tucked away in historic Grantville, Bonnie Castle is a beautiful old Victorian mansion with wrought-iron gates and manicured gardens. There is even a rounded tower with turrets! The house is comfy and relaxing and you can stroll through the historic downtown. $.

day trip 02

almost to bama:
hogansville, lagrange, west point

We'll head right up to the Alabama border on this venture from Atlanta. As with Day Trip 01, this trip takes you to a large town as well as to two small towns that you might have otherwise passed by. The first stop is Hogansville, a charming little diversion off just I-85. It's highly possible you will run into members of the Hogan family in this town founded by their ancestor almost 200 years ago.

Contrast tiny Hogansville with LaGrange, which has been a bustling center of commerce since its 1800s beginnings. It's a mixture of historic and new with international companies on the doorstep of a city with hundreds of historically registered homes and buildings.

The last stop is knocking on the door of Alabama: West Point, the most western point of the Chattahoochee River before it takes a sharp turn south.

hogansville

Hogansville bills itself as "The City of Friendly People" and there is truth in their advertising. This small town of less than 3,000 includes people who have been here for generations, and they are happy to show off their thriving little community to others.

The town takes its name from its founder, William Hogan, who got the land through an 1826 land grant. There were important crossroads on his property, including a railroad. By

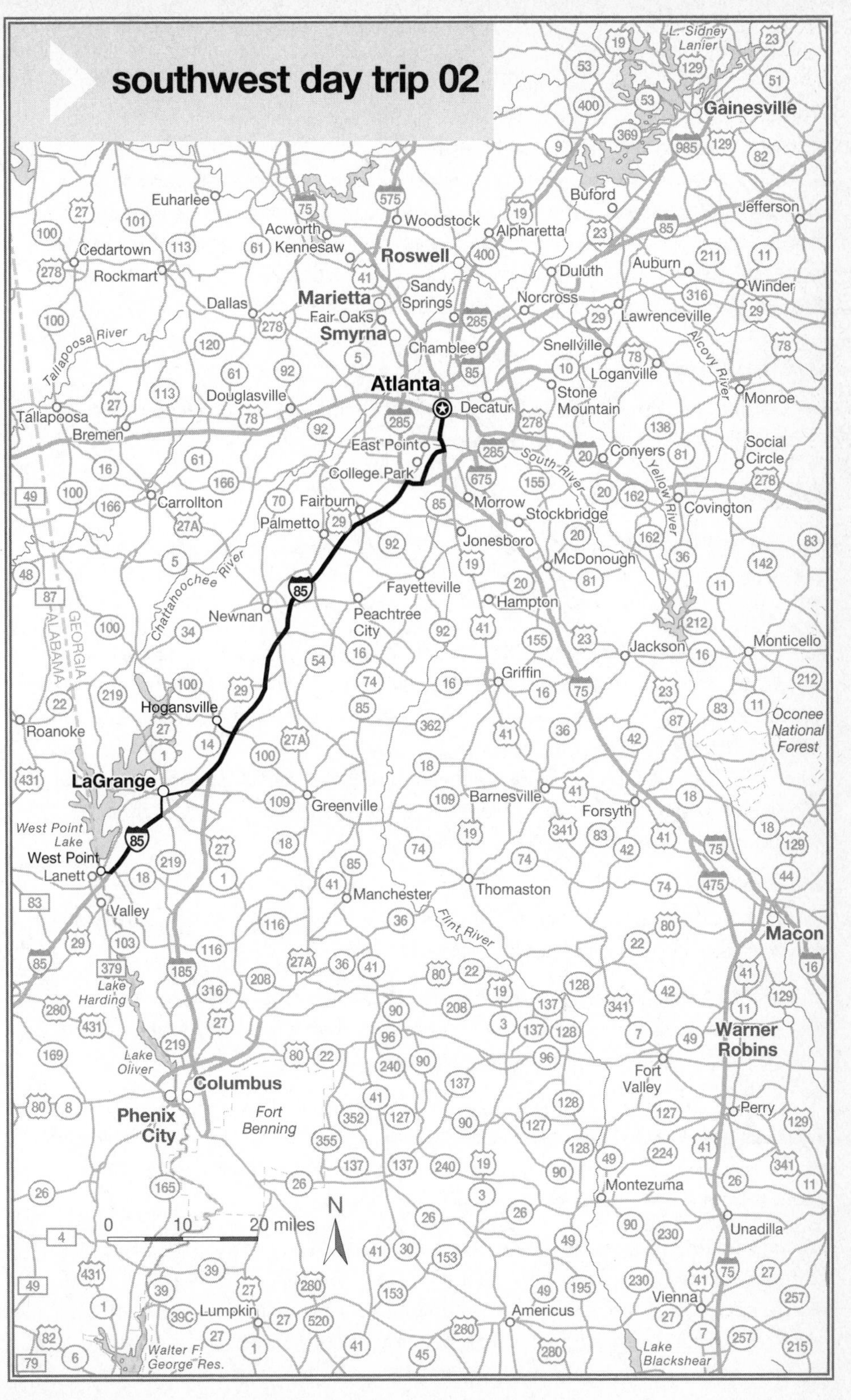
southwest day trip 02
Atlanta
Roswell
Marietta
Smyrna
Gainesville
LaGrange
West Point
Lanett
Hogansville
Newnan
Columbus
Phenix City
Macon
Warner Robins
Fort Benning
West Point Lake
Chattahoochee River
Flint River
Oconee National Forest
GEORGIA
ALABAMA
0
10
20 miles
N

striking a deal to give part of his land to the railroad, he was successful in having a depot built, which resulted in the town growing around it.

By the time it incorporated in 1870, Hogansville was a successful mill town and it grew into a center of commerce in the region. A mill still operates on the site of the original structure, but these days the town is best known for its active business community. It's a favorite place for antiques shoppers and there are countless other unique stores in the downtown area. Hogansville is also home to the annual Hummingbird Festival each October.

getting there

From Atlanta, the drive will take just under an hour. Head south on I-85 and get off at exit 29/GA 100. Go west and Hogansville is less than 3 miles off the interstate.

where to go

Hogansville Welcome Center. 306 E. Main St.; (706) 637-8013; www.hogansvillega.net. The welcome center is in among all the antiques shops so be sure to drop by for advice on where to shop and what to see. Thurs through Sat 11 a.m. to 5 p.m.

Fair Oak Plantation. 703 E. Main St.; (706) 637-8828. Now a bed-and-breakfast, this Victorian mansion was built on the site of William Hogan's original plantation home. There is a historical marker commemorating that house located just to the southwest, adjacent to the family cemetery. At one point, Hogan owned much of the present town of Hogansville. After his death in 1861, his son-in-law John Pullin sold the land for business and residential use. The building of Fair Oak was built by his granddaughter Eugenia Pullin Word in 1902 after the original home burned two years earlier.

Hogan Cemetery. 706 E. Main St. This small family cemetery is where William Hogan and numerous relatives are buried (he had 21 children by 2 wives). The historical marker nearby commemorates him and his plantation which encompassed this area.

Hogansville Amphitheater. E. Main Street. The Hogansville Amphitheater was built in the 1940s by the Civilian Conservation Corps using stone from a nearby rock quarry. It has undergone a complete restoration and is used often for local events and for concerts during the Hummingbird Festival.

Industrial Specialty Fabrics. 117 Corinth Rd.; (706) 637-0432. No tours are allowed, but this mill is a true point of interest. It was built in 1920 and is the only remaining mill in the town which once had three operating at once.

Railroad Depot. 100 Main St. The beautiful brick railroad depot served the Atlanta and Westpoint Railroad and was constructed in two stages. The freight room was built in 1890 with the passenger section being added in 1900. After the railroad vacated the depot, it had several uses before undergoing restoration in 2003 to be used as a restaurant. It is currently the largest train station/depot remaining between Chattanooga, TN, and Columbus, GA. It is now vacant but you can wander around the outside.

Royal Theater. 400 E. Main St.; (770) 637-8629. City Hall is now housed in what was once the Royal Theater. Built in 1937, by O.C. Lam, the Art Deco–style building was the center of social life in Hogansville for decades.

where to shop

Attic Treasures Uniques & Antiques Mall. 306 E. Main St.; (706) 637-8013. A wide selection of furniture, trinkets, and collectibles with several vendors. Mon through Fri 10 a.m. to 5 p.m., Sat 10 a.m. to 4 p.m.

Born Again Antiques. 304 E. Main St.; (404) 429-7191. Reborn and reclaimed furniture as well as hardware. Mon through Fri 10 a.m. to 5 p.m., Sat 11 a.m. to 2 p.m.

Hummingbird Antique Mall. 203 E. Main St.; (706) 637-4449. You'll find furniture and accessories in this little storefront that contains several vendors. Mon through Fri 10 a.m. to 5 p.m., Sat 11 a.m. to 3 p.m.

William and Mary's Antiques & Collectibles. 200 E. Main St., (706) 637-9497; www.wmandmary.com. There really are a William (Bill) and a Mary at this antiques store. Bill is the sports and memorabilia expert, while Mary loves the antique furniture, pottery, and dinnerware. Mon through Fri 10 a.m. to 5 p.m., Sat 11 a.m. to 3 p.m.

where to eat

The Grand Hotel Tea Room. 303 E. Main St.; (706) 637-8828 or (800) 324-7625; www.thegrandhotel.net. Enjoy high tea in a historic setting at the tearoom in the back of the Grand. Guests will enjoy a variety of tea settings. Reservation only. Mon through Sat 9 a.m. to 5 p.m. $$.

Hawg Heaven BBQ. GA 100; (706) 637-8990. Serving up country cooking and killer barbeque, you will be in Hawg Heaven. This is a favorite spot for motorcyclists to stop by. Tues through Fri 11 a.m. to 9 p.m., Sun 8 a.m. to 4 p.m. $.

International Cafe. 1875 E. Main St.; (706) 637-6050. You have a choice between the buffet or ordering off the menu. Either is delicious and offers a good variety of food in a number of styles. Tues through Sat 11 a.m. to 10 p.m. (lunch buffet until 4 p.m.), Sun 11 a.m. to 4 p.m. $.

Roger's Pit-Cooked Bar-B-Que. 1863 E. Main St.; (706) 637-4100; http://rogersbbq.com. Roger's has been cooking up 'que since 1945 when it was started in nearby West Point. The Hogansville location started in 1999 and is just as popular as the original. They serve up barbeque ribs, chopped pork, steak, and chicken with a wide selection of vegetables. Mon through Thurs 11 a.m. to 9 p.m., Fri and Sat 11 a.m. to 10 p.m. $.

where to stay

Fair Oaks Inn. 703 E. Main St.; (706) 637-8828. Built in 1901, Fair Oaks is on the site of the original Hogan Plantation home which burned in 1899. The existing Victorian house was built in 1901 by Hogan's granddaughter Eugenia Pullin Word. Be a part of Hogansville history by staying in this lovely B&B. Fair Oaks offers 6 guest rooms and has a pool and whirlpool on-site. $.

The Grand Hotel. 303 E. Main St.; (706) 637-8828 or (800) 324-7625; www.thegrandhotel.net. The veranda-encircled Grand Hotel was built in 1890 and maintains that old-style charm even though it is entirely updated. The Victorian building has a charming wood-paneled and brass-trimmed lobby on the second floor. It is here that guests are invited to enjoy a nightly complimentary cocktail. There are 10 rooms in the Grand and all have fireplaces with gas logs; 5 rooms have whirlpool tubs. The back of the hotel now is a Victorian tearoom, with high tea available by reservation. $$.

Woodstream Inn. 1888 E. Main St.; (706) 637-9395; www.hotelshogansvillega.com. This motel is built to fit in with the historic surroundings. Clean and convenient. Breakfast included. There is a pool on-site. $.

lagrange

LaGrange is another Georgia town that cemented its place in history early on. It was part of Indian Territory and was ceded as part of the treaties of the early 1800s. LaGrange took no time for it to be established as the county seat for Troup County and an important crossroads for commerce and industry, a tradition that has continued to this day.

The name is French, a nod to the country estate of the Marquis de Lafayette, who came through the region in 1825. During the Civil War, LaGrange was spared from destruction for the most part, and during Reconstruction established itself as a rail center. Even today, it is a major distribution center for several companies, including Wal-Mart.

But despite its industry, the core of the town has maintained its friendly atmosphere. In fact, LaGrange likes to refer to itself as a large small town. You'll find friendly pedestrian areas with great shops and restaurants and plenty of cultural experiences from which to choose.

getting there

From Atlanta, take I-85 south to exit 18/GA 109 West, which is West Lafayette Parkway. You will go less than 4 miles and arrive in Lafayette Square, which is the heart of LaGrange.

If coming from Hogansville, you may want to avoid I-85 and just take US 29 south 20 minutes to LaGrange.

where to go

LaGrange-Troup County Chamber of Commerce. 111 Bull St.; (706) 884-8671; www.lagrangechamber.com. Make this the first stop to stock up on maps and plan your itinerary. You can pick up a copy of the LaGrange Walking Tour map. Mon through Fri 10 a.m. to 5:30 p.m.

Bellevue. 204 Ben Hill St.; (706) 882-1832; www.lagrangechamber.com. Probably the prettiest building in town, Bellevue is an 1855 antebellum that was the home of Benjamin Harvey Hill, lawyer and Georgia and United States congressman. The National Register mansion features elaborate woodwork around the doorways and large windows which were hand carved by slaves. Tues through Sat 10 a.m. to 2 p.m.

Confederate Cemetery & Horace King Gravesite. Miller Street. Over 300 soldiers from every Confederate state are buried in this cemetery in the heart of town. Located just outside the walls are the graves of former slave and master bridge builder Horace King and his son Marshall. King was credited with building more than 100 covered bridges around the state of Georgia and lay in an unmarked grave until 1978.

Explorations In Antiquity Center. 130 Gordon Commercial Dr.; (706) 885-0363; www.explorationsinantiquity.com. You can step back and become a part of ancient times at this interactive museum of life in biblical lands. The exhibits are full-scale archaeological reconstructions of real discoveries and encompass several periods of both the Old and New Testament. Kids can participate in archaeological digs and sample foods typical of those times. Tues through Sat 10 a.m. to 6 p.m.

Hills & Dales Estate. 1916 Hills and Dales Dr.; www.hillsanddales.org. The Hills & Dales Estate was built as a showcase by textile magnate Fuller Callaway. Completed in 1916, the Italian villa–style home is surrounded by 35 acres of gardens cultivated over 175 years. Hills & Dales is still owned by the Callaway family. Mar through June Mon through Sat 10 a.m. to 6 p.m., Sun 1 to 6 p.m.; July through Feb, Tues through Sat 10 a.m. to 5 p.m.

Hoofers Gospel Barn. 3472 Hogansville Rd.; (800) 844-6737. If you want to get down with some great bluegrass and gospel, this is the place. The 1,200-seat venue draws nationally known artists to their huge auditorium.

Lafayette Society for Performing Arts. (706) 882-9909; www.lspaarts.com. For almost three decades the LSPA has led the way in providing cultural opportunities for residents to participate in and for others to enjoy. Year-round performances are scheduled, inviting audiences to enjoy everything from sophisticated ballet and live theater to homespun storytelling. Several arts groups operate under the umbrella of LSPA including The Lafayette

Ballet Company, The Young Singers of West Georgia, Azalea Storytelling Festival, and The Lafayette Theatre Company.

Lafayette Square. Downtown. Downtown LaGrange is centered around this charming historic square. You'll find tourists and residents alike sitting on a bench and taking in the scenery of this well manicured square. At its center is a bronze statue of the Marquis de LaFayette, who came through the area as a guest Georgia governor George Michael Troup in 1825. There is also a fountain in the square, and many of the town's most unique shops and restaurants are all within walking distance,

LaGrange Art Museum. 112 Lafayette Sq.; (706) 882-2367; www.lagrangeartmuseum.org. The LaGrange Art Museum is located in what used to be the Troup County Jail. Built in 1892, the Victorian structure alone is worth a visit, but the art museum makes it a double-do. It houses an incredible collection of contemporary art and is considered one of the state's best regional museums. Tues through Fri 9 a.m. to 5 p.m., Sat 11 a.m. to 5 p.m.

Lamar Dodd Art Center. 302 Forrest Ave.; (706) 880-8211; http://lagrange.edu. The Lamar Dodd Center houses the visual arts department of LaGrange College. Dedicated to 20th-century Southern painter Lamar Dodd, the center contains a permanent collection of his works as well as visiting artist exhibitions. Call for schedule. Open Sept through June, Mon through Fri 8:30 a.m. to 4:30 p.m.

The Legacy Museum on Main. 136 Main St.; (706) 884-1828; http://trouparchives.org. The Legacy Museum traces the history of LaGrange back to the days of Native Americans in the region and across pivotal moments over the centuries. There are permanent and temporary galleries featuring exhibits and artifacts. The museum also houses Troup County's genealogical library. Mon through Fri. 9 a.m. to 5 p.m., Sat 10 a.m. to 4 p.m. (Archives open first and third Sat only.)

Troup County Courthouse. 118 Ridley Ave.; (706) 883-1735; www.troupcountyga.org. This courthouse was built in 1939 through a New Deal work program after the previous building burned and is different from many of the other courthouses noted in this book. The marble building was designed by William J.J. Chase, who chose to a "stripped" design which blends classic and Art Deco.

where to eat

Brickhouse Grille. 141 Main St.; (706) 298-5482. Brickhouse Grille makes you feel like this is your neighborhood bar. Great sandwiches and plates. Live music on the weekend. Mon through Fri 11 a.m. to 2 a.m., Sat 11 a.m. to midnight. $$.

C Sons. 120 Main St.; (706) 298-0892; www.csons.net. Located in the heart of downtown, C Sons has an inventive menu of everything from shrimp tempura to salads and smoked duck breast. Tues through Sat 11 a.m. to 2:30 p.m., 5:30 to 10 p.m. $–$$.

Charlie Joseph's. 128 Bull St.; (706) 884-5416; http://charliejosephs.com This is as authentic a hot dog and hamburger stand as they come. Charlie Joseph's is an institution in downtown LaGrange. Walk up to the window or dine in. Mon through Sat 10 a.m. to 6 p.m. $.

Fried Tomato Buffet. 127 Commerce Ave. #G; (706) 884-8842. Country cooking with a good selection of meats and vegetables. Mon through Sat 11 a.m. to 9 p.m., Sun 11 a.m. to 8 p.m. $.

A Taste of Lemon. 204 Morgan St.; (706) 882-5382. If you have only one place to try Southern food, this should be it. Consistently good and in an elegant atmosphere. Mon through Fri 11 a.m. to 2:30 p.m. $.

Venucci. 129 Main St.; (706) 884-9393. A great little Italian bistro, complete with the brick walls, checked tables, and soft candlelight. Pasta is homemade and tasty. Mon through Sat 11 a.m. to 9:30 p.m. $–$$.

where to stay

Best Western Lafayette Garden Inn & Conference Center. 1513 Lafayette Pkwy.; (706) 884-6475; www.bestwestern.com. Convenient to the interstate, this Best Western is clean, comfortable and has a pool and fitness center on-site. $–$$.

Hampton Inn. 100 Willis Circle; (706) 845-1115; http://hamptoninn1.hilton.com. This comfortable hotel offers a continental breakfast and includes a fitness center and pool. It is also convenient to Callaway Gardens (see next day trip). $–$$.

Holiday Inn Express. 111 Lafayette Pkwy.; (706) 812-8000; www.hiexpress.com. Accessible to downtown and the interstate, the Holiday Inn Express has a fitness center and pool. $.

Thyme Away Bed and Breakfast. 508 Greenville St.; (706) 885-9625. Located in one of LaGrange's historic Greek Revival mansions, this beautifully decorated home provide comfy rooms for its guests. Each room has a separate bath with whirlpool tub and a small refrigerator. Breakfast is gourmet all the way. $–$$.

west point

Tiny West Point, Georgia, is another town that grew around a railroad stop. These days it is notable because it is on the banks of West Point Lake. Located right on the Alabama-Georgia state line, it's at the southern tip of the lake. It also got its name for being the westernmost point of the Chattahoochee River as it comes from the Appalachians and turns south.

Established in the 1800s, the town is undergoing a revitalization with the arrival of the Kia auto plant. Walk around the downtown and you'll be stunned at the beauty of some of the homes in this town that until recently had been almost forgotten.

getting there

West Point is just 11 miles from LaGrange south on I-85. Take exit 2 and make a right. It's just more than an hour directly from Atlanta down I-85 to exit 2.

where to go

West Point Depot & Visitor Center. 500 3rd Ave.; (706) 643-9404; http://westpointdepot.com. The renovated historic 1800s West Point Depot is once again the center of activity in town. Sitting on over one and a half acres, it now houses a welcome center, museum, and banquet hall. Train enthusiasts will love boxcars, a caboose, and memorabilia from both the railroads and local mills. Mon through Fri 9 a.m. to 4 p.m., first Sat of every month 10 a.m. to 2 p.m.

Fort Tyler. 6th Avenue and W. 10th Street; (706) 643-9404 or (886) 367-9792; http://forttyler.com. Built in 1863, Fort Tyler is an official Civil War Discovery Trail site. After years of use as a city reservoir, it has been reconstructed at its original location. The fort was named after Brigadier General R.C. Tyler, who on April 16, 1865, became the last general of either side killed during the Civil War. Fort Tyler was also the last fort to fall during the war. Daily dusk to dawn. Free.

West Point Lake. Just 5 minutes north of downtown is West Point Lake, an almost 27,000-acre lake created by an Army Corps of Engineers dam project on the Chattahoochee River. Stretching for almost 35 miles, it is known for boating and fishing opportunities. There are numerous places around the lake to picnic or hike, including a 6.397-acre wildlife management area. The area also has several golf courses.

where to eat

Heart of the South. 1111 2nd Ave.; (706) 643-0544. Incredible home-cooked food. Fried chicken, spoon bread, and banana pudding to die for. Tues, Wed, Fri, Sun 11 a.m. to 2 p.m.; Thurs 11 a.m. to 2:30 p.m. $.

Irish Bred Pub. 727 3rd Ave.; (706) 645-2600; www.theirishbredpub.com. There are a few of these Irish Bred Pubs around North Georgia, but each is unique and fairly authentic as US-Irish pubs go. Good pub grub and Guinness on tap. Mon through Wed 11 a.m. to 11 p.m., Thurs through Sat 11 a.m. to midnight. $.

Momma MIA Pizzeria. 21 E. 10th St.; (706) 643-7492. Not just pizza but pasta as well. Homemade and authentic Italian. Mon through Sat 11 a.m. to 9 p.m. $–$$.

where to stay

Days Inn. 2314 S Broad Ave., Lanett, AL; (334) 644-2181; http://daysinn.com. Less than 2 miles from West Point. Clean, comfortable. Continental breakfast included. Pool on-site. $.

Southern Harbor Resort and Marina. 1133 CR 294, Lanett, AL; (334) 644-3881; http://southernharbor.com. Southern Harbor is just 5 miles from West Point and offers waterfront cabins, boat rentals, and a restaurant at this full-service marina. $.

Travel Lodge. 1870 GA 18, West Point; (706) 643-9922; http://travellodge.com. Small hotel, convenient to the interstate and West Point. $.

day trip 03

gives you butterflies:
callaway gardens

Just the name Callaway rolls off the tongue in sort of a relaxing manner and that's just what this place does—relaxes you—even though with so much to do, some of you may feel you need to cram it all in. Callaway truly has it all. This is a real haven of natural beauty and even those in Atlanta know this is a place to escape to.

Callaway is technically located in Pine Mountain, which is part of Day Trip 04, and right at the front door of Columbus, which is Day Trip 05. But we felt Callaway is in a class by itself and deserves its own trip. Feel free to stay here and continue on to Day Trips 04 and/ or 05 from here.

callaway gardens

Callaway Gardens was first started in 1952 by Cason and Virginia Callaway because of their love of azaleas. That love has grown into a 13,000-acre resort complex that draws people year-round to enjoy what has been created here. Awash in color each spring with the azalea blossoms, Callaway has now combined historic buildings, championship golf, and a world-class spa all within a beautiful setting.

A nonprofit organization dedicated to horticulture, the garden hosts numerous events celebrating nature and what it offers. If you can't plan your visit around one of them, believe us, you won't be lacking for things to see and do.

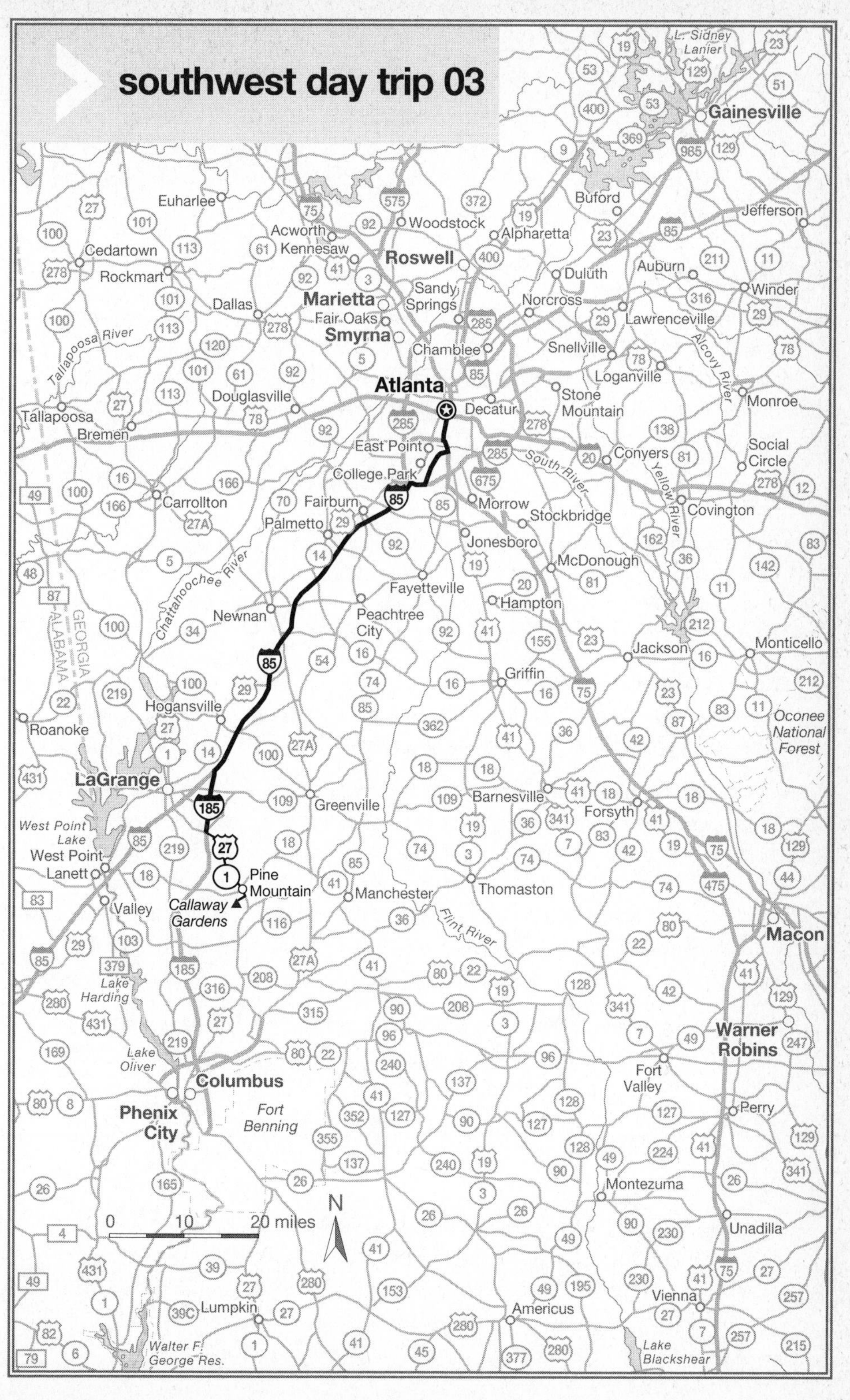
southwest day trip 03
L. Sidney Lanier
Gainesville
Jefferson
Buford
Woodstock
Alpharetta
Euharlee
Acworth
Kennesaw
Roswell
Duluth
Auburn
Winder
Cedartown
Rockmart
Marietta
Sandy Springs
Norcross
Lawrenceville
Dallas
Fair Oaks
Smyrna
Chamblee
Snellville
Tallapoosa River
Alcovy River
Loganville
Atlanta
Stone Mountain
Monroe
Tallapoosa
Bremen
Douglasville
Decatur
East Point
College Park
Conyers
Social Circle
South River
Yellow River
Carrollton
Fairburn
Morrow
Stockbridge
Covington
Palmetto
Jonesboro
McDonough
Chattahoochee River
Fayetteville
Hampton
Newnan
Peachtree City
ALABAMA
GEORGIA
Jackson
Monticello
Griffin
Hogansville
Roanoke
Oconee National Forest
LaGrange
Greenville
Barnesville
Forsyth
West Point Lake
West Point
Lanett
Pine Mountain
Manchester
Thomaston
Callaway Gardens
Valley
Flint River
Macon
Lake Harding
Warner Robins
Lake Oliver
Columbus
Fort Valley
Phenix City
Fort Benning
Perry
Montezuma
0 10 20 miles
N
Unadilla
Lumpkin
Vienna
Americus
Walter F. George Res.
Lake Blackshear

Garden gates open at 9 a.m. but closing depends on the season. Admission is $18 for adults, $9 for children. You will need to pick up a map at the entrance to track the locations of the attractions. Those staying at the resort end of the gardens can enjoy a host of amenities and activities while on the grounds.

getting there

Callaway Gardens is 80 minutes from Atlanta. Take I-85 south 55 miles to I-185, then exit 42 for US 27. Follow US 27 South to Pine Mountain. In Pine Mountain, turn right onto GA 354 West. Proceed to GA 18 and turn left into Callaway Gardens. There are two entrances. The beach entrance will get you there, but you will first have to go through the resort village. Continue past the beach entrance less than a mile to the main entrance

where to go

Callaway Gardens Entrance. GA 354 and GA 18; (800) CALLAWAY (225-5292); www .callawaygardens.com. From the moment you enter Callaway there are things to see and enjoy. The Gardens Entrance is near Mountain Creek Lake and after the entrance, the road splits in several directions. Things to do at Callaway include:

Overlook Garden. Located near the Gardens Entrance, the Overlook Garden gives you just a taste of what lies ahead. Best experienced during spring bloom, it contains thousands of carefully cultivated azaleas of more than 700 varieties.

Cecil B. Day Butterfly Garden at Callaway Gardens. (706) 663-2281. If you have never experienced a butterfly house, you may walk in here and want to spend the whole day. This 8,000-square-foot, glass-enclosed conservatory is home to 1,000 free-flying butterflies. As you walk through the lush, enclosed gardens, they will flitter back and forth in front of you and some may even land on you. Scattered among the plants and waterfalls, you may also see some ground pheasants lurking. This is the largest butterfly garden in North America.

Virginia Hand Callaway Discovery Center. The center is located at the heart of the gardens on the western shore of Mountain Creek Lake. Virginia Hand Callaway (1900–1995) was co-founder of Callaway Gardens and this 35,000-square-foot facility serves as a welcome center, museum, and a lecture hall. There is an orientation film that will help outline the history of Callaway as well as tell you all that is available. There is also a gift shop and a cafe within the center.

Discovery Bicycle Trail. Much of Callaway is accessible simply by driving, but there is a 7.5-mile Discovery Bicycle Trail that not only connects key points of interest, but will take you a bit deeper into some of the woodlands and wetlands than the car. That said, there are several places for you to access the trail from your car and give you a chance to see not just the foliage, but birds and other wildlife as well.

John A. Sibley Horticultural Center. The Sibley Horticulture Center is probably one of the most advanced greenhouse complexes in the world under one roof. Spread over 5 acres, it is all computer climate controlled. That says a lot because the center encompasses everything from native Georgian plants to Mediterranean gardens to a tropical rain forest. Inside you will find a 22-foot indoor waterfall.

Callaway Brothers Azalea Bowl. There is a reason it is called a bowl. Over 3,400 azaleas form a natural amphitheater of color here in the spring. This hiking path on the southwest shore of Falls Creek Lake also holds a wide array of trees and shrubs. When not in bloom, it is still an amazing place to be. The Callaway Brothers were Ely and Fuller Calloway, the uncle and father of gardens founder Cason Callaway

Ida Cason Callaway Memorial Chapel. Named for Callaway Gardens founder Cason Callaway's mother, this is truly one of the most peaceful areas of the garden and saying that says a lot. The Gothic-style chapel has stained-glass windows depicting the seasons of the Southern forest and sits on the edge of the woods at Falls Creek Lake. Inside the chapel is a Möller pipe organ, and you can often hear the sound of the music through the woodlands.

Mr. Cason's Vegetable Garden. This 7.5-acre garden is adjacent to the resort on the north side of the gardens. It will make you want to paint your thumb green when you see this array of fruits, vegetables, herbs, and flowers.

Pioneer Log Cabin. An authentic 18th-century structure representing the life of Georgia's early settlers.

TreeTop Adventure. Opened in May 2011, guests can take their love of adventure and nature to brand-new heights on the new TreeTop Adventure, where guests can climb, leap, swing, and whizz their way through a dizzying course of zip-lines, swinging bridges, nets, logs, and other aerial challenges in the natural forest.

Spa Prunifolia. Intersection of GA 18 and 354; (706) 663-2281. Spa Prunifolia is located in the northern end of the gardens in the resort section. The spa includes 13 treatment rooms with which to pamper guests. Daily 9 a.m. to 6 p.m.

Golf. Callaway's founder Cason Callaway believed that "playing golf should be a pleasant experience in beautiful surroundings." The result of his belief are two spectacular courses, the Mountain View Championship Golf Course and the Lake View Golf Course. Both courses were designed by world-famous architect Dick Wilson. Mountain View is a 7,057-yard par 72 course that was home to the PGA tour's Buick Challenge for over a decade. Lake View is Callaway Gardens' original golf course.

Birds of Prey. There are live shows daily featuring these magnificent birds. Guests witness the power and the beauty in free-flight shows held in the lakeside amphitheater. No two shows are the same. There are approximately a dozen birds in the program, and at each show, 3 to 5 of the raptors appear.

Mountain Creek Tennis Center. The center has helped earn Callaway *Tennis* magazine's honor of being among the "Top 50 Tennis Resorts in the Nation." There are 10 outdoor lighted tennis courts.

where to eat

Champions Grille. Mountain View Clubhouse. This sports bar is the perfect stop after hitting the links. It serves light breakfast, salads, and sandwiches and of course is the 19th hole at the end of a good round. Mon through Fri 7:30 a.m. to 5 p.m., Sat and Sun 7:30 a.m. to 6 p.m. $–$$.

Country Kitchen. Callaway Gardens Store, US 27. The Country Kitchen is one of Callaway's oldest restaurants. It serves traditional Southern food in a quaint country store setting. Selections include salads, meat-and-vegetable combinations, sandwiches, and burgers. Offers "down-home" Southern cooking enjoyed by the Georgia locals for generations. Breakfast daily 8 a.m. to 11 a.m., lunch/dinner daily 11:30 a.m. to 9 p.m. $–$$.

Discovery Cafe. Virginia Hand Callaway Discovery Center. The setting is as good as the food. The cafe can seat you inside or outside on a deck overlooking Mountain Creek Lake. Soups, salads, hamburgers, and hot dogs offered daily from 11:30 a.m. to 4 p.m. (Drinks and snacks until 5 p.m.) $.

Gardens Restaurant. Garden Clubhouse; (706) 663-2281. Located in an elegant and historic setting overlooking Mountain Creek Lake and the Lake View Golf Course, this is one of Callaway's finer resort restaurants. Entrees are created from Callaway Gardens' regional, sustainable food initiative. Many vegetables are grown right here at the gardens. Reservations strongly recommended. Tues through Sat 5:30 to 9 p.m. $$–$$$.

The Plant Room. Mountain Creek Inn, The Plant Room serves up traditional Southern food in a buffet style. Mon through Sun breakfast 6:30 to 10:30 a.m.; dinner Fri and Sat 5 to 9 p.m. $–$$.

Rockin' Robin's Malt Shop and Pizzeria. The Southern Pine Cottages. Only open during the summer months, this '50s-style malt shop serves up hot sub sandwiches, pizzas, malts, and hand-dipped ice cream, all while you are listening to a jukebox. Sun 11 a.m. to 8 p.m., Mon through Thurs 11 a.m. to 9 p.m., Fri and Sat 11 a.m. to 10 p.m. $.

Vineyard Green Restaurant and Spirits. Mountain Creek Inn. Vineyard offers a unique blend of Southern food and other offerings such as pizza, salads, and burgers. Sun through Thurs 11:30 a.m. to 9 p.m. (10 p.m. for cocktails). $$.

where to stay

The Cottages at Callaway Gardens. US 27; (706) 663-2281 or (800) 225-5292; http://callawaygardens.com. Good for a family getaway, the Cottages include 155 two-bedroom guest houses. $$.

The Lodge and Spa at Callaway Gardens. US 27; (706) 663-2281 or (800) 225-5292; http://callawaygardens.com. A Marriott property, rooms and suites at the lodge all have their own balconies overlooking the woodlands. The Spa Prunifolia is on the grounds to help pamper you. $$$.

Mountain Creek Inn at Callaway Gardens. US 27; (706) 663-2281 or (800) 225-5292; http://callawaygardens.com. Central to the shops and restaurants, the lodge has 323 rooms and includes a fitness center. $$.

The Villas at Callaway Gardens. US 27; (706) 663-2281 or (800) 225-5292; http://callawaygardens.com. The villas range in size from 1 to 4 bedrooms and feature living rooms, kitchens, and dining rooms as well as laundry facilities for a home away from home. $$$.

day trip 04

driving presidential:
pine mountain, warm springs

You'll be feeling presidential as you take this drive southwest and hit a unique part of Georgia known for its hot springs and pine trees. President Franklin D. Roosevelt brought worldwide attention to this area when he came here in 1924 to seek treatment in the springs for his polio affliction and ultimately bought a home here.

Pine Mountain and Warm Springs are cute little Southern towns in their own right, but you'll soon realize why FDR came back time and time again, not just for therapeutic purposes but because the region is just beautiful and there is much to see and do. The wooded region is both relaxing and stimulating and another of those day trips that will make you either want to stay or come back again and again as FDR did.

pine mountain

Picturesque Pine Mountain has gained a well earned reputation as being a great place to escape. Located in the foothills, it may have had its beginnings in agriculture but it has turned its attention to growing visitors. You'd swear you were much further into the mountains as you walk through the historic downtown and browse the shops and restaurants.

The town was founded under the name of Chipley in 1882 as the railroad was built through the area. When Roosevelt began coming to nearby Warm Springs, tourists followed suit to see what the appeal was. As the crowds grew, so did the attractions and

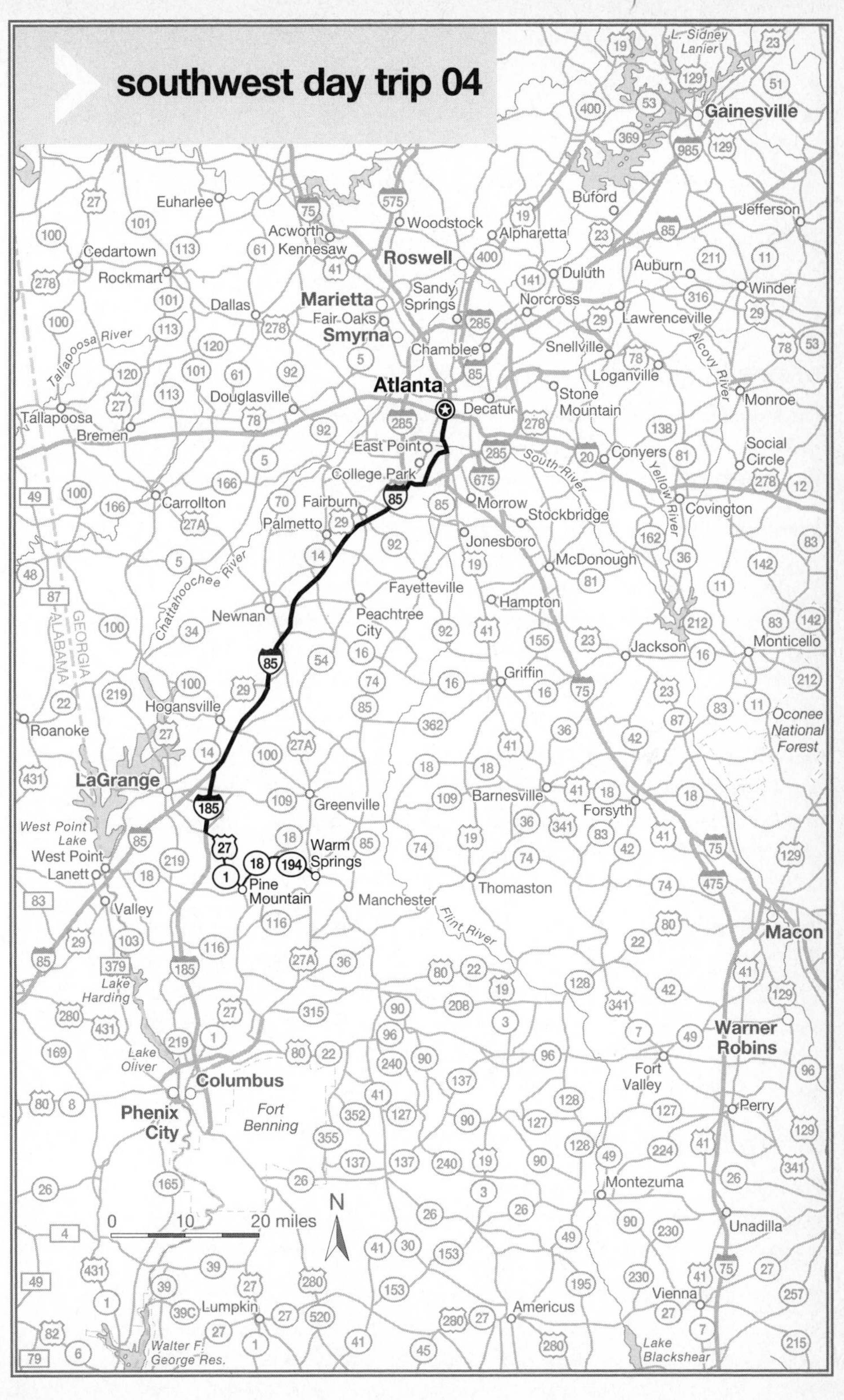
southwest day trip 04
L. Sidney Lanier
Gainesville
Buford
Jefferson
Euharlee
Woodstock
Acworth
Kennesaw
Alpharetta
Cedartown
Roswell
Duluth
Auburn
Winder
Rockmart
Dallas
Marietta
Sandy Springs
Norcross
Lawrenceville
Fair Oaks
Smyrna
Tallapoosa River
Chamblee
Snellville
Alcovy River
Loganville
Atlanta
Monroe
Douglasville
Stone Mountain
Tallapoosa
Decatur
Bremen
East Point
Social Circle
Conyers
South River
College Park
Yellow River
Carrollton
Fairburn
Morrow
Covington
Palmetto
Stockbridge
Jonesboro
McDonough
Chattahoochee River
Fayetteville
Hampton
GEORGIA
ALABAMA
Newnan
Peachtree City
Jackson
Monticello
Griffin
Hogansville
Roanoke
Oconee National Forest
LaGrange
Barnesville
Greenville
Forsyth
West Point Lake
West Point
Warm Springs
Lanett
Pine Mountain
Manchester
Thomaston
Valley
Flint River
Macon
Lake Harding
Warner Robins
Lake Oliver
Fort Valley
Columbus
Phenix City
Fort Benning
Perry
Montezuma
Unadilla
0
10
20 miles
N
Lumpkin
Vienna
Americus
Walter F. George Res.
Lake Blackshear

the town ultimately changed its name to Pine Mountain when Callaway Gardens was founded.

The name certainly suits the area, and you'll love exploring and experiencing it.

getting there

Pine Mountain is 80 minutes from Atlanta. Take I-85 south 55 miles to I-185, then exit 42 onto US 27, and follow it south to Pine Mountain.

where to go

Pine Mountain Regional Visitor Information Center. 101 E. Broad St.; (706) 663-4000 or (800) 441-3502; http://pinemountain.org. Stop in here for maps and discounts for local attractions and restaurants. Mon through Fri 9 a.m. to 5 p.m., Sat 10 a.m. to 4 p.m.

Roosevelt State Park. www.gastateparks.org/FDRoosevelt. At 9,049 acres, this is Georgia's largest state park and a place where Franklin D. Roosevelt used to come and picnic. The park is located near the Little White House historic area. Amenities include more than 40 miles of hiking trails, horseback riding, cabins, and the Liberty Bell pool which is fed by natural springs. Try to make it up to Dowdell's Knob above King's Gap. It is the highest point in the park and a favorite spot of Roosevelt's. The views are spectacular. Daily 7 a.m. to 10 p.m.

Sweet Home Plantation. 2626 Hadley Rd.; (706) 663-2486; www.sweethomeplantation.com. Sweet Home helps transport you to the Antebellum South. The National Register 1840 Greek Revival home is surrounded by 100 acres of gardens, fields, woods, and original outbuildings. Beautifully furnished, the home is welcoming and will give you a sense of the past. Visits by appointment only.

Wild Animal Safari. 1300 Oak Grove Rd.; (706) 663-8744; www.animalsafari.com. This looks more like Africa than Georgia. Wild Animal Safari allows guests to drive through or take a guided bus tour through this 500-acre park with hundreds of wild and exotic species of animals from around the world. A petting zoo on-site includes creatures such as monkeys, bears, alligators, and tropical birds. The Georgia Wildlife Museum features animal, bird, fish, and snake exhibits. Daily 10 a.m. to 5:30 p.m.

where to eat

The Bakery and Cafe at Rose Cottage. 111 E. Broad St.; (706) 663-7877; www.rosecottagega.com. All the foods here are locally grown and farm-raised products. There are microbeers and fine wine available. Daily 10 a.m. to 6 p.m. $–$$.

Carriage & Horses. 607 Butts Mill Rd.; (706) 663-4777; www.cometodagher.com. Elegant dining on the grounds of a beautiful horse farm, they feature steaks, seafood, and live entertainment in the evenings. Daily 11 a.m. until midnight. Reservations required. $$.

Cricket's Restaurant. 14661 US 18 West; (706) 663-8136; www.cricketsrestaurant.com. A great surprise with authentic Cajun food. Daily 5 p.m. until midnight. $–$$.

The Dish. 153 Main St.; (706) 663-7734. Casual atmosphere serving continental breakfast, sandwiches, hot dogs. From the fountain, ice cream, sundaes, shakes, and floats. Wed and Thurs 9 a.m. to 7 p.m., Fri through Sun 9 a.m. to 8 p.m. $.

Eddie Mae Gunn's Country Buffet. 324 Main St.; (706) 663-2640. Eddie Mae's offers up Southern-style cooking like mom used to make. Daily 6 a.m. to 8 p.m. $–$$.

Fox's Pizza. 1 Chipley Village II; (706) 663-2002. Fox's serves pizza and pasta, offering a selection of stromboli, wedgies, hoagies, breadsticks, salads, wings, spaghetti, side items, cheesecake, and more. Daily 11 a.m. to 9 p.m. $–$$.

Krispy Fried Chicken. US 27; (706) 663-4724. It's not just about the chicken. Krispy serves a variety of foods including fish, burgers, and sandwiches. Mon through Sat 11 a.m. to 10 p.m., Sun 10 a.m. to 9 p.m. $.

San Marcos Mexican Restaurante. 352 S. Main St.; (706) 663-8075. Authentic Mexican food. Mon through Sat 11 a.m. to 2 p.m. and 5 to 10 p.m. $.

Three Lil' Pigs. 146 S. Main St.; (706) 663-8423. Huge, tasty plates of barbeque. Daily 11 a.m. to 7 p.m. $.

27th Grill. 19611 US 27; (706) 663-2447. A local hangout serving steaks, salmon, salads, sandwiches, pizzas, and desserts. Sun through Thurs 11 a.m. to 10 p.m., Fri and Sat 11 a.m. to 11 p.m. $–$$.

Whistling Pig Cafe. US 27; (706) 663-4647. Barbeque sandwiches and plates, ribs, chicken, burgers, hot dogs, homemade fries, fried green tomatoes, and more. Mon through Sat 10:30 a.m. to 3 p.m. $.

where to stay

Chipley-Murrah House. 207 W. Harris St.; (706) 663-9801; www.chipleymurrah.com. Built in 1827, this beautiful Victorian bed-and-breakfast with its wraparound porch can be a great place to call home during your visit. There are 4 rooms in the home and 3 cottages on the grounds as well as a pool and manicured gardens. $$–$$$.

Fireside Inn. US 27; (706) 663-4141 or (800) 663-1414; www.fireside-pinemtn.com. Completely renovated. Comfy and clean. Pool on-site. $–$$.

Homestead Log Cabins. Pine Mountain and Warm Springs; (706) 663-4951 or (866) 652-2246. There are 3 locations in the area where you can rent 1- to 9-bedroom cabins. All self-catering. $$.

Mountain Top Inn & Resort. GA 190 and Hines Gap Road; (706) 663-4719 or (800) 533-6376; http://mountaintopinnga.com. This resort is inside Roosevelt State Park between Warm Springs and Pine Mountain. The inn includes cabins for rent and there is a pool on-site. $–$$.

Pine Mountain Club Chalets Resort. 14475 GA 18 West; (706) 663-2211 or (800) 535-7622; http://pmccresort.com. The 65-acre resort is built to resemble an alpine village. There are numerous activities on-site and rooms available in the lodge or cabin rental. $–$$.

White Columns Motel. 524 S. Main St.; (706) 663-2312 or (800) 722-5083; http://whitecolumnsmotel.com. In the heart of Pine Mountain, close to shops and restaurants. $.

worth more time

Big Bear Farm. 649 Butts Mill Rd.; (706) 881-2141; www.bigbearfarm.com. Big Bear Farm includes a faith-based Enough Ministries which is funded through the horse riding and training facilities. Located on 420 acres of rolling hills, this was the training site for both the 1996 Summer Olympic and Paralympic Games. You can come ride or just watch the horses. Big Bear Farm hosts several equestrian shows throughout the year which are free and open to the public. $$.

Butts Mill Farm. 2280 Butts Mill Rd.; (706) 663-7400. The Butts farm was established in 1830 and has been a retreat since the 1990s. The 80-acre grounds contain the historic waterwheel gristmill, a bird sanctuary, petting zoo, horseback riding, and fishing. It's a great way to see and enjoy a historic farm. $$.

warm springs

Walk around the historic district of Warm Springs and you will feel an immediate connection to its remarkable past. The springs here have been drawing people for their therapeutic purposes since the times of early Native Americans. Pumping 88-degree water at 980 gallons a minute, their constant flow brought settlers as far back as the 1700s. Buildings in the downtown reflect the fact that this started becoming a resort in the early 1800s, and business really began to boom with the coming of the railroad in the 1830s.

Warm Springs developed into a full-on resort destination in 1893 when the 300-room Meriwether Inn was built. The inn featured a dance pavilion, bowling alley, tennis, and skeet shooting to give guests other things to do when not soaking in the springs.

The area was in a decline when the resort was bought by New York philanthropist George Foster Peabody, who extolled the virtues of the springs to his friend Franklin D. Roosevelt. Having been afflicted with polio, FDR decided to try a treatment here for himself. One swim in the waters and he immediately felt an improvement. News quickly spread and others began coming.

FDR purchased the Warm Springs Center and surrounding 17,000 acres and started the nonprofit Warms Springs Foundation in 1927 to help others in need of treatment. That facility continues to operate in the historic district.

getting there

Pine Mountain and Warm Springs are just 13 miles apart. Take US 18 east 7 miles to Durand and then GA 194 to Warm Springs. From Atlanta, the drive is about 90 minutes. You would take I-85 south 34 miles to exit 41, US 27 South, towards Moreland. Follow US 27 for 35 miles to Warm Springs.

where to go

Warm Springs Welcome Center. 1 Broad St.; (706) 655-3322 or (800) 337-1927; www.warmspringsga.ws. There is a lot to see in this little town and the center will help you distinguish how to spend your time. Mon through Sat 10 a.m. to 5 p.m.

FDR's Pools & Warm Springs Museum. 401 Little White House Rd.; (706) 655-5870; http://georgiastateparks.org. Located at the Little White House, these pools were built specifically by FDR to use for his treatments. The museum helps trace the history of springs in the area and allows visitors to actually feel the warm water as it flows into a basin. Daily 9 a.m. to 4:45 p.m. Free.

Little White House. 401 Little White House Rd.; (706) 655-5870; www.gastateparks.org/LittleWhiteHouse. This little cottage was President Franklin D. Roosevelt's southern retreat and he came here often. It is also where he died on April 12, 1945, and is preserved as it was on the day he died. On display are original furniture, memorabilia, and the portrait on which Elizabeth Shoumatoff was working when the president was stricken with a massive cerebral hemorrhage. The complex includes a museum, picnic area, and snack bar as well as a theater where a film is shown about Roosevelt's life at Warm Springs and in Georgia. You can also see a display of the historic warm spring pools which drew him to the area. Daily 9 a.m. to 4:45 p.m.; closed January 1, Thanksgiving, December 25.

Roosevelt Warm Springs Institute for Rehabilitation. 6391 Roosevelt Hwy.; (706) 655-5000; http://rooseveltrehab.org. Listed as a National Historic Landmark, the rehabilitative center was founded by FDR so that others could also experience the health benefits of the warm springs. The pools are not open to the public but are available for patients of the institute. There is a full staff on-site dedicated to therapy and treatments. Open for visitors Mon through Sat 10 a.m. to 3 p.m. Guided tours are available Mon through Fri 11 a.m. to 2 p.m. Free.

where to eat

The Bulloch House Restaurant and Gift Shop. 47 Bulloch St.; (706) 655-9068. Bulloch House is probably Warm Springs' best-known restaurant. Located in the heart of town, this old house serves up a great Southern-style buffet, complete with multiple choices of meats and vegetables. Save room for dessert. Daily 11 a.m. to 2:30 p.m., Fri and Sat 5 to 8:30 p.m. $$.

Dinner's Ready. 5928 Spring St.; (706) 655-2060. Or should we say lunch? This place serves as a catering business but is open for lunch, so you can try their sandwiches, salads, and great desserts. Mon through Sat 11 a.m. to 2 p.m. $.

Mac's Barbecue and Mac's Steaks. Spring and Main Streets; (706) 655-2472. These two are next door to each other but keep different hours because they have different cuisines. Mac's BBQ serves up mouthwatering pork or beef BBQ as well as homemade desserts. Mac's Steaks is only open for dinner, but their talent with steaks makes it worth the wait. Mac's BBQ: daily 11 a.m. to 8 p.m. Mac's Steaks: Fri and Sat 5 to 9 p.m. $–$$.

Oscars Steak and Seafood. 4776 Nebula Rd.; (706) 655-2563; www.oscarssteakandseafood.com. You'll find plenty of locals at this steak and seafood restaurant. Casual atmosphere in a restaurant that is pretty much located in the middle of a cow pasture, it also features great Southern-style specials. Reservations suggested. Tues through Thurs 5 p.m. to midnight, Fri 5 p.m. to 1 a.m., Sat 5 p.m. to midnight, Sun 4 to 8 p.m. $$.

Paradise Grille. (706) 655-2260. Appropriately named, this is a great place for grilled burgers, hot dogs, hoagies, and salads. Those with a sweet tooth should try the desserts. Mon through Sat 10 a.m. to 9 p.m., Sun 11 a.m. to 9 p.m. $.

where to stay

Georgian Inn Bed and Breakfast. 566 S. Talbotton St., US 27 Alt South, Greenville, GA; (706) 977-9700. Just minutes from Warm Springs, this 1914 mansion offers 5 comfortable rooms in a relaxed, country atmosphere. $–$$.

Hotel Warm Springs Bed & Breakfast Inn. 47 Broad St.; (706) 655-2114 or (800) 366-7616; http://hotelwarmspringsbb.org. Built in 1907, this historic inn played host to all of FDR's VIP guests from kings to other presidents. Located in the heart of town, walk to attractions. $–$$.

Meriwether Country Inn. 5675 Spring St.; (706) 655-9099 or (866) 691-4061; http://meriwethercountryinn.com In the heart of downtown Warm Springs, within walking distance of shops and attractions. $.

day trip 05

outpost no more:

columbus

The city of Columbus is on the western border of the state, but it actually used to be the border of the wild frontier back in the 1800s. The city has always been a gateway of sorts because of the Chattahoochee River. This trip is only about a 90-minute drive, but you'll be on a real journey to see the past and the future because Columbus may celebrate its past, but its eyes are squarely on the future.

You'll find a fascinating science center and state-of-the-art entertainment facilities, and you'll wonder why you haven't made this journey before.

columbus

There is an incredible amount of history, culture, and industry in this small city. Columbus grew up on the banks of the Chattahoochee River at its waterfalls. South of Columbus, the river was navigable to the sea, a fact not lost on either the Creek Indian Nation which claimed this land nor the settlers who came after them.

The town was founded in 1829 and quickly grew because of its strategic location. Goods were brought here to ship, and agriculture and industry in the area both thrived. Its port made it a strategic location for shipping supplies during the Civil War, and the last land battle of the war took place here in 1865.

In 1918, the US Army presented the Columbus chamber of Commerce with a "Proposal for the Lease of Land to the U.S. Government for Establishment of School of

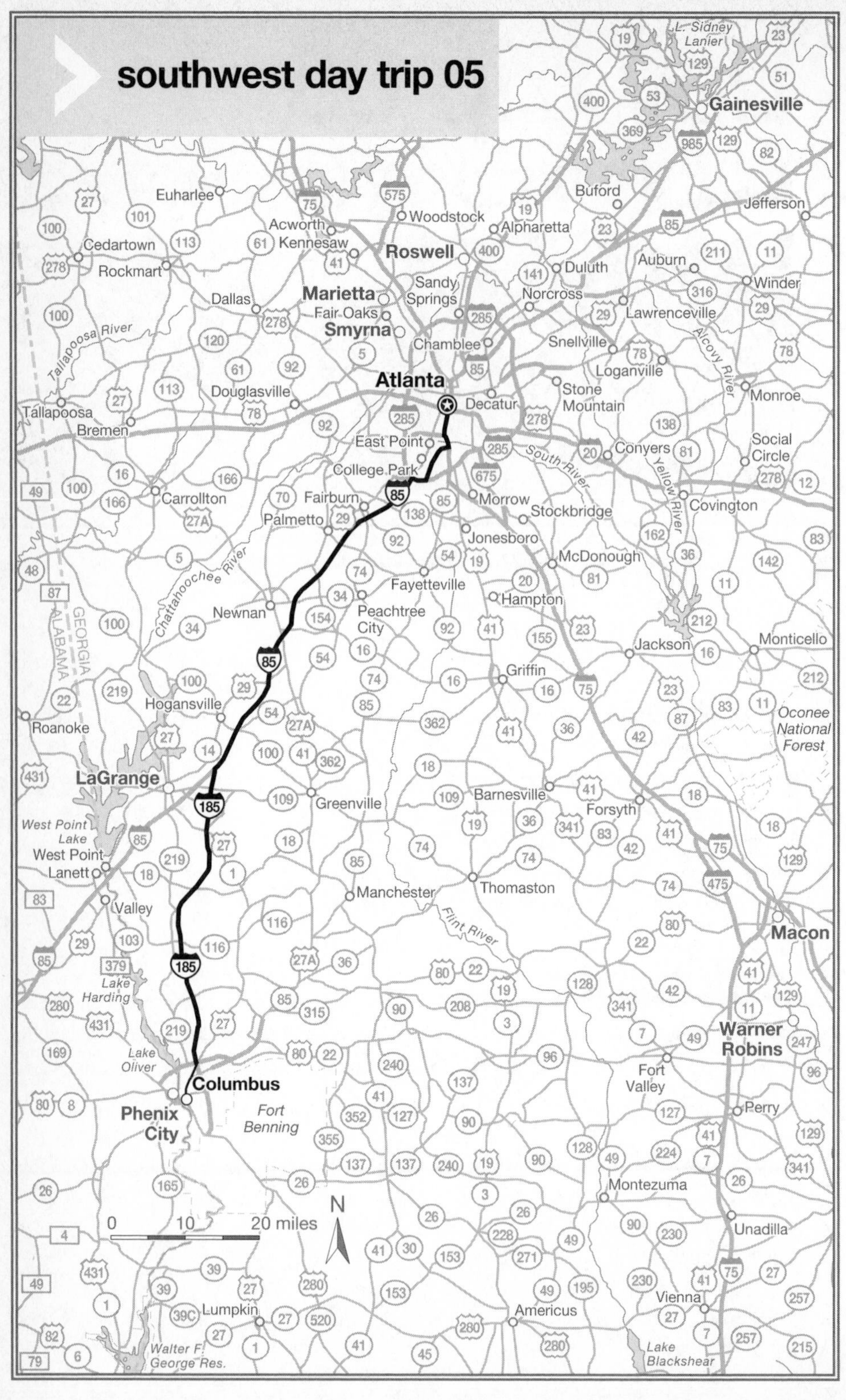

southwest day trip 05
L. Sidney Lanier
Gainesville
Buford
Jefferson
Euharlee
Woodstock
Acworth
Kennesaw
Alpharetta
Roswell
Cedartown
Rockmart
Duluth
Auburn
Winder
Sandy Springs
Marietta
Dallas
Norcross
Lawrenceville
Fair Oaks
Smyrna
Tallapoosa River
Chamblee
Snellville
Alcovy River
Loganville
Atlanta
Stone Mountain
Monroe
Tallapoosa
Decatur
Bremen
East Point
Conyers
Social Circle
South River
College Park
Yellow River
Carrollton
Fairburn
Morrow
Covington
Palmetto
Stockbridge
Jonesboro
McDonough
Chattahoochee River
Fayetteville
Hampton
Newnan
Peachtree City
GEORGIA
ALABAMA
Jackson
Monticello
Griffin
Hogansville
Roanoke
Oconee National Forest
LaGrange
Barnesville
Greenville
Forsyth
West Point Lake
West Point
Lanett
Manchester
Thomaston
Valley
Flint River
Macon
Lake Harding
Warner Robins
Lake Oliver
Fort Valley
Columbus
Phenix City
Fort Benning
Perry
Montezuma
0
10
20 miles
N
Unadilla
Lumpkin
Americus
Vienna
Walter F. George Res.
Lake Blackshear

Musketry." The result was Camp Benning, Fort Benning. Fort Benning is now a key base of operations for the US Army and encompasses 182,000 acres south of Columbus.

No longer a center for textiles, the city is now home to a diverse group of companies as well as headquarters for Aflac, Synovus, TSYS, and the Carmike Cinemas.

But all of that won't really matter when you start exploring Columbus and getting to know the city.

getting there

Columbus is 80 minutes from Atlanta. Take I-85 south 55 miles to I-185, then 44 miles to exit 7/Manchester Expressway. Take US 27 South into Columbus.

where to go

Columbus Convention and Visitor's Bureau. 900 Front Ave.; (706) 322-1613; http://visitcolumbus.com. In addition to being a great place to pick up all of the information to find your way around Columbus, the visitor center has a gift shop that is worth a visit. Mon through Fri 8:30 a.m. to 5:30 p.m., Sat 10 a.m. to 2 p.m.

Chattahoochee RiverWalk. 107 41st St.; (706) 653-4189; http://columbusga.org. With 11 access points, the RiverWalk stretches for 15 miles from Fort Benning to the old mill town of Bibb City. It is a favorite spot in town for walking, jogging, cycling, skating, and fishing. Daily 5 a.m. to 11 p.m. Free.

Coca-Cola Space Science Center. 701 Front Ave.; (706) 649-1470; www.ccssc.org. This museum is designed to get everyone excited about space science and astronomy. A division of Columbus State University, it is very much a hands-on facility. Visitors can explore the stars through the Mead Observatory or take part in a space mission in a simulator at the Challenger Learning Center. Mon through Thurs 10 a.m. to 4 p.m., Fri 10 a.m. to 8 p.m., Sat 10:30 a.m. to 8 p.m. Call for fees.

Columbus Black History Museum and Archives. 315 8th St.; (706) 507-3466. Columbus Black History Museum and Archives offers a wide variety of learning experiences related to black history in Columbus and surrounding areas. Call for hours and fees.

Columbus Botanical Garden. 3603 Weems Rd.; (706) 327-8400; http://columbusbotanicalgarden.com. First begun in 1890, the Columbus Botanical Garden sits on 22 acres of land in the heart of the city, of which most is left natural. The gardens center around an old farmhouse and are a great place to check out the more than 100 species of plants and shrubs. Office: Mon through Fri noon to 5 p.m. Grounds: daily during daylight hours. Free.

Columbus Museum. 1251 Wynnton Rd.; (706) 748-2562; http://columbusmuseum.com. This regional museum is the second largest museum in Georgia and offers up a number of diverse exhibits ranging from history to fine art. Featuring more than 14,000 artifacts, the

eat a peach

***Peaches** first came to Georgia in the 1500s from Spaniards arriving from Florida. The sweet fruit appealed to the Cherokee, who quickly started growing them. But it took a planter and Confederate officer from Columbus to come up with the idea of cultivating them and selling them commercially. In 1851, Raphael Moses started shipping peaches out of the South using champagne baskets to protect them and to preserve their flavor. By 1928, peach production in Georgia had reached a peak of almost 8 million bushels a year. These days, production is about 2.6 million bushels a year. Georgia peach season is mid-May until August.*

museum traces the history of this region of the Chattahoochee River. The art exhibits range from Impressionist to folk art to photography. There is also a hands-on gallery for children and a full schedule of educational programs, including lectures, films, and art activities. Don't forget to visit the Olmsted Garden on the museum grounds, designed by the sons of Frederick Law Olmstead, who designed Central Park. Tues through Sat 10 a.m. to 5 p.m. (Thurs until 8 p.m.), Sun 1 to 5 p.m. Call for guided tours. Free.

Heritage Park. 708 Broadway; (706) 322-0756; www.historiccolumbus.com. Walk across the street from the Space Science Center and you will find Heritage Park. This beautiful park is centered around a large man-made river/fountain which symbolizes the Chattahoochee. Dedicated to Columbus's industrial history, the self-guided tour traces 170 years of history through educational plaques, statues, and fountains. It includes exhibits on the mills, a brick kiln, and life-size statues of factory workers set into re-creations of industrial scenes.

International Marketplace. 318 10th Ave.; (706) 653-6240; http://internationalmarket place.us. Located on the grounds of the old Columbus Farmer's Market, this is a great place to view some of Columbus's most unique museums as well as do some shopping. On-site you will find the Museum of Transportation, Museum of Southern Stoneware, and even the Lunch Box Museum. Wed through Sat 10 a.m. to 6 p.m., Sun noon to 6 p.m.

Joseph House Art Gallery. 828 Broadway; (706) 321-8948; http://josephhouseartgallery .com. This artist-run gallery is located in the heart of the historic downtown. The gallery offers regional artwork including prints, watercolors, pottery, sculptures, and more. Tues through Fri 11 a.m. to 6 p.m., Sat 1 to 5 p.m.

Liberty Theatre Cultural Center. 823 8th Ave., (706) 653-7566. The Liberty was Columbus's first black theater, and just about every notable black artist of that era from Duke Ellington to Ella Fitzgerald graced the stage. Built in 1925, it was the largest movie house of any race in the city. Now on the National Register of Historic Places, it serves as a Performing Arts Cultural Center for the entire community, hosting musical events and plays. Check schedules

Linwood Cemetery. 721 Linwood Blvd.; (706) 321-8285; http://linwoodcemetery.org. It is said the city of Columbus's history can be traced in the beautifully carved stones of this historic graveyard. The first grave was that of Thurman Thomas in 1829. Thomas was the son of the surveyor who laid out Columbus and died while on the trip. Other notables include Dr. John Pemberton, the man who invented Coca-Cola. Stoll on your own or take a guided tour of this beautiful cemetery. There are numerous events held here so check the schedule.

Ma Rainey House Museum. 805 5th Ave.; (706) 653-4960. Gertrude "Ma" Rainey is known as the "Mother of the Blues." This museum was home to the colorful whiskey-slugging singer who was born and died in Columbus. The two-story wooden structure is on the National Register of Historic Places. Tues through Sat. 10 a.m. to 3 p.m. Free.

MidTown Columbus. 1236 Wildwood; (706) 494-1653. MidTown Columbus includes the oldest parts of the city and encompasses six contiguous national and state historic districts. Architecture ranges from antebellum to modern, and here you will find some of the city's most unique shops and restaurants.

Monkey Joe's–Columbus. 2453 Airport Thruway; (706) 507-5480; http://monkeyjoes.com. If you want to have your kids expend some energy, this is the place. Monkey Joe's is an indoor play center for children with inflatable slides, thrilling jumps, and party rooms. Daily noon to 6 p.m.

National Civil War Naval Museum at Port Columbus. 1002 Victory Dr.; (706) 327-9798; http://civilwarnavalmuseum.com. The 40,000-square-foot museum will astound you with all it includes. It features a full-scale reproduction of the USS/CSS *Water Witch* and a replica of the Union blockader that was captured during a Confederate raid and put into service for the CSA. There are also displays of uniforms, equipment, and weapons used by the Union and Confederate navies. Visitors can experience 19th-century naval combat firsthand through the US's only full-size ironclad Civil War simulator. Daily 9 a.m. to 5 p.m. Call for guided tours and fees.

The National Infantry Museum and Soldier Center at Patriot Park. 3800 S. Lumpkin Rd.; (706) 653-9234; www.nationalinfantryfoundation.org. The 190,000-square-foot museum is located near Fort Benning and is dedicated to all aspects of the life and training of the infantryman. It contains one of the largest collections of military art and artifacts, and follows the steps of the American infantry soldier across two centuries of courage and determination. The pivotal Battle of Antioch is depicted in the museum's award-winning exhibition, *The Last 100 Yards.* The museum also contains an IMAX theater as well as a gift shop and the Fife & Drum Restaurant. Tues through Sat 9 a.m. to 5 p.m., Sun 11 a.m. to 5 p.m.

RiverCenter for the Performing Arts. 900 Broadway; (706) 256-3612; www.rivercenter.org. The 245,000-square-foot RiverCenter is the centerpiece of Columbus's entertainment and performing arts community. The state-of-the-art facilities include the 2,000-seat Bill Heard Theatre which is the center's main venue and home to the Columbus Symphony Orchestra. Designed with orchestra, mezzanine, and balcony seating, the hall is able to accommodate Broadway shows, symphonic concerts, dance performances, pop concerts, lectures, and conferences. Check schedule for performances and tickets.

Springer Opera House. 103 E. 10th St.; (706) 327-3688; www.springeroperahouse.org. This red, plush, and gilded theater first opened its doors on February 21, 1871, and is a must-see. In its more than a century and a half of existence, it has entertained presidents and playwrights and hosted hundreds of world-class entertainers and events. Fully restored, it is the official State Theatre of Georgia. If you have the opportunity to take in a performance here, you must. Mon through Fri 10 a.m. to 10 p.m., Sat 6:30 a.m. to 10 p.m., Sun 1:30 to 5 p.m.

where to eat

Brother's General Store. 1014 Broadway; (706) 507-3503. OK, this is not so much a place to eat but a place to get every wonderful sweet thing known to man. This nostalgic general store has wonderful old-fashioned candies and treats. Mon through Sat 10 a.m. to 6 p.m. $.

The Cannon Brewpub. 1041 Broadway; (706) 653-2377; www.thecannonbrewpub.com. Their craft beers are brewed on the premises but don't just come here for the suds. They have spectacular burgers and great seafood and steaks. Mon through Thurs 11 a.m. to 10 p.m.; Fri 11 a.m. to 11 p.m.; Sat noon to 11 p.m.; Sun noon to 10 p.m. $–$$.

The Den. 1009 Broadway; (706) 507-8226. A great local market and deli for soups, sandwiches, and salads. Eat in or take out Mon through Fri 8 a.m. to 10 p.m., Sat 11 a.m. to 6 p.m. $.

Meritage Cafe. 1350 13th St.; (706) 327-0707; www.meritagecafe.net. Locally owned, Meritage serves a lot of purposes. The deli and cafe are great for a casual lunch, while Meritage itself has fine dining next door at dinner. The restaurant has a distinct New Orleans flavor. Deli and cafe Mon through Sat 11 a.m. to 3 p.m.; Meritage fine dining Thurs through Sat 5:30 to 10 p.m. $–$$$.

Minnie's Uptown Restaurant. 104 8th St.; (706) 322-2766. This home-cooking buffet restaurant allows you to get your meat-and-three lunch at a good price. Tasty chicken, country ham, and vegetables, Minnie's is a local hangout. Mon through Fri 10:30 a.m. to 2:30 p.m. $.

Skipper's Fresh Seafood Market and Deli. 3505 Buena Vista Rd.; (706) 683-0101. A hidden gem, Skipper's has great fresh fish served in a wide variety of ways from fried to broiled. Their gumbo is awesome. Friday night is a crab boil, so bring your appetite. Tues through Sat 11 a.m. to 10 p.m. $–$$.

The Speakeasy. 3123 Mercury Dr.; (706) 561-0411; www.speakeasycolumbus.com. Designed to be fun for adults and kids, there is a full bar as well as a game room. Food ranges from sandwiches to pizza and Mexican. Sun 11 a.m. to 9 p.m., Mon through Sat 11 a.m. to 10 p.m. $–$$.

12th Street Deli. 121 12th St.; (706) 576-6939; http://12thstreetdeli.com. An old-fashioned deli serving breakfast and lunch. It's not all about the sandwiches, although they are great. You must try their plates. Mon through Sat 7 a.m. to 3 p.m.

Vintage 222. 222 7th St.; (706) 507-2991; www.thepoundhouseinn.com. Located in the Rothschild Pound House Inn, Vintage 22 offers up one of Columbus's finest dining experiences. They have a wide selection of wines, and their meals are served in a setting that has been hosting guests since the 1800s. Nightly 5 p.m. to 1 a.m. $$$.

where to stay

Columbus Quality Inn. 1325 Veterans; (706) 322-2522; http://choicehotels.com. Located near the Chattahoochee RiverWalk, the Quality Inn has an outdoor pool and a free hot breakfast. $–$$.

EconoLodge. 1034 Veterans; (706) 324-3674; www.econolodge.com. Located in the historic district, this well maintained EconoLodge includes an expanded continental breakfast and a business center. $.

The Gates House B&B. 802 Broadway; (706) 342-6464. This elegant old inn in the heart of downtown Columbus will put you within walking distance of many of the attractions. There are 3 rooms from which to choose, all decorated in antiques. $–$$.

Marriott Columbus. 800 Front Ave.; (706) 324-1800 or (800) 455-9261; http://marriott.com. This Marriott is located in Columbus right near the river and affords full comfort to visitors. Fitness center and pool on the property. $$.

Rothschild-Pound House Inn. 201 7th St.; (706) 322-4075; www.thepoundhouseinn.com. This bed-and-breakfast includes not just the inn, but several cottages, and you will experience Southern hospitality at its finest. The rooms are all suites and are decorated in wonderful antiques with comfy beds and modern amenities. $$$.

worth more time

Whitewater Rafting. http://columbusgawhitewater.com. If you have the time you may want to check out what is billed as the longest urban whitewater course in the world. The course was built after the Chattahoochee River was restored to its natural state at its fall line in Columbus with the release of water from the Eagle & Phenix and City Mills Dams. Raft, tube, or kayak through the town. The Columbus Visitor's Bureau can help guide you to places to rent equipment.

west

day trip 01

west is best:
villa rica, tallapoosa, carrollton

This easy day trip will take you to some spectacular places that even most Atlantans haven't visited. Perhaps it is because they are just too close. If you head out I-20 due west toward Alabama, the interstate is flanked by quaint towns that grew up at a time when this was considered the Wild West. These days they are steeped in history but yet offer up some unexpected surprises.

Who knew that Villa Rica was a gold rush town? That Tallapoosa's frontier roots still show? Or that in Carrollton you can shop at the state's oldest bookstore and then dine on some of Georgia's most innovative cuisine? These may not be the state's best-known towns, but that is simply an oversight.

villa rica

Its name literally means "Rich Village," and Villa Rica has earned that name as the site of the great Georgia Gold Rush of 1829 (predating the California Gold Rush by almost a decade). Back then the town was called Hixtown, but as word of the gold spread, residents wanted their luck to be known. At one time, there were 19 active mines in the town.

Early Villa Rica resembled the Wild West, complete with horse thieves, Indians, and vigilante hangings. Those days are a far cry from the town of today with its genteel historic districts and picturesque homes and buildings. The gold rush is now just a theme for many things in town.

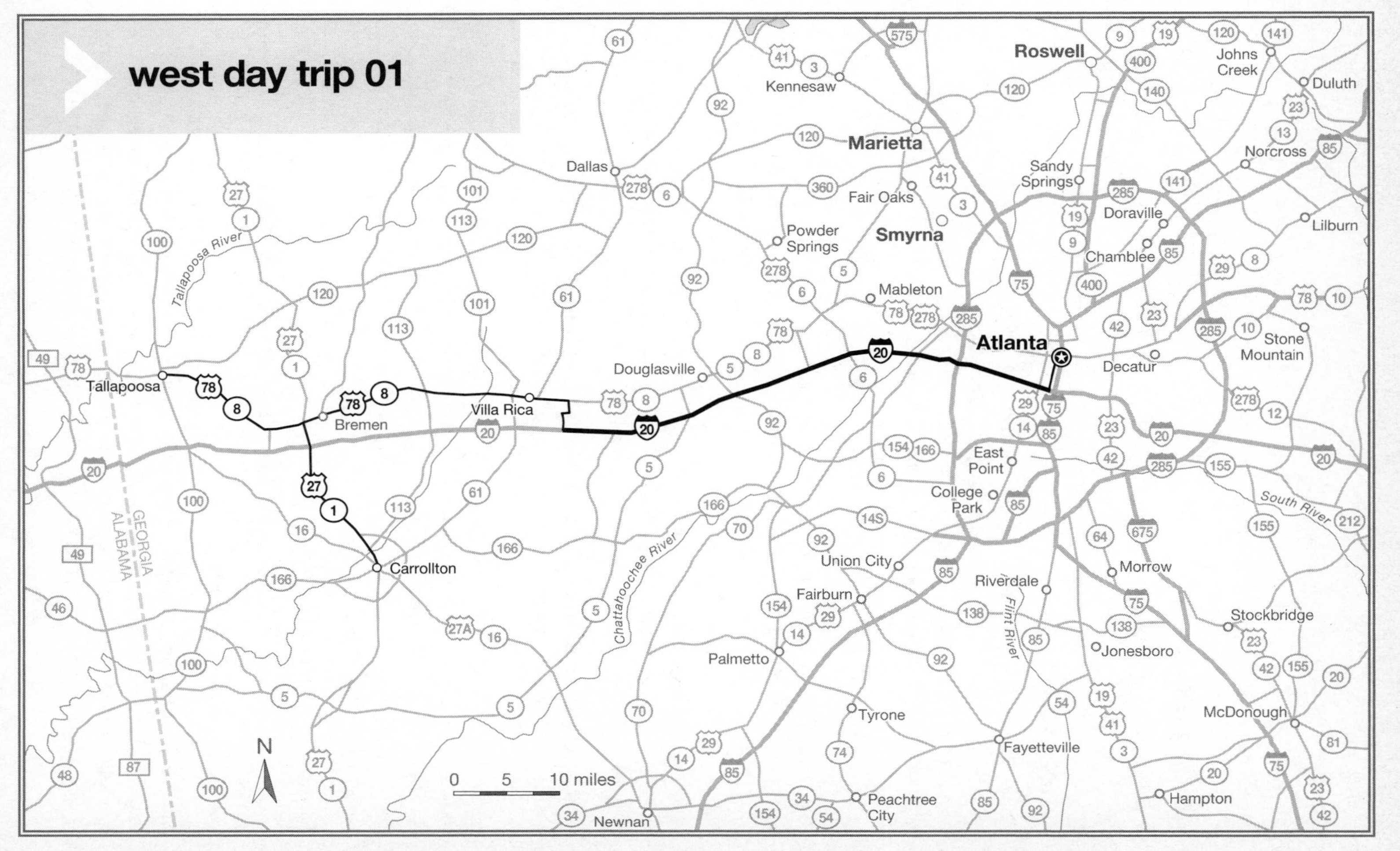
west day trip 01
Roswell
Johns Creek
Duluth
Kennesaw
Marietta
Norcross
Dallas
Sandy Springs
Fair Oaks
Doraville
Lilburn
Powder Springs
Smyrna
Chamblee
Tallapoosa River
Mableton
Stone Mountain
Atlanta
Decatur
Douglasville
Tallapoosa
Villa Rica
Bremen
East Point
College Park
South River
GEORGIA
ALABAMA
Carrollton
Chattahoochee River
Union City
Morrow
Riverdale
Fairburn
Flint River
Stockbridge
Jonesboro
Palmetto
McDonough
Tyrone
Fayetteville
N
0
5
10 miles
Peachtree City
Hampton
Newnan

Villa Rica was the birthplace of the father of black gospel music, Thomas Dorsey, and each June his birth is celebrated with a gospel music festival.

getting there

Located just 30 minutes from downtown Atlanta. Take I-20 West and get off at exit 24 on GA 101 North.

where to go

Annie Powell Berry House. 203 Peachtree St. A private residence, this beautifully restored mansion is one of the most photographed buildings in Villa Rica. Built in 1908, the home features many of the original wood floors as well as much of the millwork and beveled glass. Portions of the home were once rented to teachers visiting Villa Rica. Now on the National Historic Register, the present owner, Valerie Berry Wilhelm, is the granddaughter of the original owners.

The Dorough Round Barn and Farm. North of Hickory Level on Villa Rica Road. Just 3 miles outside of Villa Rica, this landmark is worth a look even though it is in disrepair. Built in 1917, this round barn was designed by Floyd Lovell in what was considered a progressive technique for agricultural businesses. It's 2 stories tall and is surrounded by several outbuildings of the farm including the 19th-century farmhouse. The barn and farm are privately owned, so it is not advised to wander around the property. The barn is on the National Register of Historic Places.

First Presbyterian Church of Villa Rica. 519 Main St.; (770) 459-5276; www.firstpcavillarica.org. This congregation dates back to 1855 and the building itself to 1885. Beneath the brick outer structure stands a wood-framed building that was moved to this location by parishioners in 1930. The stained-glass windows are of particular note because the formula for that color is long lost and cannot be replicated. This was the home church for the Candler family. Asa Candler moved from Villa Rica to Atlanta in 1873 to start a retail drug company, and he then started the Coca-Cola Company in Atlanta in 1892. The Candlers remain benefactors of this church.

First United Methodist Church of Villa Rica. 206 North Ave.; (770) 459-3067; http://vrfumc.net. The Methodist Church has long claimed to be the oldest church in Villa Rica, getting its start in a log cabin in 1830. The current white framed church was started in 1905 and was first used in July 1906.

Mt. Prospect Baptist Church. 133 Sunset Dr.; (770) 459-5918; www.mtprospectbaptist.org. You'll find 2 churches at this site, but the one of most interest is the smaller structure. Built in 1945, it replaced the original building which had dated to the 1890s. But the church's significance is not so much in the buildings themselves but in the fact that this was black gospel leader Thomas A. Dorsey's home church when he grew up in the early 1900s and where he learned about music.

Pine Mountain Gold Museum at Stockmar Park. 1881 Stockmar Rd.; (770) 459-8455 or (866) 514-6536; www.pinemountaingoldmuseum.com. Preserving the century-old relics of Villa Rica's gold-mining industry, the Gold Museum is on the site of an actual gold mine. The 4,800-square-foot museum includes exhibits and a 50-seat theater which traces the history of the Villa Rica mines. Guests can try their luck at panning for gold themselves or explore the nature trails surrounding the mine. Sun through Sat 10 a.m. to 4 p.m. $.

Wick's Tavern. 12 W. Wilson St.; (770) 942-2692 or (770) 328-9825. Built in 1830, Wicks Tavern is the oldest commercial structure in Carroll County and sits just outside the downtown area. The tavern was run as a bar for gold miners and hotel for travelers by former New Yorker John B. Wick. When the Georgia-Pacific Railroad built their rails in 1882, the depot was several miles from Wick's. Many of its neighbors were put on rollers and literally pushed to what is now present-day Villa Rica. The tavern was far too large and stayed put, becoming a private home. In 1998, a group called "Friends of Wick's Tavern" finally arranged a move, and it was rolled into town where it now serves as a living history museum. By appointment only.

where to eat

Blue Brick. 215 S. Carroll Rd.; (770) 459-9208; www.bluebrickfrenchrestaurant.com. Fine French dining in this tiny Southern town comes through a French native chef. The menu changes according to the seasons, and all is guaranteed from the freshest ingredients. Tues through Fri from 11:30 a.m., Sat from 4 p.m. $$.

Cafe Trading Post. 749 W. Bankhead Hwy.; (770) 456-4221. A longtime local favorite, the Cafe Trading Post serves up Southern cooking with flair. Try their barbeque, fried okra, fried catfish, butter beans, and salmon patties. Serving breakfast, lunch, and dinner. $–$$.

Dres Place BBQ. 208 Tolbert Ave.; (678) 793-4798. The best place in Villa Rica for barbeque. Hefty portions of ribs and chicken with outdoor seating available for those who make a mess with all of that great sauce. Sun 12:30 to 6 p.m., Tues through Thurs 11 a.m. to 8 p.m., Fri and Sat 11 a.m. to 10 p.m. Closed Mon. $–$$.

Martin's. 1100 US 78 West; (770) 456-0065; www.martinsrestaurants.com. This local fast-food chain started in Austell, Georgia, a few miles away in 1962, but is a local mainstay. Great homemade burgers, fries, onion rings, and dogs. Try their breakfast biscuits. Mon through Sat 5:30 a.m. to 3 p.m., Sun 6:30 a.m. to 3 p.m. $.

Ruby's Diner. 810 W. Bankhead Hwy.; (770) 459-5501. A traditional diner atmosphere with friendly folk and good food, served up fast. Mon through Fri 6 a.m. to 3 p.m., Sat and Sun 7 a.m. to 3 p.m. $.

Stix Tavern. 660 W. Bankhead Hwy., Ste. A; (678) 523-4272; www.stixbarandgrill.com. This sports bar and pool hall is a fun place to duck into for a quick bite. It has great subs and sandwiches and hand-tossed pizzas, but the dinner fare is also substantial with chicken parmesan and spaghetti. Mon through Sat 11 a.m. to 2 a.m., Sun noon to 2 a.m. $–$$.

Tin Roof Cafe. 110 Main St.; (770) 456-2474; www.tinroofcafe.com. Serving up breakfast and lunch, this place bills itself as "good food, nice people" and that's the truth. They will make you feel at home as you get served up Southern comfort food such as biscuits and gravy or banana pudding. Saturday features a breakfast buffet. Mon through Fri 7:30 a.m. to 2:30 p.m., Sat 7:30 a.m. to 2 p.m. $.

where to stay

Comfort Inn & Suites. 114 GA 61; (678) 941-3401 or (800) 4CHOICE; www.choicehotels.com. Just off the interstate, the Comfort Inn includes an indoor pool, free breakfast (including waffles), and Wi-Fi. $.

Days Inn. 195 GA 61 Connector; (770) 459-8888; www.daysinn.com/hotel/03941. Pet friendly, this Days Inn has an outdoor pool and offers a free breakfast. $.

Wyndham Resort at Fairfield Plantation. 1602 Lakeview Pkwy.; (800) 428-1932. Including rooms, condos, and studio suites, you could spend several days at this lakeside resort. There are free massages available, 2 golf courses, tennis, and a marina. $$–$$$.

worth more time

Six Flags Over Georgia. 275 Riverside Pkwy. Southwest, Austell, GA 30168-7877; (770) 948-9290. Between Atlanta and Villa Rica, the Six Flags amusement park is on 100 acres of land and has rides of all levels to enjoy. Its roller coaster collection includes the awe-inspiring *Goliath, Mind Bender,* and the 2011 addition *Dare Devil Dive. Acrophobia* was the world's first "floorless" free-fall tower ride, and the historic Riverview Carousel is actually on the National Register of Historic Places as 1 of only 3 remaining 5-abreast carousels known to exist. Season or day passes are available. Mon through Thurs 10:30 a.m. to 8 p.m., Fri and Sat 10 a.m. to 10 p.m., Sun 10 a.m. to 9 p.m. $$$.

tallapoosa

No one quite knows what the name Tallapoosa means, but it derives from a nearby river which obviously has Native American roots. And while some may find the term hard to pronounce, it sure beats one of the original names, Possum Snout. The city started in the 1830s and grew with its timber industry, becoming known as the "Yankee City Under a Southern Sun."

These days, the atmosphere is very much of the Southern bent with a heavy slant to wildlife and natural attractions. In fact, the town rings in the New Year with the Annual Possum Drop and holds a summer bluegrass concert series called "Possum Pickin'."

getting there

Tallapoosa is just 60 miles due west of Atlanta and just before the Alabama border. Take I-20 West from Atlanta or from Villa Rica and take exit 5, GA 100 North. Tallapoosa is just 5 miles from the interstate. Or, if you want to spend a little more time meandering through the countryside, you can take US 78/GA 8 from Villa Rica parallel to I-20 and that will take you directly into Tallapoosa.

where to go

Amelia's (The Homeplace). 139 Connecticut Ave.; (770) 574-7193. In the 1887 Amelia Johnson family home, Amelia's purpose is to preserve local heritage through education. Schoolchildren are brought here to experience living history and to learn about life in the area in the 1800s. By appointment.

Bud Jones Taxidermy and Wildlife Museum. 359 GA 120 East; (770) 574-7480; www.budjonestaxidermy.com. Certainly one of the more unique things to do in Tallapoosa, this is a real taxidermy shop and open to the public to give people a sense of how it all works. You'll see beasts and birds from North America and Africa, including a zebra and even an elephant head. Mon through Fri 8 a.m. to 5 p.m., Sat 9 a.m. to noon. Free.

The Building. 21790 US 78; (770) 574-5250. Built in 1891, the Building's first name was Eaton Block, and it housed a series of businesses from bars to bowling alleys and everything in between. These days the historic structure is an event venue. Check to see what is on tap there because the Building hosts small concerts, movie premiers, and parties

georgia's first wine industry

The area around the town of Tallapoosa became a prime wine-growing area in 1893 when a group of Hungarian immigrants arrived and began cultivating vines. The town boomed as the wine production grew and soon the sloping hills were covered in growing grapes. That heyday was short-lived. In 1907, Georgia passed its Prohibition Act, forbidding the making and selling of alcoholic beverages. The wine industry fell to ruins and the families who founded it moved elsewhere to continue their livelihood.

regularly so you'll never know what you may run into. The ground floor is open for tours, but call for an appointment. Upstairs is a family residence.

Helton Howland Memorial Park. US 78 East; (770) 574-2345. This public park has a great many recreational opportunities from swimming and fishing in the lake to simply picnicking. The grounds include several military vehicles you can explore, such as a tank. Open all year long, so feel free to play tennis or toss some horseshoes.

Historic Walking Trail. 388 Bowdon St.; (770) 574-3124. If you want to explore downtown Tallapoosa, there is a self-guided in-city pedestrian trail that begins behind the Tallapoosa Library and winds through the historic district.

Veteran's Memorial and Medal of Honor Park. GA 100 at Taliaferro Street; (770) 574-2482. This small memorial adjacent to Helton Howland Memorial Park is dedicated to American veterans of all wars. It includes the Wall of Tears (commemorating women in the military), the Medal of Honor Fountain, and the League-Lowe Memorial. Open daily. Free.

West Georgia Museum of Tallapoosa. 186 Mann St.; (770) 574-3125. You'll be pleasantly surprised by what all is to be found in the West Georgia Museum. Created by local residents, the museum has a bit of everything from a 30-foot-tall *Tyrannosaurus rex* to replicas of businesses from the 1800s. Old stores, barber shops, and other businesses have been replicated within the walls of this beautiful old building in the heart of town. Tues through Fri 9 a.m. to 4 p.m., Sat 9 a.m. to 5 p.m. $.

where to eat

Crossroads. 505 Bowdon St.; (770) 574-7755. This is a family-style restaurant, so it's kid-friendly, serving up country cooking and steaks. Thurs and Fri 11 a.m. to 2 p.m., Sat 5 to 9 p.m., Sun 11 a.m. to 2 p.m. Closed Mon through Wed. $–$$.

Jack's Family Restaurant. 2276 US 78; (770) 574-9760; www.eatatjacks.com. This Alabama-based hamburger chain has spilled over the border into Georgia, and you'll be glad it did. The burgers, chicken, and biscuits are all delicious. 7:30 a.m. to 9 p.m. daily. $.

Los Pinos Mexican. 105 W. Lipham St.; (770) 574-2202. Authentic Mexican food in the heart of Tallapoosa. Generous portions at good prices. Tues through Thurs 11 a.m. to 9 p.m., Fri 9 a.m. to 10 p.m., Sat 4:30 to 9 p.m.; Sun noon to 9 p.m. $–$$.

Turn Around Barbeque. 2390 US 78; (770) 574-9966. The name says it; you'll want to turn around and come back again for more. Turn Around has been around a long time, as you can tell by the faded sign. In this small shack of a restaurant, the Brunswick stew is to die for. The country ham and biscuits can only be topped by the barbeque. Breakfast and lunch only. $.

where to stay

Comfort Inn. 788 GA 100; (770) 574-5575. Right on I-20, the Comfort Inn is convenient for travelers. It's very near the Crossroads Shopping Center. There is an outdoor pool, and a free breakfast is included in your stay. $.

worth more time

Historic Haralson County Courthouse. 145 Van Wert St., Buchanan, GA. If you wanted to wander a little more off the beaten path, venture 8 miles east of Tallapoosa on GA 120 to the little town of Buchanan. Among the historic homes and businesses, you will also find the Historic Haralson County Courthouse, one of Georgia's oldest working courthouses. Built in 1891, it is on the National Register of Historic Places.

carrollton

Carrollton was named after a man who never lived here. Charles Carroll of Maryland was the last surviving signer of the Declaration of Independence when the town was chartered in 1829. It grew out of lands acquired through the 1825 Treaty of Indian Springs between the Cherokee and Creek Indian Nations.

Settlers came here because of the rich soil, and the advent of the railroad helped farmers ship their cotton and other crops, allowing the town to prosper in the late 1800s. Agriculture remains an important business in the county. You'll see a lot of cattle in the fields around town because Carrollton is home to the largest cattleman association in Georgia. In town, however, is a healthy small-town atmosphere, with the main social activities taking place on the town square. You'll find historic buildings and businesses in the heart of town and friendly folk who are glad to see you. Carrollton is also home of the University of West Georgia.

getting there

Take GA 100 south from Tallapoosa and then head east on GA 16 after you pass I-20. Carrollton is just 12 miles south of the interstate. If you are coming directly from Atlanta, it's just over an hour drive, but you may want to get off at exit 11 and head south on the 4-lane US 27/GA 1.

where to go

Carrollton Area Convention and Visitors Bureau (Log Cabin Visitor's Center). 102 N. Lakeshore Dr.; (800) 292-0871 or (770) 214-9746; www.visitcarrollton.com. As with most towns, this is a good first stop so you can get maps of the area and suggestions on how to best spend your time.

Adamson Square. Downtown. Adamson Square in the heart of Carrollton is at the center of the city's historic commercial district and is surrounded by galleries, shopping, and restaurants. The square is named for lawyer, judge, and congressman Williams Carroll Adamson, who was born nearby and buried in the Carrollton Cemetery. Carrollton's streets are quite pedestrian friendly, so start at the square and explore the town.

Carroll County Courthouse. 323 Newnan St.; (770) 830-5830. At the time this courthouse was built in 1928, it was the largest in the state. Built out of marble in an Italian Renaissance Revival style, it is still in use. One courtroom alone in the building is 3,700 square feet! Mon through Fri 8:30 a.m. to 5 p.m.

Carrollton Cemetery. Old Carrollton Road (at Villa Rica Highway). The cemetery is located on 2 hilltops at what was once the edge of town. Graves here date back to the 1700s and include some spectacular tombs and funerary art. To make the most of your grave tour, pick up the cemetery guide available at the visitor center and in many shops in town. It contains information and images on about 15 different people buried at the cemetery including congressman W. C. Adamson, Confederate Col. William Curtis, C. M. Tanner, Edwin Sharpe, and Georgia Price.

Curtis-Marlow-Perry House/Carroll County Historical Society. 226 West Ave.; (770) 834-3081; www.carrollcountyhistory.org. Built in 1830, this little white house on the hill is one of Carrollton's oldest homes and now houses the Carroll County Historical Society. The original structure was a frontier cabin made of logs and sections of those logs are visible in some areas. The home is furnished with pieces dating to the 1800s. Visitors can browse the cabin and the county archives. By appointment.

Horton's Books and Gifts. 410 Adamson Sq.; (770) 832-8021; www.hortonsbooks.com. Even if you don't think you want to shop for books, you should duck into Horton's. And if you do love books, this is paradise. First opened in 1892, it is the oldest bookstore in the state of Georgia. New books line the centuries-old shelves, and the staff can tell you just about anything about any author or publication. You will also like to spy some furry mascots. Horton's has a few cats in residence who lounge among the stacks. Mon through Thurs 9 a.m. to 7 p.m., Fri 9 a.m. to 9 p.m., Sat 10 a.m. to 10 p.m.

where to eat

Alley Cat. 120 Newton St.; (770) 834-2642. Asian fusion with a touch of burgers and sandwiches. Dine inside or out on the patio. Mon through Fri 11 a.m. to 2 a.m., Sat 5 p.m. to 2 a.m., Sun 5 p.m. to midnight. $–$$.

Blue Steakhouse. 104 Adamson Sq.; (770) 838-5559. Right on the square, Blue Steakhouse offers steaks and seafood as well as some great burgers. They also boast a pretty extensive beer and wine selection. Tues through Sat 4 p.m. to midnight. $–$$.

Corner Cafe. 304 Adamson Sq.; (770) 834-9805; www.cornercafecarrollton.com. A great little find with homemade sandwiches, soups, and salads in a great corner spot overlooking the square. Affordable and good. Mon through Sat 11 a.m. to 9 p.m. $.

J-Bo's BBQ. 422 Newnan St.; (770) 834-4540. A bit of a dive, but barbeque and hot wings are their specialty and they do them well. J-Bo's is great for a quick and good bite. Mon through Sat 11 a.m. to 7:30 p.m. $.

Little Hawaiian. 206 Rome St.; (770) 838-1220; www.littlehawaiianrestaurant.com. You wouldn't expect to find a tiki bar in the heart of historic Georgia, but here it is! In a hundred-year-old mule barn, Little Hawaiian serves up some of the best seafood you'll find this side of the South Pacific. Sun through Fri 11:30 a.m. to 2:30 p.m., Mon through Thurs 5 to 9 p.m., Fri and Sat 5 to 10 p.m. $$.

Plates on the Square. 301 Adamson Sq.; (770) 214-5531; www.platesonthesquare.com. Casual fine dining. Plates serves traditional Southern food with a contemporary twist. Mon through Sat 11 a.m. to 1:30 a.m., Sun 11 a.m. to 2 p.m. $–$$.

Sam's House Memphis BBQ. 108 Alabama St.; (770) 214-5059. Mouthwatering Memphis-style barbeque, served up with live music most nights. This place is very popular among locals. Tues 11 a.m. to 9 p.m., Wed through Sat 11 a.m. to 10 p.m. $.

where to stay

Banning Mills. 205 Horseshoe Dam Rd., Whitesburg; (770) 834-9149; www.historicbanningmills.com. Just a few miles from Carrollton is Historic Banning Mills Country Inn and Conference Center. The inn has 47 rooms, and the entire property is designed as a resort to fit your every need (see more in the next chapter). There is free Internet service, state-of-the-art meeting spaces, and on-site chef and day spa. $$–$$$.

Best Western Carrollton Inn and Suites. 1111 Bankhead Hwy.; (770) 830-1000; www.book.bestwestern.com. Set up to accommodate business travelers, this hotel has wireless Internet, a choice of rooms or suites, as well as an indoor pool and fitness center. $.

Hampton Inn. 102 S. Cottage Hill Rd., Carrollton; (770) 838-7722; www.hamptoninn1.hilton.com. With 77 rooms, the Hampton Inn includes many business traveler features such as Internet and a conference center. There is an on-site fitness center with a pool. $.

day trip 02

zip-a-dee-doo-dah:
whitesburg

The town of Whitesburg is not exactly a household name, but if you choose to take this day trip, you'll understand that those who don't make the effort are really missing out. The place itself is one of those sleepy little towns which barely have stop signs, but it sits in the middle of some beautiful county in the foothills of the North Georgia mountains.

Equally enticing is the Historic Banning Mills area which is technically in Whitesburg. This 1,200-acre reserve contains the ruins of the mills which used to thrive in the area and has been transformed into a natural retreat area. Guests can explore the Ghost Town left by the mills and enjoy a wide variety of activities from team-building sports to zip lining. Even if you do nothing but sit on the deck of the inn, it's worth a visit.

whitesburg

Whitesburg is one of those tiny Georgia country towns that you see in movies. Only about 600 people live here, but it's easy to see why they choose to stay.

On the Chattahoochee, the town was a stagecoach stop and later had its own railroad depot. Whitesburg became the distribution point for all freight in West Georgia. Goods were shipped here and then disbursed throughout the region. At one time, the bustling town had 13 businesses, a depot, a school, a restaurant, two churches, a sawmill, and three taverns.

These days, Whitesburg has a much sleepier atmosphere, and only three of those buildings remain. If you are looking for a relaxing getaway, this is the place to come.

west day trip 02

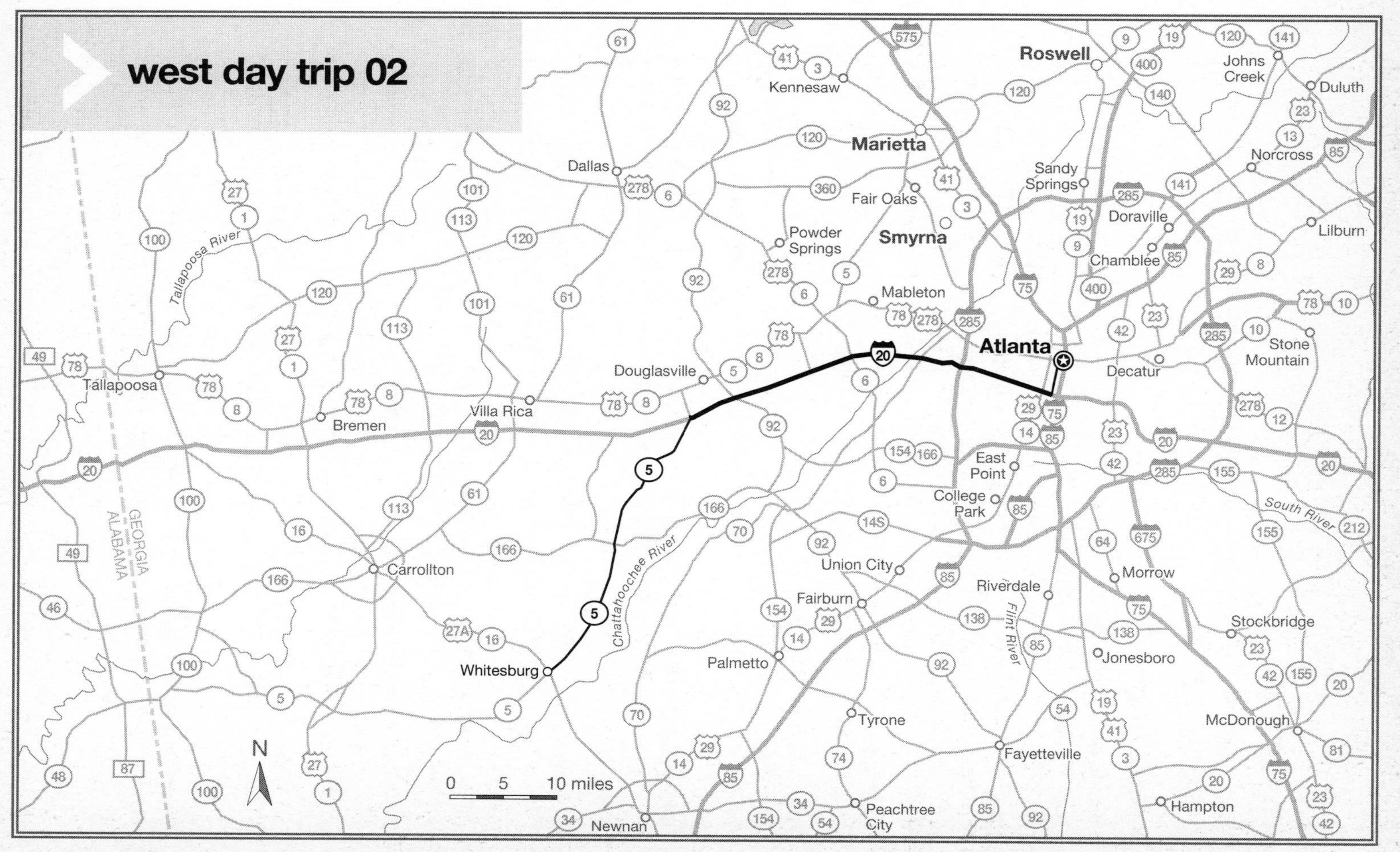

getting there

Less than an hour from downtown Atlanta, take I-20 east to exit 37 and take GA 5 south for 20 miles to Whitesburg.

where to go

Banning Mills. 205 Horseshoe Dam Rd.; (770) 834-9149; www.historicbanningmills.com. In scenic Snake Creek Gorge, Banning Mills was once the site of 10 mills, including 2 pulp mills, a paper mill, gristmill, and sawmill. For years, it was considered a ghost town, but guests are invited to roam those ruins and explore the almost countless hiking trails in the area. Banning Mills features a host of things to do while enjoying 1,200 acres of preserved North Georgia woodlands. Kayaking, canoeing, and horseback riding are all available along with a host of team-building activities. Among them is the longest zip line in the Northern Hemisphere (see below). Banning Mills features a historical interpretive center that spans the Creek Indian era through the Civil War and early industrial era of Banning Mills.

McIntosh Reserve. 1046 W. McIntosh Circle; (770) 830-5879; www.carrollcounty recreation.com. This 527-acre reserve along the Chattahoochee River was named for Chief William McIntosh of the Lower Creeks whose home was once here. McIntosh was murdered in 1826 after helping arrange the Indian Springs Treaty between the Creeks and the Cherokees. A replica of his home is on the grounds. The reserve contains 14 miles of hiking trails. Fishing, rafting, and canoeing are all permitted. Primitive camping is also available. Open daily except Christmas and New Year.

Screaming Eagle Zip Line Tour. Banning Mills, 205 Horseshoe Dam Rd.; (770) 834-9149; www.historicbanningmills.com/zipline. Perfect for adrenaline junkies, Screaming Eagle is the longest and highest canopy tour in the Northern Hemisphere, covering more than 7 miles of zip lines at up to a quarter of a mile above the ground. There are several options including all-day passes. Reservations are strongly suggested. $$.

Whitesburg Baptist Church. 662 Main St.; (770) 830-9728. Built in 1875, this little church is on the National Register of Historic Places. Its Gothic Revival arched windows and front entrance and interior make it architecturally and historically significant for its time.

The Whitesburg Depot. Depot Street; (678) 798-1152. Built in 1873, the town grew up around the railroad depot. Now an antiques store, the owners love explaining the history of their building.

Whitesburg Methodist Church. 480 Church St.; (770) 830-0461. This little brick church was built in 1913 to replace the original church which was located across the street and destroyed by fire.

where to eat

Kay's Cafe. 1150 Main St.; (770) 830-7900 This coffee shop is where you'll find the locals. Diner-style meals complete with blue plate specials are on offer. Breakfast and lunch. $.

Mojave Hotwings. 1069 Main St.; (770) 830-0488. Great wings and as many as you can eat. Dine in or take out. Daily 11 a.m. to 9 p.m. Cash only. $.

Wagon Train Cafe. 1018 Main St.; (770) 838-5660. Another local hangout, Bradley's is your typical small-town restaurant. Staples include meat-and-three. Lunch and dinner daily except Sun. $–$$.

where to stay and eat

Banning Mills. 205 Horseshoe Dam Rd.; (770) 834-9149; www.historicbanningmills.com. Historic Banning Mills also features a Country Inn and Conference Center. The lodge offers both rooms and cottages. Amenities include an on-site chef, an Olympic-size pool, and a day spa. $$–$$$.

appendix: festivals & celebrations

february

Ground Hog Day. Yellow River Game Ranch, Lilburn. Every February 2, Groundhog Beau Lee makes an appearance to determine when winter will end. (770) 972-6643; www.yellowrivergameranch.com.

march

Annual Cowboy Poetry Gathering, Cartersville. The Wild West comes to Georgia the second weekend of March. Poetry, movies, and a chuck wagon cook-off are included. (770) 387-1300; www.boothmuseum.org.

Cherry Blossom Festival, Macon. Macon is the Cherry Blossom Capital of the World, and this 10-day festival at the end of March celebrates the pink and white blossoms with a backdrop of more than 300,000 Yoshino cherry trees. (478) 751-7429; www.cherryblossom.com.

april

Big Shanty Festival, Kennesaw. Paying homage to the town's original name, this second week in April festival is one of the largest arts and crafts celebrations in North Georgia. It kicks off with a parade and features live music and tons of food. (770) 423-1330.

The Georgia Mountain BirdFest, Unicoi State Park. The last weekend in April, this unique festival involves not just birding, but an artist market, guided walks, field trips, classes, and hands-on activities. georgiastateparks.org/GaMountainBirdFest.

Sacred Heart Garden Festival, Augusta. Augusta's nickname is the Garden City and this 3-day festival at the end of April celebrates the miles and miles of greenery and flowers. (706) 826-4700; www.sacredheartgardenfestival.com.

Sunrise Service, Stone Mountain. 7 a.m. Easter Sunday morning atop Stone Mountain. http://festivals.stonemountainpark.com.

The Tubman Museum Pan African Festival of Georgia, Macon. Held each April at the Tubman Museum, the festival celebrates Pan-African culture. Featured activities include

Caribbean steel bands, reggae, African music, dancers, films, and cultural demonstrations. (478) 743-8544; www.tubmanmuseum.com.

may

Battle of Resaca Civil War Reenactment, Resaca. Two-day event held on the third weekend of May features reenactors setting the stage on the actual battlefield. It includes living history, Ladies Tea, Camp Tours, and a Period Ball. www.georgiadivision.org/bor_reenactment.html.

Blairsville Spring Arts and Crafts Festival, Blairsville. Artists and craftsmen exhibit on the square surrounding Union County's Historic Courthouse. Live performances by dancers and musicians and a variety of food vendors. www.downtownblairsville.com.

Blind Willie McTell Blues Festival, Thomson. Celebrate the life of one of the true pioneers of country blues music, Blind Willie McTell, with a day of the blues in late May. www.blindwillie.com.

Brenau Barbeque Festival, Gainesville. The 3-day festival on the grounds of Brenau University is a fund-raiser for student scholarships. (800) 252-5119; www2009.brenau.edu/bbq/index.cfm.

Canton Festival of the Arts, Canton. Held the third weekend of May and set in historic Brown Park. (770) 479-5443; www.cherokeearts.org.

Cotton Pickin' Festival, Gay. Held in the first weekend of May for planting and the first weekend in October for picking, this festival includes music, crafts, and food. (706) 538-6814; www.cpfair.org.

Mountain Flower Fine Art and Wine Festival, Dahlonega. Dahlonega's Summer Farmer's Market kicks off the third weekend of May during this festival of artists, music, and food. www.dahlonegamerchants.org/mountain-flower-art-festival.

Rutledge Country Fair, Rutledge. This 10-day event at the end of May includes bluegrass music, arts and crafts, an antique car show, rides, and entertainment for all ages. (706) 557-0211.

Taste of Sautee, Sautee Nacoochee. Wine, food, music, and art are all part of a joint collaboration between InsideOut Sautee and Yonah Mountain Vineyards. (706) 878-5522; www.insideoutsautee.com.

Tour de Moose Annual Bike Ride, Warner Robins. This annual bicycle tour the third Saturday of May begins at the Museum of Aviation and follows through Robins Air Force Base. Ride at your own leisure, kids' activities, and more. www.museumofaviation.org.

memorial day weekend

1890 Day Jamboree, Ringgold. Live music on several stages, food vendors, children's rides, a fiddle contest, crafters, and a closing night fireworks display. www.1890sday.com.

Arts in the Park, Blue Ridge. The largest collection of fine arts vendors in North Georgia come together with music and food. (478) 494-0185; http://blueridgearts.net/ArtsintheParkFestivals.aspx.

Creek Indian Wars of 1836, Lumpkin. Creek and Seminole Indians from all over the Southeast gather for battle reenactments and authentic Indian encampments. (888) 733-1850; visit www.westville.org.

Pie Baking and Tasting, Dahlonega. Everything from peach pie to shepherd's pie. Held 11 a.m. to 1 p.m. the Saturday of Memorial Day weekend. Proceeds support the Lumpkin County Literacy Coalition in operation of the Dolly Parton Imagination Library for children 0 to 5 years of age. (706) 867-9607; www.lumpkinliteracy.org.

Spring Art and Wine Festival, Young Harris. The Spring Festival at Crane Creek Vineyards includes a sampling of wines, food, art, and listening to live music. (706) 379-1236; www.cranecreekvineyards.com.

june

AthFest, Athens. Held the first week of June, AthFest features live music, movie screenings, art, and food, as well as a KidFest. (706) 548-1973; http://athfest.com.

Blairsville Scottish Festival, Blairsville. The second weekend in June, a celebration of Scottish heritage, which includes bagpipes, country dancing, caber tossing, and other live demos as well as genealogy tents. www.blairsvillescottishfestival.org.

Bulls 'N Barrels Rodeo, Young Harris. Held the first weekend in June, barrel racing, team roping, bull riding, and goat tying. (706) 379-9900; www.brasstownvalley.com.

Fried Green Tomato Festival, Juliette. Celebrating the filming of the movie *Fried Green Tomatoes,* the second weekend in June. Live music, arts & crafts, and food. (478) 992-8200; www.juliettega.com.

Georgia Fine Wine Festival, Dahlonega. Hosted on the grounds of BlackStock Vineyards and Winery the first weekend of June. (706) 219-2789; www.bsvw.com.

Georgia Peach Festival, Byron and Fort Valley. Held between the first and second weekend of June between the two cities. www.worldslargestpeachcobbler.com.

Georgia Wine Country Festival, Dahlonega. Three Sisters Vineyards' Annual Wine Festival is held the first full weekend of every June. (706) 865-9463; www.threesistersvineyards.com.

Helen to the Atlantic Balloon Race & Festival, Helen. The South's oldest balloon event and the United States' only long-distance hot air balloon race. Balloon rides available. Starts the Thurs after Memorial Day. (706) 878-2271; www.helenballoon.com.

The Twelve Oaks Barbecue and Ball, Crawfordville. Taking place mid-June at Liberty Hall, the Twelve Oaks Barbecue and Ball refers to the infamous barbeque that took place at the beginning of *Gone with the Wind.* It features 2 days of living history and Confederate encampments, along with arts and crafts. (706) 456-2273.

Thomas A. Dorsey Festival, Villa Rica. Celebrating the birthday of the Father of Black Gospel Music, this 2-day festival at the end of June offers plenty of gospel music, barbeque, and arts and crafts. (678) 697-7684; www.villaricatourism.com.

july

Georgia Mountain Fair, Hiawassee. Ten days of musical performances, fun carnival rides, unique attractions, and a glimpse into North Georgia's rich history and culture. Held the last week of July. www.georgiamountainfairgrounds.com.

Green Bean Festival, Blairsville. It's all about the bean the last weekend in July. Bean shucking contest, bean cooking contests, music, arts and crafts. (706) 994-4837; www.greenbeanfestival.com.

Sunflower Festival, Sunflower Farm, 1430 Durden, Rutledge. A 3-day festival the first weekend in July that features arts and crafts, food, and music on beautiful Sunflower Farm. (706) 557-2870; www.sunflowerfarmfestival.com.

august

Annual Big Haynes Creek Wildlife Festival, Georgia International Horse Park, Conyers. Features birds of prey, living history, wildlife exhibits, demonstrations, hands-on activities, local performances, children's activities, and arts and crafts. The last weekend of August. (770) 860-4190; http://bighaynescreekwildlifefestival.com.

Pigs and Peaches Barbeque Festival, Kennesaw. Offers up plenty of "Q" and tons of desserts with activities for all ages in this old-fashioned community celebration. Held the last weekend in August. (770) 422-9714; www.pigsandpeaches.com.

september

Battle of Tunnel Hill Civil War Reenactment, Tunnel Hill. Rain or shine, hundreds of reenactors turn out to re-create this Civil War battle. (678) 939-3679; www.tunnelhillheritage center.com.

Chattahoochee Mountain Fair, Clarkesville. Livestock shows, art show, 4-H competitions, cake walks, bingo, rodeo, entertainment on 2 stages, grounds shows, petting zoo, food and craft vendors, and a large midway for 10 days starting the weekend after Labor Day. http://chattahoocheemountainfair.org.

Marietta Antique Street Festival, Marietta. The square in Marietta is transformed into a giant antiques street market the third Saturday in September. (770) 429-1115; www.marietta antiquedealers.com.

Oktoberfest, Helen. Starting at the end of September and going throughout the month of October, the Bavarian village of Helen in North Georgia plays host to the nation's largest and longest Oktoberfest. Grab a beer and a brat and do the chicken dance. (706) 878-1619; www.helenchamber.com.

Plains Peanut Festival, Plains. Held the third weekend in September, the daylong event includes food, crafts, a fun run, and an eclectic parade that can alone be worth the trip. (229) 824-7477; www.plainsgeorgia.com/peanut_festival.html.

Powers Crossroads Festival, Newnan. Held over Labor Day weekend, this festival is listed as one of the top festivals in North America. It features history, music, food, and more than 200 artists. (770) 253-2011; http://powersfestival.org.

Pumpkin Festival, Louisville. Held the fourth weekend in September on a family farm in Louisville, the Pumpkin Festival includes seed spitting contests and pumpkin bowling. It includes a corn maze and more than 50 attractions. (478) 494-0185; www.kackleberryfarm .com.

Yellow Daisy Festival, Stone Mountain Park. One of the largest arts and crafts festival in the US is held the second week of September at Stone Mountain Park. http://festivals .stonemountainpark.com.

october

Annual Olde Town Fall Festival, Conyers. A scarecrow competition is just one of the activities as crafters and artists help raise funds for the Rockdale County Historical Society the third Saturday in October. http://visit.conyersga.com.

City Wide Yard Sale Tallapoosa, Tallapoosa. Follow the signs throughout the town for lots of treasures! Held the first Saturday in October in Tallapoosa from 8 a.m. to 3 p.m. For more information, call (770) 574-2482.

Corn Festival, Louisville. It's all things corn from a corn maze to corn-eating contests the third weekend in October at Kackleberry Farm. (478) 494-0185; www.kackleberryfarm.com.

Cotton Pickin' Festival, Gay. Held in the first weekend of May for planting and the first weekend in October for picking, this festival includes music, crafts, and food. (706) 538-6814; www.cpfair.org.

Cowboy and Indian Days, Cartersville. Themed events take place throughout the month on each weekend. Expect everything from chuck wagon cooking demonstrations to artifact identification classes. (770) 387-1357; www.notatlanta.org.

Cumming Country Fair & Festival, Cumming Fairground. Carnival Midway, Heritage & Indian Village, concerts, and food. First week of October. (770) 781-3491; www.cumming fair.net.

Georgia Mountain Fall Festival, Georgia Mountain Fairgrounds, Hiawassee. The 9-day event the first full week of October features Georgia's Official State Fiddlers' Convention, other musical performances, demonstrations, and food. (706) 896-4191; www.georgia mountainfairgrounds.com.

Hummingbird Festival, Hogansville. Celebrate flighty friends with food, music, arts, crafts, antiques, rides, vendors, and a charity auction on the third weekend in October. www .hummingbirdfestival.com.

Indian Summer Festival, Suches. The first full weekend of October, on the grounds of Woody Gap School. Event includes a car show, crafts, music, square dancing, and clogging demonstrations, as well as plenty of food. http://indiansummerfestival.org.

Peanut Festival, Sylvester. The self-proclaimed "Peanut Capital of the World" hosts this annual festival the third weekend in October to honor our local peanut farmers. Activities include parades, a 5K run, and craftsmen from all over the state. www.sylvesterworthco chamber.com/festival.aspx.

Prater's Mill Festival, Dalton. This country festival on the grounds of an 1855 gristmill celebrates life in North Georgia in the mid-1800s. Experience mountain music, Southern foods, living history exhibits, and handmade crafts and original art. Craft demonstrations include blacksmithing, spinning, quilting, rug hooking, woodcarving, and hand tufting. (706) 694-6455; www.pratersmill.org.

Ringgold Gap Civil War Festival, Ringgold. Celebrated the first weekend in October, the festival includes living history, reenactments, music, and food. (706) 965-1249; www .ringgoldgapfestival.com.

Sorghum Festival, Blairsville. Learn the art of sorghum syrup-making and enjoy greased pole climbin', biskit eatin', and log sawin' the second and third weekends of October. (706) 745-4745; www.sorghum.blairsville.com.

november

Annual Historic Acworth Holiday Tour of Homes, Acworth. Tour some of Acworth's most historic homes the second weekend of November. (770) 974-8813.

Deer Festival, Monticello. Celebrating hunting season, there are crafts, rides, a 5K Deer Dash, a parade, and a Venison Cook-off. The first weekend in November. (706) 468-8994; www.historicmonticello.com/chamberofcommerce/43rd_annual_deer_festival_plans.html.

The National BBQ Cup, Cumming. The Georgia Championship BBQ cook-off with cooking demonstrations, raffles, giveaways, BBQ sampling, award-winning food vendors, and arts and crafts vendors. All the second weekend in November. www.nationalbbqcup.com.

Old-Fashioned Christmas, Dahlonega. Starting the Friday after Thanksgiving with the lighting of the square and continuing throughout December, there are almost daily events celebrating Christmas. (706) 864-3513; www.dahlonega.org.

december

Christmas at the Cabin, Red Top Mountain State Park. An 1800s-style Christmas celebration complete with cooking, caroling, and the Clauses, held during the first weekend in December. (770) 975-4226; www.friendsofredtop.org.

Marietta Pilgrimage Christmas Home Tour, Marietta. Five homes on the National Register Historic District are featured in this holiday tradition held the first weekend in December. (800) 835-0445; www.mariettasquare.com.

Old-Fashioned Christmas, Dahlonega. Throughout December with almost daily events celebrating Christmas. An old-fashioned parade is held the first weekend in December with the arrival of Santa. (706) 864-3513; www.dahlonega.org.

index

B

C

H

I

S

T

U

V